Linguistics Studies in Phoenician

Linguistics Studies in Phoenician

In Memory of J. Brian Peckham

edited by

Robert D. Holmstedt
and
Aaron Schade

Winona Lake, Indiana
Eisenbrauns
2013

Printed in the United States of America.
www.eisenbrauns.com

Library of Congress Cataloging-in-Publication Data

Linguistics studies in Phoenician : in memory of J. Brian Peckham / edited by Robert D. Holmstedt and Aaron Schade.
pages cm
ISBN 978-1-57506-266-2 (alk. paper)
1. Phoenician language—History. 2. Phoenicians—Language. 3. Historical linguistics—Phoenicia. I. Holmstedt, Robert D. II. Peckham, Brian, 1934- honouree.
PJ4171.L56 2013
492'.6–dc23

2013009744

The paper used in this publication meets the minimum requirements of the American National Standard for Information Sciences—Permanence of Paper for Printed Library Materials, ANSI Z39.48–1984. ♾™

Contents

Preface

Four and a half years ago we decided to put together a volume of essays on Phoenician language in honor of J. Brian Peckham. Brian was an impressive scholar in both biblical studies and Northwest Semitics, and his greatest interest and love was always to be found in Phoenician language and history. He studied at Harvard with Frank Moore Cross and Thomas Lambdin, and under their tutelage, published his thesis *The Development of the Late Phoenician Scripts* in 1968, a publication that continues to be influential in the field of Phoenician language studies today. Through the following four decades after his degree, Brian's teaching and research focused regularly on Phoenician studies, resulting in his *Phoenicia: Episodes and Anecdotes from the Ancient Mediterranean,* which he submitted in September 2008 and is now in press (Eisenbrauns). His abiding and enthusiastic interest in Phoenician history and language was contagious, especially to the editors of this volume, and his vast knowledge on the subject was unparalleled. When we presented the scope of this volume, along with a list of contributors, Brian beamed. He was both honored and, of course, anxious to read the essays. The enthusiasm of his response highlighted his great passion and love for the Phoenician language, a topic he so rigorously and excitedly shared with his students and colleagues over the years.

To our great sorrow, our friend J. Brian Peckham passed away in Toronto on October 19, 2008. He had an illustrious career that influenced the field and motivated and touched people's lives. After finishing his doctoral studies in 1964 at Harvard, Brian pursued theological studies in Lyon, France. The newly ordained Father Peckham then took up the position of Professor of Bible at Regis College at the University of Toronto. He was at Regis until 1976, after which he was appointed in what is now the Department of Near and Middle Eastern Civilizations. He became Professor Emeritus in 2000, but did not retire from teaching. Indeed, it was due to Brian's love of teaching and generosity that he accepted the yearly invitation to continue teaching the Northwest Semitic epigraphy courses in Near and Middle Eastern Civilizations through

2007. Throughout these years, and up unto his death, Brian was instrumental in helping countless students complete the requirements necessary for undergraduate and graduate degrees. Most importantly, he always taught through example to approach academics and life with dignity, professionalism, and class.

Brian was an inspiring teacher, mentor, and colleague. He had acquired a depth and breadth of knowledge that represented over forty years of study, a knowledge he was always willing to share. He once said that true knowledge only comes through teaching, a principle he believed and practiced. Brian's ability to provide both an ancient and modern context for the subjects he taught contributed to this success in leaving a lasting influence on his students and colleagues. The effectiveness of his teaching was highlighted in his ability to pose thought-provoking questions that challenged his students to think, inquire, and seek for solutions. His personal anecdotes, freely shared in his office (which served as his classroom) or over casual and friendly conversations enjoyed at the nearby Madison Avenue Pub, revealed both the range of his interests and expertise, and the ease with which he combined his personal and academic lives. We will never forget the story he told (of the many) about walking into the British Museum and being denied access to study an inscription until he told the curator that the stele had been displayed upside down.

We express our appreciation to all of our contributors who accepted the invitation to contribute to this volume, once a Festchrift and now, unfortunately, a memorial. It is with gratitude and appreciation that we dedicate this volume to the memory of J. Brian Peckham. May it be a worthy and long-lasting testimony to the man and scholar we esteemed so dearly.

The editors,
Robert Holmstedt
Aaron Schade

March 2013

Abbreviations

Text Editions and Dictionaries

CIL *Corpus inscriptionum latinarum.* Berlin-Brandenburg Academy of Sciences and Humanities. Berlin: n.p., 1853–

CIS *Corpus inscriptionum semiticarum.* Académie des inscriptions et belles-lettres. Paris: n.p., 1881–

COS Hallo, W. W., and K. L. Younger Jr. *The Context of Scripture.* 3 vols. Leiden: Brill, 1997–2002

DNWSI Hoftijzer, J., and K. Jongeling. *Dictionary of the North-West Semitic Inscriptions.* 2 vols. HOSNME 21. Leiden: Brill, 1995

HNPI Jongeling, K. *Handbook of Neo-Punic Inscriptions.* Tübingen: Mohr Siebeck, 2008

IFO Magnanini, P. *Le iscrizioni fenicie dell'Oriente: Testi, Traduzioni, Glossari.* Rome: Istituto di Studi del Vicino Oriente, 1973

IFPCO Amadasi Guzzo, M. G. *Le iscrizioni fenicie e puniche delle colonie in Occidente.* Rome: Instituto di Studie del Vicino Oriente, 1967

IFPI Amadasi Guzzo, M. G. *Iscrizioni fenicie e puniche in Italia.* Rome: Libreria dello Stato, 1990

ILAfr Cagnat, René, and Alfred Merlin, with the collaboration of M. Louis Chatelain. *Inscriptions latines d'Afrique* (Tripolitaine, Tunisie, Maroc). Paris: Lerous, 1923.

ILAlg Gsell, Stéphane, I. Albertin, and H. G. Pflaum. *Inscriptions latines de l'Algerie.* 4 vols. Paris: Librairie Ancienne Honoré Champion, 1922–76

ILS Desau, Hermann. *Inscriptiones Latinae Selectae.* 3 vols. Berlin: Weidannos, 1892–1916

ILTun Merlin, Alfred. *Inscriptions latines de la Tunisie.* Paris: Presses Universitaires de France, 1944

IPT Levi Della Vida, G., and M. G. Amadasi Guzzo. *Iscrizioni puniche della Tripolitania* (1927–1967). Monografie di Archeologia Libica 22. Rome: L'Erma di Bretschneider, 1987

IRT Reynolds, Joyce Marie, and John Bryan Ward-Perkins. *Inscriptions of Roman Tripolitania.* Rome: British School at Rome, 1952

KAI Donner, H., and W. Röllig. *Kanaanäische und aramäische Inschriften mit einem Beitrag von O. Rößler.* 3 vols. Wiesbaden: Harrassowitz, 1966–69

KAI[5] Donner, H., and W. Röllig. *Kanaanäische und aramäische Inschriften*, vol. 1.5: *Erweiterte und überarbeitete Auflage*. Wiesbaden: Harrassowitz, 2002

KTU[2] Dietrich, M., O. Loretz, and J. Sanmartín. *The Cuneiform Alphabet Texts from Ugarit, Ras Ibn Hani, and Other Places.* 2nd, enlarged ed. ALASPM 8. Münster: Ugarit-Verlag, 1995

LPE Jongeling, K., and R. M. Kerr. *Late Punic Epigraphy: An Introduction to the Study of Neo-Punic and Latino-Punic Inscriptions*. Tübingen: Mohr Siebeck, 2005

MartAfr Monceaux, Paul. *Histoire littéraire de l'Afrique chrétienne depuis les origines jusquà l'invasion arabe*, vol. 3: *Le quatréime siécle, d'Arnobe Victorin*. Paris: Leroux, 1901. [Repr. Brussels, 1966]

MartEcclAfr Morcelli, Stefano A. *Africa Christiana*, vol. 1: *Martyrologium ecclesiae africanae*. Brescia: Ex officina Bettoniana, 1816

RIL Chabot, J.-B. *Recueil des inscriptions libyques.* Paris: Imprimerie Nationale, 1940–41

Other Resources

AAL *AfroAsiatic Linguistics*

AfO *Archiv für Orientforschung*

AION *Annali dell'Università degli Studi di Napoli «L'Orientale»*

AJSL *American Journal of Semitic Languages and Literature*

AKM Abhandlungen für die Kunde des Morgenlandes

ALASPM Abhandlungen zur Literatur Alt-Syrien-Palästinas und Mesopotamiens

AnOr Analecta Orientalia

AOAT Alter Orient und Altes Testament

AOS American Oriental Series

ArOr *Archiv Orientální*

AuOr *Aula Orientalis*

BA *Biblical Archaeologist*

BAC *Bulletin Archéologique du Comité de Travaux Historique et Scientifiques*

BAR *Biblical Archaeology Review*

BASOR *Bulletin of the American Schools of Oriental Research*

BDB Brown, F., S. R. Driver, and C. A. Briggs. *Hebrew and English Lexicon of the Old Testament.* Oxford: Clarendon, 1907

BibOr Biblica et Orientalia

BiOr *Bibliotheca Orientalis*

BJPES *Bulletin of the Jewish Palestine Exploration Society*

BMB *Bulletin du Musée de Beyrouth*

BZAW Beihefte zur Zeitschrift für die alttestamentliche Wissenschaft

CahRB Cahiers de la Revue biblique

CBQ *Catholic Biblical Quarterly*

CNWS Centre of Non Western Studies

CRAIBL	*Comptes rendus de l'Académie des inscriptions et belles-lettres*
CSEL	Corpus Scriptorum Ecclesiasticorum Latinorum
DS-NELL	Dutch Studies on Near Eastern Languages and Literatures
EpAn	Epigraphica Anatolica
ErIsr	*Eretz-Israel*
GKC	Kautzsch, E., ed. *Gesenius' Hebrew Grammar.* Translated by A. E. Cowley. 2nd ed. Oxford: Oxford University Press, 1910
HAR	*Hebrew Annual Review*
HOSNME	Handbook of Oriental Studies, section 1: The Near and Middle East
HS	*Hebrew Studies*
HSM	Harvard Semitic Monographs
HSS	Harvard Semitic Studies
HTR	*Harvard Theological Review*
IEJ	*Israel Exploration Journal*
IOS	*Israel Oriental Studies*
JA	*Journal asiatique*
JANES	*Journal of the Ancient Near Eastern Society*
JAOS	*Journal of the American Oriental Society*
JCS	*Journal of Cuneiform Studies*
JHS	*Journal of Hebrew Scriptures*
JNES	*Journal of Near Eastern Studies*
JNSL	*Journal of Northwest Semitic Languages*
JQR	*Jewish Quarterly Review*
JRAS	*Journal of the Royal Asiatic Society*
JS	*Journal for Semitics*
JSOTSup	Journal for the Study of the Old Testament: Supplement Series
JSS	*Journal of Semitic Studies*
KUSATU	*Kleine Untersuchungen zur Sprache des Alten Testaments und seiner Umwelt*
LA	*Liber Annus*
LAPO	Littératures anciennes du Proche-Orient
LASBF	Liber annuus Studii biblici franciscani
LCA	Langues et cultures anciennes
LSAWS	Linguistic Studies in Ancient West Semitic
MUSJ	Mélanges de l'Université Saint-Joseph
OBO	Orbis biblicus et orientalis
OEANE	Meyers, E. M., ed. *The Oxford Encyclopedia of Archaeology in the Near East.* 5 vols. New York: Oxford University Press, 1997
OLA	*Orientalia lovaniensia analecta*
OLP	*Orientalia lovaniensia periodica*
Or	*Orientalia*
OrSuec	Orientalia Suecana
OtSt	*Oudtestamentische Studiën*
PEFQS	*Palestine Exploration Fund, Quarterly Statement*
PEQ	*Palestine Exploration Quarterly*

RA	*Revue d'assyriologie et d'archéologie orientale*
RÉS	Répertoire d'épigraphie sémitique.
RIL	Recueil des inscriptions libyques
RSF	*Rivista di Studi Fenici*
RSO	*Rivista degli Studi Orientali*
SAAS	State Archives of Assyria Studies
SBLRBS	Society of Biblical Literature Resources for Biblical Study
SBLSBS	Society of Biblical Literature Sources for Biblical Study
SBLWAW	Society of Biblical Literature Writings from the Ancient World
SEL	Studi Epigrafici e Linguistici sul Vicino Oriente Antico
SM	Studi Magrebini
SSN	Studia semitica neerlandica
SubBi	Subsidia biblica
TL	*Theoretical Linguistics*
UF	*Ugarit-Forschungen*
VOK	Veroffentlichungen der Orientalischen Kommission
VT	*Vetus Testamentum*
WO	*Die Welt des Orients*
ZAH	*Zeitschrift für Althebraistik*
ZAW	*Zeitschrift für die alttestamentliche Wissenschaft*
ZDMG	*Zeitschrift der deutschen morgenländischen Gesellschaft*
ZDPV	*Zeitschrift des deutschen Palästina-Vereins*

Languages

Akk	Akkadian
Arb	Arabic
Arm	Aramaic
BH	Biblical Hebrew
CS	Central Semitic
EA	El Amarna
Eth	Ethiopic
GK	Greek
GP	Greco-Punic
Heb	Hebrew
LP	Latino-Punic
MSA	Modern South Arabian
NP	Neo-Punic
NWS	Northwest Semitic
OfA	Official Aramaic
OSA	Old South Arabian
Phoen	Phoenician
PS	Proto-Semitic
Soq	Soqotri
Syr	Syriac
Ug	Ugaritic

Miscellaneous

Assrb.	Assurbanipal
c.	century
DN	divine name
EA	El Amarna tablet
Esar.	Esarhaddon
ET	English translation
fasc.	fascicle
GN	geographical name
Hr.	Henschir
IPA	International Phonetic Alphabet
LXX	Septuagint
NWS	Northwest Semitic
pl.	plate
PN	personal name
rev.	reverse
Senn.	Sennacherib
Shalm.	Shalmaneser
SVO	Subject – Verb – Object syntax
VSO	Verb – Subject – Object syntax

Interlinear Glossing

[ ]	phonetic representation
/ /	phonemic representation
{ }	graphemic representation
.	(period) used in glossing to indicate multiple morphemes of single linguistic item
-	(hyphen) to separate segmentable morphemes
=	(equals) to mark clitic boundaries
*	ungrammatical or unattested example
1	1st person
2	2nd person
3	3rd person
ABS	absolute
ACC	accusative
ADJ	adjective
ADV	adverb
ART	article
C	common (gender)
CAUS	causative
COMP	complementizer
CONJ	conjunction
CSTR	construct
DEM	demonstrative

DU	dual
F	feminine
GEN	genitive
IMPF	imperfect(ive)
INF	infinitive (often ABS or CSTR)
INTERR	interrogative
IPFV	imperfect(ive)
JUSS	jussive
M	masculine
N/NP	noun/noun phrase
NARR	uninflected narrative verb (see also INF ABS)
NEG	negative
NOM	nominative
OBL	oblique case
P	plural
PASS	passive
PAST	past
PERF	perfect(ive)
PFV	perfect(ive)
PP	prepositional phrase
PRED	predicate/predicative
PREP	preposition
PRON	pronoun
PTCP	participle
REL	relative marker/complementizer/affix
S	singular
V	verb

Introduction

The Phoenician Language: An Overview

The Phoenician language is a member of the Semitic language family, located on the Northwest Semitic branch of Central West Semitic (see Huehnergard 1995; 2004; 2005). Within Northwest Semitic, Phoenician is part of the Canaanite dialect group, its closest linguistic relatives being Hebrew, Moabite, Ammonite, and Edomite (see Garr 1985).

Phoenician is distinguished from its sister dialects by grammatical features ranging from phonology (for example, syncopation or palatalization of /h/ in third-person singular and plural suffixes), morphology (pronominal usage, relative particles, demonstrative pronouns, declension of nouns), and syntax to discourse features, such as the the conventions of narrative sequences of clauses (imperfective, perfective, infinitival, and preterite sequences). Whatever the differences, the activities of the Phoenicians in their trade and colonization have planted their language firmly in the linguistic and sociolinguistic center of the first-millennium Near East and Mediterranean. One cannot exaggerate the linguistic and historical importance of Phoenician in this language family. Based on shear volume alone (Phoenician–Punic boasts by far the largest collection of ancient texts within the Canaanite language family, with 6,058 Phoenician or Punic texts listed in *CIS* alone; Vance 1994), Phoenician constitutes a linguistic anchor in the comparative and historical analysis of Canaanite languages within the Northwest Semitic grouping (Harris 1939; Garr 1985). Beyond the size of the corpus, the temporal distribution of Phoenician and Punic inscriptions (eleventh century B.C. to the fifth century C.E.), their geographical distribution (throughout the Near East and the Mediterranean), and the presence of bilinguals (such as at Karatepe) and mixed dialects (such as with Samalian) all reflect the influence of the Phoenicians and the critical role that their language now plays in the historical-comparative study of NWS languages.

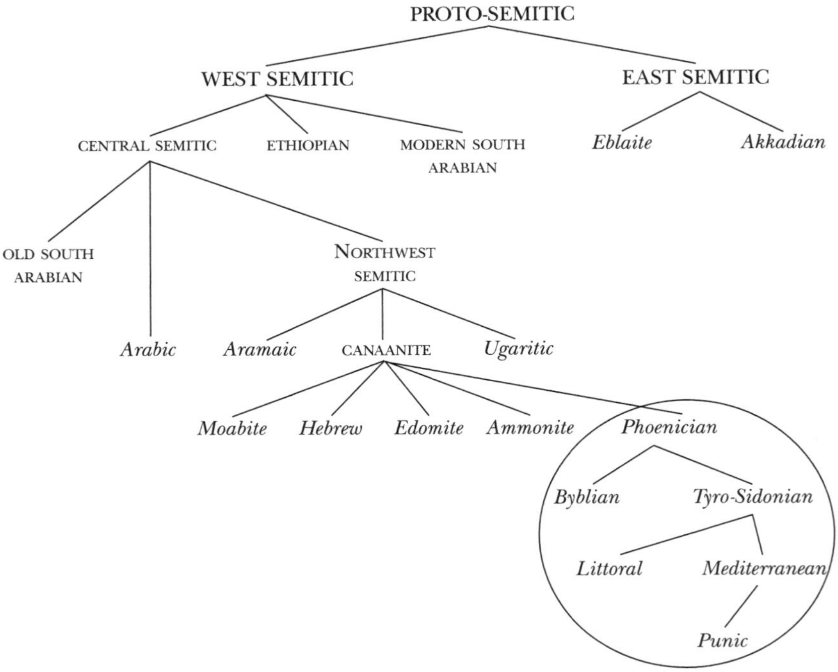

Figure 1. Phoenician within the Semitic Languages.

To summarize, thorough study of the Phoenician–Punic corpus is critical for examining and understanding important details of the larger linguistic grouping, whether in the area of formal grammar, such as phonology, syntax, pragmatics, and grammaticalization, or in the area of sociolinguistics, such as shared scribal traditions within the ancient Near East and the Mediterranean. As Garr summarizes in his study of dialect geography in Iron Age Syria–Palestine:

> According to the present evidence, the linguistic innovations in first-millennium NWS cluster principally into two dialectal groups. One set of innovations–the merger of *ḏ̣ and *ṣ (2:1), *ḏ and *z (2:2), *ṯ̣ and *ṣ (2:3), *ṯ and *š (2:4), the merger of accented *a*-vowels and *ṓ (2:5–7), monophthongization (2:8), the loss of intervocalic *he* (2:16), the personal interrogative pronoun [*mî*] the definite article *he* (3:5), etc.–occurred, in differing degrees, in the Canaanite dialects. Only standard Phoenician, however, had all these innovations as well as several that did not spread beyond Phoenician. . . . Thus, standard Phoenician and

> Old Aramaic (as a dialect group) constituted the two major linguistic centers of Syria–Palestinian NWS. In terms of a dialect continuum, standard Phoenician and Old Aramaic were the linguistic extremes. For those dialects lying between these two poles, standard Phoenician and Old Aramaic were competing forces. (Garr 1985: 227–28; numeric references are to chapters and examples within Garr—ed.)

The current volume offers a step forward in examining grammatical, typological, and historical-comparative issues concerning the Phoenician language—a language that had such a vast impact on the region as a whole.

The spread and impact of the Phoenician language can be highlighted by Phoenician expansion, colonization, and trade. Historically, the Phoenicians carved out for themselves a niche that extended from Mesopotamia to the western extent of the Mediterranean—even establishing several port settlements in Spain by the eighth century B.C. (Bierling 2002); this niche included sea-faring commerce and the transportation of goods, and their fame in these endeavors made its way into biblical accounts relating the construction of Solomon's temple. The influence of the Phoenician language expanded with their trade network and colonization activity (endeavors that required a mutual mode of communication with indigenous peoples), so much so that one may say that Phoenician achieved the status of a Mediterranean lingua franca in the first millennium (Krahmalkov 2001: 5–6).

Within Phoenician, a few major dialects emerged. The Sidonians, and thus the Sidonian dialect, moved to the northwest and had the earliest colonies in northern Syria, Cilicia (southeastern Anatolia), western Cyprus, the Aegean, Italy, and Sardinia. Tyre and its dialect (which is similar to Sidonian, and so the two are often referred to together as Tyro-Sidonian) flourished later, with the Tyrians taking a southwestern route and founding colonies in eastern and southern Cyprus, in Egypt, the coast of North Africa, in Malta, Sicily, Sardinia, and Spain. Byblos had an outpost at Larnaca tis Lapithou in western Cyprus and a colony at Pyrgi in Italy; however, the Byblian dialect seems to have been restricted to Byblos itself, with Tyro-Sidonian used elsewhere as a veritable Phoenician koine.

Despite the general ascendancy of the Sidonian dialect, some Phoenician texts (e.g., Karatepe, Çineköy) exhibit features suggesting independent dialectal development as well as non-Semitic borrowing (cf. Schmitz 2008; 2009). A refined Phoenician dialectology, based not just on purely descriptive linguistic observations but also on the ever-increasing knowledge of the complex sociopolitical situations in the various areas in which Phoenician was used, remains a desideratum.

By the fifth century, the Tyrian colony of Carthage in North Africa was an independent city-state with its own dominions in North Africa, colonies in Italy and France, and satellite cities in Sicily, Sardinia, and Spain. The Carthaginian dialect of Phoenician, which was a development of Tyro-Sidonian, is known as Punic, and thousands of Punic inscriptions have been discovered, with evidence of Punic reaching throughout the Mediterranean and as far north as Wales (Jongeling and Kerr 2005: 57; Jongeling 2008: 289). Inscriptions dating after the fall of Carthage in 146 B.C. are said to be written in Late Punic Neo-Punic, the distinction is more one of script than of dialect (Jongeling and Kerr 2005: 1). Punic inscriptions date as late as the second century C.E., and there are even later Latino-Punic (Punic written in Latin script) that date to the fourth and fifth centuries C.E. (Jongeling and Kerr 2005: 2–6; Kerr 2007: x–xviii).

In summary, the linguistic artifacts attest the breadth and temporal depth of Phoenician influence throughout the Mediterranean. Phoenician-Punic texts have been found outside the Phoenician homeland at sites in modern Turkey, Egypt, Cyprus, Tunisia, Algeria, Libya, Malta, Sardinia, Sicily, France, Spain, and the Balearics. This large-scaled distribution highlights the prominence and influence of the Phoenician language and dialects over time and territory.

The Focus of and Contributions to this Volume

This collection of studies is aimed at advancing our understanding of the grammatical features of Phoenician. Given the use of Phoenician throughout the Mediterranean littoral, this volume contains something of interest for numerous areas of investigation: comparative Semitics, Anatolian studies, early Mediterranean studies, and even Hebrew and biblical studies. The essays are grouped into two categories. The first set of studies is more narrowly concentrated on the linguistic features of Phoenician qua Phoenician. They include investigations of phonology, syntax, and pragmatics. The second set of studies seeks to situate some feature(s) of Phoenician typologically or within comparative and historical Semitics.

To maximize consistency and the target audience, the articles in this volume use a standard set of linguistic terms and glosses, listed

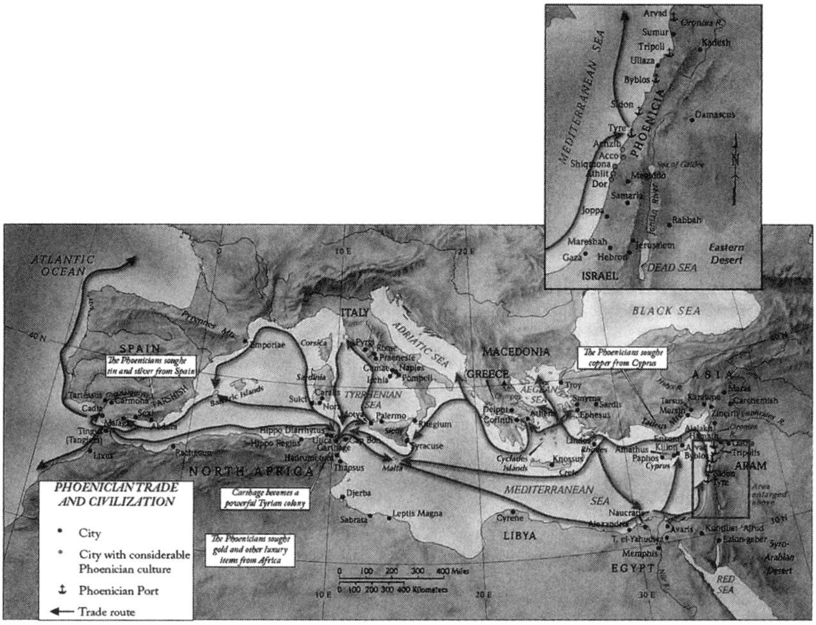

Figure 2. Extent of Phoenician and Punic Linguistic Influence.

in the Abbreviations and based on the Leipzig Glossing Rules (http:// www.eva.mpg.de/lingua/resources/glossing-rules.php, accessed January 31, 2010). Thus, the volume's format provides access for linguists and non-linguists alike who may not have studied Phoenician but who may benefit from knowledge of Phoenician linguistic features.

Robert Kerr's study begins the first part of the volume by addressing the phonology and paleography of Phoenician–Punic. He describes two subcorpora of Semitic epigraphy, the different scripts of which allow the deduction of phonological contrasts. Using /s/, /ṣ/, and /š/ as a case study, he concludes that the sibilants remained distinct, regardless of their actual realization at any given time or place throughout the long history of Phoenician–Punic. That is, the merger of sibilants in Phoenician–Punic is not a matter of phonology but of paleography.

Paul Mosca's article moves the discussion of grammar from phonology to syntax and lexicon. Mosca returns to *ʾyt* in the Çebel Ires Daği Inscription, which he identified as the independent object pronoun in the editio princeps. He argues for the correctness of his initial analysis, that *ʾyt* is an independent object pronoun rather than a simple *nota accusativi* marking the direct object.

Naʾama Pat-El continues the focus on particle syntax by examining the system of negative particles in Phoenician. In historical-comparative fashion, she demonstrates that Phoenician is unique in that it lacks both the Proto-Semitic negative particle **lʾ* and the regular Northwest Semitic negative existential *ʾyn* (Heb., Ug.).

Philip C. Schmitz provides a sociolinguistic analysis of the enigmatic lexemes *mškbm* and *bʿrrm* in the Kulamuwa inscription. He makes the case that these are not ethnic labels but refer to political standing vis-à-vis vassal loyalty (or lack thereof).

Robert Holmstedt's essay addresses the syntactic placement and pragmatic function of nonclitic subject pronouns in verbless and verbal clauses. He proposes a model for interpreting pronominal presence when it is not obligatory.

Aaron Schade examines fronted word order in Phoenician. He argues that the fronting of constituents can be triggered by either syntactic or pragmatic factors and that the resulting word order often has both an information structure function, such as Focus or Topic, and a discourse structure function, such as marking paragraph boundaries.

Andrés Piquer Otero's article continues in the syntax-discourse vein. Piquer Otero analyzes the functionality of the narrative infinitive in narrative versus direct speech contexts, in foreground or background textual units, and in introductions, bodies, and closing sections of a unit. Piquer Otero also discusses the semantic content of the actions expressed and formulaic versus nonformulaic uses.

Holger Gzella's paper signals the transition to the second section of the volume, in which the view of Phoenician is moved to the broader typological and historical-comparative context. Gzella situates Old Byblian (the earliest variety of Phoenician, commonly dated to the tenth century B.C.) within both the history of Phoenician and the broader Canaanite dialect continuum.

Rebecca Hasselbach addresses the development of morphological case marking in Phoenician. Using the common reconstruction of the Northwest Semitic case system, with three distinctly marked cases in the singular, Hasselbach traces the loss of the original case-marking system in Phoenician to the changes in the orthography of specific words and morphemes, such as weak verbs and pronominal suffixes.

The concluding article of the volume demonstrates the value of using grammar and dialectology in the study of texts. After thoroughly considering every feature of the Gezer Calendar in light of attested linguistic evidence in the larger dialect region, Dennis Pardee argues that the language of the text is more accurately classified as Phoenician than Hebrew or Philistian.[1]

References

Amadasi Guzzo, M. G., and Röllig, W.

1995 La langue. Pp. 185–92 in *La civilisation phénicienne et punique: Manuel de recherche*, ed. V. Krings. HOSNME 20. Leiden: Brill.

Bierling, Marilyn R., ed. and trans.

2002 *The Phoenicians in Spain: An Archaeological Review of the Eighth–Sixth Centuries* B.C.E.*–A Collection of Articles Translated from Spanish*. Winona Lake, IN: Eisenbrauns.

Comrie, B., Haspelmath, M., and Bickel, B.

n.d. The Leipzig Glossing Rules: Conventions for Interlinear Morpheme-by-Morpheme Glosses. http://www.eva.mpg.de/lingua/pdf/LGR09_02_23.pdf (revision, February 2008; accessed January 31, 2010).

Friedrich, J., and Röllig, W.

1999 *Phönizisch-Punische Grammatik*. 3rd ed. by M. G. Amadasi Guzzo with W. R. Mayer. AnOr 55. Rome: Pontifical Biblical Institute.

Garr, W. Randall

1985 *Dialect Geography of Syria–Palestine, 1000–586* B.C.E. Philadelphia: University of Pennsylvania Press. [Reprinted, Winona Lake, IN: Eisenbrauns, 2004.]

Hackett, Jo Ann

2004 Phoenician and Punic. Pp. 365–85 in *The Cambridge Encyclopedia of the World's Ancient Languages*, ed. R. D. Woodard. Cambridge: Cambridge University Press.

Harris, Zellig S.

1936 *A Grammar of the Phoenician Language*. AOS 8. New Haven, CT: American Oriental Society.

1939 *Development of the Canaanite Dialects: An Investigation in Linguistic History*. AOS 16. New Haven, CT: American Oriental Society.

1. As with many collections of specially commissioned essays, over two years have passed since the authors finished their research and the volume has appeared. Thus, for the sake of the contributors, the editors would like to remind the reader that subsequent studies appearing in this gap have been impossible to incorporate.

Huehnergard, John

1995 Semitic Languages. Pp. 2117–134 in *Civilizations of the Ancient Near East*, ed. J. M. Sasson. New York: Scribner.

2004 Afro-Asiatic. Pp. 138–59 in *The Cambridge Encyclopedia of the World's Ancient Languages*, ed. R. D. Woodard. Cambridge: Cambridge University Press.

2005 Features of Central Semitic. Pp. 155–203 in *Biblical and Oriental Essays in Memory of William L. Moran*, ed. A. Gianto. BibOr 48. Rome: Pontifical Biblical Institute.

Jongeling, Karel

2008 *Handbook of Neo-Punic Inscriptions*. Tübingen: Mohr Siebeck.

Jongeling, K., and Kerr, R. M.

2005 *Late Punic Epigraphy: An Introduction to the Study of Neo-Punic and Latino-Punic Inscriptions*. Tübingen: Mohr Siebeck.

Kerr, Robert M.

2007 *Latino-Punic in Its Linguistic Environment: An Investigation of the Tripolitanian Latino-Punic and Related Inscriptions from Roman North Africa with Some Reference to Libyan and Latin.* Ph.D. dissertation, Leiden University.

Krahmalkov, Charles R.

1992 Languages: Phoenician. Pp. 222–23 in vol. 4 of *The Anchor Bible Dictionary*, ed. D. N. Freedman. New York: Doubleday.

2000 *Phoenician-Punic Dictionary*. OLA 90. Studia Phoenicia 15. Leuven: Peeters.

2001 *A Phoenician-Punic Grammar*. HOSNME 54. Leiden: Brill.

Kuhrt, Amélie

1995 *The Ancient Near East, c. 3000–330 B.C.* 2 vols. London: Routledge.

Lipiński, Edward

2001 *Semitic Languages: Outline of a Comparative Grammar*. 2nd ed. OLA 80. Leuven: Peeters.

Peckham, Brian

1968 *The Development of the Late Phoenician Scripts.* HSS 20. Cambridge: Harvard University Press.

1992 Phoenicia, History of. Pp. 349–57 in vol. 5 of *The Anchor Bible Dictionary*, ed. D. N. Freedman. New York: Doubleday.

Segert, Stanislav

1976 *A Grammar of Phoenician and Punic*. Munich: Beck.

Schmitz, Philip C.

2008 Archaic Greek Words in Phoenician Script from Karatepe. *American Society of Greek and Latin Epigraphy Newsletter* 12/2: 5–9.

2009 Phoenician KRNTRYŠ, Archaic Greek ΚΟΡΥΝΗΤΗΡΙΟΣ, and the Storm God of Aleppo. *KUSATU* 11: 119–60.

Vance, D. R.

1994 Literary Sources for the History of Palestine and Syria: The Phoenician Inscriptions. *BA* 57: 2–19, 110–20.

Phoenician–Punic: The View Backward—Phonology versus Paleography

Robert M. Kerr

The grammatical discussion of Phoenician–Punic traditionally begins with the oldest monuments from the Lebanese motherland and adjacent regions that adopted Phoenician as a monumental language (e.g., Zinçirli in Syria, Anatolia).[1] Most discussions make some reference to the Western dialect of Punic and passing reference to the latest inscriptions in Neo-Punic and Latin script. The latter are often dealt with in a somewhat cursory fashion, like fairy-tale stepchildren: unwanted yet impossible to ignore entirely. Often, however, texts written in these scripts, besides being viewed as less relevant for biblical studies, are also seen as corrupt specimens produced in a period of language loss or "vulgar Punic."[2] Indeed, these texts often appear odd to to modern students of Phoenician–Punic, who are typically either Old Testament scholars or classically trained Semitists. On the one hand, the Neo-Punic script at first glance often bears little or no resemblance to traditional Northwest Semitic writing; on the other hand, for those accustomed to a solely consonantal rendition of lexemes on etymological principles, Neo-Punic texts can seem quite peculiar. The reason for this, however, is quite simple and has nothing to do with language loss but, rather, with a switch from an etymological to a phonetic spelling[3] that can employ vowel letters.

Author's note: A small contribution to the memory of an epigraphist whose contribution to Phoenician–Punic paleography remains an indispensable tool without rival. In the following, where necessary to avoid confusion, graphemes are enclosed in braces { }, phonemes between slashes / /. I wish to thank K. Jongeling for his helpful comments.

1. For Zinçirli/Zinjirli, see *KAI* 24–25. For recent Anatolian finds, see, e.g., *KAI*[5] 287 and the texts published by Tekoğlu and Lemaire 2000 and Kaufman 2007.

2. This has been proposed widely in the past. I mention here only Várhelyi 1998 and Adams 2003: 200–45, esp. pp. 242–45.

3. See, for example, written Norwegian, with its distinction between *Riksmål* and *Nynorsk*.

A necessarily more-or-less phonological spelling can be found in the Latino-Punic texts, as I have demonstrated elsewhere.[4] These texts merely render Phoenician–Punic, albeit in a different script that systematically represents vowels and other phonetic features that remain invisible in the Semitic script (such as spirantization). Here I must emphasize the fact that the terms Neo- and Latino-Punic are not linguistic but paleographical criteria, and together they form what might best be designated Late Punic.[5] Hence, there are two subcorpora of Semitic epigraphy employing different scripts that supply us with firsthand phonological information, especially with regard to vocalization, from a period when by all accounts the language was still a living language, unlike Masoretic Hebrew, Classical Syriac, or even Qurʾānic Arabic.[6] In addition, one might note that Punic epigraphy from the Roman period imitates Latin epigraphic culture and hence displays much more variation with regard to genre, grammar, and lexicon than the the texts of the preceding periods do. Although there has been considerable progress in the study of these corpora in recent years, much remains to be done; for example, phonetic spellings in hitherto unattested genres that depart from standard formulas often leave the modern epigrapher quite puzzled.[7]

The biggest barriers to the study of Neo-Punic remain the script and the lack of good photographs of the texts. Many of these inscriptions have never been published with an illustration, others with just a line drawing of the editor's interpretation or an illegible photograph. Drawings of this sort are often highly unreliable due to the idiosyncratic nature of the Neo-Punic script. Even J. Brian Peckham (1968: 177–222) in his magisterial study of the development of the Phoenician–Punic

4. Cf. Kerr 2007. Here I also demonstrate that the similarities in orthography between the *Poenulus* (930–939) and the Tripolitanian inscriptions indicate a tradition of writing Punic with Latin letters.

5. Thus, for example, *LPE*.

6. Without entering the complex problem of the origins of Classical Arabic, I merely note that different dialects are represented by the reading and written traditions of the Qurʾān. Manuscript evidence also makes it clear that the current consonant pointing (إعْجَام), vowel marks (حَرَكَات) and supplementary diacritics (تشْكِيل) are later additions to the consonantal text (رَسْم).

7. A good example of this phenomenon is, for example, *KAI* 161/Cherchel 2, from the mausoleum of Micipsa (*mkwsn*), which must postdate his demise in 118 B.C. This "official" text is well executed and full of unusual phrases that make its interpretation difficult.

script seemingly ran into difficulties when trying to describe Neo-Punic, because it did not fit into any model of supraregional linear development, as do the various Phoenician scripts. He noted that the "want of dated, or readily datable material" seriously inhibits any study of this sort for Punic (1968: 193). The same applies to Neo-Punic, and the customary epigraphical tenet that Punic inscriptions antedate the Roman destruction of Carthage in 146 B.C. and that Neo-Punic texts are posterior to this date is obviously deficient and is only maintained for lack of a suitable replacement.[8] Nonetheless, Peckham's conclusions that "Neo-Punic developed in an independent cursive tradition whose influence on Punic, particularly in the latter part of the third and in the second century, is extensive" (1968: 220) remain valid.

The precise course of development will probably always remain a mystery. Neo-Punic cursive, which was in use before 146 B.C.,[9] probably originated as a chancellery or book hand used to write on perishable materials such as papyrus, parchment, ostraca, and so on, most of which have not survived.[10] This type of writing was more common, which explains its influence on the Punic lapidary script.[11] It seems that, after the destruction of the Carthaginian hegemony in North Africa after the Third Punic War, the formal writing tradition became extinct

8. I note here the Neo-Punic texts from Carthage, which in all likelihood antedate the Roman conquest that ended the Third Punic War. An interesting case is Carthage 4 (*CIS* I 942), which commences in Punic and suddenly continues in Neo-Punic script. Of note here also is Chia 1 (*KAI* 173) from Sardinia (which had come under Roman suzerainty in 238 B.C.) and dating to the end of the first/early second century C.E., displaying its script form and using vowel letters. Although the text is from the Roman era, its script more closely resembles Phoenician than Punic, indicating a separate development paralleling its political separation from the Phoenician–Punic realm. See also the inscription mentioned in the previous note.

9. See Amadasi Guzzo: "Se la scrittura neopunica si afferma in forme monumentali ca la caduta di Cartagine, la sua origine è certo precedente. Lettere tracciate secondo semplificazioni che saranno poi neopuniche sono già attestate sia su stele della stessa Cartagine di epoca ellenistica, sia, occasionalmente, su documenti più antichi" (*IFPI*: 31–32).

10. See, esp., Amadasi Guzzo: "Alcune di esse sono tipiche della scrittura corsiva dipinta su ostraca e papiri di provenienza fenicia e, soprattutto, egiziana (in particolare da Elefantina). Tali attestazioni mostrano che la scrittura neopunica deriva da una variante corsiva della scrittura fenicia ch si forma verosimilmente già nei secoli VI–V a.C. Ed è tracciata forse a pennello su materiale non lapideo (papiro, pergamena)" (*IFPI*: 32).

11. The influence of cursive hands (now mostly lost) on lapidary ductus was a continuous feature in the evolution of the Northwest Semitic scripts.

(possibly due to the introduction of Latin, especially in the administrative sector).[12] Along with the demise of the formal written tradition, historical etymological orthography was partially replaced by an informal phonetic orthography that reflected the spoken language more closely. Hence, in both phonology and paleography, we can see only the outcome of the development and have little or no insight into the intermittent stages.

Although Peckham (1968: 177–222, pl. 17) has described the major features of Neo-Punic paleography more than adequately,[13] an often-heard complaint is that the distinction between various graphemes is often minimal: this applies especially to the differentiation between *ʾaleph* and *mem*; *bet, dalet,* and *resh; dalet* and *ʿain;* as well as *samech, ṣade,* and *šin*–depending on the inscription in question. This is partially a question of resisting overgeneralized paleographical descriptions: Neo-Punic confounds any general treatment. More often than not, local graphemic variants are quite distinct–from the impressive monumental forms from Lepcis Magna of the first century C.E. to the rough cursive employed in some Algerian backwaters such as Calama (modern Guelma). Hence, any serious treatment must often remain on the level of the individual inscription or, at best, a single, ad hoc geographical region with paleographically similar texts. The Leptian texts, which can be read without much difficulty, display for the most part a traditional historical-etymological spelling of Semitic words. The Guelma texts, on the other hand, often seem to display a bewildering array of spellings.[14]

12. Somewhat differently, for example, Amadasi Guzzo: "È presumibile che la caduta di Cartagine abbia favorito una parziale interruzione della tradizione scribale monumentale e una più rapida diffusione delle forme corsive anche su documenti in pietra" (*IFPI*: 32).

13. A recent handbook on writing systems merely states that "the Neo-Punic script of the Roman period is extremely cursive and hard to read" (Coulmas 1996: 423).

14. Although the orthography fluctuates significantly in this subcorpus, this is due solely to the absence of a standardized phonetic spelling–all the spelling variations of one lexeme are but different ways of spelling the same word phonetically (as in substandard English "nite" for *night*). Generally, Neo-Punic inscriptions display the following system of vocalization: {ʾ} for /e, o/ and sometimes /u/; {w} for /u/ (never /o/); {y} for /i/ (never /e/); and {ʿ} for /a/ (see below, n. 52; and Kerr 2007: 12–38). This can be seen in some of the more frequent words from the Guelma texts (quoted from *HNPI*): *ʾbn* 'stone,' historical-etymological (5, 6, 10, 11, 12, 14, 15, 16) versus phonetic *ʿbn* (1, 3, 4, 7, 8, 9, 17) for /abn/; *šnt* 'years,' hist.-ety. (1) versus phon. *šʿnt* (2–5, 13) /šanūθ/; *lʾdn* 'for the lord,' hist.-ety. (20, 30) versus phon. *lʿdn* (18, 19, 21, 22, 24, 25, 26, 27, 28, 32) and *lʿdʾn* (35) /ladūn/; *bʿl ḥmn* 'Bal Amun' (20, 31; cf. Hebrew בַּעַל הָמוֹן, Cant 8:11), hist.-ety. versus phon. *bʿl mn* (18, 19, 21–27, 32,

At this site, for example, {š}, {s}, and {z} are often indistinguishable at first glance, and past editors of these texts have often made the mistake of reading graphemes of this sort based on a generalized prototype form. Although one could conceivably argue that only one grapheme is rendered (that is, that these three sounds have merged), there is no support for a merger of this sort from elsewhere, and in any given text these graphemes are usually quite distinct from each other, although specific forms may have no other parallel elsewhere at Guelma.[15] The texts from this site represent two genres, funerary and *molk*-votive steles,[16] each more or less following a specific formula. In texts of the former genre, it is usually quite clear syntactically which grapheme is intended. For example:

(1) Guelma 1 (NP 22):

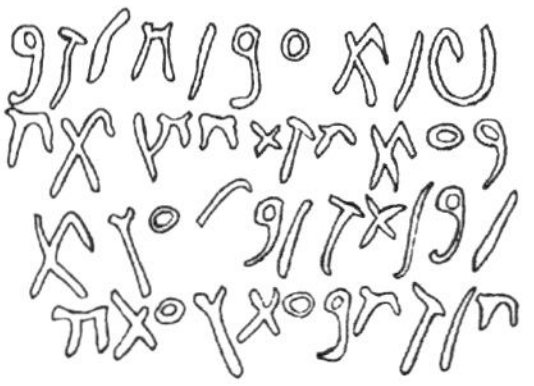

[1]*ṭnʾ*	*ʿbn*	*z*	*l=tb-*[2]*b*ᶜ
erected.PERF.PASS.3FS	stone.FS.NOM	DEM	for=Tabiba.FS.GEN
ʾš-t=m	*š*	*zwʾš-*[3]*n*	*bn*
wife-FS.GEN=his.MS	REL	Zuošan.MS.GEN	son.MS.NOM
mtnbl	*ʿwʾ*	[4]*šn-t*	
Muthunbal.MS.GEN	lived.PERF.3FS	years-FP.ACC	
šbʿ-m	*w=ʿmš*		
seventy-MP.ACC	CONJ=five.MS.ACC		

'This stone was erected for Tabiba, wife of Zuošan,[17] son of Muthunbal; she lived seventy-five years'.

34, 36), *bʿl ʾmn* (37) and *bʿl mʾn* (37) /bal amūn/; *šmʿ* 'he heard,' hist.-ety. versus *šmʾ* (22, 34, 32), *šʿmʾ* (18–20, 25, 26, 28) /šamō/ and the anomalous *šmw* /šamū/ (31); **ql* 'his voice,' hist.-ety. (not at Guelma) versus *qlʾ* (31–34), *qʾlʾ* (18), and *qwlʾ* (19, 20, 25, 26) /*qūlō*/.

15. That is, the {s} of one text may appear similar to the {z}, {ṣ}, or {š} of another and vice versa.

16. Guelma 1–17, 38–39 and 18–37, respectively.

17. I will not discuss the Libyco-Berber names here, because I have no knowledge of their etymology. Note that Jongeling in *HNPI* (ad loc.) reads *Zuosan,* but since the grapheme in question looks more like {š}, and there is no other attestation of {s} in this text, caution suggests reading *Zuošan.* Note that Libyco-Berber names

In this text, in the seventh letter of the first line there is what syntactically must be the demonstrative {z} (/zə/). Although the form is highly idiosyncratic, it is quite distinct from the various renditions of {š} in lines two and four. Although in the past, demonstratives {š} and {s} have been proposed for Late Punic, a close reading of this text shows that reading a {z} is correct. The fourth sign of the fourth line was read by Chabot 1916 as an {s}, which Friedrich and Röllig (1999: §48a) retain as its only example for a phonetic shift /š/ > /s/. Although this letter looks rather odd, it is by no means necessarily an {s} but fits in with the attested variations of {š} such as in the fourth letter of the second line (in *ʾštm*); because there are no Semitic words containing a grapheme {s}, there is no manner of establishing what such a letter would have actually looked like in this text. Hence there is no reason to read an {s} here or to suspect a sound change /š/ > /s/ based on such evidence. In the *molk*-votive texts, confusions between these two graphemes also seem to occur, for example:

(2) Guelma 19 (NP 18):

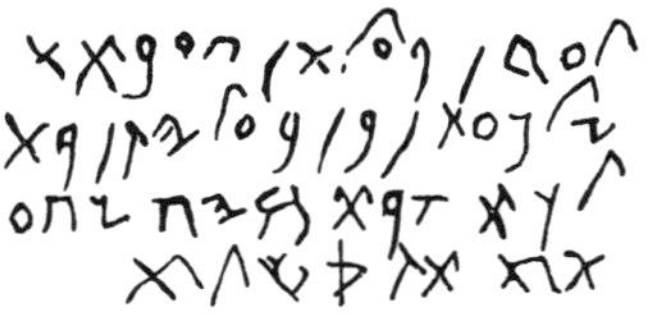

[1]*l=ʿdn*	*bʿl*	*mn*
[1]for=lord.MS.GEN	Bal.MS.NOM	Amun.MS.GEN
zʿbʾ	*m-*[2]*ylkʿtn*	*bn*
sacrificed.PERF.3MS	Milkathon.MS.NOM	son.MS.NOM
bʿlytn	*b=m-*[3]*lk*	*ʾzrm*
Balithon.MS.GEN	as=*molk*.MS.GEN	*hzrm*.MP.GEN
h=yš	*w=šʿ*[4]*mʾ*	*ʾt*
the=male.MS.GEN	CONJ=heard.PERF.3MS	ACC
qwl=ʾ		
voice.MS.ACC=his.MS		

seemingly display both the suffixes *-san* and *-šan*, seemingly in free variation; also in Libyco-Berber texts (cf., e.g., BLSN *RIL* 212, BRSN 914, BRŠN 186, BTŠN 817). Hence, the variations here are not a question of paleography, because the graphemes traditionally transcribed (see Kerr 2010) as {š} and {s} are clearly differentiated in Libyco-Berber: Ⅹ/C and ⋟, respectively.

'For the lord Bal Amun, sacrificed Milkathon, son of Balithon, as the *hzrm* molk-offering of a male, and he heard his voice'.

In this series of texts, the distinction between the two graphemes {š} and {z} is often quite hard to make. An additional problem is the etymology of the lexeme spelled *ʾzrm* or *hzrm* at Guelma—that is, determining which consonants make up the root. Here as elsewhere,[18] it is seemingly a sacrificial term and, based on these spellings, the {z} appears certain, whatever the precise derivation of the root may be.[19] In Chabot's edition of these texts, he transcribed the root as *zbḥ* (18, 19, 20, 25, 32, and 34) or as *šbḥ* (21, 26, 27, 31, and 35), depending on the letters' apparent shape and postulated an "équivalence du son attribue à ces lettres dans la prononciation de bas époque" (Chabot 1916: 79).

A general confusion of the sibilants in Late Punic, especially a realization of {š} as /s/ is often asserted in the grammatical literature on the subject.[20] Is this a question of phonology or of paleography? In my opinion, as the (easily multipliable) examples from Guelma show, only the latter can be correct. As Jongeling (2003: 121) points out, "It is of course common knowledge that *š* and *z* quite often resemble each other in Neo-Punic script, as is the case with e.g., *t* and *n*. In cases when *t* and *n* are difficult to distinguish, nobody seems to find any problems in choosing between them according to the supposed meaning of the text. The same is the case with the short forms of *b*, *d* and *r*." Indeed, a glance through the vocabulary of *HNPI* (pp. 381–410) shows that there

18. El Hofra 162; *CIS* I 3781, 3783, 5702, 5741; *HNPI* Tunisia OU 3; *KAI* 120, 121, 126. In the latter three texts, *ʾdr ʿzrm* renders Latin *præfectus sacrorum*.

19. I will address this issue in more detail in a forthcoming monograph on the *mulk/molek* sacrifices. In the meantime, I note that readings such as *ʾšrm*, such as have been proposed in the past (e.g., this text in *LPE* 49–50), should be rejected.

20. E.g., Segert 1976: §33.54: "The distinction between /s/ and /š/ came also to be overlooked" (not discussed in Segert 1997); Krahmalkov 2001: 25–26: "In Classical Phoenician, the fricative merged with simple /s/ (expressed by the grapheme *S*) but normally continued to be represented in orthography by the grapheme *Š*," et passim; Krahmalkov 2002: 209: "Phoenician did not possess the sound *sh*"; Hackett 2004: 367: "confusion of sibilants"; 2004: 369–70: "š /s/"; Haelewyck 2007: §168: "En phénicien récent et en punique, il y a une grande confusion dans les sifflantes, qui indique une tendance à la disparition de la prononciation particulière de š et de *s*." Harris (1936: 22) and van den Branden (1969: 7) are rather more cautious.

are only a few instances when, with the exception of the gutturals,[21] incorrect consonants are employed in Semitic lexemes.[22]

Do these exceptions warrant a rule? Harris's (1936: 22) warning that "every word in a language has its own history" seems sorely forgotten in much modern linguistic work. In the more recent overviews,[23] which for want of space often give no text references, anomalies are often mentioned without indication of their frequency, creating the impression that they might be frequent. An example is the alleged demonstrative pronoun {s}. Although the demonstrative {st} is a standard feature of Late Punic for both masculine and feminine nouns (Friedrich and Röllig 1999: §115: "eine selbständige Erneuerung?"), I assume that the root form originates from the {z}, /zv/, demonstrative appended with {-t} (/θ/), possibly realized as /s/ due to partial regressive assimilation to the voiceless dental fricative /θ/ (cf. Kerr 2007: 108).[24] This, however, leaves the form {s} unexplained. Friedrich and Röllig (1999: §113) mention only one example[25] (*KAI* 146 = Hr. Maktar 65, *HNPI* p. 123). Is one example, from a site that otherwise frequently employs {z} as the demonstrative,[26] valid support? If one looks at Berger's photograph made from a squeeze (1901: pl. 5:1), it is hard to read the sign in question as an {s}. A {z}, although not certain due to the poor quality of the illustration, is equally possible.[27]

Other examples of a phonetic merger of sibilants in Late Punic are either limited to specific words or of doubtful interpretation. In the latter category belongs *m'sʾ* in *KAI* 126.8 (cf. Friedrich and Röllig 1999: §48a; *HNPI* Labdah 19, pp. 27–28), which renders *merita* in the Latin

21. Which were no longer a phonetic reality and were hence either written as relics in historical spellings or as vowel letters; see above, n. 14.

22. In the Guelma texts published in *HNPI* (pp. 228–44), Jongeling rightly reads the correct historical sibilant, unlike our more hesitant approach in *LPE* 48–50.

23. E.g., Krahmalkov 2002; Hackett 2004.

24. Similarly partial contact progressive assimilation t > θ/s is reflected in the spelling of Latin names in Punic, e.g., *skstʾ* /seksθe/ 'Sextus', *rstyqʾ* /rusθike/ 'Rusticus', *pʿwstʾ* /fawsθe/ 'Faustus'; otherwise the Punic grapheme {ṯ} always renders Latin {t}, Greek τ (cf. in general Kerr 2007: 77–81, esp. pp. 79–80).

25. *HNPI* 399 also mentions Bordj Bou Chateur 1 (p. 68), but the reading of this text is so uncertain that its value in rendering support to a general sound change is nil.

26. Hr. Maktar 13–19, 22–26, 28–34, 42, 46, 48, 50, 54–58, 60–62, 125, and 133.

27. With all due respect to Berger, a century ago the orthography of Neo-Punic was still only rudimentarily understood.

parallel text (*IRT* 318b:5). Friedrich and Röllig (1999), *KAI, IPT*, and *DNWSI* derive this word from *ʿśy* (Heb. עשה), which is rather unlikely because this would be the first attestation of this Hebrew and Moabite isogloss in Phoenician-Punic which, like Arabic, employs *pʿl* (versus Aramaic *ʿbd*) in this connotation (or might this be a Hebrew loan?). Krahmalkov (2000: s.v.) wisely notes "?etym."—especially since this text is one of the Leptian Neo-Punic texts that renders elements of the Roman conceptual world in Punic linguistic guise. From the former category, Krahmalkov's prime example (2001: 22) is the spelling of *zkr* (> Semitic *ḏkr*) 'to remember' as *skr*. This, however, is not indicative of a general *Lautverschiebung* /z/ > /s/ but is exclusively limited to this one root, and one should concur with the explanation of Friedrich and Röllig (1999: §46a:) "daß die in Imperfektform wie **iazkur* > *iaskur* in unmittelbarer Berührung mit dem folgenden stimmlosen *k* lautgesetzlich entstandene Aussprache mit stimmlosen *s* in andere Stellungen übertragen wurde."

The other examples that are usually brought to bear all concern lexemes with a root consonant derived from the Proto-Semitic lateral fricative /ś/ (/s²/, IPA /ɬ/). The NWS alphabet had no separate grapheme for this sound, which only survived into (early) Classical Hebrew, Moabite, Old Aramaic, Old North and South Arabic, and Gəʿəz.[28] Old Akkadian, Ugaritic, and even Arabic lost this phoneme.[29] The fact that Phoenician-Punic does not render this phoneme is often seen as proof that the Phoenician alphabet (regardless of its precise origins) was the ultimate source of other NWS alphabets (cf. the distinction שׁ /š/ and שׂ /ś/ in Masoretic Hebrew). There is no reason to reopen the complex discussion of the *Nachleben* of the Proto-Semitic sibilants here except to note that the issue is rather complex and that a mechanical application

28. Whereas the preceding languages seem to have preserved /s/, /ś/ and /š/ (resp. s¹⁻³), Gəʿəz only preserved ሰ /s/ and ሠ /ś/, /š/ having merged with the latter phoneme. In the traditional pronunciation and successor languages (Amharic and Tigriña), both graphemes are realized as /s/ and often confused in manuscripts (we exclude here the secondary palatalization > ሸ /š/).

29. *Old Akkadian*—where it by all appearances had merged with /s/. Cf. Hasselbach 2005: 135–36; von Soden 1995: §30.

Ugaritic—generally it had merged with /š/ (and secondarily in a few cases > /θ/). Cf. Tropper 2000: §32.122.

Arabic—usually > ش, but note Guillaume (1965: 34) who gives several examples with ڢ. Note, however, that in older Classical Arabic, for example, in الكتاب of Sibawayhi, ش renders /s/ and س renders /š/, the opposite of the present situation. Hence, transcriptions such as Ibn Khaldun's rendition of St. Augustine اجوشتين ~ /agūštīn/ < /agūstīn/ remain difficult to assess.

of phonetic rules does not provide an adequate solution. With regard to Phoenician–Punic, note the numerals *‘*śr*(*t*) ‘ten’ and *‘*śrm* ‘twenty’, the spelling of which can vary between {š} and {s}. For Phoenican, there are only two relevant examples, namely, *‘sr w’rb‘* ‘fourteen’ (*KAI* 14.1) versus *‘šrt wšlšt* ‘thirteen’ (*Muséon* 51, 286, 2; that is, עשרת). In Neo-Punic, {s} is employed consistently (cf. *HNPI* p. 401 versus Friedrich and Röllig 1999: §242). In all other cases, even in Neo-Punic, the grapheme {š} is always used to render PS /ś/, for example, forms of *ś* (‘sheep’), *nś’* (‘to carry, to bring’) and *śd* (‘field’; cf. Friedrich and Röllig 1999: §46b). The question is how to interpret these seemingly conflicting data.

Krahmalkov (2001: 25–26) again mentions *‘śr*(*t*) and *‘śrm* as his prime examples,[30] but he makes no mention here of *ś*, *nś’*, and *śd*, instead referring to Latin transcriptions, especially St. Augustine's wordplay on *salus*, which he renders phonetically as /salūs/. Additionally, he refers to Judg 12:6, the classic *shibboleth*. With regard to the latter, while the dialects of Classical Hebrew, especially the Southern (Jerusalemite) dialect and a northern dialect-continuum encompassing Phoenician are becoming increasingly clear,[31] it is impossible to know whether the Ephraimite "speech impediment" was merely a local feature or was an areal feature (although, if the number of slain Ephraimites given in the biblical text, 42,000, was correct, this would point to a somewhat widespread feature).[32] Nonetheless, it cannot have been a feature of the recorded Phoenician–Punic dialects, since one would then expect a general uncertainty reflected in the orthography: Phoenician–Punic, as has been seen, never confuses the phonemes rendered by {š}[33] and {s} when writing Semitic words. For Phoenician proper, this is abundantly clear, as can be seen by the Neo-Assyrian transcriptions of Phoenician personal names where Phoenician /s/ is rendered with cuneiform signs

30. Because this feature, like *zkr* > *skr*, is limited to but one lexeme, one can only speculate about whether /ś/ > /s/ here might somehow be conditioned by the immediately following /r/. Unfortunately, comparative examples < */-śr-/ are lacking in Phoenician–Punic.

31. See, in general, Israel 1985. Also see Garr 1985, who views Northwest Semitic as a dialect continuum with Phoenician and Aramaic at opposite ends (cf. Garr 1985: 5–7, 231, et passim).

32. For a discussion of the issues and previous interpretations with bibliography, see Woodhouse 2003.

33. Note the exemplary caution of Friedrich and Röllig 1999: §44 *fine*: "In diesem Buch wird das Graphem ש einheitlich als *š* umschrieben; über die genaue Aussprache an einem bestimmten Ort oder zu einer bestimmten Zeit soll damit nicht präjudiziert werden."

of the {š} (Neo-Assyrian /s/)-series and Phoenician /š/ by signs of the {s}- series (Neo-Assyrian /š/).[34]

The Neo-Assyrian transcriptions should be a sufficient caveat when dealing with words transcribed by the script of another language. Although in principal any script can be used to render any language, one must always remember that one cannot just borrow a writing system but is also borrowing the underlying phonetic system of the language from which the writing system is borrowed. Hence modern Arabic lexemes rendered in Latin letters from North Africa often display French phonetic values, for example, the Algerian town (formerly Iol/Caesarea) *Cherchel* < شرشال ; whilst regions more influenced by Great Britain display a rendition in {sh}, for example, Sharm el-Sheikh (شرم الشيخ).[35] Akkadian was able to distinguish between /s/ and /š/, whereas Greek and Latin could not. Thus, the question is, are Latin and Greek sources that use {s} to transcribe Punic /š/ useful as phonetic information, or are these alphabets simply unable to provide reliable information in this regard?

If one looks, for example, at the Latino-Punic texts,[36] one sees the four Punic phonemes rendered either simply as {s}, digraphs or loan-graphemes in Latin script:

Punic Grapheme	*Latin Rendition*
/z/	*s, z, sd, zd,* Σ
/s/	*s*
/ṣ/	*s, st, tz, ꞩ*
/š/	*s*

Looking at the inscriptional evidence (both the Latino-Punic texts and the rendition of Punic names in Latin inscriptions from North Africa), one sees that the second sound poses no problems: Punic /s/ with Latin

34. Cf. Hämeen-Anttila 2000: 12; von Soden 1995: §30.

35. That is, Arabic words are spelled as if they were French or English lexemes, respectively; in the examples given, note the various renditions of /š/. One uses the orthography of the lender language to render phonemes of the target language. The differences in the spelling and pronunciation of sounds in the Romance languages are due to their individual development–not all of these languages ceased being "Latin" in one instant: see, for example, French *cinq* versus Italian *cinque* /'tʃiŋkwe/ and *champs* versus *campo*. The same applies, e.g., to Germanic.

36. I ignore here the two Greco-Punic texts from El-Hofra because they provide only limited information (see n. 46).

{s} (Greek σ). The phonemes /z/ and /ṣ/ can be specially rendered in Latin script, but this is by no means mandatory. Although Latin originally retained the Greek ζ for the genitive plural of the first declension in the pre-classical language, *-azom*, after rhotacism (i.e., s, z > r / V_V) the voiced sibilant became extinct. Early authors, such as Plautus,[37] wrote Greek loanwords with the nearest equivalent {s} and later *sd*.[38] In the early first century C.E., it was reintroduced, originally for Greek loanwords that were beginning to enter Latin en masse at this time. Latin {z} was hitherto not attested in the Latino-Punic corpus, but as I have shown elsewhere (Kerr 2007: 85–87), the symbol resembling the Greek sigma is actually a cursive Latin {z}.[39] Although this grapheme is mostly used in Latino-Punic to render /z/ in Libyan lexemes, it is once used (Bir Shmech LP 1:3) as an indeclinable relative particle {σy} (/zə/),[40] hitherto only attested in the early Byblos texts (*KAI* 1, 4, 6–7) and considered to be a diagnostic feature of that dialect.[41] This cannot hold true any longer: the late Latino-Punic attestations show that this is merely a regular feature of Phoenician–Punic. From a comparative Semitic perspective, this is hardly surprising because /d̲*v*/ (> /z*v*/ in Canaanite and Geʿez), originally a demonstrative pronoun, is commonly used as a relative pronoun in Semitic.[42]

Another phoneme foreign to Latin (and Greek) is /ṣ/. In Latin epigraphy, this was usually rendered {s} or sometimes {st} and once {tz}.[43] In Latino-Punic and in the Latin Bu-Ngem ostraca, the graph-

37. E.g., *Mercator* 926: "sona sonam sustuli."

38. See in general Kerr 2007: 89–91. Note that, while Latin {s} for Punic /z/ is common, {sd} is largely confined to literary sources. {zd} is only attested twice as *Azdrubal* (*CIL* V 4919, 4920) < Punic *ʿzrbʿl*. (Note the next line of the latter text, *Azrubal*.)

39. In the past, this grapheme has usually been interpreted as an attempt to render /š/ (e.g., Friedrich and Röllig 1999: §48e) possibly because the Greek letter originally derives from Northwest Semitic {š}, or due to the similarity of the Libyan grapheme {š}, i.e., ⵣ (see n. 17 above). Curiously, Krahmalkov does not mention this grapheme in his *Grammar* (2001) at all. The cursive Latin {z} of the ostraca looks much like a majescule Greek sigma—since this letter was hardly used in Latin epigraphy, the lapicide working from a cursive Vorlage was probably unable to convert this unfamiliar letter into Roman capitals.

40. Usually spelled {ys} (/əz/); see Kerr 2007: 102 sub §2.2.7.

41. Cf., e.g., Hackett 2004: §1.3.

42. E.g., Hebrew זוּ (Joüon and Muraoka 2006: §38) and זֶה (2006: §145c); and for Ugaritic *d̲*, cf. Tropper 2000: §43.2–3. On this usage in general, see Mazzini 2006.

43. This phoneme also seems to have been present in Libyco-Berber (cf. Kerr 2010: n. 54), which would make its disappearance in Late Punic due to alleged sub-

eme {s} is frequently employed (Kerr 2007: 81–84; Friedrich and Röllig 1999: §48e; Krahmalkov 2001: 24–25), which is actually a digraph {s+t}. However, this composite grapheme is not original to Latino-Punic or even Roman North Africa. Its origins seem to lie in Gaul, where it was employed to render the enigmatic *tau gallicum* (rendered with {ð} and {s} in Latin inscriptions) of Continental Celtic ({ss} in Insular Celtic), a sound by all accounts very similar to Semitic /ṣ/ (cf. Kerr 2007 83–84; Eska 2004: §3.3.1.1).

This leaves us with the Punic phoneme /š/, which is always transcribed {s} (Greek σ) in Latin and Latino-Punic (see Kerr 2007: 93 for attestations). In my opinion, this rendition is solely due to the inadequacy of the Greek and Latin alphabets and says nothing about its pronunciation in Punic. As has just been seen, Punic names in Latin inscriptions and especially Latino-Punic did employ special graphemes to render phonemes alien to Latin; however, these symbols were innovations borrowed from Europe for the rendition of foreign sounds from languages with which the Romans were very familiar (Greek) or quite familiar (Gallic). For whatever reasons, Punic (unlike, for example, Coptic) did not or could not adopt symbols from their traditional script (that is, the Demotic graphemes used to augment the Greek alphabet to render Egyptian, that is, Coptic) to render phonemes alien to the adopted Greek alphabet, in casu *šai* ϣ /š/.[44] At the same time, one must bear in mind that none of the languages with which Latin speakers regularly came into contact in Europe had a /š/ phoneme. Celtic and Greek (like Proto-Indo-European) never had this sound, and neither did the contemporary Germanic languages.[45] From this, one may conclude

strate influence unlikely. Compare the minimal pairs found in personal names from North African Latin inscriptions: *basa* (*BAC* 1941–1942: 626 n. 52), *batza* (*art. cit.* 619 n. 29), *baza* (*CIL* VIII 11646); *naltzalus* (*CIL* VIII 27524), *nartzalus* (*MartAfr* 545 -17 July), *narzales* (*MartEcclAfr* 371 -17 July), *narsalus* (*CIL* VIII 5282), *narseli* (VIII 4923); *siddin, sidin, tsidin, stidin, tziddin* etc. (cf. Kerr 2007: 88), and the numerous names rendered *tz-* (Kerr 2007: 87 n. 333; and Jongeling 1994: 194–95).

44. The other two "borrowed" graphemes are *fai* ϥ /f/ and *xai* ϧ /x/.

45. The phoneme /š/ (in Germanic studies usually transcribed as /ʃ/) is limited to High German dialects from Middle High German onward (cf. Hermann 1989: §155). In Old High German, spellings such as *skeidan, skirm, scūr, scalc, scrītan, fisk, wakan* show that the voiceless sibilant was still not fused with the following voiceless velar (cf. Braune 2004: §§146, 168). In modern High German dialects such as Swabian, s+C > šC in all positions, for example, *Straße* /štrāß/, *Fest* /fešt/, etc., while in the Low German tongues such as Frisian, Dutch, or Danish, they remain distinct, for example, *ship:* Frisian *skip* /skip/, Dutch *schip* /sxip/, Danish *skib* /skib/, etc. (High German *Schiff* /šif/).

that for contacts with Semitic languages (besides Punic in North Africa, various forms of Aramaic in the East) the Romans did not consider it necessary to render the voiceless fricative sibilant with their graphemic system. The graphemes necessary to transcribe alien Punic phonemes were borrowed from older (and possibly more intensive) contact situations in the Empire, and no real innovations occurred in Africa. Hence the Latin (and Greek) transcriptions of Punic /š/ with Latin {s} (Greek σ)[46] say nothing about the realization of this phoneme in Punic. The Latino-Punic inscriptions distinguish clearly between /z/, /s/, and /ṣ/, as do the transcriptions of Punic names in Latin (and Greek) sources on occasion (and as mentioned, rendering these phonemes with {s} is no proof of a sound merger in Punic). Furthermore, St. Augustine's testimony should not be made to provide what it cannot: he was a theologian and not a phonologist or a field linguist. His report of the "wordplay" on *salus*[47] was that the Punic word meaning 'three', that is, 'Trinity' (irrespective of its pronunciations, < /šalūš/ < /*šalōš/ < /*šalāš/ < /*ṯalāṯu/), sounded similar enough to the Latin *salus* 'salvation' to make a point, nothing more, nothing less.[48]

---

46. E.g., σαμω in El-Hofra GP 1:3 (*KAI* 175) /šamṓ/ 'he heard'.

47. *Epistolae ad Romanos inchoata expositio* 13 (CSEL 84):

> Quo loco prorsus non arbitror praetereundum, quod pater Valerius animadvertit admirans in quorumdam rusticanorum collocutione. Cum alter alteri dixisset: Salus, quaesivit ab eo, qui et latine nosset et punice, quid esset: Salus, responsus est: Tria. Tum ille agnoscens cum gaudio salutem nostram esse Trinitatem concinentia linguarum non fortuitu sic sonuisse arbitratus est, sed occultissima dispensatione divinae providentiae, ut cum latine nominatur: Salus a punicis intellegantur: Tria, et cum punici lingua sua tria nominant, latine intellegatur: salus . . .

> I most certainly do not think I should neglect to mention here something that Father Valerius noticed with amazement in the conversion of certain peasants [which was in Punic]. Overhearing one say "salus" to the other, Valerius asked the one who knew both Latin and Punic what *salus* meant. The peasant answered 'three'. Then Valerius, realizing with joy that our word for greeting, *salus*, means trinity, thought that this harmony was no accident, but rather the most hidden dispensation of divine providence. For when one says "salus" in Latin, a Carthaginian understands it as 'three'; and when a Carthaginian says "three" in his own language, it is understood as Latin 'salvation'. (translation from Landes 1982: 132)

48. One might wonder whether there is a triple pun here—that is, a reference to the Roman goddess *Salus* (Greek Ὑγιεία), associated with life-giving water, versus baptism, the true water of life; *extra ecclesiam nulla salus* in a new light. There is an interesting acrostic poem by the centurion Q. Avidivs Qvintianvs at Bu Njem in

I might be able to stop here and conclude that, since neither Punic nor Neo-Punic script confuses sibilants and since the Latin alphabet employed to write (Latino-)Punic only rendered non-Latin phonemes when there was a preexisting method from elsewhere in the Empire (for example, {z}, and {s}), one did the best one could by using the grapheme whose phonetic load (in the language providing the alphabet) most approximated the phoneme to be rendered—for example, {s}, σ for /š/. Any supposition about a sibilant merger from the Neo-Punic evidence is exclusively due to the fact that /s/, /ṣ/, and /š/ are often hard to distinguish in Neo-Punic script. This is a paleographical problem and not a phonetic issue; this would be tantamount to claiming that /w/ and /y/ had merged in the formal Hasmonean script and the Herodian book

---

the Tripolitanian pre-desert that he dedicated to her (he seems to have hailed from Eastern Europe and obviously hated his fiery posting; see Adams 1999: 110–12 with commentary):

Qvaesii mvltvm qvot memoriae tradere	I have sought much what to hand down to posterity
Agens prae cvnctos in hac castra milites	Acting in command of all the soldiers in this camp
Votvm commvunem proqve reditv exercitv	And (what) common vow, for the return of the army
Inter priores et fvtvros reddere	To render up among previous and future (vows?)
Dum qvaero meccum digna divom nomina	Whilst seeking privately worthy names of gods
Inveni tandem nomen et numen deae	I found at last the divine name of a goddess
Votis perennem qvem dicare in hoc loco	Which to consecrate, everlastingly in vows, in this place
Salutis igitvr qvandivm cvltores sient	Therefore, as long as there should be worshipers of Salus
Qua potvi sanxi nomen et covnctis dedi	I have sanctified (her) name in the way I could, and I have given to all
Veras salvtis lymphas tantis iggnibvs	The true waters of safety, amid such fires
In istis semper harenacis collibvs	In those always sandy hills
Nvtantis avstri solis flammas fervidas	Of the south wind causing to shimmer(?) the fiery flames of the sun
Tranqville ut nando delenirent corpora	So that by swimming peacefully they might sooth their bodies
Ita tu qvi sentis magnam facti gratiam	And so you who feel great gratitude for (this) deed
Aestvantis animae fvcilari spiritvm	That the spirit of your burning soul is revived
Noth pigere lavdem voce reddere	Do not be reluctant to render genuine praise with your voice
Veram qvi volvit esse te sanvm tibi	(of him) Who wanted to be healthy for your own benefit
Set protestare vel Salutis gratia	But bear witness even for the sake of Salus

hand, as evidenced, for example, by some Qumran texts (for example, the War Scroll and Thanksgiving Scroll) and other contemporary texts (for example, the Nash Papyrus), merely because {w} and {y} there are often difficult to distinguish.[49] Similarly, the use of transcribed sources supposedly supporting a similar sound shift succumb to the confusion of orthography and phonology. Any literate speaker of English is implicitly aware of the fact that how one writes a word has nothing to do with its phonetic realization: for example, 'night' (German *Nacht*) and 'knight' (German *Knecht*), both /nai:t/ (standard pronunciation).

In the preceding, I have shown that there is no valid support for a merger of sibilants as far as Semitic lexemes in neo- and Latino-Punic texts are concerned. There is, however, the troublesome issue (left unmentioned by the recent grammarians) of Latin names in Neo-Punic, where Latin /s/ is seemingly rendered by {š}.[50] This is most odd, for as I have noted above, this phoneme was by all accounts alien to Latin.[51] One could propose an indigenous non-Latin pronunciation of such names (which would prove the existence of the sound in question in Punic),[52] but this lacks sufficient support. In light of the fact that, as

49. The classical study on this matter remains the article by Peckham's teacher, F. M. Cross (1961: esp. pp. 168–70 and the drawings on pp. 138–39). See also Yardeni 1997: 170–81. The fact that in the Qumran texts these two graphemes often appear quite similar if not identical was one of the reasons why some of the Cairo Geniza fragments were considered copies from a medieval Qumran discovery (cf. Di Lella 1962: esp. pp. 259–63). Although the *waw* and *yod* are quite distinct in the book hand employed in the Geniza documents (cf. e.g., Yardeni 1997: 214–21), they are often confused or indistinguishable in the Cairene *Damascus Document* and Hebrew Sirach.

50. I ignore here some seemingly similar anomalies in the renditions of Anatolian and Libyco-Berber (cf. n. 17 above) names, because we still do not have enough knowledge of the respective source languages.

51. In Kerr 2007: 86–90, the issue was left unresolved.

52. This is not to say that non-Latinate pronunciations of Latin lexemes are unattested in Punic inscriptions. Although most recent grammarians of Phoenician–Punic claim that there is no evidence for the spirantization of the *bgdkpt* letters in Phoenician–Punic, it is certain that /b/, /g/, /k/, /p/, and /t/ had only the fricative pronunciation in Latino-Punic (cf. Kerr 2007: 65–81). Although Latin and Greek /k/ is usually rendered {q} in Punic, for example, *mʿrqʾ* 'Marcus' (/marke/; Bir Tlelsa 1/*KAI* 138), apparent anomalies such as *mʿrkʾ* /marxe/ reflect Latin spellings (limited to North Africa) such as *Marchvs* (*CIL* VIII 533, *ILTun* 499), *Marchi* (GEN) pro *Marci(us)* (*IRT* 898), *Marchial-na* pro *Marcial-na* (*CIL* VIII 23729, 27643; *ILS* 9510; *ILAfr* 204; *ILAlg* I 2604, 2632), etc. Similar oddities such as *mwnṭʿnʾ* (Hr. Guergour 4/*KAI* 144) do not reflect an irregular Punic vowel letter {w} rendering /o/ 'Montanus' (see Friedrich and Röllig 1999: §108.3; *KAI* and *HNPI* ad loc.) but, rather, the North African variant "Muntanus" (cf. Kerr 2007: 27). Other anomalies such as Punic {y}

mentioned, Punic, except for gutturals, always employs the correct consonants and even transcribes Latin lexemes systematically, this would be surprising. Hence, it might be worth taking a closer look at the alleged examples (see table 1).

Table 1. Punic Renditions of Latin /s/

Punic	*Latin*
w]*'ls/š*	Latin parallel 'Valente' (abl.) (Djebel Mansour 1:5)[a]
mṭhqš'	'Metaxus' (Sabratha 1:1)
ʿpwdnš	Latin parallel 'Pudens' (El-Amruni 1:4)
plkš	Latin parallel 'Felicis' (gen.) (Hr. Brirht 1:1)
š'w{'w}'r'!	Latin parallel 'Severus' (El-Amruni N 1:4–5)
šʿṭr	Latin parallel 'Satur' (abl.) (Djebel Mansour 1:4)[b]
šʿṭry	Latin parallel 'Saturio' (abl.?) (Hr. Brirht 1:4)
šhqndʿ	Latin parallel 'Secunda' (Hr. Brirht 1:2–3)
šqndʿ	Latin parallel 'Secundi' (gen.) (Hr. Brirht 1:3)[c]
pylkṣ	'Felix' (/filix/ -cf. n. 53) (Teboursouk N6)[d]

a. Cf. *KAI* 140, *LPE* 31f, *HNPI* 73–74. This is a classic case of the indistinguishabilty of {s} and {š}.
b. Jongeling (*HNPI* 73–74) reads *sʿṭr* as "*šʿṭr* seems to be either non-existent or rare." *KAI, LPE,* and others read *šʿṭr*. On the photograph, the initial grapheme is damaged; thus it actually provides no evidence either way.
c. Oddly enough, *HNPI* 81 reads this example as *sqndʿ* and the previous as *šhqndʿ, sʿṭry* in line 4, but *plkš* in line 1. This seems to contradict his statement that the distinction between {s} and {š} seems to be clearly marked. Bron (2006), who provides a good photograph, reads all the preceding names with {š} without comment.
d. As read by Fantar 1974: 407; Garbini 1978: 7–8; and Jongeling 1984: 105. In *HNPI* 178, Jongeling reads /s/ because it is "more probable and also possible." Unfortunately, this text has no {s} or another {ṣ} for comparison.

This list of exceptions to the usual rendition of Latin /s/ with Punic {s} (Kerr 2007: 86–87) is striking because only five specific inscriptions are involved. As mentioned above concerning Guelma, Neo-Punic paleography must be pursued on an inscription-by-inscription basis. The problem shared by all five texts, however, is that none of them attests any Semitic lexemes containing an {s} that could serve as a comparison. The only basis, then, for actually reading an {š} (and in one case {ṣ}) is that these graphemes more closely resemble this grapheme on other inscriptions from other sites. As has been demonstrated in the preceding, sibilants are usually uniquely distinguished in a particular text, and

representing /e/ (see Friedrich and Röllig 1999: §108.2) can be explained by developments in vulgar Latin; for example, *pylks* (Teboursouk 6) renders /filix/ (cf. *ILAlg* ii/1 326) and not /felix/; similarly *synṭr* (*CIS* I 304) renders /sinator/ (cf. *ILAlg* i 26), not /senator/.

confusion only results when one attempts to transfer paleographical findings from one text to another because the {š} of one might appear similar to an {s} or even {ṣ} or {z} of another, and vice versa. Hence there is no good reason not simply to read {s} in the preceding examples. Thus, one may conclude that the sibilants remained distinct, regardless of their actual realization at any given time or place, throughout the long history of Phoenician–Punic. Although Late Punic may not appear to be a Semitic language outwardly, based on the scripts employed to write it, it certainly remained Semitic internally with regard to phonology and morpho-syntax. The merger of sibilants in Phoenician-Punic as alleged by some is not a phonological issue but solely a paleographical problem.

Bibliography

Adams, J. N.

1999 The Poets of Bu Njem: Language, Culture and the Centurionate. *Journal of Roman Studies* 89: 109–34.

2003 *Bilingualism and the Latin language*. Cambridge: Cambridge University Press.

Berger, P.

1901 Mémoire sur la grande inscription dédicatoire et sur plusieurs autres inscriptions néo-puniques du temple d'Hathor-Miskar à Maktar. *Mémoires de l'Académie des inscriptions et belles-lettres* 36: 135–78.

Branden, A. van den

1969 *Grammaire phénicienne*. Beirut: Bibliothèque de l'Université Saint-Esprit Kaslik.

Braune, W.

2004 *Althochdeutsche Grammatik I*. 15th edition by Ingo Reiffenstein. Tübingen: Max Niemeyer Verlag.

Bron, F.

2006 La stèle bilingue latine et néo-punique de Henchir Brighita (*KAI* 142). *AuOr* 24: 142–44.

Chabot, J.-B.

1916 Punica. *JA* 11/7 (188): 77–109.

1916 Punica. *JA* 11/8 (189): 77–109, 483-520.

1917 Punica. *JA* 11/9 (190): 145-66.

1917 Punica. *JA* 11/10 (191): 5–79.

1918 Punica. *JA* 11/11 (192): 249-302.

Coulmas, F.

1996 *The Blackwell Encyclopedia of Writing Systems*. Oxford: Blackwell.

Cross, F. M.
1961 The Development of the Jewish Scripts. Pp. 133–202 in *The Bible and the Ancient Near East: Essays in Honor of William Foxwell Albright*, ed. G. E. Wright. London: Routledge & Kegan Paul.
Di Lella, A. A.
1962 Qumran and the Geniza Fragments. *CBQ* 24: 245–67.
Divjak, J., ed.
1971 *Sancti Aureli Augustini Expositio quarundam propositionum ex epistola ad Romanos epistolae ad Galatas expositionis liber unus epistolae ad Romanos inchoata expositio*. CSEL 84. Vienna: Hölder-Pichler-Tempsky.
Eska, J. F.
2004 Continental Celtic. Pp. 857–80 in *The Cambridge Encyclopedia of the World's Ancient Languages*, ed. R. D. Woodard. Cambridge: Cambridge University Press.
Fantar, M.
1974 Stèles anépigraphes et stèles à inscriptions néopuniques. *Mémoires de l'Académie des inscriptions et belles-lettres* 16: 379-431.
Friedrich, J., and Röllig, W.
1999 *Phönizisch-Punische Grammatik*. 3rd edition by M. G. Amadasi Guzzo with W. R. Mayer. AnOr 55. Rome: Pontifical Biblical Institute.
Garbini, G.
1978 Epigrafia punica nel Magreb (1977-1978). *SM* 10: 1-12.
Garr, W. R.
1985 *Dialect Geography of Syria–Palestine, 1000–586 B.C.E.* Philadelphia: University of Pennsylvania Press. [Repr. Winona Lake, IN: Eisenbrauns, 2004.]
Guillaume, A.
1965 *Hebrew and Arabic Lexicography: A Comparative Study*. Leiden: Brill.
Hackett, J. A.
2004 Phoenician and Punic. Pp. 365–85 in *The Cambridge Encyclopedia of the World's Ancient Languages*, ed. R. D. Woodard. Cambridge: Cambridge University Press.
Haelewyck, J.-C.
2007 *Grammaire comparée des langues sémitiques: Éléments de phonétique, de morphologie et de syntaxe*. LCA 7. Brussels: Safran.
Hämeen-Anttila, J.
2000 *A Sketch of Neo-Assyrian Grammar*. SAAS 13. Helsinki: Neo-Assyrian Text Corpus Project.
Harris, Z. S.
1936 *A Grammar of the Phoenician Language*. AOS 8. New Haven, CT: American Oriental Society.
Hasselbach, R.
2005 *Sargonic Akkadian: A Historical and Comparative Study of the Syllabic Texts*. Wiesbaden: Harrassowitz.

Hermann, P.
1989 *Mittelhochdeutsche Grammatik*. Tübingen: Max Niemeyer.
Israel, F.
1985 Geographic Linguistics and Canaanite Dialects. Pp. 363–87 in *Current Progress in Afro-Asiatic Linguistics: Papers of the Third International Hamito-Semitic Congress (London, 1978)*, ed. J. Bynon. Amsterdam Studies in the Theory and History of Linguistic Science, Series 4. Current Issues in Linguistic Theory 28. Amsterdam: Benjamins.
Jongeling, K.
1984 *Names in Neo-Punic Inscriptions*. Groningen: Groningen University.
1994 *North-African Names from Latin Sources*. CNWS Publication 21. Leiden: Research School CNWS.
2003 Use of Vowel Letters in Neo-Punic Texts from Guelma. *DS-NELL* 5: 117–36.
Joüon, P., and Muraoka, T.
2006 *A Grammar of Biblical Hebrew*. Rev. ed. SubBi 27. Rome: Pontifical Biblical Institute.
Kaufman, S.
2007 The Phoenician Inscription of the Incirli Trilingual: A Tentative Reconstruction and Translation. *Maarav* 14: 7–26.
Kerr, R. M.
2007 *Latino-Punic and Its Linguistic Environment*. Leiden: Leiden University.
2010 Some Thoughts on the Origins of the Libyco-Berber Alphabet. Pp. 41–68 in *Études berbères V: Essais sur des variations dialectales et autres articles—Actes du «5. Bayreuth-Frankfurt-Leidener Kolloquium zur Berberologie», Leiden, 8–11 octobre 2008*, ed. H. Stroomer et al. Cologne: Rüdiger Köppe.
Krahmalkov, C. R.
2000 *Phoenician-Punic Dictionary*. OLA 90. Studia Phoenicia 15. Leuven: Peeters.
2001 *A Phoenician-Punic Grammar*. HOSNME 54. Leiden: Brill.
2002 Phoenician. Pp. 207–22 in *Beyond Babel: A Handbook for Biblical Hebrew and Related Languages*, ed. J. Kaltner and S. L. McKenzie. SBLRBS 42. Atlanta: Scholars Press.
Landes, P. F.
1982 *Augustine on Romans: Propositions from the Epistle to the Romans, Unfinished Commentary on the Epistle to the Romans*. Early Christian Literature Series 23. Chico, CA: Scholars Press.
Mazzini, G.
2006 D-Base pronominal system in Qatabanic. Pp. 475–88 in *Loquentes linguis: Studi linguistici e orientali in onore die Fabrizio A. Pennacchietti*, ed. P. G. Borbone, A. Mengozzi, and M. Tosco. Wiesbaden: Harrassowitz.
Peckham, J. Brian
1968 *The Development of the Late Phoenician Scripts*. Cambridge: Harvard University Press.

Segert, S.
1976 *A Grammar of Phoenician and Punic.* Munich: Beck.
1997 Phoenician and the Eastern Canaanite Languages. Pp. 174–86 in *The Semitic Languages*, ed. R. Hetzron. New York: Routledge.
Soden, W. von
1995 *Grundriß der akkadischen Grammatik.* 3rd ed. AnOr 33. Rome: Pontifical Biblical Institute.
Tekoğlu, R., and Lemaire, A.
2000 La bilingue royale louvito-phénicienne de Çineköy. *CRAIBL* 2000: 960–1006.
Tropper, J.
2000 *Ugaritische Grammatik.* AOAT 273. Münster: Ugarit-Verlag.
Várhelyi, Z.
1998 What Is the Evidence for the Survival of Punic Culture in Roman North Africa? *Acta Archaeologica Academiae Scientiarum Hungaricae* 38: 391–403.
Woodhouse, R.
2003 The Biblical Shibboleth Story in the Light of Late Egyptian Perceptions of Semitic Sibilants: Reconciling Divergent Views. *JAOS* 123: 271–89.
Yardeni, A.
1997 *The Book of Hebrew Script: History, Paleography, Script Styles, Calligraphy and Design.* Jerusalem: Carta.

The Road Not Taken: An Independent Object Pronoun in Cebel Ires Dağı 7A–7B?

Paul G. Mosca

Two roads diverged in a wood, and I—
I took the one less travelled by,
And that has made all the difference.

—Robert Frost

1. Introduction

More than two decades have now passed since the publication of the *editio princeps* of the Phoenician inscription from Cebel Ires Dağı (Mosca and Russell 1987; *KAI* 287). While many minor corrections have been suggested over the years (with varying degrees of cogency), it is safe to say that the most controversial section of the text has been the subordinate clause in lines 7A–7B. Alternative interpretations have been offered by G. A. Long and D. Pardee (1989), A. Lemaire (1989), and E. Lipiński (2004). Of these, the most influential thus far has been that of Long and Pardee, whose solution has been adopted by I. Kottsieper (2001), K. L. Younger Jr. (*COS* 2.137–39), and (with modifications) C. R. Krahmalkov (2000; 2001). The aim of the present study is to review these various proposals and explain why I continue to prefer the solution offered in the *editio princeps*. It is dedicated to the memory of J. Brian Peckham, S.J., in gratitude for his many contributions to Phoenician-Punic epigraphy.

2. The Context

Some years ago, at the beginning of his study of the Nora "puzzle" (*KAI* 46), Bruce Zuckerman (1991: 270) observed that ancient scribes did not set out to create puzzles: "despite all appearances to the contrary, whoever composed a given inscription meant it to be understood by a given audience." The same is undoubtedly true of the Cebel Ires Dağı inscription. To be sure, many of its puzzles still await definitive solutions; but at least the broad outlines and purpose of the text are clear enough. The stone records a series of land grants by a royal official and by the king himself. Rather like the Mesopotamian *kudurru*, it provides us not with the original title deeds, which would presumably have been housed in the archives of the parties involved, but with a selective summary that was put on display in order to support the claims of a certain MSNZMŠ (his name is also spelled MSNʾZMŠ) to ownership of various allotments of land. The following outline of the text summarizes the contents of the text on which there seems to be more or less general agreement:

I. *Lines 1A–3A:* ʾŠLPRN, the governor of YLBŠ, gave allotments of land to MSN(ʾ)ZMŠ in TMRS, in ʾDRWZ, and in KW.

II. *Lines 3A–7A:* This same governor gave land in WRYKLY to MTŠ and KLŠ. MTŠ in turn gave a portion of land to KLŠ, settled BʿL KR (meaning disputed) in it, and pronounced a strong curse on anyone who should wrongfully seize any of it from KLŠ's family.

III. *Lines 7A–8B*: The king transferred ownership of this land to MSN(ʾ)ZMŠ.

IV. *Lines 9A–C1*: Three witnesses are named.[1]

V. *Lines C1–C2*: MSN(ʾ)ZMŠ also received MSD, the daughter of MTŠ and wife of KLŠ.

VI. *Line C3*: The text closes with the colophon of PHLʾŠ, the scribe responsible for the document.

1. Only B. Margalit (1996: 125–26) would deny that the three persons named served as witnesses, but his grounds for doing so are based on a misunderstanding of my position. While our text is not a legal document in the strict sense, its assertions are rooted in a series of legally documented grants and transfers. The three persons named were not, I argue, witnesses to all these transactions but only to the last-named (and apparently most controversial) transaction—namely, King WRYK's transfer of land to MSN(ʾ)ZMŠ. This accounts for their position in the inscription. Regarding PHLŠ, the mention of his title 'the envoy' (*hmlʾk*, line 9B) need not exclude his serving here as a witness; the title may have been added simply to distinguish him from PHLʾŠ 'the scribe' (*hspr*, line C3). Nor does Margalit's (1996: 127) proposed translation inspire great confidence.

3. The Problem

There is general agreement that lines 7A–8B are crucial to our understanding of the inscription. The material reading of the stone is clear and undisputed; the analysis of the reading is the opposite. In the *editio princeps* (Mosca and Russell 1987: 9–10, 17–18), I proposed a translation consistent with the glossing in (1) (the raised vertical line ' represents the word dividers in the text):

(1) Cebel Ires Dağı (*KAI* 287), lines 7A–8B

w=km ' *ʾš* ' *y-gl* ' *ʾyt* '
and=when that CAUS-exile.PERF.3MS ACC=him.3MS
msnzmš ' *b=ym-t* ' *ʾzwšš* ' *w* '
MSNZMŠ.NOM in=day.MP.GEN ʾZWŠŠ.MS.GEN then
y-sb ' *mlk* ' *wryk* [']
CAUS-transfer.PERF.3MS king.MS.NOM WRYK.MS.NOM
l=msnʾzmš ' *kl* ' *h-šdy-t* ' *ʾl*
to=MSNʾZMŠ.MS.GEN all.ACC ART-field-FP.GEN this.DEM.P
'And when MSNZMŠ exiled him [i.e., KLŠ] in the days of ʾZWŠŠ, then King WRYK transferred to MSNʾZMŠ all these fields'.

In choosing to analyze *ʾyt* as an independent object pronoun rather than as a simple *nota accusativi* marking *msnʾzmš* as the direct object, I was aware that I was going down a road "less travelled by." Although one example of this sort of object pronoun existed in Punic, no clear example had been found in Phoenician.[2] It was my sense of context that forced me down this road, for it seemed to me that the coherence and continuity of the inscription demanded it. Indeed, I maintain that grammar and context are mutually enriching and that they make equally important contributions to the process of decipherment. If grammatical rules and expectations now control our initial steps in deciphering a new

2. It is worth noting, however, that M. Lidzbarski (1902: 157) was willing to restore a 3MS object pronoun (*ʾy*[*ty* . . .]) in the damaged area of a Phoenician inscription from Memphis (*KAI* 48.3) and that his restoration was accepted by W. Röllig (*KAI* 2.64–65), although the latter scholar rightly preferred to analyze *ʾy*[*ty*] as 1CS rather 3MS. To be sure, Krahmalkov (1992: 229–30) has suggested a restoration for this portion of the Memphis inscription that eliminates the independent pronoun in favor of a simple *nota accusativi*. Yet even if Krahmalkov's restoration is correct, the fact remains that both Lidzbarski and Röllig were open to the possible existence of an independent object pronoun in Phoenician.

inscription, this is only because they have been shown to make sense of previously known texts. They have been built up slowly and inductively over many generations. When, however, the application of recognized rules undermines the continuity and coherence of a new text, we must be prepared to expand our grammars, however slightly. In the following two sections, I shall attempt first to explain my dissatisfaction with the alternative explanations that have been proposed for the subordinate clause in lines 7A–7B and then to defend my analysis of *ʾyt* against the grammatical objections raised by Long and Pardee.

4. Competing Solutions

4.1. E. Lipiński

In the most recent study of lines 7A–8B, E. Lipiński describes my original proposal as "unsatisfactory" and the proposal of A. Lemaire as not only "unsatisfactory" but "farfetched" (Lipiński 2004: 129 n. 125). He does not elaborate on the reasons for his dissatisfaction, nor does he mention the studies of Long and Pardee (1989) and of Long (1991). Instead, he has tried to cut the Gordian knot of *ʾyt* by taking it as a plural noun rather than as the *nota accusativi* with or without a pronominal suffix. The translation proposed by Lipiński (2004: 129) is: "but when they brought to light the proofs of Masanazimiš in the days of Azawašuš, then king Wariyka turned over to Masanaʾzimiš all these fields."

When read in isolation, this interpretation seems to make good sense and would be at home in a legal or quasi-legal text. Even in isolation, however, there are two obvious irritants. To begin with, there is the problem of *ygl* in line 7A. There is no difficulty in reading the verb as plural ('they') rather than singular ('he'), since Phoenician orthography would not distinguish between the two. Indeed, Krahmalkov (2000: 140, 231, 339, 456; 2001: 268, 296) had already analyzed the verb as 3MP. (Neither scholar clarifies who 'they' are.) The difficulty is, rather, with the meaning that Lipiński assigns to the verb: 'bring to light' rather than 'exile'. When the verbal root *gly* 'reveal' appears in Phoenician, it is used in either the Qal (*DNWSI* 223–24) or the Piel (so Krahmalkov 2000: 140) but not in the Yiphil. This distinction is consistent with the Hebrew and Aramaic evidence, where the G-stems and D-stems are both used for 'uncover, reveal', but the G-stems and C-stems for 'go into exile' and 'exile', respectively. To find the Yiphil form *ygl* used with the meaning 'they brought to light' would thus be anomalous. As for *ʾyt* 'signs', one can indeed "posit a Phoenician singular *ʾāwīt, written *ʾwt* like *swt* 'purple-red robe'" (Lipiński 2004: 140). The plural of *swt*, however, is *swyt* (see, e.g., Krahmalkov 2000: 341); and so Lipiński is also forced to posit for *ʾ*wt* "a plural *ʾawyōt > *ʾayyōt, with assimilation like in *ḥwy* > *ḥy* 'life'." So convoluted a development undermines its attractiveness.

These two irritants might be remotely tolerable if the result were a manifestly superior reading, but such is not the case. In fact, even more—and more serious—problems arise when we attempt to reconcile Lipiński's reading of lines 7A–8B with their wider context. Although Lipiński (2004: 129) claims that the inscription as a whole "records the settlement of a dispute," in reality there has been no hint of a dispute thus far in the text, which has spoken consistently of outright gifts (*ytn*: lines 1A–1B, 2B, 3B, 4A). Since the first three gifts are clearly stated to be grants from the royal governor to MSN(ʾ)ZMŠ, and the fourth, which may well be connected directly or indirectly to the marriage of KLŠ and MSD (line C1), is a free gift between individuals related by marriage, it is difficult to imagine what could be in dispute. What proofs could MSN(ʾ)ZMŠ bring forward, and what could they be intended to prove? Nor is it clear, in Lipiński's scenario, why the scribe, who clearly presents MSN(ʾ)ZMŠ as the protagonist and unifying personality of the inscription, would include a lengthy paraphrase of MTŠ's curse (lines 5B–7A). In short, Lipiński's proposed solution, for all its ingenuity, has failed in its attempt to resolve the puzzles of lines 7A–8B. The lexical and, especially, contextual difficulties that it creates are too serious to be ignored.

4.2. A. Lemaire

Turning to the suggestion of Lemaire (1989), we find a far less radical reinterpretation of lines 7A–8B. Lemaire (1989: 125*–26*) adopted the syntax of the subordinate clause proposed in the *editio princeps* and readily accepted *ʾyt* as our first clear Phoenician example of the independent object pronoun 'him'. He preferred, however, to connect the Yiphil verb *ygl* to the root g*ʾl* 'redeem, buy back' rather than to *gly* 'go into exile'. The resultant translation would thus be: "quand Massanazêmis le 'racheta' (ou 'agit en *gōʾēl* pour lui'), le roi Urikki transféra à Massanazêmis tous ces champs." (I have here combined the subordinate and main clauses that Lemaire treated separately [1989: 125* and 126*].)

Long (1991) argued forcefully against Lemaire's suggestion on linguistic grounds. Long rightly noted (1) that in Phoenician proper there is little or no evidence for "the syncope of *aleph* in a post-consonantal, syllable-initial environment" (1991: 422); (2) that the Semitic lexemes elsewhere in the Cebel Ires Dağı inscription itself show no syncope of the *ʾaleph*, whether word-initial, postconsonantal, or intervocalic (1991: 423); and (3) that the root *gʾl* is attested only in the Qal and–aside from two Amorite personal names–only in Hebrew and in Jewish Aramaic (1991: 422 n. 7).

The problems with Lemaire's proposal only multiply when we move from the linguistic realm explored by Long out into the "real world" of the text and the society that produced it. Lemaire (1989: 128* n. 19) notes "l'existence probable d'une sorte de lévirat dans la tradition Hittite," but this hardly justifies postulating the existence of the distinct sociolegal practice of redemption in WRYK's kingdom many centuries later, let alone its existence in the very different environment of the Phoenician city-states. Nor is there any hint elsewhere in the text that MSN(ʾ)ZMŠ and KLŠ are kinsmen. It is true that the curse of MTŠ mentions not simply KLŠ but *špḥ klš* 'the family of KLŠ' (line 6B), but this need only reflect the fact that MTŠ intended his gift to be passed on to KLŠ's heirs following his death.

The mention of death raises another difficulty. According to Lemaire (1989: 125*), MSN(ʾ)ZMŠ exercised his duty as redeemer "vraisemblablement à la suite du décès de KLŠ." Why would so pivotal an event as the death of KLŠ not be explicitly mentioned? Moreover, biblical laws and narratives concerning redemption regularly speak of the practice in terms of buying and selling: *qānâ* 'buy' in Lev 25:28, 30; Jer 32:7 (2×), 8 (2×), 9; Ruth 4:4, 5, 8, 9; *mākar* 'sell' in Lev 25:25, 27, 29, 34; Ruth 4:3. Such language is completely absent from our inscription; instead we have land 'transferred' (*ysb*, line 8A) by a king–a figure never mentioned in connection with Israelite redemption–to a subordinate. All these suppositions, silences, and deviations from Israelite practice are quite a burden to put on the shoulders of a syncopated *ʾaleph*. We can only conclude that Lemaire's analysis of *ygl* collapses under the linguistic and contextual weight.

4.3. G. A. Long and D. Pardee

The position defended by Long and Pardee (1989) inverts Lemaire's position. Lemaire accepted my analysis of *ʾyt* and rejected my analysis of *ygl*; Long and Pardee accepted my analysis of *ygl* and rejected my analysis of *ʾyt*. In their opinion, *ʾyt* can only be the *nota accusativi* marking *msnzmš* as the direct object of *ygl*. Their translation of lines 7A–8B thus reads: "When, however, he (KLŠ) exiled MSN(ʾ)ZMŠ during ʾZWŠŠ's term of office, King WRYK turned all these fields over to MSNʾZMŠ" (1989: 213). It is somewhat ironic, of course, that Long and Pardee's conclusion was my own starting point (Mosca and Russell 1987: 17), as they themselves (1989: 207) were aware. To read *ʾyt* here as a simple *nota accusativi* results in a translation that is grammatically impeccable.[3] I acknowledged then and readily concede now that elsewhere in the Phoenician corpus *ʾyt* is regularly followed by a nominal direct object. My problem is with *what* is being said in the subordinate clause, not with *how* it is said, for it seems to me that it clashes both with the main clause and with the inscription as a whole.

To begin with, the transition from the subordinate clause to the main clause is simply too abrupt. If KLŠ (or anyone else) had exiled MSN(ʾ)ZMŠ, we would expect the inscription to mention MSN(ʾ)ZMŠ's return from exile explicitly before reporting King WRYK's transfer of land to him. To be sure, Long and Pardee (1989: 214), in their outline of the text, summarize the main clause in lines 7B–8B (their C[lause]13) as "MSN(ʾ)ZMŠ's Reinstatement." In this, they are followed by Kottsieper and Younger. The former speaks of a "Rechtsvorgang" by which MSN(ʾ)ZMŠ's exile "rückgängig gemacht wurde" (Kottsieper 2001: 184); the latter speaks of "a royal reinstatement of Masanazamis by King Awariku" (*COS* 2.137). In fact, however, the clause says nothing of MSN(ʾ)ZMŠ's being recalled from exile or of his reinstatement. It is precisely the absence of an explicit notice of MSN(ʾ)ZMŠ's exoneration and return from exile that I found (and continue to find) so astonishing. MSN(ʾ)ZMŠ is, after all, the central figure in the inscription, and it is his narrative that orders the text from beginning to end. Why would so important a detail, a detail so favorable to MSN(ʾ)ZMŠ's land claims, be passed over in silence?

Second, if it was KLŠ who exiled MSN(ʾ)ZMŠ, what would the basis for the royal transfer of KLŠ's land to MSN(ʾ)ZMŠ have been? Long and

3. I challenge Long and Pardee's decision, however, to render the phrase *bymt PN*, both here and throughout the inscription, as 'during PN's term of office' (1989: 213–14, lines 2A–2B, 7B, C2). (In this, they have been followed by Younger [*COS* 2.137–39].) Although it gives the inscription a curiously contemporary ring, it is inappropriate, for the phrase 'term of office' in English denotes a definite period of time, having a specified limit (Black, Nolan, and Connolly 1979: 1318a). Since we have no evidence that the "governors" of our inscription held office for a fixed period, it is safer to retain the original's 'days' or some equally vague synonym.

Pardee (1989: 210) claim that WRYK's intervention "on the one hand, righted an injustice and, on the other, served as punishment for the initial deposer." This claim, however, ignores the force of the verb *ygl*. In the Neo-Assyrian and Neo-Babylonian empires, exile was viewed as a legitimate punishment for rebellious vassals. In the Hebrew Bible, *heglâ* consistently has as its subject a state, a king (including Yhwh), or a royal representative (Clines 1995: 351). Thus exile in biblical texts, as in Mesopotamia, was implicitly recognized as being, from the ruler's perspective if not the victims', a legally sanctioned use of force. If KLŠ were no more than an illegitimate "deposer," we would expect a more neutral or even negative term to be used to describe his action, for example, *grš* 'expel, drive out' or *gzl* 'steal, seize by force' (used in line 6A). Just as the use of *gzl* in MTŠ's curse is aimed at any illegal use of force or abuse of authority (Westbrook 1988: 23–30), so, too, the use of *ygl* underlines the legitimacy of the action in question; and, in light of the main clause, this action can only be attributed to MSN(ʾ)ZMŠ, not to KLŠ.

Last, there is the matter of the curse in lines 5B–7A. With regard to my own interpretation, Long and Pardee (1989: 209) ask: "why should the land originally given to KLŠ be legally given to MSN(ʾ)ZMŠ without explicit reason in the face of an explicitly stated curse?" They (1989: 210) claim that their own interpretation "answers this basic question," since "the curse uttered by MTŠ on KLŠ's behalf . . . must be considered as having been rendered null and void by KLŠ's participation in the exiling of MSN(ʾ)ZMŠ" (1989: 212). As we have just argued, however, the use of *ygl* implies legitimacy, and so KLŠ's participation should not have nullified the curse. If, on the contrary, KLŠ was not exiling but exiled, then the act of rebellion that ended in his exile would also result in the forfeiture of his lands to the crown. The king's action in transferring ownership to MSN(ʾ)ZMŠ serves as confirmation that the curse was no longer operative.

In sum, Long and Pardee's reading does manage to retain the usual morphosyntactic usage of simple *ʾyt*, but it creates serious difficulties for the comprehensibility and coherence of lines 7A–8B, whether viewed in isolation or within their wider context.

4.4. C. R. Krahmalkov

Krahmalkov's translation of our lines (2000: 140, 231, 339, 456; 2001: 268, 296) is similar to the translation defended by Long and Pardee, but it differs from theirs in a number of details. First, as already mentioned, he takes the verb *ygl* as 3MP, 'they exiled'. Since Krahmalkov, like Lipiński, does not indicate who "they" are, we can only await a full-scale treatment of the inscription before commenting further on this detail. A second difference is Krahmalkov's consistent reading of *mlk wryk⟨ly⟩* 'the king of WRYKLY' in lines 8A–8B. It is true that the place-name WRYKLY is mentioned in line 3B of our inscription. The emendation of lines 8A–8B on the basis of its earlier appearance is, however, gratuitous; and the restoration of the royal title at the expense of the king's personal name is equally unnecessary. What I find most interesting, however, is that on one occasion, Krahmalkov (2001: 274) translates our lines "When they exiled MSNZMS (*?read MTS*) in the days of ʾZWSS, the king of WRKLY returned all these fields to MSNʾZMS" (emphasis added). This second attempt at textual emendation clearly reflects Krahmalkov's unease with Long and Pardee's interpretation and implicitly acknowledges the force of my own reasoning. At the same time, Krahmalkov undermines his own rendering of *ysb* as 'returned'. Since "these fields" were not previously owned by MSN(ʾ)ZMŠ, they could only be "turned over" or "transferred" to him, not "returned."

5. An Independent Object Pronoun in Phoenician?

In the study of the Nora Stone mentioned at the beginning of §2 of this essay, Bruce Zuckerman (1991: 270) sketched three "rules of thumb" that "can allow one at least to evaluate potential solutions and thereby come to better choices". The first is simplicity, the third is what he called "fruitfulness," but it is the second that is of immediate concern here. According to Zuckerman (1991: 270–71), "[a] solution is not to be trusted if it creates grammatical problems–whether epigraphic [i.e., the physical data of the inscription], phonological, morphological, syntactical or lexical. In other words, a solution which compels one to rewrite the grammar books in order for it to 'work' is probably a bad choice." I find this "rule of thumb" to be in need of qualification, for the fact is that we do rewrite the grammar books of Northwest Semitic epigraphic languages at irregular intervals, as new inscriptions provide us with new evidence or force us to revise old formulations. The three editions of Friedrich's Phoenician grammar published between 1951 and 1999 (each longer, more detailed, and in almost every way more accurate than its predecessor) provide sufficient proof of this reality. Nor is this in any way surprising. The corpus of Phoenician texts (*sensu stricto*) is actually quite small. Almost all the inscriptions on which the grammars repeatedly draw for their examples are included in the most recent (5th) edition of *KAI*, and they occupy at most 20 pages—somewhat less if we discount the Greek and Cypro-syllabic texts provided in bilinguals, not to mention the large areas of white on most of these pages. It would be foolhardy indeed to think that so small a corpus can exhaust all possible features of Phoenician grammar. "A given solution which compels one to rewrite the grammar books" may well be "a bad choice." This sort of solution should not, however, be prematurely categorized as "not to be trusted." It must, rather, be carefully examined and weighed. If it results in a demonstrably superior understanding of the text in which it is embedded, then we may well have to adjust our grammar books. This is why, in the preceding section, I placed as much emphasis on context as on grammar.

The Cebel Ires Dağı inscription serves as a good illustration of the approach that I am trying to defend. When, in the *editio princeps* (Mosca and Russell 1987: 17–18), I proposed that we see *ʾyt* not as a simple object marker but rather as an independent object pronoun, I was well aware that this would meet with some opposition. And this opposition was not long in coming. While Lemaire (1989: 125*) and B. Margalit (1996: 128–29 n. 32) readily accepted my analysis, Long and Pardee (1989: 208–9) forcefully objected to it. They offered three lines of argument: (1) the usage of *ʾyt* elsewhere in Phoenician; (2) the syntactical strings attested in Phoenician for clauses involving *ʾyt*; and (3) the morphosyntax of pronominal direct objects in Phoenician and Punic. None of the three is without its problems.

5.1. ʾyt *in Phoenician*

According to Long and Pardee (1989: 208), "[t]he extant Phoenician corpus [i.e., Byblian, Tyro-Sidonian, and Cypriot] indicates that where a PN, GN, DN or a gentilic is the direct object, it is normally governed by a NA."[4] This is a reasonably accurate statement of the situation in

4. In order to facilitate the comparison of our opposing positions, I shall employ the same abbreviations as Long and Pardee:

> S = SUBJECT constituent expressed by a noun phrase in concord with the verb; V = a VERBAL PREDICATE expressed by a finite verbal form having, of course, an intrinsically marked subject; NA = *NOTA ACCUSATIVI*; O = OBJECT, the adverbial component depending on a transitive verb and expressed by a noun phrase; AM = ADVERBIAL MODIFIER, an adverbial component. (Long and Pardee 1989: 208 n. 9)

Phoenician, although I am puzzled by their penchant, both here and elsewhere, for ignoring or marginalizing the evidence available from Punic and Late Punic sources. I have recently been compiling the data for the NA in all its forms: *ʾyt* (rarely *ʾt*) in Phoenician, *ʾyt*/*ʾt*/*t* in Punic, and *ʾt*/*t* (very rarely *ʾyt*) in Late Punic. Interim statistics indicate a remarkable continuity between Phoenician and Punic in the use of the NA immediately before PNs (6× in Phoenician, 6× in Punic), DNs (1× in Phoenician, 1x in Punic), GNs (2× in Phoenician, 1× in Punic), as well as before *kl* 'all' (3× in Phoenician, 2× in Punic). Worth noting, too, is that the NA occurs most frequently immediately before a simple noun and demonstrative adjective, whether the noun is preceded by the definite article *h-* (11× in Phoenician, 6× in Punic, and 5× in Late Punic) or the *h-* is omitted (4× in Phoenician, 6× in Punic, and 2× in Late Punic).[5]

I mention these data because they help reveal a significant gap in Long and Pardee's first argument. In comparing the use of the supposed NA in lines 7A–7B with its use elsewhere in Phoenician, they failed to consider the rest of the Cebel Ires Dağı inscription itself. There we have, as direct objects of transitive verbs, a PN (MSD, line C1), a GN (*wlwy*, lines 3A–3B),[6] possibly a DN (*bʿl kr*, line 5B), *kl* 'all' (line 8B), and

Long and Pardee also use PN to indicate a personal name, GN a geographical name, and DN a divine name. I am grateful to the editors for their kind permission to deviate from the abbreviations used elsewhere in this volume.

5. These statistics do not include the rare occurrences of more-complex uses of the NA, for example, before construct chains or compound objects with the demonstrative following the second of the coordinated nouns. Full documentation for all occurrences will be given in the separate study devoted to the NA that is being prepared by Robert Kerr and me. For the present, the following small sampling must suffice:

1a. NA before PNs in Phoenician: *KAI* 26 A III.3 = Pho/B Orthostat 7 (restored; Röllig 1999: 56) = *KAI* 26 C III.17 (Karatepe); *KAI* 10.8–9 (Byblos); *KAI* 60.2 (Piraeus); Moraleda de Zafayona (Ruiz Cabrero 2003; Lemaire 2007; Amadasi Guzzo 2007);

1b. NA before PNs in Punic: *KAI* 295.1–2, 3 (Grotta Regina); *CIS* I 4862.2–3 (Carthage); *KAI* 89.2, 3 (Carthage); *CIS* I 5689.4–5 (Carthage);

2a. NA before DN in Phoenician: *KAI* 14.16 (Sidon);

2b. NA before DN in Punic: *CIS* I 5511.4 (Carthage);

3a. NA before GN in Phoenician: *KAI* 14.19 (Sidon); Karatepe S.I.a.1 (Röllig 1999: 69);

3b. NA before GN in Punic: *KAI* 302.10 (Carthage).

6. Long and Pardee (1989: 210, 211, 213, 214), followed by Younger (*COS* 2.138 and n. 12), agree that *wlwy* is best taken as a GN (Mosca and Russell 1987: 6, 12). Lemaire (1989) does not comment on the issue. Margalit (1996: 126) translates it 'WLWY(-rights?)' but nowhere explains what exactly he means by this translation.

the sequence definite article + noun + demonstrative (*hspr z*, line C3). Not once has the scribe employed the NA to mark any of these direct objects. In other words, the isolated appearance of *ʾyt* in line 7B, which seems so normal to Long and Pardee in the context of other Phoenician (and, I would add, Punic) texts, is in fact anomalous in the context of the Cebel Ires Dağı inscription itself. I submit that the simplest explanation of this anomaly is that *ʾyt* in line 7B is not the simple NA but the NA+3MS pronominal suffix, that is, an independent object pronoun.

5.2. Syntactic Strings

According to Long and Pardee (1989: 208–9), the syntactic strings involving the NA and a finite verb argue against taking *ʾyt* as a pronominal object. They allow for only six such strings:

1. V – NA – O	1′. V – S – NA – O
1A. V – AM – NA – O	1A′. V – AM – S – NA – O
2. NA – O – V	2′. S – NA – O – V

My objection is not to the evidence compiled, which is admittedly useful and reasonably accurate.[7] Long and Pardee, however, then seek to rule out the possibility that new evidence may alter or enlarge our syntactic knowledge in any significant way, for they mark other strings with an asterisk, which for them "specifies the syntax as unattested *and presumably ungrammatical*" (Long and Pardee 1989: 209 n. 16; emphasis added). I can only protest against this equation of "unattested" with "ungrammatical." The extant Phoenician corpus is simply too small to support so radical a claim. This seems evident from the fact that three of the syntactic strings isolated by Long and Pardee—1A, 1A′, and 2—are attested only by single examples. Had any one of these inscriptions not

Krahmalkov (2001: 270) and Kottsieper (2001: 185 and n. B3a) read *wlwy* as a PN, but neither addresses the objections raised to this in the *editio princeps* (Mosca and Russell 1987: 12). In any case, Krahmalkov's attempt to insert "<this same land>" as the implicit object of the verb is simply wrong, for the lands given to MSN(ʾ)ZMŠ were in TMRS, in ʾDRWZ, and in KW (lines 1A–3A), while the lands given to MTŠ and KLŠ were in WRYKLY (line 3B). The parcels of land can hardly be the same.

7. Two modifications are called for. First, in support of string 2′ (S – NA – O – V), Long and Pardee (1989: 209 n. 15) cite both *KAI* 15 and *KAI* 16. The latter inscription is a clear example of string 2′. The syntax of the former inscription, however, is debated. A lengthy prepositional phrase (beginning *bṣdn ym*) follows the subject in *KAI* 15. This may be adnominal, as Long and Pardee think; but others take it as adverbial, for example, W. Röllig (*KAI* 2.23–24) and P. Magnanini (*IFO*: 7–8). It seems safer, therefore, to set this text aside for the time being. The second modification, which centers on *RÉS* 1204.5–6, will be discussed below.

been found, its syntactic string would remain "unattested and presumably ungrammatical."

There are other reasons for questioning the specifics of Long and Pardee's claim. In their reading of the data, "where the constituent 'S' appears (1′, 1A′, 2′), it always immediately preceded the NA (-O)" (Long and Pardee 1989: 209). They can make this claim only because of their analysis of the two examples of the NA in *RÉS* 1204.5–6, both of which they group under V – NA – O: *pʿl* (V)–*ʾyt* (NA)–*ḥṣy hsp z* (O) [line 5] and *ytn* (V)–*ʾyt* (NA)–*hḥṣy hsp z* (O) [line 6] (Long and Pardee 1989: 208 n. 10). Long and Pardee simply assume that there is only an intrinsically marked subject and translate 'he made half of this basin' and 'he gave (the) half of this basin', respectively. The inscription, however, is badly damaged, with the beginnings (right side) of all lines missing. Most translators have assumed that lines 5 and 6 are referring to "half of this basin" and "the (other) half of this basin" and that the two verbs had one or more PNs as their respective subjects (so, for example, *RÉS* 1204; *IFO*: 17–18; Krahmalkov 2000: 347). Even if their first assumption is wrong and the lines are speaking of the making and giving of the same half of the basin, as Long and Pardee imply, it still remains likely that at least the first verb had a separate PN (or PNs) as subject. It is thus premature to declare that the string *V – NA – O – S or *S – V – NA – O is ungrammatical.

There is still another reason to question Long and Pardee's reading of the evidence. They are forced to concede that the syntactic string V – O – S does occur in Phoenician but hasten to add that "in no instance is the NA part of the clause" (Long and Pardee 1989: 209). However, if V – O – S is permissible in Phoenician, why should *V – NA – O – S be ungrammatical, especially when the latter string occurs frequently in Punic (*KAI* 72 B.1–2; *KAI* 80.1; *IFPCO*: 109–10 [Sardegna 32.7–8], and almost certainly *KAI* 303.1)?

Last, Long and Pardee claim that their data argue against the possibility of *V – NA+suffix – S: "if 'S' were to be independently expressed, it would not follow the NA (+suffix)" (Long and Pardee 1989: 209). They would expect *V – S – NA+suffix or * S – NA+suffix – V instead. Yet Biblical Hebrew regularly displays exactly the syntactical variation that Long and Pardee deny to Phoenician; one need go no further than the opening chapter of Genesis to find examples of (2) V – S – NA – O and (3) V – NA+suffix – S:

(2) *wa=yyi-brāʾ* *ʾĕlōh-îm* *ʾet* *hā=ʾādām*
and=3MS-create.PAST god-MP ACC ART=human.MS
'and God created the human race'. (Gen 1:27)

(3) *wa=yĕ-bārek* *ʾōt=ām* *ʾĕlōh-îm*
and=3MS-bless.PAST ACC=3MP god-MP
'and God blessed them'. (Gen 1:28)

Since the NA+suffix in both languages is replacing a pronominal object suffix attached directly to the verb, it would not be surprising if in both languages it occupied the same position as the verbal suffix.

5.3. Morphosyntax of Pronominal Direct Objects

It is an incontrovertible fact that, in both Phoenician and Punic, the pronominal direct object is normally affixed to the verb. On this point, I am in complete agreement with Long and Pardee. We also agree that there is one clear exception to the norm in Punic: in *CIS* I 580.3, the pronominal object is expressed by the NA+suffix (3FS).[8] Disagreement arises only concerning the evaluation of this piece of evidence. Long and Pardee, having conceded one example of NA+suffix, seek immediately to undermine its relevance to the Cebel Ires Dağı inscription.

First, they note that the syntax of the Punic clause differs from the syntax in lines 7A–7B of our text. This is indeed a fact but not an argument. Since the Phoenician clause has a PN as the independent subject and the Punic clause has only the pronominal subject inherent in the verb itself, the syntax of the two clauses must differ a priori.

Second, Long and Pardee (1989: 209) caution us "to take *ʾtʾ* for what it is—a solitary occurrence among all the extant Phoenician and Punic corpus in what seems to be a late Punic text." *CIS* I 580 does not "seem to be" late or Punic; it *is* manifestly both. If, however, Long and Pardee mean to imply that its *ʾtʾ* should therefore be taken as indicative of a late and exclusively Punic development, the implication must be rejected as improbable. The available comparative evidence suggests

8. Since we wrote our respective studies, several scholars have tried to alter this picture either by adding a second example of the NA+suffix in Punic or by eliminating the one that we have. Elsewhere (Mosca 2005) I have tried to show that none of these suggestions can be judged successful. Frustrating though it may be, the situation has remained unchanged in the last two decades. We have at present one—and only one—clear example of a NA+suffix in Punic.

rather that *ʾtʾ* is the survival of an earlier form that developed first in Phoenician and continued into Punic, for it is in Northwest Semitic languages of the Iron Age that we find the NA+suffix appearing alongside the much older use of pronominal suffixes attached directly to verbs. In Samalian, we have an example of the NA *wt=h* in the mid-eighth-century Hadad inscription (*KAI* 214.28).[9] In Old Aramaic, again from the mid-eighth century, we have two examples in the Sefire inscriptions (*KAI* 224.11, 13); the former is damaged (*ʾy*[*t*]*y*), the latter misspelled (*ʾy<t>h*), but in both instances the restoration and analysis are uncontested. And in Hebrew, both biblical and epigraphic, the NA+suffix is too well known to require documentation; it is first attested in the early eighth century (*brkt.ʾtkm* 'I blessed you' [Kuntillet ʿAjrud Pithos A]) and employed repeatedly thereafter.

To be sure, the frequency of the NA+suffix in Phoenician-Punic more closely approximates the situation in Samalian and Old Aramaic than Hebrew. If anything, its use in written Phoenician and Punic was even rarer, but this is hardly surprising when we consider the extreme conservatism of the scribal tradition in Phoenician and (to a lesser extent) Punic. Still, the presence of this form in both the Cebel Ires Dağı inscription and *CIS* I 580 does suggest that it continued to be a feature of the spoken language. On the basis of the limited evidence available at present, it seems that this feature broke through into the written language only on the fringes, whether geographical (in the case of the former) or chronological (in the case of the latter). Nor should we forget that the Cebel Ires Dağı text was written by a scribe with an Anatolian name, for whom Tyro-Sidonian Phoenician was presumably a second language. His mastery of the literary language was certainly good but not necessarily perfect. This may help to explain not only the unusual use of the NA+suffix but also the absence of the simple NA in environments where we expect it to appear.

6. Conclusions

Ancient Phoenician inscriptions rarely, if ever, tell us all that we should like to know about the people, places, and events summarily treated in them, let alone about the wider social and historical matrices

---

9. At the 2008 annual meeting of the Society of Biblical Literature, Pardee announced the appearance of a second Samalian example of NA+suffix (*wt=h*) in a newly discovered inscription from Zinçirli; see now Pardee 2009.

from which they emerged. We do, however, expect that a correct lexical and grammatical analysis will reveal the internal logic and coherence of any inscription, including that from Cebel Ires Dağı. It was precisely this search for logic and coherence that led me 25 years ago to analyze *ʾyt* as our first clear Phoenician example of a NA+suffix 'him' (i.e., KLŠ) and *ygl* as a Yiphil 3MS of *gly* 'go into exile'. Having explained my dissatisfaction both with the later readings that reject one or both of these analyses (§3 above) and with Long and Pardee's arguments against the possible existence of the NA+suffix in Phoenician (§4), I maintain that my analysis of lines 7A–8B best fits the context. If MSN(ʾ)ZMŠ exiled KLŠ, it was appropriate within the logic of the inscription that a grateful monarch rewarded him with the rebellious subject's lands. This scenario also accounts for the careful tracing of KLŠ's holdings in lines 3A–5A, since KLŠ could only forfeit what was rightfully his. Last, it explains the scribe's summary of MTŠ's curse in lines 5B–7A.[10] As I noted in the *editio princeps*, the curse "establishes KLŠ's exclusive ownership of the lands in question" (Mosca and Russell 1987: 17).[11] In sum, I still prefer to walk the road "less travelled by."

10. I hope to return in the near future to the much debated BʿL KR in line 5B and the clause in which it is embedded.

11. It would be equally true to say that the curse served to undercut any claim that MTŠ might have put forward for the return of these lands following KLŠ's exile.

Bibliography

Amadasi Guzzo, M. G.

2007 Une lamelle magique à inscription phénicienne. *Vicino Oriente* 13: 197–206.

Black, H. C.; Nolan, J. R.; and Connolly, M. J.

1979 *Black's Law Dictionary: Definitions of the Terms and Phrases of American and English Jurisprudence, Ancient and Modern.* 5th ed. St. Paul, MN: West Publishing.

Clines, D. J. A., ed.

1995 *The Dictionary of Classical Hebrew,* vol. 2: ב–ו. Sheffield: Sheffield Academic Press.

Kottsieper, I.

2001 Eine phönizische Rechtsurkunde aus Kilikien. Pp. 184–86 in *Texte aus der Umwelt des Alten Testaments: Ergänzungslieferung,* ed. M. Dietrich et al. Gütersloh: Gütersloher Verlag.

Krahmalkov, C. R.

1992 Phoenician *ʾyt* and *ʾt*. *RSO* 66: 227–31.

2000 *Phoenician-Punic Dictionary*. OLA 90. Studia Phoenicia 15. Leuven: Peeters.
2001 *A Phoenician-Punic Grammar*. HOSNME 54. Leiden: Brill.

Lemaire, A.
1989 Une inscription phénicienne découverte récemment et le marriage de Ruth la Moabite. *ErIsr* 20 (Yadin Volume):124*-29*.
2007 L'inscription phénico-punique de la lamelle magique de Moraleda de Zafayona. *Or* 76: 53–57.

Lidzbarski, M.
1902 Eine phönizische Inschrift aus Memphis. Pp. 152–58 in *Ephemeris für semitische Epigraphik*, vol. 1: *1900–1902*. Giessen: J. Ricker (Alfred Töpelmann).

Lipiński, E.
2004 *Itineraria Phoenicia*. OLA 127. Studia Phoenicia 18. Leuven: Peeters.

Long, G. A.
1991 A Kinsman-Redeemer in the Phoenician Inscription from Cebel Ires Daği. *ZAW* 103: 421–24.

Long, G. A., and Pardee, D.
1989 Who Exiled Whom? Another Interpretation of the Phoenician Inscription from Cebel Ires Dağı. *AuOr* 7: 207–14.

Margalit, B.
1996 Philological Notes on a Recently Published Phoenician Inscription from Southern Anatolia. Pp. 119–29 in *"Dort ziehen Schiffe dahin . . .": Collected Communications to the XIVth Congress of the International Organization for the Study of the Old Testament, Paris 1992*, ed. M. Augustin and K.-D. Schunck. Frankfurt am Main: Peter Lang.

Mosca, P. G.
2005 The Independent Object Pronoun in Punic. *Or* 74: 65–70.

Mosca, P. G., and Russell, J.
1987 A Phoenician Inscription from Cebel Ires Dağı in Rough Cilicia. *EpAn* 9: 1–27, pls. 1–4.

Pardee, D.
2009 A New Aramaic Inscription from Zincirli. *BASOR* 356: 51–71.

Röllig, W.
1999 Appendix I: The Phoenician Inscriptions. Pp. 50–81 in H. Çambel, *Corpus of Hieroglyphic Luwian Inscriptions*, vol. 2: *Karatepe-Aslantaş—The Inscriptions: Facsimile Edition*. Untersuchungen zur indogermanischen Sprach- und Kulturwissenschaft/Studies in Indo-European Language and Culture n.s. 8/2. Berlin: de Gruyter.

Ruiz Cabrero, L. A.
2003 El estuche con banda mágica de Moraleda de Zafayona (Granada): una nueva inscripción fenicia. *Byrsa* 1: 85–106.

Westbrook, R.
1988 *Studies in Biblical and Cuneiform Law*. CahRB 26. Paris: Gabalda.

Zuckerman, B.
1991 The Nora Puzzle. *Maarav* 7: 269–301, pls. 1–2.

On Negation in Phoenician

Na'ama Pat-El

1. *Introduction*

For a survey and reconstruction of phonology and morphology, no more than several attestations of each form are required to set a reasonably accurate paradigm; for a syntactical survey, however, there is a need for many examples. This makes any syntactic analysis and subsequent reconstruction of a poorly attested language almost impossible. In Phoenician, much of the indigenous syntax is poorly attested. For example, there are not enough attestations of adverbial subordinating particles for a complete analysis of the Phoenician system of subordination: *mʾš* and *km ʾš* occur only once each, and thus their exact meaning and function are hard to determine. Furthermore, since a large portion of the language is formulaic, it is not always easy to evaluate the productivity of a certain pattern. Unlike Epigraphic Hebrew and some Aramaic dialects, there are no long narratives in Phoenician that can support our efforts to corroborate or contradict what we think we know about Phoenician syntax (Hackett 2002: 57).

This state of affairs renders certain aspects of the syntactical description of Phoenician, not to mention the explanation of the data, difficult and occasionally unfeasible. Therefore, syntax is the least described and, consequently, least explained part of Phoenician grammar. Furthermore, since it is very difficult to conduct internal reconstruction when the evidence is largely unavailable or only partially available (Hackett 2004: 381), Phoenician can offer clues but rarely any answers. This is where the comparative method is especially useful; if we are lucky, there are enough related languages to be able to reconstruct a system from what clues we do have.

Phoenician resembles its sister language, ancient Hebrew, in many aspects of its grammar. When it comes to syntax, negation in Phoenician is a major difference between it and ancient Hebrew, its better documented Canaanite

Author's note: I would like to thank John Huehnergard for his helpful remarks and notes on an earlier version of this paper. Any remaining errors are my own.

sister, and therefore of particular interest to Semitic historical linguistics: *bl* in Phoenician versus *lōʾ* in ancient Hebrew. The lack of the particle **lā* in Phoenician is a well-known problem in comparative Semitic linguistics (cf. Faber 1991: 424; reacting to Hetzron 1976). Hence, Phoenician shows an innovation (verbal negative *bl*) and a significant loss, unattested in any other Northwest Semitic language (loss of **lā*).

In this essay, I will attempt to examine the set of negative particles in Phoenician, using the comparative method, with particular emphasis on *bl* and its derivations in the Semitic language family.

2. *The Data*

Phoenician has three negative particles, *bl*, *ʾy*, and *ʾl* (Harris 1936: 62; Friedrich and Röllig 1999: 178, §249). Their distribution is outlined below.

2.1. bl

The particle *bl* is used to negate (1) the indicative perfect verb, (2) the indicative imperfect verb, and (3) nouns.

(1) *bl* *pʿl*
NEG did.PFV.3MS
'he did nothing'. (*KAI* 24.2, 3)

(2) *bl* *t-drkn*
NEG 2MP-walk.IPFV
'you do not tread'. (*KAI* 27.8).[1]

(3) *bl* *ʿt-y*
NEG time-my
'before my time'. (*KAI* 14.3, 12)

The exact vocalization of this particle can only be assumed, but as we shall see below, on the basis of cognates in other Semitic languages, the vocalized form /*bal/ is a reasonable reconstruction.

2.2. ʾl

The particle *ʾl* is used to negate (4) an imperative and (5) is used in modal contexts before an imperfect/jussive verb.

1. There are not many examples of negated indicative imperfect; however, the text quoted above contains two examples (lines 6 and 8). See also *KAI* 69.15 and *KAI* 74.6.

(4) *ʾl ʾl t-ptḥ ʿlt-y w-ʾl t-rgz-n*
NEG NEG 2MS-open.IPFV tomb-my and-NEG 2MS-upset.IPFV-me
'do not open my sarcophagus and do not upset me'. (*KAI* 13.3–4)

(5) *ʾl y-kn l-m mškb*
NEG 3MS-be.IPFV to-them resting.place
'may there not be for them a resting place' (*KAI* 14.8)

2.3. ʾy

The particle *ʾy* is used (6) as a negative existential:[2]

(6) *ʾl y-bqš b-n mnm k ʾy šm*
NEG 3MS-ask.IPFV in-it something because NEG there
b-n mnm
in-it something
'he should not search for something in it, because nothing is in it there [lit., there-is-not something in it there]'. (*KAI* 14.5).

The particle *ʾy* as an independent form is only found in inscriptions from Sidon and Cyprus. Krahmalkov (2001: 277–78) claims that this particle negates verbal forms; however, in none of the three existing examples is there a certain verbal form. It also appears once (7) attached to *bl*, where the function is that of *bl*—that is, negating a finite verb:[3]

(7) *w-ʾm ʾbl t-št šm ʾt-k*
and-if NEG 2MS-put.IPFV name with-you.2MS
'if you do not put my name with yours'. (*KAI* 10.13)[4]

2. There are 3 examples of *ʾy*, one with *šm* (*KAI* 14.5) and two with *ʾdln* (*KAI* 35.3–5). While *ʾdln* is usually understood to be a preposition, the exact identification of *šm* is less clear. Friedrich and Röllig (1999: 166) take it to be a verbal form, (cf. Hebrew √*śym*). Avishur (e.g., 2000: 118) thinks that *ʾy* is the Hebrew *ʾî*, not *ʾên*. This particle is common in several Semitic languages as the negation of nominal forms (e.g., Akkadian, Aramaic, and Hebrew). I have chosen to treat *šm* as an adverb (cf. Hebrew *šām/šāmmā*, Arabic *ṯumma*), because I think it fits the context better; neither *ʾî* nor *ʾên* negates finite verbs in related languages (with the exception of Gəʿəz, where *ʾî* has become the only verbal negation particle; Pat-El 2012: 22). Therefore, I do not see any convincing argument to read a finite verb in this example.

3. This analysis of {ʾbl} as *ʾy-bl* is found in Friedrich and Röllig 1999 (178, §249) as well as *DNWSI* 5, *ʾbl*$_5$.

4. In Punic, *ʾybl* /ʾībal/ is common. Whether this particle is related to Hebrew *ʾăbāl* 'but' is unclear.

Due to the poor attestation of this particle in Phoenician, I will not discuss it further.

3. The Problem

As was mentioned above, two important deviations are immediately evident in Phoenician: the lack of the general Semitic negative particle **lā* and the use of *bl* as a general negative particle for finite indicative verbs as well as for nouns. Among the Semitic languages, the Common Semitic **lā* is missing only in Ethiopic and Old South Arabian, where one negative particle—*ʾi*/*ʾal* and *ʾl*, respectively—is the negative for all verbal forms. Since Phoenician retained the difference between modal negative, {ʾl}, and indicative negative, {bl}, it must be considered a different case from Ethiopic and Old South Arabian, which show generalization.[5]

The particle **lā* is the regular Northwest Semitic negative particle for the indicative verb.[6] Moreover, all the modern descendants of the Northwest Semitic languages retain the particle **lā* (see Neo-Aramaic and Modern Hebrew). Therefore, the complete loss and replacement of **lā* in Phoenician is rather odd and requires an explanation.

4. The Distribution of *bal-

The particle **balV* occurs in several languages with slightly different functions.[7] In Akkadian, *balu*(*m*) 'without' is a preposition that negates nouns (cf. Arb and OSA *ġayr*-); in Ethiopic, it appears as a component in a complex preposition **ʾin*(*a*)-*bala* > *ʾənbala* 'without, except' (cf. Akk *ina balu*[*m*]);[8] in

5. Faber (1991: 424) objected to using the loss of **lā* as a feature for subgrouping Phoenician with South Semitic, because apart from the loss of **lā*, there is no reason to assume that Phoenician is South Semitic and not Canaanite. Therefore, Faber claimed that the existence or absence of **lā* cannot be used as a diagnostic feature for subgrouping. However, even the loss of **lā* does not indicate a relation: while Ethiopic shows loss, Phoenician shows lexical replacement (**lā* > *bal*) rather than loss. The distribution of negative particles in Phoenician remained intact; only the grammatical elements were replaced.

6. Within Central Semitic, the use of **lā* sets the Northwest Semitic languages apart from Arabic (pf. *mā*, impf. *lā* only in Classical but not in later dialects) and Old South Arabian (*ʾl* for all verbal forms), both of which use another negative particle for the negation of the indicative verb (Pat-El 2012: 36).

7. See table 2 on p. 63 for a summary of the forms.

8. See Huehnergard 2006: 16. It may also negate *yəqtəl* forms as a conjunction, 'before'. A function of this sort further emphasizes the nominal nature of this particle, as Gai (1985: 125) notes about Akkadian and Ethiopic: "[a] preposition

Soqotri (MSA), we again find a preposition, *di-bal* 'without'. That this preposition originated from a nominal, possibly **bal*, is suggested by its appearance in the construct state, as the case endings on both Akkadian and Ethiopic show.[9] In Central Semitic, however, this preposition has acquired some additional functions, though indications of a prepositional use are still attested (see below).

Arabic has two forms used as a response: (8) *bal* 'no, to the contrary'[10] and (9) *balā* 'yes, indeed' (as a reply to a negative question; compare French *si*).

(8) *qāl-ū* *ttağada* *l-raḥmān-u* *walad-an*
said.PFV-3MP adopted-PFV.3MS DEF-merciful-NOM son-ACC
suḥān-a-hu *bal* *ʿibād-un* *makram-ūna*
praise-ACC-his nay servants-NOM.P honored-NOM.MP
'They said, "The Merciful has a son. Praise be to him!" Nay, they are honored servants'. (Qurʾān 21:25)

(9) *ʾa-ya-ḥsab-u* *l-ʾinsānu* *ʾan* *lan* *na-ğmaʿa*
INTERR-3M-think.JUSS-P DEF-people COMP NEG 1CP-gather-IPFV
ʿiḍām-a-hu *balā*
bones.ACC-his yes
'Do people think we will not gather his bones? Yes, indeed'. (Qurʾān 75:3)

The use of *bal* in some Middle Aramaic dialects is very similar to Arabic. In these dialects—Hatran, Nabatean, and Palmyrene—the particle occurs exclusively in funerary texts, in all of them in an identical context.

(10) Hatran
bl *dkyr* *šmʿny* *l-ṭb*
indeed remembered.PASS.PTCP.MS PN to-good
'May Š. be remembered for the best'. (Vattioni 1981: text 24:3)

---

cannot subordinate a sentence; it is only the nominal part of a 'prepositionized combination' (= additional preposition), which can fill this role." Note also that the conjunction function is not attested in any modern Ethio-Semitic language.

9. In Ethiopic, the ending of a construct noun is always *-a*, while in Akkadian, a lack of mimation indicates a construct state.

10. There are possible biblical attestations of this (for example, in Gen 42:21), where *ʾăbal* is used in speech as a response to a previous assumption or sentence to contradict a previous assumption ("to the contrary").

(11) Palmyrene

bl	*dkyr*	*yrḥu*	*br*	*nšʾ*	*mky*
indeed	remembered.PASS.PTCP.MS	PN	son.CSTR	PN	PN
b-ṭb					
in-good					

'May Y. son of N. of M. be remembered for the best'. (*CIS* II: 4207.1)

(12) Nabatean

bl	*dkrt*	*ʾlt*
indeed	memory.FS.CSTR	PN

'To the memory of A.'. (Jaussen and Savignac 1914: vol. 2, text 213)[11]

Aggoula (1975–76: 475) notes the orthography {bly dkyr} in several Nabatean texts, which is identical to the Arabic spelling of *balā*, with final *yāʾ* (known as *ʾalīf maqṣūra* in Arabic grammars): {bly}; some examples with final {ʾ} are also attested in Nabatean (e.g., *CIS* 246). These dialects are all attested in an Arabic-speaking area and thus may reflect Arabic influence.[12]

Nevertheless, several Aramaic dialects exhibit complex prepositions, with *bal* as one of its components: *bal-ʿad* 'except' (cf. Heb *bilʿădê* or *balʿădê* 'without'). This preposition is found with the same meaning in Official Aramaic and later also in Samaritan Aramaic, Nabatean,[13] and Syriac. The use of *bal-* as an independent particle to negate either verbs or nouns is unattested in any Aramaic dialect. The existence of *balʿad* should, therefore, be considered the relic of a nominal negative function that *bal* previously had.[14]

---

11. The addition of {bl} is by no means obligatory; many similar funerary texts do not use it with the *dkyr* formula, as in (i):

(i) Hatran

dkyr	*šmšʿqb . . .*
remember.PASS.PTCP.MS	PN

'let Š. be remembered'. (Vattioni 1994: 41, line 10)

12. In Old Syriac, another Middle Aramaic dialect of the region, there is only one relatively certain form {blʾ} with the same function (Drijvers and Healey 1999: As 22:2); however, the inscription where it is attested is quite difficult and thus not likely to serve as good evidence (Drijvers and Healey 1999: 83). Payne-Smith (1879: 1.527) records *bal*, found only in a Syriac-Arabic dictionary.

13. This is not an Arabism in Nabatean, since Arabic does not have a similar form.

14. See also *bal-ḥūd* in Middle and Late Aramaic.

However, in Ugaritic and Hebrew, this particle is occasionally used to negate verbs, though it is quite restricted. Neither of these languages uses *bl* for responses, as it is used in Arabic. In Ugaritic, *bl* negates (13) nouns and (14) predicates of nominal sentences as well as (15) verbs.

(13) *bl-mlk*
NEG-king
'not a king'. (*KTU* 1.4.vii.43)

(14) *bl* *iṯ*
NEG there-is
'there is not'. (*KTU* 1.17.i.20)

(15) *bl* *n-mlk*
NEG 1CP-enthrone.IPFV
'we shall not enthrone'. (*KTU* 1.6.i.48)

In Biblical Hebrew, *bal* occurs 69 times, mostly in poetry and later material. It negates nonverbal forms in only 4 of the Biblical Hebrew examples and, as in Aramaic, the relic *bilʿădê* (or *balʿădê*) is attested (16) in Hebrew. In most of the Hebrew examples, *bal* negates either (17) an imperfect or (18) a perfect verb.[15]

(16) *mî* *ʾēl* *mib-balʿădê* *yhwh*
who god from-except YHWH
'Who is god, except YHWH?' (2 Sam 22:32)

(17) *mēt-îm* *bal* *yi-ḥy-û* *rəpāʾ-îm* *bal* *yā-qūm-û*
dead-MP NEG 3M-live.IPFV-P deceased-MP NEG 3M-rise.IPFV-P
'the dead shall not live; the deceased shall not come to life'. (Isa 26:14)

(18) *yu-ḥan* *rāšāʿ* *bal* *lāmad*
3MS-grant.amnesty.IPFV.PASS evil NEG learn.PFV.3MS
ṣedeq
justice

15. The distribution is as follows: *bal* + imperfect occurs 50 times; *bal* + perfect occurs 15 times (Isa 26:10, 33:23, 40:24 [3×], 44:8, Pss 10:11, 17:5, 21:3, 58:9, 147:20; Prov 9:13, 14:7, 23:35 [2×]); *bal* + preposition occurs twice (Ps 16:2; Prov 23:7); *bal* + infinitive construct occurs once (Ps 32:9); *bal* + adjective occurs once (Prov 24:23).

'Grace is given to the evil person, [though] he does not learn justice'. (Isa 26:10)

5. The Origin and Development of *bal-

A common etymology given to *bal-* is a derivation from the root *bly* 'to be worn, corrupt'. Brockelmann (1928: 75a) lists Syriac *blay* under √*bly* and Aggoula (1975–76: 477) similarly connects the particle *bal*/*balā* in Arabic and Aramaic to this root. Tromp (1981: 281–82) argues that, since Hebrew shows forms with and without a final *-y*, like other prepositions with weak roots (for example, *ʿad*, *ʾel*), it should be assumed that the particle originated from a substantive derived from √*bly*.

There are, however, good reasons to treat *bal-* as a biradical root that originally did not have a verbal form associated with it (compare **sum*).[16] Whenever vocalization is available, in Hebrew, for example, these forms do not fit the vocalization of a triradical root. Note, for example, that Hebrew *biltî* has an underlying form **belet* (<√*bl*), while III-weak roots should have a different pattern, for example √*bky* > *běkît*; thus, **belet* is similar to *delet* (<√*dl*), rather than to *běkît* (√*bky*). In Syriac, a III-*y* root *bly* is expected to have an absolute form *bel^y*, not *blay* (compare *šelyā* 'peace, rest', abs./cnst. *šel^y*). In languages where **balʿad* is attested, it does not show any long form, as expected from a III-weak construct noun; similarly in Ethiopic (*ʾən*)*bala* is not a normal derivation from a III-weak verb.[17] All known biradical roots in Semitic are very old, and with its wide distribution in the oldest Semitic languages, *bal* seems to fit.[18]

Faber (1991: 421) connects Central Semitic {bl} to a variety of Afro-Asiatic particles. She does not list Akkadian and Ethiopic **bal* under Afro-Asiatic's **bV* negative particles (Faber 1991: 415–16) but includes Arabic *bi-lā* and *mā b-NP* (but not Heb *bě-lōʾ*). Ultimately, Faber assumes

---

16. See the discussion in Fox 1998, listing a large number of isolated nouns with two or three radicals that developed verbal forms later in their history but did not have them originally. Fox notes that "[i]n a synchronic analysis of any of the Semitic languages, there are almost no truly isolated nouns . . . since the Semitic languages can extract roots from any word and create verbs and nouns on the basis of the new roots" (1998: 4).

17. III-*w*/*y* roots in Ethiopic behave like sound roots. For most nonaffixed nouns from III-*w*/*y*, the final consonant is either pronounced (*maṣaw* √*mṣw* 'spring') or expressed as a vowel, a contraction of a diphthong (*dawe* √*dwy* 'disease').

18. Biradical roots in Semitic are known to be nominal. See Testen 1985 for **bn* 'son' and **tn* 'two' and Fox 1998.

that *bal* and its other derivations are compound forms based on **ba-*.[19] Though she assigns {bl} an Afro-Asiatic etymology, Faber suggests that the polar-negation function found in Central Semitic for this particle is a Central Semitic innovation.

A major flaw in the diachronic scenario suggested by Faber is that, as was mentioned above, the particle **bal-* occurs outside Central Semitic, namely, in Akkadian and Ethiopic, in both of which it is a negative preposition.[20] It means, of course, that **bal-* is an inherited form in Central Semitic, not an innovation. This seems quite reasonable since, except for the function of the forms in Arabic, which is slightly harder to explain, all other **bal-* particles are negative particles wherever they are attested. In addition, where we have evidence for vocalization, the vowel of the basic form, *-a-*, is consistent across all languages (for deviations in Hebrew, see below). Thus, we have correspondence of sound, correspondence of meaning, and partial correspondence of function, which as I will show below, can be accounted for. The connection between East Semitic **bal-* and West Semitic **bal-* seems, therefore, very likely.

In light of the evidence presented above, Faber's suggestion that **bal* is a Central Semitic innovation should be rejected for two reasons. First, **bal* is attested in East Semitic and West Semitic and thus should be considered common Semitic. Second, the function of **bal* as a verbal negative is not common Central Semitic: *bal* negates verbs only in Northwest Semitic, so this particular innovation is restricted to Northwest Semitic (except Aramaic), rather than Central Semitic, where it is a negative particle but not a verbal negative particle. In fact, since Aramaic does not share this innovation, it is perhaps wiser to consider it an areal feature.

---

19. Among the forms that Faber lists as *b*-based negation alongside Central Semitic *bal* are several Cushitic, Berber, and Egyptian particles with either a prefix or a suffix *ba-*. Faber claims that Central Semitic *bal* is related to these Afro-Asiatic *ba* negation affixes. However, these very particles are the basis of Faber's reconstruction of the proto-Afro-Asiatic polar negation particle *(m)ba*, which later Faber connects to the Arabic negation *mā* and other *m*-based polar particles. It is, therefore, quite hard to see how both Central Semitic *bal* and *mā* are related to Beja *bā*. In a later work (Faber 1997: 9), Faber suggests that the "reinforcement of an inherited Afroasiatic negative marker *b" is a Central Semitic feature.

20. See also Lipiński (2001: 566) who connects the Central Semitic particle **bal* with the Akkadian preposition *balu*.

6. *Etymology*

Tropper (2000: 836) suggests that the final *-t* on the form *blt* in Ugaritic is the same enclitic *-t* that is found on some demonstrative pronouns (e.g., *hnk-t*) and, most tellingly, on adverbs (e.g., *km-t*). Tropper connects this suffix to Akkadian *-ti* (for example, on the personal pronoun *šuā-ti, šunī-ti*, etc.; and on other pronouns, like *miya-ti*).[21] The only problem with this reconstruction is that the Akkadian ending *-ti* is typically restricted to the pronominal system and does not occur with nouns; in fact, the Akkadian preposition *balūt* seems to indicate that nominal derivational suffixes are preferred.

As was briefly suggested above, the particle *biltî* seems like the dependent form of a hypothetical segolate noun **belet* from a biradical root (<**bil-t*). I suggest, therefore, that this final *-t* is the feminine *-t*, frequently added to nominal patterns of the type **qvtl* from weak and biradical roots: **lid-t* (√*wld*) > *ledet* 'birth', **bakīt* (√*bky*) > *bĕkît* 'weeping', **dalt* (√*dl*) > *delet* 'door'.[22] Attaching the feminine suffix *-t* on **bal* would produce a *qatl* pattern, which in Canaanite should result in the form **belet*, with the possible construct **bal-t-*. There are a number of ways to explain the actual form *bilt-*: the obvious analogy would be to another biradical noun with a feminine ending, namely, *bat, bitt-* 'daughter' < **bin-t*. This falls nicely with the construct form of *bal* in *bilʿădê* < **bil-ʿaday*;[23] that this is an internal Hebrew change is made clear by the cognate Aramaic form *balʿad-* 'without'.

21. Similar endings are attested for the oblique demonstratives in OSA in both genders: MS *hw-t*, FS *hy-t*, CDU *hmy-t*, MP *hm-t*, FP *hn-t*; and also in Gəʾəz *zən-ti, zā-ti, yəʾə-ti, wəʾə-tu*.

22. √*dl* without the feminine ending appears in Biblical Hebrew (Ps 141:3) as well as Phoenician (*KAI* 37 A 6, pl. *dlht*; *KAI* 18.3). Other relevant forms are *qešet* 'bow' (√*qwš*), *šōqet* 'manger' (*šqy*), **śepet* 'lip' (P *śiptôt*; √*śpy*). Of course, feminine *-t* is not restricted to weak and biradical roots (e.g., *šibōlet* < **šibōl* 'ear of grain'). Note that other languages tend to use final feminine endings with weak roots. For example, Eth *fənot* (√*fnw*) 'road', *rəmet* (√*rmy*) 'throw'; Arb *ʿidatun* (√*wʿd*) 'promise', *diyatun* (√*wdy*) 'blood money'.

23. The alternation *a~i* is attested in the construct of the segolate pattern; note that Hebrew *delet* 'door', suffixed *dalt-* (< **dal-t*) is **dil-t* in Phoenician, as Greek *delta* shows. Another possibility is an analogy with forms of **qatl* segolates that change to **qitl* in Hebrew, such as *beṭen* 'intestine', suffixed *biṭn-* (cf. Arb *baṭnun*); or even variation within Hebrew itself: *šemeš* 'sun', pausal *šāmeš* (e.g., Exod 17:12) < **šamš*, but *šimšôn* 'Samson' (Judg 13:24), *šimšōtayk* (Isa 54:12), *šimšāh* (Jer 15:9) < **šimš* (cf. Arb *šamsun*).

We are left with the problem of final *-y* at the end of {blty}.[24] In Hebrew, there are examples of prepositions from construct nouns with final long *ī*: *zûlātî* (< *zûlat-*) 'except', *minnî* (*min-*) 'from'. This final *-î* suffix, known as *ḥiriq compaginis*, occurs mostly on construct nouns; it appears on many personal names: *malkîṣedeq*, *gabrîʾēl*, and so on. The orthography {blty} fits neatly with other prepositions that developed from construct nouns, such as *zûlātî*. I do not presume to solve the perennial problem of *ḥiriq compaginis* in Biblical Hebrew; I merely note that there is nothing special about attaching a long *ī* to a construct noun serving as a preposition, such as *biltî*.

Hebrew *bĕlî* and Syriac *blay* are identical to what is expected from a construct form of a biradical **bal* (cf. Heb *ʾăbî-;* Syr *ʾĕḥay-*) and thus further substantiate my suggestion above that these forms are related to a Proto-Semitic biradical noun **bal-*.[25]

7. Phoenician Verbal Negative {bl}

The use of *bal* to negate indicative verbs is unique to Northwest Semitic and does not occur in other Semitic languages.[26] But how does

---

24. Old South Arabian, where an occasional orthography {blty} is attested, often has variant prepositions with final *-y*: *ʿd/ʿdy*, *ʿl/ʿly*, *bʾṯr/bʾṯry*, *qbl/qbly*, *tḥt/tḥty*. Old South Arabian does not normally mark long *ī* with a *-y*. For example, the external nominal absolute masculine plural morpheme is written as final {n}. Compare Arm {yn}, Heb {ym}, and Arb {wn} (nominative). Thus, the appearance of *-y* on *blty* is probably unrelated to Hebrew. A possible explanation for the final *-y* in Old South Arabian is that it is a construct plural. The prepositions that show this ending are all of nominal origin (*b-*, *l-*, and *k-* never show it). Prepositions of nominal origin may have plural or singular bases in all the Semitic languages. Compare Heb *ʿad/ʿădê*, *ʿal/ʿălê*, *ʾel/ʾĕlê*, Syriac *ʿlay* and most importantly: *men blay* 'without'.

25. The connection to the III-weak root *bly* is unclear. It may be the case that the verb is denominal (compare denominal verbs for 'to name' in Semitic: Arm √*šmh* < *šəmā*, Eth √*smy* < *səm*) or that it is unrelated to *bal*.

26. This is nicely shown in a similar pattern found in Phoenician, Akkadin, and Ugaritic: Avishur (2000: 214–15) notes a similarity between the Phoenician phrase in (i) and Ugaritic and Akkadian phrases such as in (ii). In Ugaritic and Akkadian, either *lā* or *ʾul* is used, depending on the language's syntax.

(i)	*bt*	*ʾ-bʾ*	*bl*	*t-bʾn*
	house.CSTR	1CS-come.IPFV	NEG	2MS-come.IPFV

'the house I enter, you do not enter'. (*KAI* 27.5–6)

(ii)	*ašar*	*e-rrub-u*	*lā*	*te-rrub*
	place.CSTR	1CS-come.DUR.SUB	NEG	2MS-enter.PRET

'to the place I come, you shall not come'. (Uttukî Limnūti IV.9; apud Avishur 2000: 215)

a preposition turn into a verbal negative? There is some evidence to allow us a reasonable reconstruction, and I suggest that the movement from nominal negative to verbal negative was motivated by the ability of the preposition *bal* to negate nominal predicates. Ugaritic negates its existential particle with *bl* (*bl ʾiṯ*; cf. Old Arm *l-yš*),[27] but also (19) other predicative nominals:

(19) *bl* *bnš* *hw*
NEG man PRON.3MS
'he is not a man'. (*KTU* 2.45.27)

Hebrew has several examples of a predicative adjective and prepositional phrase negated with *bal*:

(20) *wĕ-libb-ô* *bal* *ʿimm-āk*
and-heart-his NEG with-2MS
'His heart is not with you'. (Prov 23:7)

(21) *hakkēr* *pān-îm* *be-mišpāṭ* *bal* *ṭôb*
recognize.INF.CSTR face-MP in-law NEG good.MS
'It is not good to be partial in justice'. (Prov 24:23)[28]

Hebrew and Ugaritic never generalized this particle for all predicates, and **bal* remains only a marginal negative particle in the verbal system

27. There is only one such example in Biblical Hebrew: *lō yēš* (Job 9:33). Normally the negation of the existential in Hebrew is with an unrelated lexeme, *ʾên* (cf. Ug. *ʾin*).

28. See also Pss 16:2, 32:9 (with an infinitive). Note also that the prepositions *biltî* and *bĕlî* are used to negate verbs, as in (i) and (ii) (see Isa 32:10 for a nunsubordinated verb).

(i) *way-yi-gnōb* *yaʿăqōb* *ʾet* *lēb* *lābān* *hā-ʾăramî*
CONS-3MS-steal.PRET PN ACC heart.CSTR PN DEF-Aramean
ʿal *bĕlî* *higgîd* *l-ô* *kî* *bōrēaḥ* *hûʾ*
because NEG tell.PFV.3MS to-him COMP flee.PTCP.MS PRON.3MS
'Jacob deceived Laban the Aramean, because he did not tell him that he was running away'. (Gen 31:20)

(ii) *û-ba-ʿăbûr* *ti-hyê* *yirʾāt-ô* *ʿal* *pĕn-ê-kem* *lĕ-biltî*
and-in-for 3FS-be.IPFV fear.FS-his over face-CSTR-2MP to-NEG
te-ḥĕṭāʾ-û
2M-sin-IPFV-P
'and in order that his [= god's] fear will be with you so that you will not sin'. (Exod 20:20)

of these languages. It is possible, however, that in Phoenician **bal* had a much wider distribution with predicative elements and subsequently replaced *lā* as a negative particle of the indicative verb, the predicate par excellence:[29]

Table 1. The Distribution of Negatives in Northwest Semitic

	Nominal Predicate	Indicative	Non-Indicative
NWS	**bal*	**lā*	**ʾal*
Phoenician	**bal* ————–>		**ʾal*

8. *Is {bl} One Particle or Two?*

The above scenario may explain the use of {bl} as a verbal negative, but is it the same <BL> that negates nouns in Phoenician? After all, except for relics, **bal* is not normally used anymore for nominal negation in Central Semitic, except perhaps in Ugaritic. To decide whether we have one {bl} particle in Phoenician or several, we should investigate the situation in other related languages.

---

29. A similar process is attested in Qumran Hebrew, where (i) *llʾ* and (ii) *blʾ* may also negate finite verbs:

(i) *w-zqy-m* *l-lwʾ* *y-šwbr-w*
and-fetter-MP to-NEG 3M-break.IPFV.PASS-P
'fetters will not be broken'. (1QH^{a} 13:37)

[ʾyk]h *ʾ-byṭ* *b-lwʾ* *gly-th* *ʿyn-y*
how 1CS-look.at.IPFV in-NEG reveal.PFV-2MS eye.FP-my
'how shall I see and you have not uncovered my eyes'. (1QH^{a} 21:4)

Note also that, in Mishnaic Hebrew, *bal* replaces *lōʾ* in biblical quotations (iii).

(iii) *wa-hărê* *hûʾ* *ʿôber* *ʿal* *bal* *t-ôsîp*
and-INTJ PRON.3MS transgress.PTCP.MS over NEG 2MS.add.IPFV
'Look—he transgresses "do not add"'. (*m. Zebaḥ.* 8:10)

This mishnaic passage quotes Deut 13:1, *lōʾ tōsēp*, but the reason for the change from *lōʾ* to *bal* is not clear. Mishnaic Hebrew does not use *bal* productively outside of quotations.

Another example of movement from nominal negation to verbal negation is Gəʿəz *ʾi-*, which is attested in Northwest Semitic: Heb *ʾî-nāqî* 'not clean' (Job 22:30); Phoen *ʾbl*/ʾī-bal 'no'; Old Arm *ʾ-šm* 'no-name' (Sefire 1 C 24; Fitzmyer 1995). In Ethiopic, *ʾi-* is used as the negative of all verbal forms as well as nominal; that is, the negative *ʾi-* spread to the verbal system but was not lost to the nominal system. This is identical to the distribution of {bl} in Phoenician. For another possible case of nominal-to-verbal negation, see Pat-El 2012: 38.

There seem to be two other nominal negatives in Central Semitic corresponding to Hebrew *bĕlî* {bly} and *bĕlō*ʾ {blʾ}. The Biblical Hebrew prepositions *bĕlî* and *biltî* (compare with once in Phoenician *blt* [*KAI* 13.5]) are also attested in Old South Arabian (*blty* or *bltn* and once *bly;* Beeston 1984: 57). Like Hebrew and Old South Arabian, Ugaritic uses *blt* for nominal negation (Tropper 2000: 818).

In addition, Ugaritic has a nominal negative {bl}, which Tropper (2000: 771) suggests vocalizing as two separate particles: /bali/ or /balu/, alongside /balî/ (Tropper 2000: 817). Both of these prepositions may negate nominals in Ugaritic, but one of them is (22) proclitic, while the other one is, at least orthographically, (23) independent.

(22) *bl-mlk*
NEG-king
'not a king'. (*KTU* 1.4.vii.43)

(23) *bl ṭl*
NEG dew
'without dew'. (*KTU* 1.19.i.44)

The syntactic difference between them is that the nonproclitic {bl} may be preceded by another preposition: *l-*. The proclitic prepositions will be discussed below.

In Biblical Hebrew, these {bl-} prepositions may be preceded by an additional preposition (e.g., Gen 3:11 *lĕ-biltî;* Job 38:41 *li-blî*), which is very similar to Ugaritic {l-bl} (Tropper 2000: 780), as in (24) (which may be compared to the Heb example in [25]).

(24) *l bl ḥrb*
to NEG sword
'without sword'. (*KTU* 1.96 4)

(25) *li-blî ḥōq*
to-NEG rule
'without measure'. (Isa 5:14)

Syriac has a complex preposition (26) *men blay* 'without'.

(26) *men blay yātēb*
from NEG sit.PTCP.MS.ABS
'without resident'. (Isa 6:11; cf. Heb *mēʾên yôšēb*)

Superficially, these prepositions seem related to Akkadian *balu* and *balūt*—both meaning 'without'.[30]

There is, however, another particle with a similar orthography that is found in (27) Hebrew, (28) Classical Arabic, and (29) Aramaic: {blʾ}, where the preposition **bi* is followed by the Semitic negative **lā*; **bi-lā* (Heb *bĕ-lōʾ*) is commonly used to negate nominal elements. The earliest attestation of this compound preposition in Aramaic is in Official Aramaic, where there is one example of *b-lʾ* negating a prepositional phrase, even though the normal nominal negative in Aramaic is *d-lā* (cf. Akk *ša lā*):

(27) Biblical Hebrew
bĕ-lō ʾêbā
in-NEG hostility
'without hostility'. (Num 35:22)

(28) Classical Arabic
bi-lā šakk-in
in-NEG doubt-GEN.INDEF
'without a doubt'. (Fischer 2001: 154)

(29) Official Aramaic[31]
w-t-hk [b-]lʾ b-ywm-y-k
and-2MS-go.IPFV in-NEG in-day-MP-2MS
'you go away before your time'. (*Aḥiqar* 102)

In these languages the consonantal structure contains a final glottal stop {blʾ}; however, the Semitic negative **lā* is written with final quiescent {ʾ} only in Hebrew, Arabic, and later dialects of Aramaic, but as a proclitic *l-* in Ugaritic, Deir Alla, and Old Aramaic. Moreover, even where final {ʾ} is a part of the orthography of the independent negative **lā*, certain compounds clearly indicate that the final {ʾ} is not etymological, for example, Aramaic *layt/lēt* (< **lā ʾīt*) 'there is not',[32] and in Nabatean

30. The vocalization of the preposition *balūt* was suggested by John Huehnergard (private communication), who thinks that the ending is the abstract suffix *-ūt*. The dictionaries vocalize this preposition with a short *u*: *balut*.

31. Note Late Biblical Hebrew *bĕlōʾ kakātūb* 'not as it is written/prescribed' (1 Chr 30:18). This prepositional phrase is also attested in many Middle and Late Aramaic dialects, among which are the Aramaic of the Targums *Onqelos*, *Neofiti*, *Pseudo-Jonathan*, as well as Syriac and Jewish Babylonian Aramaic.

32. Classical Arabic *laysa* 'not, there is no', which is probably borrowed from Aramaic, also attests a **lā* that lacks a final etymological {ʾ}.

the negative before the 3MS independent pronoun is written {lwʾ} (< *lā hūʾ).[33] In Arabic, the negative of the subjunctive *lan* is probably from *lā ʾan* (Wright 1967: 2.300). Thus, *lā* may be written with or without final {ʾ} in Central Semitic and is probably an orthographic representation of an open long syllable (CV:) rather than a closed syllable (CVC).[34]

As was mentioned above, the Ugaritic proclitic nominal negative *bl-*, which Tropper suggests is vocalized *balî* (Tropper 2000: 817), is different from the negative particle, *bl*, which is not proclitic and may follow other prepositions, such as *l-*, and may negate nominal predicates; incidentally, the regular Ugaritic negative, *l- /lā/,* as was mentioned above, is also proclitic.[35] We may, therefore, suggest that Ugaritic, like Hebrew, has a tripartite set of particles that in Ugaritic are homographic {bl}: *bal* negating verbs, *balî* (independent), and *bilā* (proclitic); the latter two negate nominals (nouns, adjectives and prepositional phrases). All three are attested in Hebrew with the same functions found in Ugaritic, as in examples (30)–(32).

(30) *bal yi-rʾ-û*
NEG 2MS-see.IPFV-P
'they will not see'. (Isa 44:9)

(31) *bĕlî māqôm*
NEG place
'without space'. (Isa 28:8)

(32) *bĕ-lōʾ ʾêbā*
in-NEG hostility
'without hostility'. (Num 35:22)

33. Note also that *lō* 'to him' and *lōʾ* 'not' are confused even in Biblical Hebrew: {lʾ} for {lw} is found 15 times in the Bible (Exod 21:8; Lev 11:21, 25:30; 1 Sam 2:3; 2 Sam 16:18; Isa 9:2, 63:9; Pss 100:3, 139:16; Prov 19:7, 26:2; Job 13:15, 41:4; Ezra 4:2; 1 Chr 11:20). {lw} for {lʾ} is found only 2× (1 Sam 2:16, 20:2). A prothetic {ʾ} may be added to indicate final long vowels (GKC 81): *haləkû*, written {hlkwʾ} (e.g., Josh 10:24); *ribbô*, written {rybwʾ} (e.g., Ezra 2:64); *lû*, written {lwʾ} (e.g., 1 Sam 14:30); and so on.

34. Garr argues that the {ʾ} found in Hebrew and Arabic of forms such as *lā* is not etymological but, rather, "a merely phonetic, syllable closing aleph" (Garr 1985: 199 n. 65).

35. The vocalization suggested by Tropper ignores the fact that *bĕlî* is not proclitic.

If indeed Ugaritic had a set of three negative particles, as Hebrew does, it may be reasonably suggested that Phoenician also had a similar set. It is possible that, while the verbal negative particle in Phoenician is Semitic **bal*, the nominal negative particle is a combination of a preposition and a negative particle: /*bĕlō*/.[36] This fits well with other Semitic languages that use prepositions (Arb and OSA *ġayr*, Akk *balû-*), prepositional phrases (Heb *bĕ-lōʾ*, Arb *bi-lā*, Arm *b-lā*), and adnominally marked negatives (Akk *ša lā*, Arm *d-lā*) to negate nouns and adjectives.[37] This suggestion also accounts for the alleged disappearance of **lā*: it is not missing but is restricted to nominal negation as *bĕ-lō*.

Table 2 shows the distribution of the negative particle written as <BL-> in the different Semitic languages.

Table 2. The Distribution of {bl} in Semitic

	***bl+N/PP 'without'**[a]			***bl*+Verb**	**Other Functions**
	***bal**	***bal-t**	***bi-lā**		
Akk	*balu , bal-ūt*				
Eth	*ʾənbala*				
MSA	*di-bal* (Soq)				
OSA	*bly*	*blty, bltn*			
Arb			*bi-lā*		*bal* 'on the contrary' *balā* 'yes, indeed'
Ug	*bl-*	*blt*	*b-l-*	*(bl)*	
Arm	*balʿad-* *men blay*		*b-lʾ*		*bl, bly* 'yes, indeed'
Heb	*bilʿadê* *balʿadê*	*bĕlî, biltî*	*bĕ-lōʾ*	*(bal)*	*ʾăbāl* 'but, however'
Phoen	?	*blt*	*b-l*	*bl*	

a. Forms in parenthesis are not common.

36. This idea that **lā* is still attested in Phoenician is first found in Eitan (1928), who suggested that all occurrences of {bl} in Phoenician should be presumed to stand for *bĕlōʾ*. Eitan in fact suggested that other derived forms, such as *bĕlî* and *biltî*, derive from *lōʾ*. A similar suggestion is found in Gibson (1982: 109) for the phrase *bl ʿty*, which he, like Eitan, compares to Hebrew *bĕlōʾ ʿittekā* 'before your time' (Eccl 7:17). Gibson, however, concedes that *lōʾ* is not found elsewhere in Phoenician.

37. In Old South Arabian, *dʾ* or *dk* are used for nominal negation (Beeston 1984: 47). The exact etymology of these forms is unknown.

On the basis of this distribution, we may suggest that the Semitic preposition **bal-* is indeed used in a variety of derivations. It was used to negate nominal predicates, and subsequently its function was extended to negate verbs in Northwest Semitic, attaining complete generalization only in Phoenician. Several other derivations from the original noun **bal* are well attested in the family.

In addition, several Central Semitic languages use the prepositional phrase **bi-lā*, which is unrelated to **bal*, although it is often orthographically identical. When we note the distribution of these various elements in Central Semitic, especially in Northwest Semitic, the existence of a similar set of particles in Phoenician seems likely.

9. Conclusions

In this paper, I suggested that, although the main difference between Hebrew and Phoenician is in its negative particles, Phoenician is in fact much closer to Biblical Hebrew in its use of negative particles than its orthography suggests. The main grammatical difference between the two languages remains the fact that Phoenician generalized *bal* for indicative negation and almost completely lost the negative particle **lā*, while in Hebrew *bal* is only a minor negative particle and **lā* (> *lōʾ*) is the common one.

I have shown that **bal* is not a Central Semitic innovation but a common Semitic particle, probably from a biradical origin, used in all branches for negation. The innovation recorded in some Northwest Semitic languages is the use of this particle to negate verbs rather than (its more common function) as a nominal negative preposition (cf. Akk *balû-*). Phoenician generalized this particle to become the only verbal negative particle, while in other Northwest Semitic languages it remained a marginal verbal negative. I have demonstrated that replacement of indicative negative particles with a nominal negative particle is attested elsewhere in Semitic (Eth *ʾi-*).

I have suggested that the particle *lā* was not completely lost in Phoenician but was restricted to a prepositional phrase used to negate nouns and adjectives, a function attested in Hebrew (*bĕ-lōʾ*), Aramaic (*b-lʾ*), and Arabic (*bi-lā*), and potentially in Ugaritic (*b-l-*). The set of Phoenician negative particles should, therefore, be reconstructed as in (34) the triad.

(34) Reconstructed Phoenician System of Negation

indicative negative:	**bal* (cf. Heb *lōʾ*)
modal negative:	**ʾal* (cf. Heb *ʾal*)
nominal negative:	**bĕlō* (cf. Heb *bĕlōʾ*)

Bibliography

Aggoula, B.
1975–76 Remarques sur les inscriptions hatréennes (IV). *MUSJ* 49: 471–88.
Avishur, Y.
2000 *Phoenician Inscriptions and the Bible.* Tel Aviv–Jaffa: Archaeological Center Publication.
Beeston, A. F. L.
1984 *Sabaic Grammar.* Manchester: University of Manchester Press.
Brockelmann, C.
1928 *Lexicon Syriacum.* M. Niemeyer.
Cantineau, J.
1930 *Le nabatéen.* Paris: Leroux.
Drijvers, H. J. W., and Healey, J. F.
1999 *The Old Syriac Inscriptions of Edessa and Osrhoene.* Leiden: Brill.
Eitan, I.
1928 Hebrew and Semitic Particles (Continued). *AJSL* 44: 254–60.
Faber, A.
1991 The Diachronic Relationship between Negative and Interrogative Markers in Semitic. Pp. 411–29 in *Semitic Studies in Honor of Wolf Leslau on the Occasion of His Eighty-Fifth Birthday,* ed. A. S. Kaye. Wiesbaden: Harrassowitz.
1997 Genetic Subgrouping of the Semitic Languages. Pp. 3–15 in *The Semitic Languages,* ed. R. Hetzron. New York: Routledge.
Fischer, W.
2001 *A Grammar of Classical Arabic.* New Haven, CT: Yale University Press.
Fitzmyer, J. A.
1995 *The Aramaic Inscriptions of Sefire.* Rome: Pontifical Biblical Institute.
Fox, J.
1998 Isolated Nouns in the Semitic Languages. *ZAH* 11: 1–31.
Friedrich, J., and Röllig, W.
1999 *Phönizisch-Punische Grammatik.* 3rd edition by M. G. Amadasi Guzzo with W. R. Mayer. AnOr 55. Rome: Pontifical Biblical Institute.
Gai, A.
1985 Prepositions-Conjunctions in Akkadian and Geʾez. *WO* 16: 123–25.
Garr, W. R.
1985 *Dialect Geography of Syria–Palestine, 1000–586 B.C.E.* Philadelphia: University of Pennsylvania Press. [Repr. Winona Lake, IN: Eisenbrauns, 2004.]

Gibson, J. C. L.
1982 *Textbook of Syrian Semitic Inscriptions*, vol. 3: *Phoenician Inscriptions*. Oxford: Clarendon.

Hackett, J. A.
2002 The Study of Partially Documented Languages. Pp. 57–78 in *Semitic Linguistics: The State of the Art at the Turn of the Twenty-First Century*, ed. S. Izre'el. IOS 20. Winona Lake, IN: Eisenbrauns.
2004 Phoenician and Punic. Pp. 365–85 in *The Cambridge Encyclopedia of the World's Ancient Languages*, ed. R. D. Woodard. Cambridge: Cambridge University Press.

Harris, Z. S.
1936 *A Grammar of the Phoenician Language*. AOS 8. New Haven, CT: American Oriental Society.

Hetzron, R.
1976 Two Principles of Genetic Reconstruction. *Lingua* 38: 89–108.

Huehnergard, J.
2006 Proto-Semitic and Proto-Akkadian. Pp. 1–18 in *The Akkadian Language in Its Semitic Context: Studies in the Akkadian of the Third and Second Millennium*, ed. G. Deutscher and N. J. C. Kouwenberg. Leiden: Nederlandse Instituut voor het Nabije Oosten.

Jaussen, A., and Savignac, R.
1909–20 *Mission archéologique en Arabie: Mars–Mai 1907*. 3 vols. Paris: Leroux.

Johnstone, T. M.
1975 The Modern South Arabian languages. *AAL* 1/5: 1–29.

Krahmalkov, C.
2001 *A Phoenician-Punic Grammar*. HOSNME 54. Leiden: Brill.

Leslau, W.
1995 *Reference Grammar of Amharic*. Wiesbaden: Harrassowitz.

Lipiński, E.
2001 *Semitic Languages: Outline of a Comparative Grammar*. 2nd ed. OLA 80. Leuven: Peeters.

Pat-El, N.
2012 On Verbal Negation in Semitic. *ZDMG* 162/1: 17–45.

Payne Smith, R., ed.
1879–1901 *Thesaurus syriacus*. Oxford: Clarendon.

Qimron, E.
1986 *The Hebrew of the Dead Sea Scrolls*. HSS 29. Atlanta: Scholars Press.

Soden, W. von
1995 *Grundriss der akkadischen Grammatik*. 3rd ed. AnOr 33. Rome: Pontifical Biblical Institute.

Testen, D.
1985 The Significance of Aramaic *r* < **n*. *JNES* 44: 143–46.

Tromp, N. J.
1981 The Hebrew Particle בל. Pp. 277–87 in *Remembering All the Way: A Collection of Old Testament Studies*. OtSt 31. Leiden: Brill.

Tropper, J.
2000 *Ugaritische Grammatik*. AOAT 273. Münster: Ugarit-Verlag.

Vattioni, F.
1981 *Le inscrizioni di Ḥatra*. Naples: Istituto Orientale di Napoli.
1994 *Hatra*. Naples: Instituto Universitario Orientale.

Waltke, B. K., and O'Connor, M. P.
1990 *An Introduction to Biblical Hebrew Syntax*. Winona Lake, IN: Eisenbrauns.

Wright, W.
1967 *A Grammar of the Arabic Language*. Cambridge: Cambridge University Press.

The Phoenician Words mškb *and* ʿrr *in the Royal Inscription of Kulamuwa (KAI 24.14–15) and the Body Language of Peripheral Politics*

Philip C. Schmitz

The ninth-century Phoenician inscription of Kulamuwa is well known to specialists and students. Found in 1902, the inscribed orthostat was one of nine inscriptions or fragments discovered during excavations by the German Orient-Comité (von Luschan and Jacoby 1911: 374–77) at Zinçirli and other local sites.[1]

The general understanding of the two Phoenician words that constitute the main topic of the present discussion is clearly represented in a summary by T. Bryce (2012: 169), himself not a Semitist or specialist in the inscription's language.[2] The prevailing view among ancient historians is that the Samalian kingdom was ethnically diverse. In his famous inscription,

---

Author's note: The author is indebted to the editors of this volume for valuable remarks that improved the text of this chapter. Special thanks go to M. G. Amadasi Guzzo, whose wise questions about an earlier draft prompted the author to improve the argument. Jim Eisenbraun and the publisher's editorial staff accommodated final changes gracefully as well. Only the author deserves blame for errors or criticism for arguments and conclusions in the text as it stands.

1. Other epigraphic finds are discussed by V. Herrmann (2011: 27). The Kulamuwa inscription was found *in situ* in building J. See von Luschan's summary in von Luschan, Schrader, and Sachau (1893: 1–10) for a brief introduction to the site and the excavation's early progress. Note also the detailed descriptions of the Phoenician inscription by Tropper (1993: 27–28) and Brian Brown (2008: 341–44). For a succinct description of the site of Zinçirli, its discovery, and its Neo-Hittite context, see Bryce (2012: 170).

2. Concerning the language of the inscription, see, among others, Tropper (1993), Röllig (2004) and Younger (2013).

> . . . Kilamuwa identifies two population groups in his kingdom—the *Baʿririm* and the *Muškabim*.[3] Whatever this passage actually means—it appears to hint at the possibility of hostilities between the two groups if the king's successors do not honour the terms of his inscription—the *Baʿririm* are generally considered to represent an Aramaean group from an originally nomadic or semi-nomadic pastoralist background who became dominant in the land, while the *Muškabim*, [Edward] Lipiński suggests,[4] were perhaps descendants of the original Luwian inhabitants of the region 'of old sedentary and partly urbanized'. (Bryce 2012: 169)

The author just cited controls the current and past literature by Semitic specialists concerning the pair of Phoenician words, *mškbm* and *bʿrrm*, that are at issue, and he presents the consensus accurately. A few additional citations of the relevant literature will demonstrate this assertion. For example, the assumed correspondence of *mškbm* with a sedentary population and *bʿrrm* with a nomadic group arose in the earliest discussions of this text.

Less than two years after the publication of Kulamuwa's orthostat inscription,[5] Mark Lidzbarski wrote, "[*bʿrr*] heisst 'wild, unkultiviert. *bʿrr* muss hier eine Bevölkerungsschicht im Lande bezeichen, die den *mškb* gegenüberstand" (1909–15: 3.235). He attributed the dimorphic social interpretation to discussion with von Luschan and its philological explanation to discussion with Nöldeke.

Two years after the text's publication, Hans Bauer regarded the view as already widely held, as his comments on the word *mškb* imply: "Das hier an eine bestimmte Menschenklasse zu denken ist, haben mehrere Erklarer ausgesprochen" (Bauer 1913: 687). In the same paragraph, Bauer considers Theodor Nöldeke's derivation of *bʿrr* from Syriac *baʿrar* to imply ">>wild, unkultuviert<< . . . , hier wohl von der nomadischen Bevolkerung gemeint" (Bauer 1913: 687).[6]

---

3. Here Bryce is depending on Younger's translation of *KAI* 24 in Hallo and Younger 2000: 147–48 §2.30 [= *COS* 2.147–48].

4. Bryce cites Lipiński (2000: 236).

5. Lidzbarski received a copy of von Luschan and Jacoby's volume in December 1911 (1909–15: 3.220). I deduce from his discussion, which (consistent with Lidzbarski's usual practice) is bibliographically comprehensive, that the text was composed before Bauer 1913 appeared, for this article is not mentioned. Lidzbarski's citation of the earliest literature on the inscription occurs on p. 220, n. 1. Bauer does cite and discuss Lidzbarski's publication (Bauer 1913: 684).

6. Paraphrasing Lidzbarski's comment above. Note also Brockelmann (1928: 85 s.v. *baʿrar*).

Half a century later, Wolfgang Röllig offered a much briefer but similar interpretation of these words (*KAI* 2.34), citing the views of Lidzbarski and Landsberger (1948: 52–53). J. C. L. Gibson elaborated on this scenario by adding an ethnic identifier: "[*mškbm*] is a designation of the conquered indigenous population, . . . [*bʿrrm*] may refer to the dominant but minority Aramaean element" (1982: 38).[7] Schade (2006: 84–85) explains Kulamuwa's apparently conciliatory role between these presumed ethnic constituencies as the influence of his paternal Aramaean and maternal Anatolian parentage.

The historical literature does not deviate from the philological interpretations. F. M. Fales (1979: 8 n. 8) follows this interpretation, and J. Tropper (1993: 13) expresses a view close to the later, somewhat more complex views of Lipiński (2000: 236) already cited.[8] The current excavators of the site of Zinçirli, Schloen and Fink, discuss the word pair *mškbm*/*bʿrrm* in the context of Luwian–Aramaean relations in the area (2009: 10). Most recently, an exemplary doctoral dissertation completed by a member of the current Neubauer Expedition to Zinçirli presents such a view, extensively documented:

> In the inscription of Kulamuwa from the second half of the ninth century BC (*KAI* 24), this king mentions two sectors of society in the kingdom: the *bʿrrm* and the *mškbm*, the latter of whom were "living like dogs" (line 10) before the king "took [them] by the hand" (line 13). It has often been proposed to see in these enigmatic terms socioeconomic euphemisms for the dominant Aramaean seminomadic pastoralist "roamers" (*baʿrīrīm*?) and the subjugated Luwian population of "sedentists" (*muškabīm*?) (Tropper 1993: 41, 45; Dion 1997: 286 n. 67; Lipiński 2000: 236; Landsberger 1948: 54–56).[9]

Without sustained critical challenge, the ruminations of nineteenth-century orientalist scholars have become accepted fact about ancient history for twenty-first-century historical interpreters.[10]

7. Gibson's derivation "[*baʿrīrīm*] 'savage, cruel ones'; cp. Syriac" entails dependence on Nöldeke.

8. Brian Brown shows greater hesitation: "we can't be sure what these designations [*mškbm* and *bʿrrm*] actually mean—that is, we don't know if they have any ethnic implications or not" (2008: 345–46). Note also Novák 2005.

9. This passage is from V. Herrmann 2011: 32–33.

10. I do not intend the word 'orientalist' as a term of derogation. The early scholars cited were among the greatest of their generations. While they could not hold views that have developed after the world wars, their vast erudition and keen judgment deserve to be emulated and honored by us in appropriate degrees.

It may also prove significant that the social scenario imagined by philological interpreters changed over time. If von Luschan appears to have had in mind the contrast between settled and nomadic populations,[11] Lidzbarski's presentation of that notion uses terms more suggestive of social conflict between "Semiten, solange er noch in beduinischen Anschauungen lebt" (that is, *bʿrrm*) and "die im Lande vorgefundene, wohl im Wesentlichen 'chetische' Bevölkerung" (that is, *mškbm*; Lidzbarski 1909–15: 3.235–36). The views of Tropper and Lipiński sketched above involve a somewhat more explicit updating of Lidzbarski's scenario, while Gibson's spare comments add little detail. Schloen and Fink (2009: 10) view the basic dimorphism as ethnic. Virginia Herrmann's summary retains the dimorphism (2011: 32–33).

Does any version of this developing discourse approach historical verity? The prevailing interpretations of *KAI* 24.14–15 are symptomatic of a problem inherited from earlier philological approaches to ancient texts: the tendency to concentrate interpretation at the lexical level was occasionally too limited. The development of linguistic approaches to text interpretation has involved a process of expanding the interpreter's attention from the lexicon alone to the lexicon in conjunction with analysis of syntax and discourse structure. The larger perspective offered by these other levels of the text can be conducive to alternative solutions to apparent problems.[12]

In advocating this kind of analysis, I am attempting to implement an approach to Phoenician texts advised by one of their exemplary interpreters: "I am convinced that the way to improved grammatical and substantival understanding of the content of the sometimes very condensed texts (which can only be understood with difficulty) is through paying attention to the literary structure of the inscriptions" (Röllig 1995: 211). The remainder of this study will attempt, by drawing attention first to the probable lexical meaning of key words and then to the linguistic analysis of phrase structure in a single sentence, to explicate the literary structure of the passage more clearly.

To demonstrate the analysis I propose, let us return to the Phoenician text. The word *mškbm* appears early in the second section of the

11. Lidzbarski says, "v[on] Luschan schlug mir vor, *bʿrr* als die nomadische, *mškb* als die ansässige, ackerbautreibende Bevölkerung anzusehen" (1909–15: 3.235).

12. The procedure I suggest is compatible with the syntactic-literary approach of Schade (2006) and is also similar to to the corpus-driven approach to Phoenician taken by Booth (2007: 20–22).

inscription, in a passage that contrasts Kulamuwa's own reign with the conditions experienced by former kings (*KAI* 24.9b–10a; example 1):[13]

(1) *lpn hmlkm hlpnym ytlkn mškbm km klbm*
lə-pānē *ha-mmalk-īm ha-llə-pnay-īm*
to-face.of DEF-king-PL DEF-to-face.of-PL
yi-t-allək-ū-nū *maškəb-īm* *kə-mō* *kal(lă)b-īm*
PFV.3.C-CAUSE-go-PL-1PL suzerain-PL like, as-ADV 'dog'-PL
'In front of the former kings[14] suzerains (routinely) marched us like *dogs*'.

The verb *ytlk̊n* (√*hlk*) is a *Yitpael* suffixing form, third-person plural, with a first-person plural pronominal suffix.[15] In Biblical Hebrew, the Hithpael of *hlk* describes the movements of David's armed band of retainers (1 Sam 25:27). Similar use of the Hithpael stem in Biblical Hebrew (2) expresses routine behavior, and the prepositional phrase לִפְנֵי introduces a locative expression indicating the position of the movement.

(2) מָרְדֳּכַי מִתְהַלֵּךְ לִפְנֵי חֲצַר בֵּית־הַנָּשִׁים
'Mordecai (routinely) walked before the women's house'. (Esth 2:11)

The analogy supplied by this biblical sentence supports an interpretation of *lpn hmlkm hlpnym* as a locative expression, "In front of the former kings," so translated above. The concern underlying this statement is not interethnic relationships but the undefended position of vassal forces in military formations.

Lidzbarski (1909–15: 3.233) favored the reading *ytlk̊n* over *ytln̊n* or *ytlẘn*. Although the other readings were more generally followed,[16] Lid-

13. The examples that follow are transcribed without diacritic marks that indicate the certainty of readings, such as the circule over a letter.

14. The syntax of the phrase *hmlkm hlpnym,* with repetition of the definite article, is characteristic of later Tyrian-Sidonian Phoenician. Note, for example, *hʾlnm hqdšm* 'the holy deities' (*KAI* 14.9). Tropper (1993: 39) notes the contrasting syntax of archaic Byblian *ʾl gbl qdšm* (*KAI* 4.4–5, 7).

15. This differs from the analysis by Tropper (1993: 41).

16. For example, see S. Herrmann 1953. See also the meticulously documented histories of interpretation of this passage by Tropper (1993: 39–41) and Green (2010: 138–42).

zbarski's reading was revived by Tropper (1993: 39–40), then adopted by Krahmalkov (2000: 158), Younger (*COS* 2.148) and, with excellent comparative use of high-resolution photographs, Booth (2007: 167–69).[17] It is also implicit in V. Hermann's summary cited above. On the basis of the photographic images provided in Booth's text, I think the reading of the damaged letter as {*k̊*}, a three-stroke *kap* whose second stroke is partly obliterated,[18] is preferable to either the reading {*n*} or the reading {*w*}. This reading also enables a superior contextual interpretation.

From the perspective of semantics, or meaning, the form *mškbm* is particularly elusive. All interpreters derive *mškb* from √*škb* 'lie down'. I interpret the word as a causative (*Yiphil*) participle /maškēb-/ lit., 'oppressor/conqueror'.[19] A relevant biblical passage, as most commentators have observed, is 2 Sam 8:2, a scene in which David, victorious over Moab, *haškēḇ ʾôtām* 'forced them to lie down'. Hints of canine behavior nuance this vocabulary and emerge to the surface in *KAI* 24.10 in the simile *km klbm* 'as *infantry*' (see n. 24 below), immediately following.

The inscription's first half develops large themes directed to political concerns with government and international relations. According to the segmentation of units proposed by Schade (2006: 69), these concerns are: the ineffectiveness of former kings of Samʾal (*KAI* 24.2b–5a [Segment 2]); the weak position of Kulamuwa's paternal lineage (*bt ʾby*) in confronting aggression from powerful kings in the region, contrasted with his own aggressiveness (*KAI* 24.5b–7a [Segment 3]); the specific case of the superior military capability of the Danunian king, solved by Kulamuwa's voluntary submission to Assyria (*KAI* 24.7b–8

17. The photographs are available through the Inscriptifact Database (http://www.inscriptifact.com/) associated with the West Semitic Research Project at the University of Southern California, whose principal researchers are Bruce Zuckerman and Marilyn Lundberg.

18. Hence the transliteration here as *ytlk̊n*, marked with a circule. Tropper's transliteration *ytlk!n* represents his conclusion, based on his examination of the original, that the stonecutter either corrected an original {*w*} to {*k*} or misinterpreted the written copy of the text from which the inscription was carved (1993: 40). I think this caution may be greater than necessary because the damage to the letter could have occurred at any number of later times. Note the bad condition of the inscription *in situ* and also Tropper's concern about the worsening modern condition of the inscription's inscribed surface, especially during and after World War II (1993: 38).

19. The analysis by Gibson (1982: 37–38) represents earlier views. Schade (2006: 81 n. 32) points out that Tropper's analysis as a G passive participle (1993: 41) fails to account for the *m*- preformative.

[Segment 4]).[20] These themes, considered in view of the explicit mention of the "king of Assyria" in line 8, suggests the historical context for interpreting the canine imagery that emerges in line 10, where *klbm* 'dogs' are represented as hurrying around, either at the feet of their master[21] or fending off an intruder.

The larger context is the first phase (900–750 B.C.) of the Assyrian domination of Syro-Anatolian city-states (Van de Mieroop 2004: 216–22), more specifically, the campaign of Shalmaneser III against Que (*Ḫiyawa* in Cilicia)[22] in his twentieth year (839 B.C.) and in succeeding campaigns.[23] Yamada (2000: 199) refers to the Assyrian policy of "mobilisation of vassal states" in this campaign, and this policy provides the background of the term *mškbm*: the subjection and consequent military obligations imposed by suzerains on vassal states. V. Herrmann (2011: 37) examined the sources in detail and reached this conclusion:

> The king of Samʾal had . . . been compelled under threat to enter into a relationship of clientage or vassalage with the king of Assyria. In addition to the payment of a large tribute of submission, the agreement to send annual tribute, and the sending of his daughter to the Assyrian court as a bride/hostage, it is hard to imagine that the relationship was not also sealed by either the imposition of a vassal treaty or the swearing of an oath of loyalty (*adê*) (Yamada 2000: 305–6).

The political posture of vassalage would be salient among the concerns of a young(?) ruler in the position of Kulamuwa, so it makes good sense to look for that high-status term in the enigmatic word *mškbm*. I submit that *mškbm* should be construed 'suzerains'.

The word *klbm* may also involve a subtle pun. The Akkadian military term *kallābu* 'member of the light troops' (*AHw* 425; *CAD* K 77–78)

20. The content summaries of each segment are mine and, although they may not differ radically from the views of Schade, should not be understood to represent his views entirely.

21. Such movement is more clearly implied in the Biblical Hebrew verbal image *hammithalləḵîm bəraḡlê ʾădōnî* lit. "(the young men) that go around the feet of my lord," abstractly rendered in most English translations, e.g., "(the young men) who are the followers of my lord" (1 Sam 25:27 NJPS). Tropper (1993: 41) rejects the nuance of movement in favor of the broader sense "wandeln, leben." Younger's and Booth's translations also reflect this view.

22. Note especially the discussion by Lemaire (2000: 54–62).

23. On this period as background to *KAI* 24, see Tropper 1993: 12; Yamada 2000: 198–99, 237–39 (specifically about the inscription, p. 199 n. 422); and Schade (2006: 91–96). V. Herrmann (2011: 43 table 1.7) provides a full list of Assyrian synchronisms with the rulers of Samʾal/Zinçirli.

is also attested somewhat later in Northwest Semitic texts as a loanwor spelled *klb*, probably meaning 'infantry'.[24] The conceptual overlap of 'infantryman' and 'dog' can be traced in near-universal word associations. I submit that *km klbm* should be construed 'like/as infantry/mercenaries'.

The second occurrence of *mškbm* is (3) in the first part of line 13:

(3) *wʾnk tmkt mškbm lyd*
wa-ʾanēk *tamak-tī* *maškəb-īm* *la-yad*
and-I grasp.PFV-1CS suzerain-PL to-hand
'But I grasped suzerains by the hand'.

The element *mškbm* is logically the object of the verb *tmk*. The prepositional phrase *lyd* is adverbial. The collocation *tmk . . . lyd* may imply the gesture of grasping or touching the hand of another as a sign of agreement.[25] Here again the meaning "suzerains" for *mškbm* suits the context as established above. The narrative in line 7 about conflict with the more powerful king of the Danunians (apparently Katê), and Kulamuwa's collaboration with the Assyrian overlords (line 8), offers a background against which *mškbm* in this instance makes sense as the plural 'suzerains'. Kulamuwa has voluntarily submitted to Assyrian rule and advises his peers to ally with him rather than with other potential allies.

The element *mškbm* occurs twice again in the Phoenician text of *KAI* 24.13b–15a: *wmy bbny ʾš yšb tḥtn wyzq bspr z mškbm ʾl ykbd l bʿrrm wbʿrrm ʾl ykbd l mškbm*. Gibson's translation of this sentence is representative: "Now, if any of my sons who shall sit in my place does harm to this inscription, may the *mškbm* not honor the *bʿrrm*, nor the *bʿrrm* honor the *mškbm*!" (1982: 35). The concluding tautology seems odd, and the vocabulary, involving two otherwise unattested ethnonyms, is somewhat

24. In Phoenician, the plural *klbm* occurs in *lklbm wlgrm* "For light troops and for archers" (*CIS* 86 B.10 [Kition]; Schmitz forthcoming), and is probably to be restored in *CIS* 86 A.15, giving the same text: *[lklbm] wlgrm*. F. M. Fales has identified the same loanword in the Aramaic word *klbyʾ* (Berlin, Ägyptisches Museum P. 13495; AP 30; *TAD* 1 A 4.7; Fales 1987: 468–69), and in the Assur Ostracon (Lidzbarski 1921: 5–15; *KAI* 233.7; Fales 2009: 92 n. 34; 2010: 195–96 and n. 36). He advises the translation "(regular) infantry" (2010: 196 n. 36).

25. Most relevant to this discussion is the relief portrayal of a handclasp or handshake as part of a treaty negotiation between Shalmaneser III and Marduk-zakir-shumi. The relief, in the collection of the Iraq Museum, Baghdad (ND 1 1000 = IM 65574), adorned the throne base in the palace at Fort Shalmaneser (Nimrud). On the gesture more generally, see Seely 1995: 417–18.

strange. Its gnomic quality as translated creates the impression of a *non sequitur* in the argument of the inscription.

Understanding the phrase structure of this passage requires further analysis of the relationship between syntactic arguments, such as complements and adjuncts. Let us begin by noting features of the text as written. The verb *ykbd* takes an adverbial complement of manner introduced by the preposition *l*, which I understand to carry a prepositional suffix. The complement is immediately followed by a temporal adverbial adjunct introduced by the preposition *b*, *bʿrrm*. The constituent order complement-adjunct follows from constraints on syntax expected in minimalist linguistic theory.[26] In the present example, the complement *l* /lō/ 'to him' precedes the adjunct *bʿrrm*, whose meaning will be established.

In Biblical Hebrew, the verb *kbd* takes an adverbial complement of manner introduced by the preposition *li-* in Ps 86:9: *wiyḵabbədū lišmeḵā* "and they will pay honor to your name" (NJPS). The same prepositional complementation, *kbd l*, occurs twice in Dan 11:38.[27] Interpreted in light of this syntactic framework, the segment *mškbm ʾl ykbd l* can be translated "suzerains will not ascribe honor *to him*." The pronoun is coreferential with *my bbny* 'whoever among my sons'.

The phrase *bʿrrm* can now be seen as an adjunct: *b* (= in, among) + *ʿrrm* 'the destitute'. The form *ʿrr* is cognate to the Biblical Hebrew *ʿărîrî* 'stripped, childless' (*HALOT* 884), implying loss and degradation.[28] Public humiliation by divestiture—stripping off clothing—was part of the ceremonial chastisement visited by Assyrian suzerains on vassals who were held in violation of their treaty obligations.[29]

The same verbal root (*ʿrr*) is employed (4) in the Old Aramaic inscription from Sefire to portray the ritual divestiture of a vassal's spouses as a result of a (hypothetical) treaty violation:

26. This analysis is consistent with minimalist linguistic theory of phrase structure that distinguishes heads, intermediate projections, and maximal projections (Hornstein, Nunes, and Grohmann 2005: 186). Some implications of this theoretical model are that complements must precede adjuncts, and that adjuncts may be recursive.

27. Tropper (1993: 45) has noted these syntactic parallels.

28. Compare Biblical Hebrew *ʿrr* 'strip, denude' (*HALOT* 889) and Old Aramaic *ʿrr* 'to be denudated, to be stripped' (*DNWSI* 890 s.v. *ʿrr*$_2$).

29. Berlejung (2010: 24) surveys Assyrian punishments for treaty violation. Vogelzang and van Bekkum (1986) discuss the symbolism of clothing in the ancient Near East. Chapman (2010: 8 n. 16) observes that denudation removed any signals of ethnicity that clothing may have provided.

(4) *kn yʿrrn nšy mtʾʾl*
kēn *yu-ʿrər-ān* *nəš-ēy* *matīʾʾēl*
ADV IPFV.3.C-strip.IPFV wife_of.OBL.PL PN
So shall the wives of Matiʿel be stripped naked[30]

This passage establishes a ground for translating (5) as follows:

(5) *mškbm ʾl ykbd l bʿrrm*
muškəb-īm *ʾal* *yi-kabbəd-ū* *l-ō* *ba-ʿarīr-īm*
suzerain-PL NEG IPFV.3.PL-honor.RES-PL to-him in-stripped.PL
'Suzerains will not ascribe honor to him among the destitute'.

The converse clause *wbʿrrm ʾl ykbd lmškbm* must mean 'and among the destitute he will not bring honor to suzerains'.

Once recognized, this reference to the Assyrian practice of divestiture as part of the public humiliation and chastisement of disloyal vassals allows us to place the seemingly gnomic statement of line 8 in historical context. This passage follows Kulamuwa's admission that the king of the Danunians had grown too powerful against him (line 7), provoking him to "hire" (*škr*) the king of Assyria against his rival (lines 7–8).[31] Without further introduction comes the following statement (6), with the customary analysis underlying translations of this passage provided below:

(6) *ʿlmt ytn bš wgbr bswt*
ʿalmat *yutan* *bə-śe* *wa-gibbar*
young_female give.PFV.PASS for-sheep and-young_man
bi-suwat
for-garment

30. The translation is by Gibson (1975: 33). See also *DNWSI* 890 s.v. *ʿrr*$_2$.

31. "This king of Assyria is unnamed, and no Assyrian inscription records this event. It is usually assumed, however, that the rescue of YʾDY must have taken place during one of Shalmaneser III's four campaigns to Cilicia, in 839, 833, 832, or 831 B.C. (Hawkins 1982: 397–98; Dion 1997: 108; Lipiński 2000: 242; Yamada 2000: 197–205, 218–21). In the first three campaigns, he plundered several Cilician cities and set up steles, while in the last campaign he seems to have finally succeeded in ousting Katê and promoted Katê's brother Kirri to the throne" (V. Herrmann 2011: 38).

Translations have varied:

> "One had to pay a young woman for a sheep and a man for a garment" (O'Connor 1977: 19).
> "He gave a maid for the price of a sheep, and a man for the price of a garment" (Gibson 1982: 35).[32]

Phoenician orthography is conservative, and does not mark third-person pronominal suffixes on subject nouns. We could analyze *ʿlmt* with a third-person pronoun as /ʿalmatō/ 'his girl', and *gbr* as /gibbarō/ 'his young man/warrior' to give a rendering such as (7):

(7) *ʿalmat-ō* *yutan* *bə-śe*
young_female-his give.PFV.PASS for-sheep
wa-gibbarō *bi-suwat*
and-young_male-his for-garment
'His girl was sold for a sheep, his young man for a garment'.

With this slight grammatical change in example (7), the scene becomes an episode of divestiture; the girl is possibly the daughter of the Danunian king, the *gbr* either his elite corps of warriors or his royal scion. The chilling message emphasizes by understatement the consequences of overreaching–an act of disloyalty to the Assyrian crown–by vassal rulers.[33]

Should the analyses proposed above find acceptance, what gains and losses are entailed for historians interested in the message of this inscription? The primary gain is coherence. That is, the inscription concerns the situation of vassal rulers in the relatively new circumstance of subjection to Assyrian intervention. The inscription portrays the actions of local and regional Anatolian participants with a concern for their political consequences. The theme of ethnicity and interethnic competition is not absent, but it arises elsewhere than was long assumed. As demonstrated above, the words *mškbm* and *bʿrrm* are not obscure ethnic labels. The word *mškbm* probably stands for the political class of conquering rulers, or suzerains, and the phrase *bʿrrm* concerns one of the consequences of disloyalty by vassals.

---

32. Tropper's German translation (1993: 37) is essentially identical to Gibson's.
33. This possibility has repeatedly been discussed in the literature. See O'Connor 1977: 22; and V. Herrmann 2011: 38–39, with comparative examples.

The interpretation argued herein provides a somewhat expanded context for understanding the act of defacement of a royal inscription, the concern expressed in *KAI* 24.13b–15a, discussed above. Acts of this sort would be part of a forcible shift of political loyalties by local rulers and would constitute violation of treaty obligations from the Assyrian perspective.[34] Unsuccessful rebels would face public chastisement.

Ethnicity is probably expressed very subtly in this document. Kulamuwa identifies himself as *br ḥy* 'son of Ḥayya' in the opening line of the text (*KAI* 24.1)[35] but also as *br tml* in line 4.[36] Lidzbarski (1909–15: 227) proposed that Kulamuwa referred to his mother's name to distinguish his maternal lineage from that of his (half-)brother *šʾl* (line 4), and a number of scholars have followed this interpretation.[37] Schade (2006: 72 n. 10) sees Kulamuwa's purpose as accentuating "the failures of the . . . Aramaean dynasties," which are contrasted with "the rise of the Anatolian lineage (*br tml*)."[38] Kulamuwa, having deposed his ineffective half-brother, won Assyrian support with a "promise of support [for Assyrian interests] of the Anatolian people" (Schade 2006: 95). While the details remain obscure, the argument has merit. The change of lineage effected by Kulamuwa's accession to the throne probably implies a shift in ethnic affinities as well.

Finally, a subaltern voice emerges in the text's observation that *ytlkn mškbm* 'suzerains (routinely) marched us' (or 'made us march'). Precisely what are the bounds of the first-person reference in this claim? Is the semantic domain regional (Anatolians?), ethnic (Luwians?), or national (Samalians?). We must leave this determination to future research.

34. On this theme, see Schade 2006: 95.

35. The patronym appears in Aramaic orthography as *ḥyʾ* in lines 3 and 9 (Tropper 1993: 30–31; Schade 2006: 71 n. 5).

36. The restoration was established by Young (1993) and, simultaneously, by Tropper (1993: 33).

37. For example, Young (1993: 95 n. 2); Lipiński (2000: 242). Note the potential specification of parental lineage in the 9th-century Luwian inscription of Halparuntias III: *|wa/i-mu |á-mi-i-zi |tá-ti-zi DEUS-ni-zi-i |(LITUUS)á-za-ta* 'My paternal gods loved me' (MARASH 1; Payne 2010: 87). I thank Ilya Yakobuvich for helpful advice concerning this sentence.

38. Schade (2006: 72 n. 10, 93–94) does not propose an Indo-European etymology for the name. Young (1993: 96–97) offered a Semitic etymology (< *mlʾ*), although he considers Luwian also possible (1993: 98 n. 17; 2002). I am unaware of a Luwian etymology for this name.

Bibliography

Bauer, H.
1913 Die *klmw*-Inschrift aus Senschirli. *ZDMG* 67: 684–91.
1914 Die *klmw*-Inschrift aus Senschirli. *ZDMG* 68: 227.

Berlejung, Angelika
2010 Assyrians in the West: Assyrianization, Colonialism, Indifference, or Development Policy? Pp. 21–60 in *Congress Volume Helsinki 2010*, ed. Martti Nissinen. Leiden: Brill.

Booth, Scott W.
2007 Using Corpus Linguistics to Address Some Questions of Phoenician Grammar and Syntax Found in the Kulamuwa Inscription: Identifying the Presence and Function of the Infinitive Absolute, the Suffixed Conjugation, and the *wāw*. M.A. Thesis, Trinity International University.

Brockelmann, C.
1928 *Lexicon Syriacum*. 2nd ed. Halle: Max Niemeyer.

Brown, Brian
2008 The Kilamuwa Relief: Ethnicity, Class and Power in Iron Age North Syria. Pp. 339–56 in *Proceedings of the 5th International Congress on the Archaeology of the Ancient Near East, Madrid, April 3–8 2006*, ed. Joaquín M. Córdoba, Miquel Molist, M. Carmen Pérez, Isabel Rubio, and Sergio Martínez. Madrid: UAM.

Bryce, Trevor
2012 *The World of the Neo-Hittite Kingdoms: A Political and Military History*. Oxford: Oxford University Press.

Chapman, Cynthia R.
2010 Sculpted Warriors: Sexuality and the Sacred in the Depiction of Warfare in the Assyrian Palace Reliefs and in Ezekiel 23:14–17. Pp. 1–17 in *The Aesthetics of Violence in the Prophets*, ed. Julia M. O'Brien and Chris Franke. Library of Hebrew Bible/Old Testament Studies 517. New York: T. & T. Clark.

Dion, Paul-Eugène
1997 *Les Araméens à l'âge du fer: histoire politique et structures sociales*. Paris: Gabalda.

Fales, Frederick Mario
1979 Kilamuwa and the Foreign Kings: Propaganda vs. Power. *WdO* 10: 6–22.
1987 Aramaic Letters and Neo-Assyrian Letters: Philological and Methodological Notes. *JAOS* 107: 451–69.
2009 The Assyrian Words for "(Foot) Soldier." Pp. 71–94 in *Homeland and Exile: Biblical and Ancient Near Eastern Studies in Honour of Bustenay Oded*, ed. G. Galil, M. Geller, and A. Millard. Leiden: Brill.
2010 New Light on Assyro-Aramaic Interference: The Assur Ostracon. Pp. 189–204 in *CAMSEMUD 2007: Proceedings of the 13th Italian Meet-*

ing of Afro-Asiatic Linguistics Held in Udine, May 21st–24th, 2007, ed. Frederick Mario Fales and Giulia Francesca Grassi. History of the Ancient Near East Monograph 10. Padua: S.A.R.G.O.N.

Gibson, J. C. L.

1975 *Textbook of Syrian Semitic Inscriptions*, vol. 2: *Aramaic Inscriptions*. Oxford: Clarendon.

1982 *Textbook of Syrian Semitic Inscriptions*, vol. 3: *Phoenician Inscriptions*. Oxford: Clarendon.

Green, Douglas J.

2010 *"I Undertook Great Works": The Ideology of Domestic Achievements in West Semitic Royal Inscriptions*. FAT 2. Reihe 41. Tübingen: Mohr Siebeck.

Greenstein, E. L.; Huehnergard, J.; Zevit, Z.; and Rainey, A. F.

1988 Symposium: The *yiqtol* in Biblical Hebrew. *Hebrew Studies* 29: 7–42.

Hawkins, John David

1982 The Neo-Hittite States in Syria and Anatolia. Pp. 372–441 in *The Cambridge Ancient History*, vol. 3/1: *The Prehistory of the Balkans; and the Middle East and the Aegean World, Tenth to Eighth Centuries B.C.*, 2nd ed., ed. J. Boardman, I. E. S. Edwards, N. G. L. Hammond, and E. Sollberger. Cambridge: Cambridge University Press.

Herrmann, Siegfried

1953 Bemerkungen zur Inschrift des Königs Kilamuwa von Senğirli. *Orientalische Literaturzeitung* 48: 295–97.

Herrmann, Virginia Hudson Rimmer

2011 Society and Economy under Empire at Iron Age Samʾal (Zincirli Höyük, Turkey). Ph.D. dissertation, University of Chicago.

Hornstein, Norbert; Nunes, Jairo; and Grohmann, Kleanthes K.

2005 *Understanding Minimalism*. Cambridge: Cambridge University Press.

Krahmalkov, C. R.

2000 *Phoenician-Punic Dictionary*. OLA 90. Studia Phoenicia 15. Leuven: Peeters.

Landsberger, Benno

1948 *Samʾal: Studien zur Entdeckung der Ruinenstätte Karatepe*. Veröffentlichungen der Türkischen historischen Gesellschaft, 7th ser., 16. Ankara.

Lemaire, André

2000 Tarshish-*Tarsisi*: Problème de topographie historique biblique et assyrienne. Pp. 44–62 in *Studies in Historical Geography and Biblical Historiography Presented to Zecharia Kallai*, ed. Gershon Galil and Moshe Weinfeld. SVT 81. Leiden: Brill.

Lidzbarski, M.

1909–15 *Ephemeris für semitische Epigraphik*, vol 3. Giessen: Alfred Töpelmann.

1921 *Altaramäische Urkunden aus Assur*. WVDOG 38. Leipzig: J. C. Hinrichs.

Lipiński, E.
2000 *The Aramaeans: Their Ancient History, Culture, Religion*. OLA 100. Leuven: Peeters.
Luschan, Felix von; Schrader, E.; and Sachau, Eduard
1893 *Ausgrabungen in Sendschirli*, vol. 1: *Einleitung und Inschriften*. Königliche Museen zu Berlin. Mittheilungen aus den orientalischen Sammlungen 11. Berlin: W. Spemann.
Luschan, Felix von, and Jacoby, Gustav
1911 *Ausgrabungen in Sendschirli*, vol. 4: Königliche Museen zu Berlin. Mittheilungen aus den orientalischen Sammlungen 14. Berlin: Georg Reimer.
Novák, Mirko
2005 Arameans and Luwians—Processes of an Acculturation. Pp. 252–66 in *Ethnicity in Ancient Mesopotamia: Papers Read at the Forty-eighth Rencontre Assyriologique Internationale, Leiden, 1–4 July 2002*, ed. W. H. van Soldt, R. Kalvelagen, and D. Katz. Leiden: Nederlands Instituut voor het Nabije Oosten.
O'Connor, M.
1977 The Rhetoric of the Kilamuwa Inscription. *BASOR* 226: 15–29.
Orthmann, Winfried
1971 *Untersuchungen zur späthethitischen Kunst*. Bonn: Habelt.
Pardee, Dennis
2009 A New Aramaic Inscription from Zincirli. *BASOR* 356: 51–71.
Payne, Annick
2010 *Hieroglyphic Luwian: An Introduction with Original Texts*. Subsidia et instrumenta linguarum orientis 2. Wiesbaden: Harrassowitz.
Röllig, Wolfgang
1995 Phoenician and the Phoenicians in the Context of the Ancient Near East. Pp. 203–14 in *I Fenici: Ieri, oggi, domani*, ed. S. Moscati. Rome: Accademia Nazionale dei Lincei, Commissione per gli studi Fenici e Punici.
2004 Sprachen und Schriften der Levante in Anatolien. Pp. 205–17 in *Die Außenwirkung des späthethitischen Kulturraumes*, ed. M. Novák, F. Prayon, and A.-M. Wittke. AOAT 323. Münster: Ugarit-Verlag.
Sader, Hélène S.
1987 *Les états araméens de Syrie: Depuis leur fondation jusqu'à leur transformation en provinces assyriennes*. Beiruter Texte und Studien 36. Beirut: Orient-Institut der Deutschen Morgenländischen Gesellschaft.
Schade, Aaron
2006 *A Syntactic and Literary Analysis of Ancient Northwest Semitic Inscriptions*. Lewiston, NY: Edwin Mellen.
Schloen, J. David, and Fink, Amir S.
2009 New Excavations at Zincirli Hüyük in Turkey (Ancient Samʾal) and the Discovery of an Inscribed Mortuary Stele. *BASOR* 356: 1–13.

Schmitz, Philip C.
Forthcoming The Ritual Accounts from Kition (*CIS* I 86 = *KAI*[5] 37) in Historical Context. *KUSATU* Beiheft B.
Seely, David Rolph
1995 The Raised Hand of God as an Oath Gesture. Pp. 411–21 in *Fortunate the Eyes That See: Essays in Honor of David Noel Freedman in Celebration of His Seventieth Birthday*, ed. Andrew H. Bartelt, Astrid B. Beck, Chris A. Franke, and Paul R. Raabe. Grand Rapids: Eerdmans.
Tropper, J.
1993 *Die Inschriften von Zincirli: neue Edition und vergleichende Grammatik des phönizischen, samʾalischen und aramäischen Textkorpus.* Münster: Ugarit-Verlag.
Van de Mieroop, Marc
2004 *A History of the Ancient Near East, ca. 3000–323 BC.* Malden, MA: Blackwell.
Vogelzang, M. E., and Bekkum, W. J. van
1986 Meaning and Symbolism of Clothing in Ancient Near Eastern Texts. Pp. 265–84 in *Scripta Signa Vocis. Studies about Scripts, Scriptures and Scribes, and Languages in the Near East. Presented to J. H. Hospers by His Pupils, Colleagues and Friends*, ed. H. L. J. Vanstiphout et al. Groningen: John Benjamins.
Wartke, Ralf-B.
2005 *Samʾal: Ein aramäischer Stadtstaat des 10. bis 8. Jhs. v. Chr. und die Geschichte seiner Erforschung.* Mainz: Philipp von Zabern.
Yamada, Shigeo
2000 *The Construction of the Assyrian Empire: A Historical Study of the Inscriptions of Shalmanesar III Relating to His Campaigns in the West.* Culture and History of the Ancient Near East 3. Boston: Brill.
Young, Ian
1993 *KLMW BR TML. Syria* 70: 95–98.
2002 The Languages of Ancient Samʾal. *Maarav* 9: 93–105.
Younger, K. Lawson, Jr.
2013 The Languages of North Syria. In *Bible et Proche-Orient: Volume d'hommages pour André Lemaire.* Edited by Jean-Marie Durand and Josette Elayi. Paris.
Zevit, Ziony
1988 Talking Funny in Biblical Henglish and Solving a Problem of the YAQTUL Past Tense. *Hebrew Studies* 29: 25–33 (part of Greenstein et al. 1988 above).

The Syntax and Pragmatics of Subject Pronouns in Phoenician

Robert D. Holmstedt

1. Introduction

Grammatically speaking, pronouns are odd items. In traditional descriptions, pronouns are defined as words that "stand for nouns" (see, for example, Waltke and O'Connor 1990: §16.1 on pronouns in Biblical Hebrew). Syntactically, pronouns do appear in many similar (but not all the same) positions as nouns and noun phrases, but semantically and pragmatically, the "standing for nouns" definition is simply wrong. Consider for a moment the clause in example (1).

(1) *k* *mlk* *ṣdq* *h̲ʾ*
because king righteous PRON.3MS
'because a righteous king is *he*'. (*KAI* 10.9)

Does the pronoun *hʾ* contain any descriptive content? Do we know to whom or what *hʾ* refers? No. The pronoun provides some morphological agreement features that limit the choices, in this case, to a single male who is not the speaker or addressee (at least, within the deictic bounds of the clause). Beyond this, the pronoun is semantically empty and illustrates how pronouns are unlike nouns by lacking descriptive content. And yet, the 3MS pronoun *hʾ* in (1) does identify an object within the discourse context: it clearly picks out *yḥwmlk*, the king of Byblos, as its referent. This is the *anaphoric* function of third-person pronouns, which, interestingly, sets them apart from first- and second-person pronouns. Consider the statements in (2) and (3).

Author's note: I am grateful to Aaron Schade, Philip Schmitz, and Holger Gzella for feedback on my argument. I alone am responsible for the analyses given in the essay as well as any errors.

(2) *k*[1] *ʾnk* *nḥn*
because PRON.1CS pity.PASS.PTCP.MS
'because I am pitied'. (*KAI* 14.12)

(3) *qnmy*[2] *ʾt*
whoever PRON.2MS
'whoever you are'. (*KAI* 14.20)

Like the third-person pronoun in (1), the first-person pronoun in (2) and the second-person pronoun in (3) provide us some information via morphological agreement features, but beyond this we do not know the descriptive content of *ʾnk* or *ʾt*. Whereas the third-person pronoun is anaphoric and thus refers back to another expression (one with descriptive content) that occurred in the discourse, the first- and second-person pronouns are not anaphoric. The first- and second-person pronouns, rather, identify the two principal speech roles, the "speaker" and the "addressee."

Note also how the first- and second-person pronouns cannot be replaced by a noun phrase in the same way that the third-person pronoun can and produce the same meaning for the clause. That is, in (1) the 3MS *hʾ* could be replaced by *yḥwmlk*, leaving the clause semantically identical.

1. Although the majority stance seems to be to take *k* as a noncausal particle here (see *KAI* 2.21–22; Faber 1986: 427 n. 12; Krahmalkov 2001: 286–87; Schade 2006: 171–72; compare with Cooke 1903; Gibson 1982; and Avishur 2000: 135). But in my opinion, Krahmalkov's "presentative function" (as well as most others' noncausal analyses) is a struggle to produce a good English rendering rather than to understand *k* in Phoenician. Whatever the motivation, these authors are constraining the semantics of the *k* subordinate clause too narrowly. Muraoka (2006: §170da) makes an insightful and relevant comment on *kī* in Biblical Hebrew:

> In some cases, what follows כי is not a logical cause of an event or circumstance, but the evidence of, or an argument for, the preceding assertion: 1Kg 1.24f. "My lord, O king, you did say that Adonijah should reign after you and sit upon your throne. For (כי) he is gone down this day, and has slaughtered oxen . . . ," cf. also 1Sm 26.151.

So, too, in the ʾEshmunʿazor text (and also for the Karatepe example that Krahmalkov cites; 2001: 187), the *k* clause relates back to the larger argument of the text section or even the entire text and provides the reason or motivation for the action: "[do or do not do these things, or, these things have been done] because . . ."

2. Concerning *qnmy*, I follow Friedrich and Röllig 1999: §124 in taking it as a compound interrogative, rather than Krahmalkov (2000: 428; 2001: 109), who takes *qnmy* as two separate words, *qn* and *my*, and translates it "O acquirer <of this resting-place>, whoever you may be."

In contrast, replacing the 1CS *ʾnk* with *ʾšmnʿzr* (the speaker in *KAI* 14) in (2) or the 2MS *ʾt* with *kl mmlkt wkl ʾdm* (the following appositional noun phrase) in (3) destroys the "speaker versus addressee" distinction provided by the pronouns. Another feature that divides the third-person from other personal pronouns is its demonstrative use, illustrated in example (4).

(4) *w=y-qṣn* *h=mmlk-t* *h*ʾ
and=3-cut.off.IPFV.PASS.MP the=king-FS DEM.3MS
w=h=ʾdm-m *hmt* *w=zrʿ=m* *l=ʿlm*
and=the=man-MP DEM-MP and=seed=their.3MS for=ever
'and *that* king or *those* men and their seed shall be cut off forever'. (*KAI* 14.22)

The third-person pronouns *hʾ* and *hmt* are not primarily anaphoric here but *deictic*: they point to particular instances of the nouns they modify. In Phoenician and related languages (for example, Hebrew, Aramaic, Syriac), the third-person pronouns are often used specifically for distal deixis, 'that, those'. Cross-linguistically, it is not unusual for third-person pronouns to overlap with demonstrative pronouns or to be derivationally related (see Bhat 2004: chap. 6).[3] And it is not difficult to see how anaphora and deixis meet in the function of third-person pronouns: in both cases, the pronouns "are used for locating the participants of events . . . with reference to the speech context" (Bhat 2004: 9). A description and analysis of the Phoenician pronouns must take into account the full range of pronoun functions.

Another complicating factor is the use of personal subject pronouns with verbs that are highly inflected. It is standard among the Semitic languages for the finite verbs to carry morphological agreement features

3. The demonstrative use of the third-person pronouns is well attested outside Semitic (see Bhat 2004: chap. 6) and is the norm within Semitic, even though, for Phoenician, none of the commonly used grammars includes these pronouns in descriptions of demonstratives. For example, Segert (1976: §61.15) has one sentence indicating that the third-person pronouns are also demonstratives and Friedrich and Röllig (1999: §§111.3, 114) also mention it only in passing. Although Krahmalkov's treatment (2001) is more substantive, it is given in the chapter on the "independent personal pronoun" instead of the "demonstrative" and introduced with the confusing (and inaccurate) subtitle "Expressing the Anaphoric Pronoun" (§3.5). The problem is that grammarians confuse etymology and syntax. It does not matter whether, for example, *hʾ* is also the anaphoric 3MS pronoun, if it serves in other contexts as a demonstrative, it should be included in the description of demonstrative pronouns.

matching the person, number, and gender of the subject. As such, the Semitic languages are among those that are "pro-drop" or 'null subject" languages, in which a subject, whether a full NP or a pronoun, does not need to appear overtly in the syntax.[4] The way that this is articulated in generative syntax is that subject NPs and overt subject pronouns are in complementary distribution with a "covert" or "null" pronoun referred to as "little *pro.*"[5] The general *pro*-drop feature of Phoenician (as with all Semitic languages) explains why the epigraphic texts covered in this study exhibit numerous clauses that lack an overt subject. The representative Byblian (5), Tyro-Sidonian (6b), and Anatolian (7) examples below illustrate the generalization.

(5) *km=ʾš* *qrʾ-t* ____ *ʾt* *rb-t=y* *bʿlt*
like=REL call.PFV-1CS ACC mistress-FS=my.1CS Baʿalat.of
gbl *w=šmʿ* ____ *ql* *w=pʿl*
Byblos and=heard.PFV.3FS voice.my.1CS and=did.PFV.3FS
l=y *nʿm*
to=me.1CS goodness
'at (the time) that *pro* (I) called on my mistress, Baʿalat of Byblos, *pro* (she) heard my voice and *pro* (she) did goodness for me'. (*KAI* 10.7–8)

(6) *w=yšb-n=y* ____ *šm-m* *ʾdr-m*
and=settle.PFV-1CP=him.3MS heaven-MP mighty-MP
'and *pro* (we) settled him ['Eshmun] (in) the mighty heav ens'. (*KAI* 14.16)

4. The *pro*-drop parameter was formulated within the early Government-and-Binding framework of generative linguistics, although it is now recognized more broadly. The theoretical context of the *pro*-drop parameter is critical since, contrary to some nongenerative linguistic approaches (particularly the early twentieth-century approach of Jespersen, which is sometimes still used in Biblical Hebrew studies), the generative view of inflectional affixes on verbs, such as those in Hebrew, is that they differ syntactically and semantically from independent pronouns. That is, inflectional affixes on verbs are taken not as cliticized pronouns, which is sometimes the view in Hebrew studies but, rather, as morphologically realized agreement features. The subject pronouns, in contrast, are full syntactic constituents. On *pro*-drop in Hebrew, see Holmstedt forthcoming.

5. The null subject *pro* is present when an overt (pronominal or full NP) subject is absent in order to fulfill the "extended projection principle" (EPP) requirement (that is, every clause must have a syntactic subject) and to check both person, gender, and number agreement and nominative case features (see, e.g., Haegeman 1994: 19–25, 454–58; Cook and Newson 2007: 87–99, 293).

(7) *w=b=rb-m* *y-ld* ____ *w=b=rb-m*
and=in=many-MP 3-bear.IPFV.MP and=in=many-MP
y-ʾdr ____ *w=b=rb-m* *y-ʿbd* ____
3-be.powerful.IPFV.MP and=in=many-MP 3-serve.IPFV.MP
l=ʾztwd *w=l=bt* *mpš*
to=ʾAzatiwada and=to=house.of Mpš
'and in many *pro* (they) were bearing (children), and with many *pro* (they) were becoming powerful, and with many *pro* (they) were serving ʾAzatiwada and the house of Mpš'. (*KAI* 26.AIII.9–11)[6]

As we see in (5)–(7), it is most common for an overt subject NP or pronoun to be dropped when the agent/patient subject of the verb is the most recently used verbal subject. Moreover, the data suggest that the identification of the covert pronoun is related to the discourse: *pro* is used with an inflected finite verb when its ability to access its antecedent within the discourse is high, whereas the referring NP subject is used when the discourse accessibility is low, and an overt pronoun is used when the antecedent is marked for Topic or Focus (see Gutman 1999, 2004 for a similar analysis of modern Israeli Hebrew).

In the following sections (§§2–6), I describe my findings for the use of subject pronouns in Phoenician epigraphic texts, divided chronologically and geographically. The final section, §7, is a brief summary of resumptive pronouns and object pronouns. For all their linguistic oddities, pronouns are central to both the linguistic system of Phoenician languages and the organization of information within stretches of discourse. And yet, the syntax and pragmatics of pronouns are just a sample of linguistic phenomena for which the description in our Phoenician grammars[7] must now move beyond the strong philological tradition to linguistic analyses grounded in both modern theory and the insights and generalizations gained from cross-linguistic studies.

6. Although all recent treatments have taken the verbs in this section of the Karatepe text to relate to a future time (see, among others, Younger 1998; Röllig 1999; Avishur 2000; Schade 2006), I have taken the verbs in (7) as imperfectives used for past conditions. In my opinion, past events or conditions continue to be related until the *ʾm* conditional clause in A III.12 marks the transition to the curse that ends the text.

7. See Harris 1936: §15; Segert 1978: §§51, 61; Friedrich and Röllig 1999: §§110–11, 286–87; Krahmalkov 2001: 38–49.

2. *Early Byblian: Ittobaal b. Aḥirom* (KAI *1) and Yaḥimilk* (KAI *4)*

We have little relevant data from the earliest Phoenician inscriptions, the tenth-century Byblian texts. The genre of these texts is dedicatory, and the narratorial voice does not use first-person presentation in the same way that memorial inscriptions, such as the Byblian inscription of Yaḥawmilk (*KAI* 10) or the Anatolian inscriptions of Kulamuwa (*KAI* 24), ʾAzatiwada (*KAI* 26), and Warika (Çineköy; see Tekoğlu and Lemaire 2002) do. Moreover, there is often no need in the early Byblian texts for Topic or Focus, since these texts are not long and often lack multiple agents who take differing stances or actions. Thus, there are only two overt pronouns from these early texts, given in (8) and (9):

(8) *w=h̠ʾ* *y-mḥ* *spr=h*
and=PRON.3MS 3-efface.IPFV.PASS.MS inscription=his.3MS
l=pp *šbl*
to=edge.of path
'and as for *him*—may his inscription be effaced by the edge (?) of the road?'. (*KAI* 1.2)

Example (8), from the tenth-century sarcophagus of Aḥirom, exhibits an anaphoric 3MS pronoun, which points back to the previously mentioned person who dares to uncover the sarcophagus. Although the pronoun could be the subject of the following verb, I take it as a left-dislocated element that is resumed by the genitive clitic pronoun in the noun phrase *sprh̠* 'his inscription'. However, for the pragmatic analysis of this overt pronoun, it matters little whether the pronoun is part of the clause proper or is a left-dislocated constituent; in both cases, it serves as a Topic and thus marks a shift from one agent to another—from what the transgressor's scepter and rule will suffer to what the dastardly fellow himself will suffer. Presumably, to have one's burial inscription erased is a severe and very personal punishment.

(9) *h̠ʾt* *ḥwy* *kl* *mpl-t* *h=bt-m* *ʾl*
PRON.3MS restore.PFV.3MS all ruin-FP the=house-MP DEM.P
'he (alone) has restored all the ruins of the these houses'. (*KAI* 4.2–3)

In (9), the sole overt pronoun in the tenth-century Yaḥimilk inscription is also a 3MS anaphoric pronoun and is inserted into the clause to carry Focus. It is not a Topic pronoun because there is no agent shift at this point; rather, the Focus helps the narrator assert that it was Yaḥimilk and no other possible candidate who rebuilt the houses.[8]

3. *North Syrian: Kulamuwa (*KAI *24)*

The next text in chronological sequence that exhibits adequate pronoun evidence is the late ninth-century Kulamuwa text, from Zinjirli (ancient Samʾal) in northern Syria. In (10a–b), the 1CS pronouns are required for the self-identification of the speaker and as subjects for the two null-copula clauses.

(10a) *ʾnk* *klmw* *br* *ḥy*[ʾ]
PRON.1CS Kulamuwa son.of Hayyaʾ
'*I* am Kulamuwa, son of Hayyaʾ'. (*KAI* 24.1)

(10b) *w=ʾnk* *klmw* *br* *tm*
and=PRON.1CS Kulamuwa son.of TM
'but *I* am Kulamuwa, son of TM'. (*KAI* 24.4)

Similarly obligatory is the 1CS pronoun following the uninflected narrative verb (NARR)[9] in (10c):

8. In the Nora Stele (ca. 820 B.C.; *KAI* 46), there is a possible 3MS pronoun *hʾ* in lines 2 and 3–4. If this is the correct interpretation of the text (see Schmitz in this volume for an alternate reading), the pronouns follow a perfective verb (*grš hʾ garriš=ô* drive.out.3MS=him he.3MS 'he drove out') and an adjective (*šlm hʾ* save.MS he.3MS 'he is safe/well''; see Zuckerman 1991). In the second clause, the pronoun is syntactically obligatory to represent the subject of the null-copula clause; its position after the predicate adjective presumably represents Focus-marking on the adjective, thereby indicating that the status of the subject of the inscription was what was being "emphasized." It is much more difficult to explain the postverbal placement of the pronoun in the first clause, since the subject pronoun is optional and, when present with a finite verb, almost always precedes the verb to signal a focused subject. Thus, if the pronoun readings in the Nora Stele are correct, I suggest that *grš* might be our earliest example of the uninflected narrative verb that appears so prominently a century later in the Karatepe text. Notably, with the uninflected narrative verb, the pronoun is obligatory to provide the grammatical information concerning the verbal subject *and* overwhelmingly follows the verb.

9. On the issue of the "uninflected narrative verb," see below, examples (11e,f), and the subsequent discussion.

(10c) *w=ʾdr* *ʿl=y* *mlk*
and=be.powerful.PFV.3MS upon=me.1CS king.of
dnn-ym *w=škr* *ʾnk* *ʿl=y*
Danunian-MP and=hire.NARR PRON.1CS over=me.1CS
mlk *ʾšr*
king.of ʾAshur
'and the king of the Danunians was more powerful than me so *I hired* against him the king of ʾAshur'. (*KAI* 24.7–8)

Note that, with the uninflected narrative verb, the pronoun always follows the verb (see the numerous examples in the Anatolian texts, below; Krahmalkov 2001: 46). the common use of the pronoun to signal Topic or Focus and the assocation of Topic and Focus with the left-periphery of the clause (that is, the fronted position), I suggest that the postverbal order in the uninflected narrative verb clauses is intentional in order to signal that the pronouns are pragmatically unmarked.

In (10d–e) fully inflected finite verbs are used, indicating that the pronoun is syntactically unnecessary.[10] Thus, in both cases, the presence of the pronoun signals a pragmatic function.

(10d) *l=pn* *h=mlk-m* *h=l=pn-ym* *y-tlwn*[11]
to=face.of the=king-MP REL=to=face-MP 3-writhe.MP
mškb-m *km* *klb-m* *w=ʾnk* *l=my*
lower.class-MP like dog-MP and=PRON.1CS to=who
k-t *ʾb* *w=l=my* *k-t* *ʾm*
be.PFV-1CS father and=to=who be.PFV-1CS mother
w=l=my *k-t* *ʾḥ*
and=to=who be.PFV-1CS brother

10. In line 9, there is another occurrence of the 1CS pronoun: *ʾnk klmw br ḥyʾ yšb-t ʿl ksʾ ʾb=y*. The syntax is ambigous, however: it is possible to take the 1CS pronoun as the subject of a null copula clause ('I am Kulamuwa; *pro* (I) sat upon my father's throne'; see, e.g., O'Connor 1977a; de Moor 1988; Avishur 2000; *COS* 2.147–48; Schade 2006) or as the subject of the inflected verb ('I, Kulamuwa, sat upon my father's throne'; see, e.g., Collins 1971; Gibson 1982; Sperling 1988; Parker 1996). Whatever option was intended by the author, the choice likely related to whether this first statement in the second half of the text was meant as an opening identification, parallel to the opening statement of the entire text, 'I am Kilumuwa', or as a statement of accomplishment (since the speaker's identity has been well established by this point).

11. See O'Connor 1977a: 22 for discussion of *ytlwn*.

'before the kings who were beforehand the lower class writhed like dogs, but *I* was father to whomever, a mother to whomever, and a brother to whomever'. (*KAI* 24.9–11)

In (10d), the Focus signaled by the presence of the 1CS pronoun is strengthened by its fronted position: it has been raised above the prepositional phrase with the interrogative *lmy* 'to whomever'. The intended contrast is clear: Kulamuwa sets his compassion and magnanimity over against the fear induced in the "lower class" by his precedessors (on the identity of the *mškbm*, see Schmitz's essay in this volume).

(10e)	*w=ʾnk*	*tmk-t*	*mškb-m*		*l=yd*
	and=PRON.1CS	hold.PFV-1CS	lower.class-MP		to=hand
	w=hmt	*št*	*nbš* *km*	*nbs*	*ytm*
	and=PRON.3MP	set.PFV.3CP	life like	life.of	orphan
	b=ʾm				
	in=mother				

'and *I held* the lower class by the hand and *they set* (for me) affection like the affection of an orphan for a mother'. (*KAI* 24.13)

In (10e), the two pronouns, the 1CS *ʾnk* and the 3MP *hmt*, work together but are not contrastive with each other. Rather, the 1CS pronoun presents Focus on Kulamuwa, the speaker, and again contrasts him with his precedessors. The 3MP pronoun in the following clause is a Topic in that it marks a shift in the agent from the speaker to "they," which is clearly anaphorically linked to "the lower class" in the first clause.

*4. Anatolian: Karatepe (*KAI *26), Çineköy, and Çebel Ires Daği (*KAI *287)*

The artifacts from the Anatolian sites of Karatepe, Çineköy, and Çebel Ires Daği (modern Çebelireis Daği) have provided us with the largest extant Phoenician texts to date. At first glance, the numerous pronouns, especially in the Karatepe texts, suggest great potential for exhibiting innovative pronominal syntax or pragmatics. However, the pattern remains the same as we have seen so far. Consider the representative examples from mid-eighth-century Karatepe texts:

(11a) *ʾnk* *ʾztwd* *hbrk*[12] *bˁl* *ˁbd* *bˁl*
PRON.1CS ʾAzatiwada steward.of Baˁal servant.of Baˁal
'*I* am ʾAzatiwada, steward of Baˁal, servant of Baˁal'.
(AI.1–2//BI.1, CI.1)

(11b) *yḥw* *ʾnk* *ʾyt* *dnn-ym*
revive.NARR PRON.1CS ACC Danunian-MP
'*I revived* the Danunians'. (AI.3–4//BI.2, CI.5)[13]

In these first two examples, the pronoun is required by discourse to specify the speaker role and by the syntax to serve as a subject for both null-copula clauses (11a) and clauses with the uninflected narrative verb (11b). The vast majority of subject pronouns are used this way in Karatepe. Only a few instances reflect the pragmatics of Topic or Focus (11c–g).

(11c) *w=ʾnk* *ʾztwd* *št=nm* *tḥt*
and=PRON.1CS ʾAzatiwada set.PFV.1CS=them.3MP under
pˁm=y
foot.MP=my.1CS
'but *I*, ʾAzatiwada, *set them* under my feet'.
(AI.16–17//BI.9, CII.5)

(11d) *w=ʾnk* *ʾztwd* *ˁn-t=nm*
and=PRON.1CS ʾAzatiwada oppress-1CS=them.3MP
'and *I*, ʾAzatiwada, *oppressed them*'. (AI.19–20//BI.11, CII.11)

There is an ambiguity to the syntax of both (11c) and (11d), just as there was with the example in line 9 of Kulamuwa (*KAI* 24.9, see above, n. 6). There are three possibilities: (1) the 1CS pronoun is the subject as a null-copula clause, followed by a separate finite verbal clause, 'I am ʾAzatiwada; *pro* (I) did x'; (2) the pronoun and proper name are left-dislocated, 'As for me, ʾAzatiwada–*pro* (I) have oppressed them' (see

12. On *hbrk* as 'steward', see Pardee 1983: 64–65; Röllig 1999: 58; Lipiński 2004: 123–27; Schade 2006: 21–22; on *hbrk* as 'blessed of', see O'Connor 1977b.

13. See also AI.4 (//BI.2, CI.5), AI.6 (//BI.3–4, CI.10), AI.6–7 (//BI.4, CI.11), AI.9 (//BI.5), AI.9–10 (//BI.5), AI.10 (//BI.5–6, CI.18), AI.11 (//BI.6, CI.19), AI.11–12 (//BI.6, CI.19–20), AI.13–14 (//BI.8, CII.1), AI.17 (//BI.9–10, CII.6), AI.18 (//BI.10, CII.8), AII.9 (//BI.15, CIII.7), AII.9–10 (//BI.15), AII.11–12 (//BI.17, CIII.9), AII.17 (//BII.4–5, CIII.14–15), AII.17–18 (//BII.5–6, CIII.15–16), AII.18–19 (//BII.6, CIII.16).

Dunand 1944; 1946; Dupont-Sommer 1948; the problem with this analysis is that there is no resumptive constituent in the core clause, which is required in structures of this sort); (3) the pronoun is the syntactic subject of the verbal clause, with the proper noun in apposition: 'I, ʾAzatiwada, did x' (see, e.g., Marcus and Gelb 1948; 1949; Gordon 1948; 1949; Alt 1949; Honeyman 1949; O'Callaghan 1949a, b; Younger 1998; *COS* 2.148–50; Avishur 2000; Schade 2005; 2006). The clear weight of scholarship is on the side of the third option (with no one who takes the first, and only Dunand and Dupont-Sommer who opt for the second).

I also take the third analysis to be the most felicitous within the context; the speaker is not reidentifying himself but, rather, making an assertion about his achievements. If this is correct, then the pronoun is not syntactically required as a subject for the two inflected finite verbs in (11c) and (11d). Rather, it serves two purposes, one strictly pragmatic and one related to the discourse function of first-person pronouns. In pragmatic terms, the insertion of the 1CS pronoun serves to mark the speaker with Focus, thereby aiding ʾAzatiwada in asserting how he, unlike previous rulers, accomplished these things (for example, subduing brigands). In its nonpragmatic role, the 1CS pronoun also provides a suitable position to host the appositional proper noun, ʾAzatiwada, thereby allowing the speaker (for good rhetorical measure) to assert himself as the speaker of the narrative (the "I") and remind the audience who he is ("ʾAzatiwada"). This latter function is not related to Topic or Focus but is an inherent feature of the pronominal system.

The next two pronoun examples in Karatepe are hardly less troublesome (11e–f), since the verbs have been analyzed as participles or infinitives absolute with object suffixes:

(11e) *yrd=m* *ʾnk*
bring.down.NARR=them.3MP PRON.1CS
'*I brought them down*'. (AI.20//BI.11, CII.11–12)

(11f) *yšb=m* *ʾnk* *b=qṣ-t*
settle.NARR=them.3MS PRON.1CS in=end-FP.of
gbl=y
border.MP=my.1CS
'*I settled them* in the ends of my borders'. (AI.20//BI.11, CII.12)

It is often recognized (often implicitly) that, if the verb in both (11e) and (11f) is the "infinitive absolute" with object suffixes, then the Phoenican grammar represented in Karatepe differs in this regard from Hebrew, in which the adverbial infinitive does not allow affixation (see, e.g., Obermann 1950: 96; O'Callaghan 1949b: 239; Gordon 1949: 114; Bron 1979: 74; Garr 1985: 183–84; Friedrich and Röllig 1999: 103, 126, 130; Krahmalkov 2001: 72). Yet, if these are to be analyzed as the "infinitive absolute," or better, an "uninflected narrative verb" (see, e.g., Marcus 1969: 60 n. 23; Ginsberg 1973: 144 n. 56; Gibson 1982: 37), then the presence and position of the subject pronoun is uncontroversial. In contrast, if these forms are participles (see, e.g., Obermann 1950), the affixation of object pronouns is normal, but the placement of the pronoun following the participle is problematic: while pronouns are obligatory with participles in main clauses (they may be dropped in relative clauses and small clauses), they are typically placed *before* the participle. The placement after a participle suggests that the participles would be raised for Focus, which makes no sense in the context. I tentatively suggest that the two verbs in (11e, f) are not participles but rare cases of the uninflected verb with object suffixes.[14]

The final example of the subject pronoun in Karatepe, given in (11g), lies within an interpretive crux (see Bron 1979: 78–85).

(11g) *w=b=ym-t=y* *ʾnk* *ʾš-t* *t-k*
and=in=day-FP=my.1CS PRON.1CS woman-FS 3-walk.IPFV.FS
l=ḥd=y *dl* *plk-m*
to=alone=her.3FS with spindle-MP
'but in my days, *mine*!, a woman walked by herself with spindles' (AII.5//BI.13, CIII.3)

Whatever the correct interpretation of *tk lḥdy dl plkm* (see, among others, Bron 1979: 78–85; Swiggers 1980; Younger 1998: 32–33),the role of the 1CS pronoun seems clear: it is inserted for Focus. The initial prepositional phrase *wbymty* 'and in my days' is a scene-setting Topic constituent, and yet the speaker, ʾAzatiwada, wants to draw attention to

14. Note that I eschew the label "infinitive absolute" for this verb in Phoenician (as well as in Amarna Canaanite and Biblical Hebrew). The form functions as a finite, narrative verb that simply lacks full agreement and, regardless of any homophony with the adverbial "infinitive absolute," should be recognized as part of the finite verbal system.

the fact that this positive situation (whatever it was) happened only on *his* watch (for a similar construction, see *KAI* 10.12–13, given below in [16f]).

In the recently published text from Çineköy (mid- to late eighth century B.C.) there are three examples of a subject pronoun, all in the first-person singular (12a–c):

(12a)	*ʾnk*	*w[rk*	*bn —-]*
	PRON.1CS	Warika	son.of

‘*I* am Wa[rika, son of . . .]’. (line 1)

(12b)	*w=pʿ]l*	*ʾnk*	*ʾp*	*ss*	*[ʿl*	*ss]*
	and=do.NARR	PRON.1CS	also	horse	on	horse

‘[and] *I* [*add*]*ed* also horse [upon horse]’. (lines 5–6)

(12c)	*w=bn*	*ʾnk*	*ḥmy-[t]*
	and=build.NARR	PRON.1CS	wall=FP

‘and *I built* fortifications’. (line 10)

In the first example, in (12a), the pronoun is the subject of a null-copula clause and, like the two similar examples in Kulamuwa in (10a–b), is required both for the self-identification of the speaker and as the syntactic subject. In the second and third examples, in (12b–c), the pronouns are similarly obligatory; the only difference is that, instead of the null-copula in (12a), the predicate in (12b–c) is the uninflected narrative verb. As in the lone occurrence in Kulamuwa (10c) and the numerous examples in Karatepe (see [11b] and n. 5), the pronoun follows the uninflected narrative verb and does not signal Topic or Focus.

The final Anatolian pronoun example comes from the mid- to late seventh-century text from Çebel Ires Dağı (*KAI* 287):

(13)	*nṭʿ*	*hʾ*	*mṭʿ-m*	*b=šd*	*bkr*
	plant.PFV.3MS	PRON.3MS	plantation-MP	in=field.of	BKR
	b=ym-t	*ʾšlprn*			
	in=day-FP.of	ʾŠlprn			

‘*He planted* plantations in the field of BKR in the days of ʾŠlprn’. (*KAI* 287 AB.1–2)

The nature of (13) is not entirely clear. On the one hand, it looks like a simple case of the uninflected narrative verb with the pronoun required for the syntactic subject. If the verb were the 3MS perfective (so Mosca and Russell 1987; Friedrich and Röllig 1999: 77), the postverbal position of the pronoun would be extremely unusual since it would only be inserted for Topic or Focus and both positions are preverbal. On the other hand, nowhere else in the text is the uninflected narrative verb used (that is, the inflected perfective verb is preferred); moreover, this would constitute the only example of the uninflected verb with anything other than a first-person pronoun. If it is the inflected 3MS perfective verb, it is possible that the pronoun is used for Focus to contrast the activities of one of the protagonists, MSNZMŠ, with the activities of the others.

*5. Sidonian: Tabnit (*KAI *13) and ʾEshmunʿazor (*KAI *14)*

After the Anatolian texts, we need to move to later texts from Sidon for additional examples of pronoun usage. First is the early fifth-century Sidonian inscription of Tabnit (*KAI* 13). In this short text, there are three overt pronouns, given in (14a–c):

(14a)

ʾnk	*tbnt*	*khn*	*ʿštrt*	*mlk*	*ṣdn-m*
PRON.1CS	Tabnit	priest.of	ʿAshtart	king.of	Sidonian-MP
bn	*ʾšmnʿzr*	*khn*	*ʿštrt*	*mlk*	
son.of	ʾEshmunʿazor	priest.of	ʿAshtart	king.of	
ṣdn-m	*škb*	*b=ʾrn*	*z*		
Sidonian-MP	lie.PTCP.MS	in=sarcophagus	DEM.S		

'*I*, Tabnit, priest of ʿAshtart, king of the Sidonians, son of ʾEshmunʿazor, priest, *am lying* in this sarcophagus'. (*KAI* 13.1–3)

(14b)

my	*ʾt*	*kl*	*ʾdm*	*ʾš*	*t-pq*	*ʾyt*
who	PRON.2MS	any	man	REL	2-find.IPFV.MS	ACC
h=ʾrn	*z*	*ʾl*	*ʾl*	*t-ptḥ*		
the=sarcophagus	DEM.S	NEG	NEG	2-open.IPFV.MS		
ʿlt=y						
over=me.1CS						

'Whoever *you* are—any man—who find this sarcophagus—do not, do not open (what is) over me!' (*KAI* 13.3–4)

The 1CS pronoun *ʾnk* in (14a) is necessary not only to specify the subject of the participle *škb*, which does not exhibit the same full agreement features of the finite verbs, but also so that the ostensible speaker of the text can assert himself–in this case to identify who he is. Placing a referential noun phrase, such as a proper name, in apposition to a first- or second-person pronoun is the only way to specify the speaker or addressee (Bhat 2004: §2.2.3), since these two pronouns are tied to the two speech roles of a discourse and have no anaphoric feature. In (14a), the 1CS pronoun *ʾnk* is followed by the appositional proper name *tbnt* and later in (14b) the 2MS pronoun *ʾt*, representing the addressee, is followed by the appositional noun phrase *kl ʾdm ʾš tpq ʾyt hʾrn z* 'any man who finds this sarcophagus' in order to specify the type of addressee with which Tabnit is concerned. There is no Topic or Focus function associated with either pronoun in (14a) or (14b). However, the use of the 2MS pronoun in (14b) to address the reader directly has great rhetorical effect, as does the redundancy of the appositional noun phrase, since anyone reading the text would logically need to have found the sarcophagus. The effect, in my opinion, is to put the reader on the spot, so to speak, and give the following entreaty and threat all the more shock value.

The third example of a subject pronoun in the Tabnit text is (14c):

(14c)	*w=kl*	*mnm*	*mšr*[15]	*blt*	*ʾnk*	*škb*
	and=all	nothing	riches	NEG	PRON.1CS	lie.PTCP.MS
	b=ʾrn	*z*				
	in=sarcophagus	DEM.S				

'and no riches at all, but *me*, are lying in this sarcophagus'. (*KAI* 13.5)[16]

The 1CS subject pronoun in (14c) is in what is structurally a non-nominative position, since it follows what appears to be the bound *blt* 'except'. In Hebrew, the parallel expression is *biltî* 'besides me', with the 1CS enclitic pronoun (as in Hos 13:4, *ûmôšîăʿ ʾayin biltî* 'there is no savior besides me', // *wēʾlōhîm zûlātî lōʾ tēdāʿ* 'and no god but me do you know'). Since it is likely that the exceptive particle *blt* is a bound form and requires a clitic host, then the 1CS pronoun in this case fulfills a syntactic requirement and thus has no pragmatic function by itself (although the

15. See Lipiński 1974: 55–56; *DNWSI* 705–6 (s.v. $mšr_2$).

16. So Krahmalkov 2001: 118, 239. See Schade 2006: 144–48 for the argument that *blt* begins a new clause; so also Gibson 1982: 103–4, Avishur 2000: 115–20.

entire exceptive phrase, which as a parenthetical statement disrupts the syntax, may be associated with some sort of Focus).

Tabnit's son, ʾEshmunʿazor II, also left an early fifth-century Sidonian inscription (*KAI* 14), and the use of pronouns in this text is syntactically similar to the Tabnit text. The relevant clauses are given in (15).

(15a) *w=škb* *ʾnk* *b=ḥl-t* *z* *w=b=qbr*
and=lie.PTCP.MS PRON.1CS in=box-FS DEM.S and=in=grave
z
DEM.S
'and *I* am lying in this box and in this grave'. (*KAI* 14.3)

(15b) *qnmy* *ʾt* *kl* *mmlk-t* *w=kl* *ʾdm* *ʾl*
whoever PRON.2MS any king-FS and=any man NEG
y-ptḥ *ʾyt* *mškb* *z*
3-open.IPFV.MS ACC resting.place DEM.S
'whoever *you* are, any king or any man—let *pro* (him) not open this resting-place!' (*KAI* 14.4; see also line 20)[17]

(15c) *k* *ʾnk* *nḥn*
because PRON.1CS pity.PASS.PTCP.MS
'because *I* am pitied'. (*KAI* 14.12)

(15d) *bn* *ʾlm-t* *ʾnk*
son.of widow-FS PRON.1CS
'a son of a widow am *I*'. (*KAI* 14.13)

(15e) *k* *ʾnk* *ʾšmnʿzr* *mlk* *ṣdn-m . . .*
indeed PRON.1CS ʾEshmunʿazor king.of Sidonian-MP
w=ʾmy *ʾmʿštrt . . .* *ʾ⟨š⟩* *bn-n*
and=mother-my.1CS ʾImmi-ʿAshtart REL build.PFV-1CP

17. Friedrich and Röllig 1999: §326 classifies the shift in person in (15b) as anacoluthon, but this is not strictly correct since the deictic shift does not formally disrupt the syntax. Comparing this example to the similar one in (14b) suggests that, while the expected antecedent is in the second person, as in (14b), the third-person appositional phrase provides a closer antecedent for the following verb, and this is the likely explanation for (15b). Moreover, it is also likely the text has both an implied addressee (second person) and *witness* (third person), thus making the deictic shifts here and elsewhere in *KAI* 14 a matter of whether the speaker is addressing the addressee directly or talking about the addresse to the witness.

ʾyt bt ʾln-m
ACC house.of god-MP
'indeed, *I*, ʾEshmunʿazor, king of the Sidonians . . . and my mother, ʾImmi-ʿAshtart . . . who *pro* (we) have built the house of the gods'. (*KAI* 14.13–16)

(15f) *w=ʾnḥn ʾš bn-n bt l=ʾšmn*
and=PRON.1CP REL build.PFV-1CS house for=ʾEshmun
'and *we* are (those) who built a house for ʾEshmun'. (*KAI* 14.16–17; see also lines 17–18)

In the ʾEshmunʿazor text, covert pronouns predominate, but the overt pronoun is used as the subject with participles (15a, c) and in null-copula clauses (15d, e). The 1CS *ʾnk* is used for the ostensible speaker and the 2MS *ʾt* in (15b), in a similar construction to the example we saw in Tabnit (above, in [14b]). The predicate-pronoun order of the participial clause *škb ʾnk* 'I am lying' (15a) and the null-copula clause *bn ʾlmt ʾnk* 'a son of a widow am I' (15d) may both reflect Focus-raising of the predicate. I propose this for two reasons: (1) the dominant order with finite verbs, participles, and in null-copula clauses is pronoun-predicate; (2) the participle in (15a) is separated from its oblique (locative) PP complement *bḥlt z wbqbr z* 'in this box and in this grave' (and since a verb and its complement constitute a single constituent, the fact that they are separated in [15a] suggests that the participle has been raised out to a higher position). With the phrase *bn ʾlmt ʾnk* in (15d), the Focus-fronting of the predicate serves to contrast his status as a fatherless boy to any other status.[18]

One final feature of the pronouns in ʾEshmunʿazor to note is the use of the 1CP pronoun *ʾnḥn* in (15f). Note that it is the subject of a null-copula clause in which the predicate is a relative clause. Since a simple

18. In Biblical Hebrew studies, Andersen's (1970) word-order-based distinction between "classifying" (= predicate-subject order) and "identifying" (subject-predicate order) null-copula clauses has become the generally accepted analysis. However, not only do the numerous exceptions doom this distinction, there is a much simpler analysis: null-copula clauses are subject-predicate order unless the predicate has been fronted for Topic or Focus; any correlation with the discourse-semantic notions of "classifying" and "identifying" are by-products and not directly involved in the syntactic and pragmatic operations acting upon the word order (see Buth 1999 for both an extended critique of Andersen's distinction and a Topic and Focus analysis of Biblical Hebrew null-copula clauses).

verbal clause could have sufficed (as it does in line 16 with *wyš<b>n ʾštrt* 'and we settled Ashtart'), the use of the pronoun and the relative clause here suggests that the pronoun not only functions as the subject of the null-copula clause but also carries Focus. And in the context, this makes sense, particularly if the latter part of the inscription was added by ʾEshmunʿazor's mother and regent upon his death in a last-gasp attempt to immortalize herself (so Parker 1999).

6. *Late Byblian: Yaḥawmilk (*KAI *10)*

Contempory with the Sidonian texts, the Late Byblian Yaḥawmilk text (early fifth century B.C.) presents the final set of subject pronouns that I will discuss in this study. As with the other texts discussed above, the Yaḥawmilk "drops" the pronoun (that is, uses covert *pro*) widely; overt pronouns are often used to fulfill the requirement for a syntactic subject in null-copula clauses, illustrated in (16a, b):

(16a)	<u>*ʾnk*</u>	*yḥwmlk*	*mlk*	*gbl*
	PRON.1CS	Yaḥawmilk	king.of	Byblos

'*I* am Yaḥawmilk, king of Byblos'. (*KAI* 10.1)

(16b)	*k*	*mlk*	*ṣdq*	<u>*hʾ*</u>
	because	king	righteous	PRON.3MS

'because a righteous king is *he*'. (*KAI* 10.9)

In (16a) the 1CS pronoun *ʾnk* is used as the subject of a null-copula clause in the first clause, and in (16b) the 3MS pronoun is used anaphorically to link with the speaker, who refers to himself in the third person. The Focus-fronting of the predicate in the null-copula clause serves to assert that he was nothing if not a righteous king.

In addition to the null-copula clauses, the Yaḥawmilk text also exhibits the subject pronoun following the uninflected narrative verb (which we have not seen since the much earlier Anatolian texts):

(16c)	*w=*<u>*qrʾ*</u>	<u>*ʾnk*</u>	*ʾt*	*rb-t=y*
	and=call.NARR	PRON.1CS	ACC	mistress-FS=my.1CS
	bʿlt	*gbl*		
	Baʿalat.of	Byblos		

'and *I called* my mistress, Baʿalat of Byblos'. (*KAI* 10.2–3)

(16d) *w=p̱ʿl* *ʾnk* *l=rb-t=y*
and=make.NARR PRON.1CS for=mistress-FS=my.1CS
bʿlt *gbl* *h=mzbh* *nḥš-t* *zn*
Baʿalat.of Byblos the=altar bronze-FS DEM.S
'and *I made* for my mistress, Baʿalat of Byblos, this bronze altar'. (*KAI* 10.3–4)

(16e) . . . *p̱ʿl* *ʾnk* *yḥwmlk* *mlk* *gbl*
make.NARR PRON.1CS Yaḥawmilk king.of Byblos
l=rb-t=y *bʿlt* *gbl*
for=mistress-FS=my.1CS Baʿalat.of Byblos
'[this doorway, etc.] *I*, Yaḥawmilk, king of Byblos, *made* for my mistress, Baʿalat of Byblos'. (*KAI* 10.6–7)

A final example presents an unusual use of the pronoun:[19]

(16f) *šm* *ʾnk* *yḥwmlk* *mlk* *gbl*
name.my.1CS PRON.1CS Yaḥawmilk king.of Byblos
[*t-št* *ʾt*]*=k* *ʿl* *mlʾk-t* *hʾ*
2-set.IPFV.MS with=you.2MS on work-FS DEM.S
'my name, *mine*!–Yaḥawmilk, king of Byblos–*pro* (you) should set with you on that work'. (*KAI* 10.12–13)

In (16f), the 1CS pronoun *ʾnk* is used appositionally to *šm* 'my name' (Segert 1976: §61.16; Friedrich and Röllig 1999: §286; Krahmalkov 2001: 47). Like the similar example from Karatepe (see above, [11g]), the pronoun in this example serves no syntactic role within the clause, which is unusual; even so, its pragmatic role appears to be as a Focus constituent, strengthening the 1CS suffix on "my name" by asserting that the one whose name is in question is none other than the speaker, the king. Note that the 1CS pronoun, because it is not anaphoric, is followed by its own appositional phrases, the personal name *yḥwmlk* and the NP

19. There are also two 1CS pronouns in the Yaḥawmilk funerary inscription (*KAI* 280, "Byblos 13"), both in the first line. Since the beginning of the first line is broken, the context of the first pronoun is lacking. But the context for the second case of the pronoun is clear–and it is an obligatory pronoun both for a subject for the participle and for the identification of the first-person speaker: *w=kn hn ʾnk škb b=ʾrn zn* 'and so, here *I am lying* in this coffin'. Similar to this example is the single pronoun in the fourth-century Batnoʿam text (*KAI* 11.1–2): *bʾrn zn ʾnk btnʿm ʾm mlk ʿzbʿl mlk gbl bn pltbʿl khn bʿlt škbt* 'In this ark *I*, Batnoʿam, mother of King ʿAzbaʿal, king of Byblos, son of Paltibaʿal, priest of Baʿalat, *am lying*' (*KAI* 11.1–2).

mlk gbl, both of which identify the speaker, just in case the addressee forgot.[20]

7. Resumptive and Object Pronouns

Among the epigraphic Canaanite texts of the first millennium, only Phoenician has left us with unambiguous cases of RC resumption, but even in the Phoenician texts the examples are limited, though they appear to increase over time. Two Byblian examples exist, presented in (17) and (18):[21]

(17) B. Shiptibaal III, ca. 500 B.C.

b=mškb	*zn*	*ʾš̱*	*ʾnk*	*škb*	*ḇn*[22]
in=resting.place	DEM.S	REL	PRON.1CS	lie.PTCP.MS	in.it.3MS

'in this resting-place *that* I lie in *it*'. (*KAI* 9 A.3)

(18) Yeḥawmilk, ca. 450 B.C.

ʾnk	*yḥwmlk*	*mlk*	*gbl*	*bn*	*yḥrbʿl*
PRON.1CS	Yeḥawmilk	king.of	Byblos	son.of	YḤRBaʿal
bn	*bn*	*ʾrmlk*	*mlk*	*gbl*	*ʾš̱*
son.of	son.of	ʾUrimilk	king.of	Byblos	REL
pʿl-t=ṉ	*h=rb-t*	*bʿlt*	*gbl*		
make.PFV-3FS=me.1CS	the=mistress-FS	Baʿalat.of	Byblos		

20. Isolated occurrences of pronouns also appear in the following nonexhaustive list of texts: Chytroi (Cyprus, ca. 650 B.C.), line 2; *CIS* 113 (ca. 550 B.C.), line a; *KAI* 50 (ca. 550 B.C.), obv. line 2; *KAI* 49.4–6, 7 (2×), 8, 9, 11 (2×), 12, 13, 19, 22, 25–28, 34 (2×), 35–41, 45–49; the silver amulet (ca. 500 B.C.), lines 6–8; *RES* 1513 (5th–4th c. B.C.); Ostracon A from Dor (33608/1, 5th–4th c. B.C.), line 5; the Milkyaton trophy inscription (Cyprus, early 4th c. B.C.), line 4; *RES* 1213, line 6; the Byblian altar inscription of *ʿbdʾšmn* (3rd c. B.C.), lines 1–2; *KAI* 35.1 (3rd c. B.C.); *KAI* 43.1, 5 (ca. 275 B.C.); *KAI* 17.2 (2nd c. B.C.); *KAI* 48.1 (1st c. B.C.), *KAI* 54.1, 2 (1st c. B.C.); *KAI* 59.1 The syntax and pragmatics of the pronouns in these texts appear to follow the same pattern that we have seen in the larger texts.

21. Segert (1976) suggests that the Nora Stele (9th c. B.C., Sardinian; *KAI* 46) contains an instance of subject-resumption in a relative clause. His reading of lines 2–3, which follows *KAI*, is at odds with the readings of, for example, Peckham 1972 and Cross 1972. Based on my own reading of Peckham's original 1972 photograph, I concur with the readings of Peckham 1972; Cross 1972; and Zuckerman 1991; against that of Segert 1976; and *KAI*: there is no relative clause and therefore no subject-resumption in this inscription. It is also worth noting that three later Phoenician instances of resumption, one oblique and two subject, are from Cyprus and date to the 3rd c. B.C. (*KAI* 40.2; 43.4–5, 12–3).

22. On the preposition *bn*, see Krahmalkov 2001: 232.

mmlk-t *ʿl* *gbl*
king-FS over Byblos
'I am Yeḥawmilk, king of Gubl, son of YḤRBaʿal, grandson of ʾUrimilk, king of Gubl, *who* the Ba'alat of Gubl made *me* king over Gubl'. (10.1–2)

Both Byblian examples are from the second half of the first millennium. The example in (17) is obligatory, since the whole PP (which itself requires a complement) is an oblique (locative) complement of the verb. The resumption at the accusative position in (18) is not syntactically obligatory, but it is nonetheless required for semantic interpretation, since without the resumption the entity to which the object of the verb refers would be ambiguous–did Ba'alat of Gubl make the speaker, Yeḥawmilk, king or one of the closer potential antecedents, his father or grandfather? With the insertion of "me" as the resumptive pronoun, the antecedent is specified, and the clause is rescued from fatal ambiguity.

There are no clear cases of resumption in Early Tyro-Sidonian or Anatolian texts;[23] the earliest examples are from later in the first millennium (19)–(20):

(19) Oblique Resumption:
Cyprus-Lapethos ii (c. 274 B.C.)

23. There is one example in the first Arslan Tash text (*KAI* 27.16), but the authenticity of the two Arslan Tash texts has been questioned (see Teixidor 1983; cf. van Dijk 1992), and thus I have excluded it from consideration above. However, I will briefly describe the example here (with some details changed from Holmstedt 2008):

(i) *[ʾ]š-t* *ḥwrn* *ʾš* *tm* *p=y̱*
wife-FS.of Hawran REL true command=her.3FS
'Hawran's wife, who *her* [= whose] command is true'. (*KAI* 27.16)

The resumptive element in (i) is the clitic (possessive) pronoun on the subject noun in the relative clause, *py̱* '*her* command'. In Phoenician, as in all NWS languages, this genitive type of resumption is obligatory (see Holmstedt 2008), since without the resumptive possessive suffix coreferential with the relative head, *ʾšt ḥwrn* 'wife of Hawran', the noun in the relative clause would have no syntactic or semantic connection to the matrix clause. This kind of resumption illustrates the most common function of resumptive pronouns in NWS–as a "last resort" strategy to save a construction that would otherwise fail grammatically. In contrast, in languages with true relative pronouns the possessive or genitive relationship is manifested by agreement features on the relative pronoun itself; the remnants of a system of this sort are still visible in English *whose*, as in "Hawran, whose command is bound."

h=dl-t *h=nḥš-t* . . . *ʾš* *bn* *mnḥ-t*
the=plaque-FS the=bronze-FS REL in.it.3FS detail-FP.of
ḥn=y
generosity=my.1CS
'the bronze plaque . . . that *in it* (are) the details of my generosity'. (*KAI* 43.12–13)

(20) Subject Resumption

a) Cyprus-Idalion (254 B.C.)
b=šn-t *31* *l=ʾdn* *mlk-m* *ptlmys* . . . *ʾš*
in=year-FP 31 to=lord.of king-MP Ptolemy REL
hʾ *š-t* *57* *l=ʾš* *kty*
PRON.3MS year-FS 57 to=man.MP.of Kition
'in year 31 of the Lord of Kings, Ptolemy, . . . which *it* is year 57 of the Kitionite'. (*KAI* 40.2)

b) Cyprus-Lapethos ii (274 B.C.)
b=šn-t *11* *l=ʾdn* *mlk-m* *ptlmyš* . . . *ʾš*
in=year-FP 11 to=lord.of king-MP Ptolemy REL
hmt *l=ʿm* *lpš* *šn-t* *33*
PRON.3MP to=people.of Lapethos year-FS 33
'in year 11 of the Lord of Kings, Ptolemy, . . . which *they* (are) year 33 of the people of Lapethos'. (*KAI* 43.4–5)

The relative clause in (19) exhibits resumption in the oblique (object of preposition) position inside the relative clause. The preposition and thus the resumptive pronoun as its complement fill the syntactic role of the copular predicate and are thus syntactically licensed. The two cases of subject resumption in (20a, b)—the only two Phoenician examples of subject resumption I have yet to find—are not syntactically necessary; moreover, I see no pragmatic explanation and can only conjecture that the late date and language contact are involved.

The use of resumptive pronouns in Phoenician is, on the one hand, similar to the use of subject pronouns (they are almost always required for the grammaticality or felicitousness of the clause in context) and, on the other hand, more constrained. That is, there are no clear cases (among the admittedly rather small selection) of resumptive pronouns inserted for Topic or Focus.

As best we can tell, object pronouns operate similarly to resumptive pronouns. Representative examples are provided in (21)–(23) (examples [23a] and [23b] repeat [11c] and [11f], respectively).

(21)	*ʾrn*	*z*	*pʿl*	*[ʾ]tbʿl*	*bn*	*ʾḥrm*
	sarcophagus	REL	make.PFV.3MS	ʾIttobaʿl	son.of	ʾAḥirom

mlk	*gbl*	*l=ʾḥrm*	*ʾb=h*	*k*
king.of	Byblos	for=ʾAḥirom	father=his.3MS	when

št=h	*b=ʿlm*
set.PFV.3MS=him.3MS	in=eternity

'The sarcophagus that ʾIttobaʿl, son of ʾAḥirom, king of Byblos, made for ʾAḥirom, his father, when he set *him* in eternity'. (*KAI* 1.1)

(22)	*w=my*	*bl*	*ḥz*	*pn*	*š*
	and=who	NEG	see.PFV.3MS	face.of	sheep

št=y	*bʿl*	*ʿdr*
make.PFV.1CS=him.3MS	owner.of	flock

'and one who had not seen the face of a sheep—I made *him* the owner of a flock'. (*KAI* 24.11)

(23a)	*w=ʾnk*	*ʾztwd*	*št=nm*	*tḥt*
	and=PRON.1CS	ʾAzatiwada	set.PFV.1CS=them.3MP	under

pʿm=y
feet.MP=my.1CS

'but I, ʾAzatiwada, set *them* under my feet'. (*KAI* 26 AI.16–17//BI.9, CII.5)

(23b)	*yšb=m*	*ʾnk*	*b=qṣ-t*
	settle.NARR=them.3MS	PRON.1CS	in=end-FP.of

gbl=y
border.MP=my.1CS

'I settled *them* in the ends of my borders'. (*KAI* 26 AI.20//BI.11, CII.12)

In all four examples, the enclitic object pronoun provides a syntactic complement for each of the transitive verbs. Even in the case of left-dislocation in (22), since the initial noun phrase sits at the edge of the clause and has no formal syntactic role within it, the resumptive pronoun is obligatory to fulfill the accusative case role of the verb *št* 'I made'. It is also true, however, that the choice of left-dislocation often sets up the resumptive pronoun as a Focus constituent, so that the dislocated element functions as a Topic (for example, "as for this fellow") and the resumptive pronoun provides the focal contrast (for example, "I made him [and no other person] the owner").

There remain many questions about Phoenician object pronouns, many of which, unfortunately, will remain unanswered due to the lack of orthographic representation for many third-person enclitic pronouns. That is, since Phoenician does not exhibit the same use of matres lectionis as ancient Hebrew, enclitic pronouns that are manifested as word-final syllables are simply not represented by the writing convention (for a convenient list followed by discussion, see Krahmalkov 2001: 68–74). Moroever, unlike the prolific use of the nota accusativi *ʾt* with an enclitic pronoun in ancient Hebrew, such usage in Phoenician is arguably nonexistent (although it does occur in Punic; see Mosca, this volume, for a discussion). Thus, it is quite possible that Phoenician uses zero anaphora much more widely than Hebrew (on zero anaphora in Biblical Hebrew, see Creason 1991). Even with the orthographic obstacles, a thorough study of the limited available evidence on the syntax and pragmatics of object reference in Phoenician is needed.

Bibliography

Alt, A.
1949 Die phönizischen Inschriften von Karatepe. *WO* 1: 272–87.
Andersen, F. I.
1970 *The Hebrew Verbless Clause in the Pentateuch.* JBL Monograph 14. Nashville: Abingdon.
Avishur, Y.
2000 *Phoenician Inscriptions and the Bible: Select Inscriptions and Studies in Stylistic and Literary Devices Common to the Phoenician Inscriptions and the Bible.* Tel Aviv–Jaffa: Archaeological Center Publications.
Bhat, D. N. S.
2004 *Pronouns.* Oxford: Oxford University Press.
Bron, F.
1979 *Recherches sur les inscriptions phéniciennes de Karatepe.* Geneva: Droz.
Buth, R.
1999 Word Order in the Verbless Clause: A Generative-Functional Approach. Pp. 79–108 in *The Verbless Clause in Biblical Hebrew: Linguistic Approaches*, ed. C. L. Miller. LSAWS 1. Winona Lake, IN: Eisenbrauns.
Collins, T.
1971 The Kilamuwa Inscription: A Phoenician Poem. *WO* 6: 183–88.

Cook, V. J., and Newson, M.
2007 *Chomsky's Universal Grammar: An Introduction*. 3rd ed. Malden, MA: Blackwell.
Cooke, G. A.
1903 *A Text-Book of North-Semitic Inscriptions: Moabite, Hebrew, Phoenician, Aramaic, Nabataean, Palmyrene, Jewish*. Oxford: Clarendon.
Creason, S.
1991 Discourse Constraints on Null Complements in Biblical Hebrew. *University of Chicago Working Papers in Linguistics* 7: 18–47.
Cross, F. M.
1972 An Interpretation of the Nora Stone. *BASOR* 208: 13–19.
Dijk, J. van
1992 The Authenticity of the Arslan Tash Amulets. *Iraq* 54: 65–68.
Dunand, M.
1944–45 Les inscriptions phéniciennes de Karatepe. *BMB* 7: 81–97.
1946–48 Une nouvelle version des inscriptions phéniciennes de Karatepe. *BMB* 8: 17–36.
Dupont-Sommer, A.
1948 Azitawadda, roi des Danouniens. *RA* 42: 161–88.
Faber, A.
1986 On the Structural Unity of the Eshmunᶜazor Inscription. *JAOS* 106: 425–32.
Friedrich, J., and Röllig, W.
1999 *Phönizisch-Punische Grammatik*. 3rd ed. by M. G. Amadasi Guzzo with W. R. Mayer. AnOr 55. Rome: Pontifical Biblical Institute.
Garr, W. R.
1985 *Dialect Geography of Syria–Palestine, 1000–586 B.C.E.* Philadelphia: University of Pennsylvania Press. [Repr., Winona Lake, IN: Eisenbrauns, 2004.]
Gibson, J. C. L.
1982 *Textbook of Syrian Semitic Inscriptions*, vol. 3: *Phoenician Inscriptions*. Oxford: Clarendon.
Ginsberg, H. L.
1973 Ugaritico-Phoenicia. *JANES* 5: 131–47.
Gordon, C. H.
1948 Phoenician Inscriptions from Karatepe. *JQR* 39: 41–50.
1949 Azitawadd's Phoenician Inscription. *JNES* 8/2: 108–15.
Gutman, E.
1999 *Null Subjects: A Theory of Syntactic and Discourse-Identification, Linguistics*. Ph.D. diss., University of Delaware.
2004 Third Person Null Subjects in Hebrew, Finnish and Rumanian: An Accessibility-Theoretic Account. *Journal of Linguistics* 40: 463–90.
Haegeman, L.
1994 *Introduction to Government and Binding Theory*. 2nd ed. Oxford: Blackwell.

Harris, Z. S.
1936 *A Grammar of the Phoenician Language*. AOS 8. New Haven, CT: American Oriental Society.

Holmstedt, R. D.
2008 The Relative Clause in Canaanite Epigraphic Texts. *JNSL* 34/2: 1–34.
2009 Word Order and Information Structure in Ruth and Jonah: A Generative-Typological Analysis. *JSS* 54: 111–39.
forthcoming Pro-Drop. In *Encyclopedia of Hebrew Language and Linguistics*, ed. G. Khan. Leiden: Brill.

Honeyman, A. M.
1949 Epigraphic Discoveries at Karatepe. *PEQ* 81: 21–39.

Joüon, P., and Muraoka, T.
2006 *A Grammar of Biblical Hebrew*. Rev. ed. SubBi 27. Rome: Pontifical Biblical Institute.

Krahmalkov, C. R.
2000 *Phoenician-Punic Dictionary*. OLA 90. Studia Phoenicia 15. Leuven: Peeters.
2001 *A Phoenician-Punic Grammar*. HOSNME 54. Leiden: Brill.

Lipiński, E.
1974 From Karatepe to Pyrgi: Middle Phoenician Miscellanea. *RSF* 2: 45–61.
2004 *Itineraria Phoenicia*. Studia Phoenicia 18. Leuven: Peeters.

Marcus, D.
1969 Studies in Ugaritic Grammar I. *JANES* 1/2: 55–61.

Marcus, R., and Gelb, I. J.
1948 A Preliminary Study of the New Phoenician Inscription from Cilicia. *JNES* 7/3: 194–98.
1949 The Phoenician Stele Inscription from Cilicia. *JNES* 8/2: 116–20.

Merwe, C. H. J. van der; Naudé, J. A.; and Kroeze, J. H.
1999 *A Biblical Hebrew Reference Grammar*. Sheffield: Sheffield Academic Press.

Moor, J. C. de
1988 Narrative Poetry in Canaan. *UF* 20: 149–71.

Mosca, P. G., and Russell, J.
1987 A Phoenician Inscription from Cebel Ires Dagi in Rough Cilicia. *EpAn* 9: 1–28 + 4 plates.

Obermann, J.
1950 Phoenician YQTL ʾNK. *JNES* 9/2: 94–100.

O'Callaghan, R. T.
1949a The Great Phoenician Portal Inscription from Karatepe. *Or* 18: 173–205, figs. 1–9.
1949b The Phoenician Inscription on the King's Statue at Karatepe. *CBQ* 11: 233–48.

O'Connor, M.
1977a The Rhetoric of the Kilamuwa Inscription. *BASOR* 226: 15–29.

1977b The Grammar of Getting Blessed in Tyrian-Sidonian Phoenician. *RSF* 5: 5–11.

Pardee, D.

1983 Review of *Recherces sur les inscriptions phéniciennes de Karatepe* by François Bron. *JNES* 42/1: 63–67.

Parker, S. B.

1996 Appeals for Military Intervention: Stories from Zinjirli and the Bible. *BA* 59: 213–24.

1997 *Stories in Scripture and Inscriptions: Comparative Studies on Narratives in Northwest Semitic Inscriptions and the Hebrew Bible*. New York: Oxford University Press.

Peckham, B.

1972 The Nora Inscription. *Or* 30: 457–68.

Röllig, W.

1999 The Phoenician Inscriptions. Pp. 50–81 in *Corpus of Hieroglyphic Luwian Inscriptions, Volume II: Karatepe-Aslantaş, The Inscriptions: Facsimile Edition*, ed. H. Çambel. Berlin: de Gruyter.

Schade, A.

2005 A Text Linguistic Approach to the Syntax and Style of the Phoenician Inscription of Azatiwada. *JSS* 50/1: 35–58.

2006 *A Syntactic and Literary Analysis of Ancient Northwest Semitic Inscriptions*. Lewiston, NY: Edwin Mellen.

Segert, S.

1976 *A Grammar of Phoenician and Punic*. Munich: Beck.

Sperling, S. D.

1988 KAI 24 Re-examined. *UF* 20: 323–37.

Swiggers, P.

1980 A Note on the Phoenician Inscription of Azitiwada. *UF* 12: 440.

Teixidor, J.

1983 Les tablettes d'Arslan Tash au Musée d'Alep. *AuOr* 1: 105–8.

Tekoğlu, R., and Lemaire, A.

2002 La bilingue royale louvito-phénicienne de Çineköy. *CRAIBL* 2000: 960–1006.

Waltke, B. K., and O'Connor, M.

1990 *An Introduction to Biblical Hebrew Syntax*. Winona Lake, IN: Eisenbrauns.

Wiese, H., and Simon, H. J.

2002 Grammatical Properties of Pronouns and Their Representations: An Exposition. Pp. 1–21 in *Pronouns: Grammar and Representation*, ed. H. J. Simon and H. Wiese. Amsterdam: Benjamins.

Younger, K. L., Jr.

1998 The Phoenician Inscription of Azatiwada: An Integrated Reading. *JSS* 43: 11–47.

Zuckerman, B.

1991 The Nora Puzzle. *Maarav* 7: 269–301.

Fronted Word Order in Phoenician Inscriptions

Aaron Schade

1. Introduction

The study of fronted word order in Phoenician is a topic that is relatively unexplored.[1] While some Phoenician grammars make brief mention of constructions of this sort in clauses and sentences, few explanations are given with regard to their function, and rarely do the observations go beyond the sentence level.[2] As meaningful and useful as these grammars are, the purpose of this essay is to move beyond the sentence-based observations about the occurrence of fronted word order to defining their text-level functions within the Phoenician inscriptional material. This study will thus provide linguistic explanations surrounding the function of fronted clause types (which are generally supplied in broad, taxonomic listings) and describe how they operate within the text as a whole.

In taking this approach, we will discuss questions that arise while examining syntax and fronted constructions such as what normal word order is, what linguistic triggers influence word order variation, what role pragmatics plays in the development of information structure, how literary devices influence the text's linguistic make-up, and how syntax and stylistic factors operate interdependently within a text. In this examination, I will work from two starting points: (1) that Phoenician is a verb-initial language, and (2) that "triggers" induce deviations from that

1. In Biblical Hebrew (BH), fronted constructions have received a significant amount of attention. See, for example, Buth 1990: 9–16; van der Merwe 1991: 129–44, 1999a: 277–300; Bandstra 1992: 109–24; Heimerdinger 1999; van der Merwe and E. Talstra 2002–3: 68–107; Floor 2003: 197–236, 2005: 23–58; and Holmstedt 2009: 111–39.

2. See the approaches in Krahmalkov 2001: 290–95 and Friedrich and Röllig 1999: 222–33.

norm—deviations that simultaneously exhibit detectable syntactic and pragmatic text-level features.[3] I will thus examine how fronted constructions operate and influence the development of the information structure of entire texts and how such constructions act as syntactic descriptors that appear to be driven by pragmatic motivations within the text. The relationship between syntax and pragmatics finds support in the fact that many fronted constructions tend to occur where one expects a new unit of text to begin or end (and are thus marked). That being said, it should be remembered that fronted constructions do not always mark these boundaries, because they also occur in subordinate clauses (which exhibit both VX and XV tendencies), and in these constructions the fronting may also be influenced by pragmatic functions. Syntax and pragmatics thus cannot be divided when analyzing texts. The necessity for an approach that examines the interdependence of both the syntax and text-level functions of fronting is described by Myhill (1995: 139) in relation to BH:

> There are cases of 'emphatic' fronting, for which discourse factors alone can explain what is fronted. However, for the great majority of clauses with non-verb-initial order, discourse and syntactic factors operate together. This type of complex interaction between discourse and syntactic properties has not to my knowledge been reported in the literature; word orders in particular constructions have been reported to be controlled by either syntactic factors or discourse factors, but not both. It is not clear at this stage how common the type of phenomenon I have described here is, because studies have typically only gone into detail about either the effect of discourse factors or the effect of syntactic factors, but not both, so that perhaps linguists have not investigated the possibility of this type of complex interaction.[4]

The present examination of Phoenician inscriptions will take into consideration both syntactic and pragmatic factors, and the way the two

3. In BH, most assume that the language demonstrates a "basic" Verb-Subject order. For those who advocate a "basic" Subject-Verb order, see, for example, Joüon 1923; DeCaen 1995; and Holmstedt 2005; 2009. For Phoenician, Friedrich and Röllig (1999: 222) list Verb-Subject-Object as the standard word order, and Krahmalkov (2001: 290–93) writes more in terms of verbs "without syntactic restriction" but does not explain in much detail about how or why these variations occur.

4. See also Heimerdinger (1999: 32), who states, "Discourse is a sized unit of language use. It is a stretch of language use with a beginning, a middle and an end. It is also characterized by sequentiality and connectivity: sequences of utterances have a non-random character and are connected syntactically, semantically and pragmatically."

relate in the makeup of a text. Syntax should be primary in a study of this sort, because syntax, though flexible, does have certain limitations. Holmstedt (2009: 112) correctly summarizes syntactic priority in analyzing texts:

> The relationship between syntax and semantics, on the one hand, and pragmatics, on the other, is primarily unidirectional; in other words, pragmatics necessarily accesses the syntactic and semantic features of a text, but not vice versa. It stands to reason, then, that any model of information structure can only be as accurate as the syntactic and semantic model upon which it builds.[5]

It thus becomes necessary to examine fronted word order based on multiple variables.[6] Subsequently, though not a primary focus of this study, syntax and literary style work interdependently to convey, not prohibit, the flow of a text, and fronted word order often offers linguistic signals at crucial transitions within the writings.[7]

---

5. See also Talstra 1999: 101. In Schade 2006a, I describe the syntactic structure of Phoenician inscriptions, and the current essay draws on that model in defining the discourse functions in these compositions.

6. So Buth 1990: 15. Van der Merwe (1999b: 173–74) writes that fronting has been referred to as "topicalization" and can be governed by multiple variables including syntax, literary devices, and linguistic signaling of the information structure.

7. Floor (2005: 23–24) offers the following remark in his study on fronting in Proverbs:

> . . . almost every verse contains a fronted constituent. Is this markedly higher occurrence only due to poetic freedom and relatively meaningless stylistic considerations, just to create an aesthetic form of art, or does it rather point to the fact that the poet exploited available grammatical structures for rhetorical and thematic purposes? If the latter suggestion is correct, what then are the forms and the meanings of these available grammatical structures so exploited? A related issue is the thematic segmentation of a text. Many segmentations can easily be intuitive and subjective, and then differ from analyst to analyst. Are there any clues in the text that provide a more objective explanation of where the thematic boundaries lie? I will argue in this article that an information structure approach to fronting and marked word order in Biblical Hebrew can partly explain why the poet exploited those devices for thematic reasons, as well as for text segmentation. Information structure analysis allows the analyst to explain word order variation in terms of the interaction between topic and focus, and how the poet uses topics and focus structures for specific thematic purposes.

The use of fronted word order for thematic reasons and text segmentation also occurs in Phoenician inscriptions. See Schade 2006a, where I describe this interrelationship between syntax and style.

2. *Methodological Framework*

In describing aspects of discourse linguistics, O'Connor (2002: 20–21) states that an "area of discourse linguistics concerns the working of grammatical elements over entities larger than the clause or sentence, including problems of topic, theme, reference, and time structure." In the course of this study, I will examine some of the larger Phoenician inscriptions, which offer the greatest amount of data for discourse and syntactic observations. I will intentionally avoid drawing upon specific discourse methodologies and appellations that have been applied in BH studies and that have led to convoluted discussions yielding few definitive conclusions.[8] Instead, I will use a broad set of descriptors such as those outlined in Holmstedt (2009: 128) and provided in table 1.[9]

Table 1. Discourse-Pragmatic Functions

Theme	Old/known (or presupposed) information
Rheme	New/added (or reinvoked) information
Focus	Information contrasted with possible alternatives
Topic	Thematic information used to (1) isolate one among multiple Themes, or (2) set the scene (e.g., time, place)

Specifically, I will examine issues surrounding Theme, Rheme, Focus, and Topic in relation to marked syntactic units within the texts and the ways that syntactic variations such as Subject-Verb, Object-Verb, Prepositional Phrase-Verb, and Adverb-Verb are used–for example, for presenting new characters or information, for drawing our attention to references of time and place, or for marking contrast in the events of the text–and are thus linked to pragmatic features.[10] In some instances,

8. On the lack of agreement on labels in discourse functions, Moshavi (2006: 232) writes, "Despite much impressive work, however, considerable disagreement still exists as to the linguistic framework most appropriate for analyzing word order, as well as the meanings of discourse concepts topic and focus." For critiques of some of the proposed models in BH and the difficulties with sufficiently defining discourse-related terms and their functions, see van der Merwe 1999a: 277–300; Eskhult 1992; and Holmstedt 2003.

9. Holmstedt applies these concepts in terms of layers: Theme/Rheme and Topic/Focus.

10. By employing these broad terms here, I will try to avoid getting caught up in the semantics of the undecided. I will thus attempt simultaneously to describe in practical terms the relationship of the syntax and pragmatics of fronted constructions.

it will be observed that fronted constructions frequently occur in the genre of dedicatory inscriptions and in anterior constructions in conditional clauses and that, in these constructions, discourse functions can be detected within the syntactic variations.

3. The Data

3.1. Introductions/Presentations

At the beginning of Phoenician inscriptions, a pronoun followed by a nonverbal copula clause may introduce the main character:

(1) *ʾnk* *klmw* *br*
I.PRON.1CS.NOM Kilamuwa.MS.NOM son.of.MS.NOM
Ḥy[ʾ]
Hayyaʾ.MS.GEN
'I am Kilamuwa, son of Hayyaʾ'. (*KAI* 24.1)

It is more common in introductions for the pronoun to be followed by a noun phrase(s) and a relative clause that describes what a deity (or a king) has done to support the honoree. In this manner, the individual (usually the king or one who has been empowered by royalty or set in place by a deity) thus becomes activated in the narrative with the introduction, or presentation of the character:

(2) Azatiwada (second half eighth-century Phoenician)
ʾnk *ʾztwd* . . .[11] *ʾš*
I.PRON.1CS.NOM Azatiwada.MS.NOM whom.REL
ʾdr *ʾwrk* *mlk*
empowered.PFV.3MS Awariku.MS.NOM king.MS.NOM
dnny-m
Danunians.MP.GEN
'I am Azatiwada . . . whom Awariku, king of the Danunians empowered'. (*KAI* 26.I 1–2)

(3) Yeḥawmilk (mid-fifth-century Byblian)
ʾnk *yḥwmlk* . . .[12] *ʾš*
I.PRON.1CS.NOM Yeḥawmilk.MS.NOM whom.REL

11. In the text, a series of titles follows the name of Azatiwada.
12. The title of king and patronymics follow the name of Yeḥawmilk.

pʿl-t=n *h=rb-t* *bʿl-t*
made-PFV.3FS=me.PRON.1CS ART=lady-FS.NOM Baalat-FS.NOM
gbl *m-mlk-t* *ʿl* *gbl*
Byblos.FS.GEN kingship-FS.ACC over.PREP Byblos.FS.GEN
'I am Yeḥawmilk . . . whom the Lady, Baalat of Byblos, made king over Byblos'. (*KAI* 10.1–2)

While constructions of this sort may not constitute fronted word order, they do offer an important starting point in the introduction of characters. They employ the personal pronoun and a proper name in a nonverbal construction to activate a character in the text. When a verbal constituent does occur in the introductory portion of an inscription, the result is a fronted construction:

(4) Tabnit (early fifth-century Sidonian)
ʾnk *tbnt* . . .[13] *škb*
I.PRON.1CS.NOM Tabnit.MS.NOM lie.MS.PTCP
b=ʾrn *z*
in.PREP=coffin.MS this.DEM.MS
'I, Tabnit, . . . lie in this sarcophagus'. (*KAI* 13.1–3)

Here the syntactically fronted word order would be discourse driven and thus carries the pragmatic feature of formally introducing and activating the character into the text.[14] The fronted construction thus functions pragmatically similar to its nonverbal counterparts in examples

13. Titles and the patronymic follow here.

14. In this example, the syntactically fronted participle is driven by pragmatic motivations. The participle is not always fronted in Phoenician and this highlights the instance here. See, for example, *KAI* 14.3, where the participle is not fronted. Krahmalkov (2001: 294) observes the difference in the syntactic positioning of these two examples of the participle but does not explain why they take different positions in these clauses. The opening lines of *KAI* 14 are awkward, and a pronominal suffix is used instead of the personal pronoun in the introduction of Eshmunazor (Avishur [2000: 134] translates this pronominal suffix, and McCarter [*COS* 2.182] does not), an introduction that subsequently follows a prepositional phrase providing a date, which also serves a pragmatic function in the inscription (example 23 in the text). When the participle is encountered, it is in the initial position of the clause and is followed by a tripartite string of prepositional phrases aligned according to anabasis (a deliberate literary device drawing attention to the phrases), which seems to highlight the location of the listed items within this clause (where Eshmunazor lies) and not the unmarked verbal constituent describing the act of lying. See also example (19) for the pragmatically motivated fronting of the participle.

(1)–(3), and in all of these examples (1)–(4) the information at the beginning of the inscription would be rhematic (introduction of new material–Rheme).[15]

3.2. Subject Fronting in Reinvoking Information (Rheme)

The presentation of new information at the beginning of an inscription was just discussed, and there are also instances of reintroducing characters within a text after the plot has developed. Fronting of this sort frequently occurs when the subject is an individual who has not been mentioned by name for several paragraphs, or an element of Focus is present. The example from Eshmunazor in example (5) provides an instance of subject fronting for reinvoking material (Rheme):

(5) Eshmunazor (fifth-century Sidonian)
k[16] *ʾnk* . . .[17] *w-ʾm=y*
I.1CS.PRON.NOM and.CONJ=mother.FS.NOM=PRON.1CS
ʾš *bn-n*
who.REL built.1CP.PFV
'I . . . and my mother . . . are the ones who built . . .' . (*KAI* 14.13–15)

The fronted subject in (5) marks the beginning of a new syntactic unit and reintroduces Eshmunazor by name. This is rhematic material, because the king has not mentioned his name since the beginning of the inscription.[18] The introduction of Eshmunazor's mother as part of the subject is additionally rhematic material. These plural constituents

15. For the fronting of the subject in BH "presentational" constructions or the "beginning" of a discourse paragraph see van der Merwe 1999a: 294; 2002–2003: 76. For subject fronting in introducing an entity in the Jerusalem Amarna letters see Gianto 1994: 224, and in the Shechem letters see van der Westhuizen 2002: 20.

16. I have not provided a gloss here, because the use of (*k*) in this scenario is too infrequently attested (only here and in line 12) to draw definitive conclusions. For a few possible explanations of this occurrence of (*k*), see Krahmalkov 2000: 221; 2001: 286–87; *DNWSI* 482–83; and Schade 2006a: 171–74.

17. The text includes an extended noun phrase as subject preceding the relative clause and contains titles and patronymics, as well as the mention of Eshmunazor's mother.

18. Some commentators see similarities at this juncture with the beginning of the text (here, the reintroduction), because spaces for two or three letters separate the writing between this and the previous paragraph, working to mark a significant transition. Avishur (2000: 129) argued that this portion of the text was taken from a separate account. Parker (1999: 57–60) supported the unity of the text and attributed the new direction of the author to genre-mixing.

stand as the subjects of the relative clause, and a Focus seems apparent: they were the ones (and no one else) who built the listed objects. This interpretation seems supported by the following clauses in this paragraph, given in examples (6)–(7):

(6) Eshmunazor
w=ʾnḥn *ʾš* *bn-n*
and.CONJ=we.1CP.PRON.NOM who.REL built.1CP.PFV
'And we are the ones who built . . .' (*KAI* 14.16–17)

(7) Eshmunazor
w=ʾnḥn *ʾš* *bn-n*
and.CONJ=we.1CP.PRON.NOM who.REL built.1CP.PFV
'And we are the ones who built . . .' (*KAI* 14.17)

In both of these sequences, the plural pronoun is used to reference the king and his mother, who were just introduced by a singular pronoun and a noun. The pronouns are in the initial position of the clause and supply thematic information with Focus. Again, this highlights that Eshmunazor and his mother were the ones who built (and not anybody else).

A few more examples of subject fronting for reinvoking a character occur in the Azatiwada inscription (8):

(8) Azatiwada (second half eighth-century Phoenician)
w=ʾnk *ʾztwd*
and.CONJ= I.PRON.1CS Azatiwada.MS.NOM
št=nm *tḥt* *pʿm=y*
set.PERF.1CS=PRON.3MP under.PREP foot.DU.GEN=my.PRON.1CS
'Now I, Azatiwada, set them under my feet'. (*KAI* 26.I 16–17)

The fronted word order in (8) syntactically marks, or signals, a new unit of text. The previous clauses were dependent on the narrative infinitive as the main verb, a feature that is common in the Azatiwada inscription. Through fronting, Azatiwada is reintroduced (rhematic material) by name—a name that has not been mentioned since its introduction at the beginning of the inscription, five paragraphs earlier. There is also an element of Focus, because Azatiwada states that it was he, and no other, who was able to overcome the malefactors who had been causing so much trouble.[19] The contrast is heightened later in the paragraph when Azatiwada specifically states that he humbled lands that no king before him did. When syntactic and discourse functions are considered together, the complexity of their harmony is exactly what one would expect.

In the very next paragraph of Azatiwada's inscription (*KAI* 26.I 19–20), the subject-fronted construction occurs again (9):

(9) Azatiwada
w=ʾnk *ʾztwd*
and I.CONJ=PRON.1CS Azatiwada.MS.NOM
ʿn-t=nm
subdued.PFV.1CS=PRON.3MP
'Now I, Azatiwada, subdued them'. (*KAI* 26.I 19–20)

The fronted word order in (9) again marks a new syntactic unit, following a series of narrative infinitive clauses.[20] The fronted subject contains both a pronoun and the name of Azatiwada. As in the previous paragraph, there seems to be an element of Focus (he was the one, not anyone else, who subdued).[21] Additionally, through the use of the pronominal suffix, the reader is referred back to the previous paragraph, which describes Azatiwada subduing lands that no other king could. The subsequent material discussed in this unit of text deals specifically with movement and location: where Azatiwada settled those whom he subdued.[22]

19. I believe that the combination of the conjunction, pronoun, and the personal name would have made this contrast apparent in the intonation and intention of the text. Younger (*COS* 2.149) ultimately translates the opening conjunction 'But, I', highlighting this contrast.

20. Commenting on a similar phenomenon in BH, Heimerdinger (1999: 17) states, "Other clause types (subject-predicate clauses, for example) are most of the time situated at the margins of vayyiqtol clause clusters: their function is to indicate the boundaries of these clusters. Thus, clearly delinated episodes or paragraphs can be identified. The non-vayyiqtol clauses mark either episode onset, interruption or close out." In the Shechem letters, "Subject fronting facilitates two discourse functions, namely to highlight the identity of the subject and to mark a transition to a new subject matter in a discourse." (van der Westhuizen 2002: 4).

21. Younger (*COS* 2.149) again translates the initial conjunction with this contrast, "But I, Azatiwada, have humbled them."

22. Floor (2005: 26) states, "Topic [in this essay equated with Theme] is defined as the presupposed referent–already identifiable and activated–about which

Later on in the inscription, another fronted subject occurs (10):

(10) Azatiwada, III 7–8

w=ʿm	*z*	*ʾš*	*yšb*
and.CONJ=people.MS.NOM	this.DEM.MS	who.REL	dwell.MS.IPFV
b=n	*y-kn*	. . .	
in.PREP=it.3FS.PRON	be.3MS.JUSS		

'And may this people who dwell in it become . . .' .[23] (*KAI* 26.III 7–8

The rhematic subject in example (10) is fronted and syntactically marks a new unit of text. The preceding clauses of the previous paragraph were verb initial and concluded with the desire that the *city* become an owner of abundance. Thus, a new logical subject is introduced with the fronted constituent (*the people* living in the city). This complex subject is followed by a jussive verb form and a complement describing what the subject is to become.

Example (11) represents rhematic material being reintroduced for Focus:

(11) Kilamuwa (last half of ninth-century Samalian)

w=ʾnk	*klmw*	*br*	
but.CONJ=I.1CS.PRON.NOM	Kilamuwa.MS.NOM	son.MS.NOM.of	
tml	*m=ʾš*	*pʿl-t*	. . .[24]
TML.FS.GEN	what=which.REL	did.1CS.PFV	

'*But I, Kilamuwa, son of TML, what I did,* those before me did not do'. (*KAI* 24.4–5)

In (11), Kilamuwa is reintroduced by name (Rheme), and the name TML is also rhematic information. The naming of Kilamuwa at this juncture following the pronoun is no coincidence, and the Focus structure is presented in a logical order, because all of the individuals and

something new is asserted. The newly asserted information 'says something about' the topic in order to enrich it semantically. A topic is a topic when some new information is attributed to it." Though I define Topic differently, in the Azatiwada inscription subsequent paragraphs and material within paragraphs build on the preceding ones and tend to use fronting to initiate this process.

23. The text continues with a description of the people becoming owners of various objects.

24. The text follows with what Kilamuwa's predecessors did not do.

their failures with which Kilamuwa will be contrasted have been listed in the preceding lines of text, and the focused constituent follows here, introduced with the fronted word order.[25] The previous sentences listing his predecessors' failures are presented with a perfective verb + subject syntactic ordering, and the fronted construction cited above works to mark the end of the paragraph syntactically and pragmatically to Focus the contrasting accomplishments of Kilamuwa (a contrast that is explicitly stated in the text).

3.3. Thematic Subject Fronting

An instance of a fronted Theme (old information) occurs in the example from Eshmunazor given in example (12):

(12) Eshmunazor (fifth-century Sidonian)
k[26] *ʾnk* *n-ḥn*
I.1CS.PRON.NOM pitied.MS.PASS-PTCP
'I am to be pitied'. (*KAI* 14.12)

The fronted word order in (12) serves syntactically to mark a new unit of text. The previous paragraph consisted of curses (a different mood) that were conveyed by jussive verb forms. The fronted construction here functions pragmatically to isolate thematic material as Topic by the use of the pronoun, and a new logical subject is directly referenced (this is the first time Eshmunazor has been referred to directly since the introduction four paragraphs earlier, and the previous paragraph references individuals who will be cursed for opening up Eshmunazor's resting place).[27] The verb then supplies rhematic information.[28] It is possible that Focus is implied in the fronted subject, but there are no visible signs in the text of contrast or comparison with other individuals who are to be pitied, and Eshmunazor seems to hope that his readers will pity him.[29]

25. Younger (*COS* 2.147) also reflects the contrast in his translation, "But I . . ."
26. As with the occurrence of (*k*) in line 13 (see above, example [5]), I have omitted any gloss here.
27. It could be argued that the subject is rhematic information and that Eshmunazor is being reintroduced. However, this usually occurs with a proper name included in the text and with some element of Focus.
28. The rhematic information supplied by the verb is a crucial element here and provides the real intent of this unit.
29. The passive verb used here may also couch this nuance.

Below is another example of a fronted subject for Topic:

(13) Kilamuwa (last half of ninth-century Samalian)

w=kl *šlḥ* *yd*
and.CONJ=each.MS.NOM sent.3MS.PFV hand.FS.ACC
l=lḥm
to.PREP=consume.INF
'[The house of my father was in the midst of mighty kings,] *and each stretched forth a hand*[30] *to consume*'. (*KAI* 24.4–5)

The clause in (13) follows the mention of the house of Kilamuwa's father amid mighty kings. The fronted subject uses a general, singular designation to isolate each of the previously mentioned plural kings. It has thus become thematic information fronted for Topic, as each of the kings, one at a time, becomes subject to the verb.[31]

Later on in Kilamuwa's inscription (*KAI* 24.13), there are additional examples of subject fronting for Topic, as in example (14):

(14) Kilamuwa

w=ʾnk *tmk-t* *mškb-m*
and.CONJ=1CS.PRON.NOM took-1CS.PFV Mushkabim-MP.ACC
l=yd
by.PREP=hand.FS
'And I took the Mushkabim by the hand'. (*KAI* 24.13a)

In (14), the fronted subject introduces a new syntactic unit.[32] The pronoun isolates Kilamuwa as a thematic entity (the verb containing rhematic information) and constitutes a new logical subject from the previous material. The subsequent clause, given in example (15), then presents thematic material, the pronoun referring back to the Mushkabim. The constituent has been fronted for Topic, isolating it as the new subject (line 13).

30. It is possible that the 3MS pronoun is present here ("his hand").

31. The Kurkh Monolith, describing events from the reign of Shalmaneser III, offers some interesting insights into the way that this process of fighting and consuming may have unfolded among these kings. See Younger (*COS* 2.262) for a translation of the inscription and Schade (2006a: 91–97) for a few remarks on these conflicts.

32. Younger (*COS* 2.148) also distinguishes a new unit here.

(15) Kilamuwa
w=hmt *št* *nbš*
and.CONJ=3MP.PRON.NOM set.3MP.PFV soul.FS.ACC
'and they [the Mushkabim] showed a disposition [like the disposition of an orphan toward its mother]'. (*KAI* 24.13b)

These elements ultimately work together to form a chiastic/concentric pattern in the unit and describe a cause-and-effect relationship, with the fronted constituents playing a vital role in the process (Schade 2006a: 84–86).

One last example, (16), will demonstrate a fronted Theme for Topic:

(16) Ahirom (tenth-century Byblian)
w-hʾ *y-mḥ*
and.CONJ=he.3MS.PRON efface.3MS.IPFV/JUSS
spr=h . . .[33]
inscription.MS.NOM=his.GEN
'And as for him, may[34] his inscription be effaced'. (*KAI* 1.2)

If we accept this translation of the text, it seems necessary for *ymḥ* to be a passive verb, and *hʾ* would reference the possessive pronoun attached to *spr*—the subject of the verb. This would carry the nuance of the previous paragraph, which used *t*-stem forms. The Topic fronting here would isolate the thematic material that is referenced pronominally (any king, governor, or commander who should rise against Byblos and uncover Ahirom's sarcophagus, mentioned in the previous unit) and acts as a specific, new logical subject. As Topic, the subject is now isolated and begins this last unit of text in the inscription.

3.4. Fronted Direct Object as Thematic Topic

Clear cases of fronted direct objects occur less frequently, but example (17) is illustrative:

33. The last two words of the inscriptions are notoriously problematic and have been excluded here.

34. This translation is from McCarter (*COS* 2.181). This prefixed form may be a jussive (as is usually reflected in translations); however, a wish seems out of place here and this may be more an issue of epistemic modality with the imperfective verb ('shall efface').

(17) Azatiwada (second half eighth-century Phoenician)

w=dnny-m	*yšb-t*	*šm*
and.CONJ=Danunians-MP.ACC	settled.PFV.CAUS-1CS	there.ADV

'Now[35] the Danunians I had settled there'. (*KAI* 26.I 21–II 1)

The fronted direct object in (17) marks a new syntactic unit and serves the purpose of thematic Topic structure. The immediately preceding material had been highlighting the fact that Azatiwada had subdued bad men and leaders of gangs, he had subdued strong lands that other kings could not, and he had displaced and settled his opponents throughout his borders. It is at this point that the syntactically marked fronted direct object is introduced, and the Danunians are isolated as the ones being settled. The marked word order and the introduction of the topical direct object constitute a new unit in the text that subsequently describes the state of the Danunians living without fear in places that were formerly feared, as a result of the bad men, gangs, etc. (rhemetic material that builds upon the information already provided). Thus, the syntactically marked fronted word order is motivated to fulfill pragmatic purposes.

3.5. Fronted Adverbial Focus

There are a few instances in the Phoenician inscriptions where an adverb is used to provide Focus. Semantically, these adverbs provide focal nuances, and the fronted syntax in these occurrences is driven by pragmatic considerations.

(18) Azatiwada

ʾps	*šm*	*ʾztwd*	*y-kn*	. . .
only.ADV	name.MS.NOM	Azatiwada.MS.GEN	be.3MS.IPFV	

'Only the name of Azatiwada shall be. . .' .[36] (*KAI* 26.IV 1–2)

The fronted sentence in (18) concludes the inscription and follows a very complex paragraph that consists of an anterior construction with a protasis/apodasis and an extensive chiastic structure (see Schade 2005:

35. I have used 'now' in the translation to offer some sort of discourse beginning, which isolates the Danunians (and not some other group) that Azatiwada has settled there.

36. The text continues that only his name shall be "forever like the name of the sun and the moon."

53–56). That paragraph uses the conditional element "if" followed by the pronouncement of being effaced for breaking the prohibitions. The syntactically fronted construction here marks a new unit of text that has pragmatic Focus.[37] The subject (the focused constituent) follows the adverb used to set up this Focus, and it is only the name of Azatiwada, and no other name, that shall exist forever. In the previous paragraph, kings, people, and rulers were prohibited from removing Azatiwada's name, and the focal element associated with Azatiwada is an appropriate conclusion to the text and immortalizes his name (and no other).

In example (19), there is another example of the fronted adverbial used in Focus structure:

(19) Tabnit (early fifth-century Sidonian)

blt	*ʾnk*	*škb*	*b=ʾrn*
only.ADV	I.1CS.PRON.NOM	lie.MS.PTCP	in.PREP=sarcophagus

z
this.DEM.MS
'Only I lie in this sarcophagus'. (*KAI* 13.5)

The focused subject follows the adverb and highlights that nothing else lies in the coffin with Tabnit, and there is thus no need to disturb it. This sentence follows a paragraph that is directed at "whoever you are, any person" who might find the coffin, and contains a prohibition not to disturb the coffin because there is nothing valuable with it. The fronted constituents syntactically mark a new paragraph and pragmatically signal a new logical subject from information provided in the previous paragraph.[38] Rhematic material is then introduced after another prohibition, with religious connotations of infringing upon the tomb being described as "an abomination of Astarte."

3.6. Fronted Prepositional Phrases

Pragmatic influences can also be detected in the syntactic fronting of prepositional phrases. This phenomenon occurs in several different contexts, and the following examples are illustrative of this:

---

37. Younger (*COS* 2.150) also sees a break in the text here and describes this last sentence as a "Climactic Invocation."

38. Immediately preceding the fronting and marking of this new logical subject, there is a tripartite construction listing gold, silver, and any sort of riches. These items subsequently form a paradigmatic list where anabasis is present, thus offering a logical break in the text with the introduction of the new fronted subject.

(20) Azatiwada

w=b=rb-m	*y-ld*
and.CONJ.in.PREP=great.ADJ.MP	bear.3MS.JUSS
w=b=rb-m	*y-ʾdr*
and.CONJ.in.PREP=great.ADJ.MP	be.powerful.3MS.JUSS
w=b=rb-m	*y-ʿbd*
and.CONJ.in.PREP=great.ADJ.MP	serve.3MS.JUSS

'And may they abundantly bear children; and may they immensely become powerful; and may they greatly serve Azatiwada'. (*KAI* 26.III 9–10)

The tripartite series of fronted prepositional phrases in (20) can best be associated with thematic Topic. The previous sentence begins a new unit and consists of a fronted subject describing the people who live in the city becoming owners of livestock and abundance (expressed in the form of a wish employing the jussive).[39] Here the jussive verbs (which introduce rhematic material) are preceded by the prepositional phrases used adverbially, expressing quantitative measures. The subjects of the verbs are not referenced by name or pronominally and constitute thematic information. These prepositional phrases modify what the thematic subjects are going to do, isolating and quantitatively describing the desired outcome of the actions. The inscription is about Azatiwada's reversing the state and fate of the land, and here the fronted constituents quantify the greatness of the desired blessing invoked on the thematic individuals already activated (through fronting) in the paragraph. They are to prosper greatly in the wished endeavors, and it is concluded in the paragraph that this will occur "by the grace of Baal and the gods."

Example (21) is another prepositional phrase fronted for Topic, but Focus also seems to be involved:

(21) Azatiwada

w=b=ym-t=y	*ʾnk*
and.CONJ.in.PREP=days.MP=my.1CS.PRON	I.1CS.PRON.NOM

ʾšt	*tk*
woman.FS.NOM	walk.3FS.IPFV

'and in my very days a woman could walk alone'. (*KAI* 26.II 5)

39. See example (10).

In the clause in (21), there are multiple fronted constituents. The fronted prepositional phrase is a thematic Topic used to set the scene in time (Azatiwada's days). However, the suffixed, pronominal reference in conjunction with the independent personal pronoun seems to add an element of Focus: "it was in my very days" and not some other time.[40] The introduction of the woman being able to walk alone is for rhematic Focus and contrasts the environment where a man used to fear walking (mentioned in the previous clause).[41] This fronted subject is followed by a modal imperfective verb expressing ability and helps highlight the Focus contrast. The fronted syntax and change in aspect with modality also serve to mark the end of the syntactic unit. Again, syntactic variations and pragmatic functions work hand in hand in conveying certain nuances in the text.

In the next scenario, the fronted prepositional phrase conveys rhematic information and modifies what Azatiwada (referenced pronominally as the object of the verb) is to become:

(22) Azatiwada, I:12

w=ʾp	*b=ʾb-t*
and.CONJ=also.CONJ	in.PREP=fatherhood-FS.GEN

pʿl=n	*kl*	*mlk*
make.PFV.3MS=PRON.1CS	every.MS.NOM	king.MS.NOM

'And moreover, every king made me as a father' (*KAI* 26.I 12)

The fronted syntax in (22) marks a new unit and introduces a new logical subject, building upon the thematic material present in the rest of the clause.

(23) Eshmunazor

b=yrḥ	*bl*	. . .[42]	*dbr*
in.PREP=month.MS.GEN	Bul.MS.GEN		spoke.3MS.PFV

40. Younger's (*COS* 2.149) translation reflects such Focus: "But in my days, (especially) mine." Rather than just considering the focal element, I have attempted to describe the layers of the fronted constituents.

41. Kienast (2001: 314, 267.2a) describes the imperfective verb conveying this previous information as occurring in the durative.

42. The subsequent text contains an extended noun phrase describing the name of the king, his reign, and his patronymic.

mlk . . .
king.MS.NOM
'In the month of Bul . . . King Eshmunazor spoke . . .'.
(*KAI* 14.1–2)

In the opening line of this inscription, there are multiple fronted constituents. The prepositional phrase in (23) begins the text and then introduces Eshmunazor by name. This introduction provides all new information to the reader/listener (Rheme). The pragmatic feature that underlies this fronted prepositional phrase seems to be associated with providing a reference of time, a function that is generally associated with Topic fronting. When it comes to initiating a text with a date, this type of formulaic presentation of the prepositional phrase appears to be frozen in this syntactic position and pragmatically serves to situate the inscription in time.[43] The presentation of Eshmunzor by name then follows the general pattern of introductions in the inscriptional material.

4. *Genre of Dedicatory Inscriptions*

Situating dedicated objects in the initial position in the dedicatory portions of Phoenician inscriptions serves pragmatic features, and these objects seem to be syntactically frozen within the dedicatory formulas.[44] There are several examples of dedicatory inscriptions in the Phoenician corpus,[45] but I will use the following example as an illustration because it contains another fronted constituent in the text:

(24) Yeḥimilk (tenth-century Byblian)
bt *z=bny* *yḥmlk* . . .[46]
house.MS.NOM that.REL.built.3MS.PFV Yeḥimilk.MS.NOM
'Temple that Yehimilk, [king of Byblos,] built'. (*KAI* 4.1)

Syntactically, the dedication in (24) begins with the object that is being dedicated in the initial position. Because this is a dedication, the

43. The introduction of Phoenician inscriptions with the use of a prepositional phrase associated with time reference is not common, but it does occur in other ancient Near Eastern inscriptions. Syntactically frozen positioning in the genre of dedicatory inscriptions will also be discussed in §4.

44. For a treatment on dedicatory inscriptions, see Lewis 1989: 76.

45. See, for example, *KAI* 1, 5, 6, 7.

46. The title 'king of Byblos' follows here.

object holds a place of prominence, and its initial positioning draws the reader's attention directly toward it. This clause occurs at the beginning of the inscription, so the information is rhematic. What is of particular importance about this inscription occurs in the next clause and offers us clues in the use of fronted constructions, syntax, and information structure. Consider (25):

(25) Yeḥimilk
hʾt *ḥwy* *kl* *mpl-t*
he.3MS.PRON.NOM restore.3MS.PFV all.MS.ACC ruin-FP.ACC
h=bt-m *ʾl*
the.ART=temple-MP.GEN these.DEM.MP
'he restored all the ruins of these temples'. (*KAI* 4.2–3)

The fronted subject in (25) presents the thematic Focus, highlighting with pronominal reference the rhematic information supplied in the previous clause. Here Yeḥimilk is focused as the one who restored the temples, the emphasis on the doer rather than the object.[47] The clauses in (24)–(25) subsequently combine to form a chiastic/concentric pattern (see Schade 2006b: 119–22), where the Focus constituent begins the inversion of the chiastic structure.[48] This coordination of pragmatically driven syntactic fronting across clauses demonstrates that literary style is not the constructing force behind the development of a text but that literary structure is formed by drawing upon syntactic and pragmatic features available to the author. All of these elements should work cooperatively and should be examined interdependently when one works with the texts.

5. Other Fronting Triggers

The conditional conjunction 'if' (*ʾm*) is syntactically restricted to the initial position in the clause. It may occur multiple times in a paragraph, and its first occurrence tends to mark a new unit of text syntactically.[49] In the earlier Phoenician inscriptions, "if" and other conditional

47. The intonation of the reader/listener may have accentuated this.

48. In the chiastic structure, the fronted objects (the temple and Yeḥimilk) are assigned positions that help accentuate their relevance in the text and place them in elevated areas of importance on par with one another (object and doer).

49. Conditional clauses marked with "if" generally occur in the protasis and are followed by an apodasis.

conjunctions are generally followed by other fronted constituents. Consider example (26):[50]

(26) Azatiwada

w=ʾm	*mlk* . . .[51]	*ʾš*	*y-mḥ* . . .
and.CONJ=if.CONJ	king.MS.NOM	who.REL	efface.3MS.IPFV

'*Now, if there is a king* [among kings or a ruler among rulers, if there is a man who is a person of name] *who might efface* . . .' . (*KAI* 26.III 12–13)

The unit of text prior to (26) contained jussive verbs and desired wishes to be brought upon the dwellers in the city. The trigger 'if' in (26) syntactically marks a new unit,[52] and the fronted subject explicitly introduces a new logical subject and rhematic material. What is insightful about the use of this trigger in the text is that it occurs again in the next sentence with an implicit subject, still referencing the material just introduced. The very next time this trigger is used (it occurs twice), it is followed by another fronted constituent:

(27) Azatiwada

ʾm	*b=ḥmd*	*y-sʿ*
if.CONJ	from.PREP=desire.MS.GEN	remove.3MS.IPFV

'If out of desire he should remove . . .' . (*KAI* 26.III 17a)

The fronted prepositional phrase in (27) is used as thematic Topic highlighting the motivation for removing Azatiwada's gate and name. Previously, the fronted construction was associated with the subject; here the emphatic nature revolves around the action of the doer. This pattern follows in the next clause, given in example (28):

50. I will only provide a few illustrative examples. Conditional clauses are quite common in Phoenician inscriptions, and their complexity and volume require an extensive treatment of their own. The examples I provide here only begin to explain the syntactic and pragmatic features that come into play in conditional clauses. These clause types are generally prohibitions, injunctions, or warnings with consequences, all of which contain a protasis and an apodasis. In Schade 2008, I proposed the possibility of a subjunctive form that is used in conditional clauses where a protasis and apodasis are present.

51. An extended noun phrase as subject occurs here preceding the relative clause.

52. Younger (*COS* 2.150) also sees a marked unit here.

(28) Azatiwada
ʾm *b=šnʾt*
if.CONJ from.PREP=hate.FS.GEN
w=b=rʿ *y-sʿ*
and.CONJ=from.PREP=malice.MS.GEN remove.3MS.IPFV
'If out of hate or malice he should remove . . .' . (*KAI* 26.III 17b)

Again, this is an element of Topic fronting associated with what the individual is doing (the motivations), not focusing on the individual. Subsequently, this entire paragraph forms a complex chiastic pattern executed by drawing on the aforementioned syntactic and pragmatic features (see Schade 2005: 53–57).

In the examples of the trigger "if" in (26)–(28), each case had additional fronted constituents. In later texts, this is not always the case, as seen in (29)–(30):

(29) Yeḥawmilk
w=ʾm *ʾbl* *t-št*
and.CONJ=if.CONJ not.NEG set.2MS.IPFV
'And if you should not set . . .' . (*KAI* 10.13)

(30) Tabnit (early fifth-century Sidonian)
w=ʾm *ptḥ* *t-ptḥ*
and.CONJ=if.CONJ open.INF.ABS open.2MS.IPFV
ʿlt=y
upon.PREP=me.1CS.PRON
'And if you open up upon me . . .' . (*KAI* 13.6–7)

In both of these examples, the conditional conjunction helps mark a new unit of text. In the former example, the conditional clause appears in the protasis, and in the latter, the clause is anterior to the negative jussive expressing desire.

Another fronting trigger is the use of the interrogative in prohibitions, curses, blessings, and injunctions. When this fronted constituent occurs it constitutes an anterior element relative to the prohibition/blessing. It may occur as the subject preceding a relative clause, and/or as the fronted referent of a prohibition. The initial location of the interrogative and the fronted construction marks a syntactic and pragmatic signal that a new unit, with a new logical subject (often introducing new rhematic material) has been set in place. Consider the following representative examples in (31)–(33):

(31) Eshmunazor

qnmy	*ʾt*	. . .[53] *ʾl*
whoever.INTERR	you.2MS.PRON.NOM	not.NEG
y-ptḥ	*ʿlt=y*	
open.3MS.IPFV/JUSS	upon.PREP=me.1CS.PRON	

'Whoever you are . . . do not open upon me . . .' . (*KAI* 14.4, 20)

The interrogative trigger marks a syntactic break in the text, a shift to a prohibition (mood), and introduces a new logical subject in relation to the previous material.

(32) Yeḥawmilk

qnmy	*ʾt*	. . .[54] *ʾš*
whoever.INTERR	you.2MS.PRON.NOM	who.REL
y-sp	. . .	
multiply.3MS.IPFV		

'Whoever you are . . . who might continue . . .' . (*KAI* 10.11)

The trigger marks a syntactic break in the text, shifts the mood from a previous paragraph that contained wishes expressed by means of jussive verb forms to an injunction expressed with the modal imperfective, and introduces a new logical subject.

Following this complex subject, and additionally preceding the main verbal clause, the direct object is also fronted for Topic in conjunction with the injunction to include the king's name with any additional work that is done to the temple complex:

(33) Yeḥawmilk

šm	*ʾnk*	*yḥwmlk*	*mlk*
name.MS.ACC	I.PRON.1CS	Yeḥawmilk.MS	king.MS

53. More referents (any king or any person) follow in the text.

54. More referents (any king or any person) follow in the text. I am using *qnmy ʾt* here–a restoration of a damaged portion of the inscription that was adopted by Prof. Peckham and that we worked with as his students.

gbl *t-št* *ʾt=k*
Byblos.FS.GEN set.2MS.IPFV with.PREP=you.2MS.PRON
'My very name, Yeḥawmilk, king of Byblos, you shall set with you'. (*KAI* 10.12–13)

The fact that the king mentions setting his name "with you" seems to exclude the possibility of Focus fronting and solidifies the interpretation of Topic, because the king's name is isolated through fronting.

The interrogative (*my*) 'who' also marks new syntactic units and introduces new logical subjects, and in most cases, changes mood in relation to adjacent material.[55] Note the following case in point in (34):

(34) Tabnit
my *ʾt* . . .[56] *ʾl* *ʾl*
whoever.INTERR you.2MS.PRON not.NEG not.NEG
t-ptḥ *ʿlt=y*
open.2MS.IPFV upon.PREP=me.1CS.PRON
'Whoever you are . . . do not open up upon me . . .'. (*KAI* 13.3–4)

The fronted constituents in example (34) mark a new unit of text that contains rhematic information and a new logical subject, and they introduce a new mood from previous material.

6. The Subordinating Conjunction (*k*)

Beyond the brief comments provided below, I will not include the subordinating conjunction (*k*) in this study because it does not always "trigger" fronted word order. When fronted elements do follow the conjunction (*k*) the driving force appears to be more pragmatic than syntactic, and pragmatic factors can be detected. Note the following examples:

(35) Azatiwada
k *bʿl* *w=ršp*
because.CONJ Baal.MS.NOM and.CONJ=Rešep.MS.NOM
ṣpr-m *šlḥ=n*
stags-MP.GEN send.PFV.3MP=me.PRON.1CS

55. *my* ('who') can occur in parallel with other clauses initiated by this word. See, for example, *KAI* 24.11–12, 13–15; and 13.3.

56. Another referent occurs in the text here.

'because Baal and Rešep of the stags sent me'. (*KAI* 26.II 10–11)

In the subordinate clause in (35), a causal relationship is formed in the text. Azatiwada is attributing his success to being sent by the gods. The names of the deities are fronted and constitute rhematic material. This fronted construction not only introduces these gods into the text, it highlights them as the senders whose power underlies Azatiwada's actions and establishes his legitimacy. An element of Focus is thus present.

In the next example, (36), the Topic is fronted with a prepositional phrase, setting the scene in the time of Azatiwada's days.

(36) Azatiwada

k	*b=ym-t=y*	*kn*
because.CONJ	in.PREP=days.MP.GEN=my.1CS.PRON	be.3MS.PFV
l=ʾrṣ	*ʿmq*	*ʾdn*
for.PREP=land.FS.GEN	valley.MS.GEN	Adana.MS.GEN

'because there was in my days for the land of the valley of Adana'. (*KAI* 26.II 15–16)

In (36), there is additionally an element of Focus inherent in the suffix pronoun. In the previous material, Azatiwada describes all the good that he has accomplished, as well as the benefits he has brought to the land. Here the fronted word order reiterates this focal element–that it was in *his days* that this was achieved.

7. *Conclusion*

In the course of this essay, I have examined fronted word order, simultaneously considering both the syntactic and the pragmatic functions underlying this phenomenon. I have concluded that syntax and pragmatics work cooperatively to convey and establish the information structure of Phoenician inscriptional material. Too often examinations of inscriptions are subjective, and opinions vary when solely based on subject matter. When syntax and discourse features align, we are left with a more accurate reading of a text, and we more clearly perceive the nuances intended by the original author. Within the inscriptions, fronted subjects frequently mark new syntactic units, and often introduce (or reintroduce) information that is fronted for Focus contrast–or in the case of thematic material, fronted for Topic. The fronted constituent is thus intentional and is a syntactic descriptor motivated by pragmatic features.

In the inscriptions, we also witness fronted prepositional phrases, adverbs, and direct objects. In each instance, one can detect layers of Rheme and Theme; and often in conjunction with these elements, Focus or Topic. In a significant number of these occurrences, the fronted constituent is instrumental in marking the onset of a new syntactic unit or its conclusion. Other "triggers" such as conditional conjunctions also often carry fronted constituents and syntactic significance. In the case of subordinate clauses where fronting occurs, the fronted item seems to be more a function of pragmatics, because (*k*), for example, does not always trigger fronted word order. In dedicatory inscriptions, the dedicated objects appear to be syntactically set in the initial position of the clause, and the information structure aligns with the rules of pragmatics outlined in this paper. Taking all things into consideration, the simultaneous precision, accuracy, and alignment of syntax and discourse factors in the inscriptions are astounding and leave little doubt that authors carefully crafted the texts, hoping that their readers would comprehend the nuances of the intended meaning and intentions of their compositions.

Bibliography

Avishur, Y.
2000 *Phoenician Inscriptions and the Bible: Select Inscriptions and Studies in Stylistic and Literary Devices Common to the Phoenician Inscriptions and the Bible.* Tel Aviv–Jaffa: Archaeological Center Publication.

Bandstra, B.
1992 Word Order and Emphasis in Biblical Hebrew Narrative: Syntactic Observations on Genesis 22 from a Discourse Perspective. Pp. 109–24 in *Linguistics and Biblical Hebrew*, ed. W. R. Bodine. Winona Lake, IN: Eisenbrauns.

Buth, R.
1990 Word Order Differences between Narrative and Non-narrative Material in Biblical Hebrew. Pp. 9–16 in *Proceedings of the 10th World Congress of Jewish Studies*, Division D, vol. 1: *The Hebrew Language – Jewish Languages*, ed. D. Assaf. Jerusalem: World Union of Jewish Studies.

DeCaen, V.
1995 *On the Placement and Interpretation of the Verb in Standard Biblical Hebrew Prose.* Ph.D. dissertation, University of Toronto.

Eskhult, M.

1992 Text Structure in Focus: A Discussion of Alviero Niccacci's *Lettura sintattica della prosa ebraico-biblica*. *OrSuec* 40: 95–101.

Floor, S. J.

2003 From Word Order to Theme in Biblical Hebrew Narrative: Some Perspectives from Information Structure. *JS* 12: 197–236.

2005 Poetic Fronting in a Wisdom Poetry Text: The Information Structure of Proverbs. *JNSL* 31: 23–58.

Friedrich, J., and Röllig, W.

1999 *Phönizisch-Punische Grammatik*. 3rd ed. by M. G. Amadasi Guzzo with W. R. Mayer. AnOr 55. Rome: Pontifical Biblical Institute.

Gianto, A.

1994 Subject Fronting in the Jerusalem Amarna Letters. *Or* 63: 209–25.

Heimerdinger, J. M.

1999 *Topic, Focus and Foreground in Ancient Hebrew Narratives*. JSOTSup 295. Sheffield: Sheffield Academic Press.

Holmstedt, R. D.

2003 Adjusting Our Focus (review of Katsuomi Shimasaki, *Focus Structure in Biblical Hebrew: A Study of Word Order and Information Structure*). *HS* 44: 203–15.

2005 Word Order in the Book of Proverbs. Pp. 135–54 in *Seeking Out the Wisdom of the Ancients: Essays Offered to Honor Michael V. Fox on the Occasion of His Sixty-Fifth Birthday*, ed. R. L. Troxel, K. G. Friebel, and D. R. Magary. Winona Lake, IN: Eisenbrauns.

2009 Word Order and Information Structure in Ruth and Jonah: A Generative-Typological Analysis. *Journal of Semitic Studies* 54 (1):111–39.

Joüon, P.

1923 *Grammaire de l'hébreu biblique*. Rome: Pontifical Biblical Institute.

Kienast, B.

2001 *Historische Semitische Sprachwissenschaft*. Wiesbaden: Harrassowitz.

Krahmalkov, Charles R.

2000 *Phoenician-Punic Dictionary*. OLA 90. Studia Phoenicia 15. Leuven: Peeters.

2001 *A Phoenician-Punic Grammar*. HOSNME 54. Leiden: Brill.

Lewis, T. J.

1989 *Cults of the Dead in Ancient Israel and Ugarit*. HSM 39. Atlanta: Scholars Press.

Merwe, C. H. J. van der

1991 The Function of Word Order in Old Hebrew with Special Reference to Cases Where Syntagmeme Precedes a Verb in Joshua. *JNSL* 17: 129–44.

1999a Towards a Better Understanding of Biblical Hebrew Word Order. *JNSL* 25: 277–300.

1999b Explaining Fronting in Biblical Hebrew. *JNSL* 25: 173–86.

Merwe, C. H. J. van der, and Talstra, E.
2002–3 Biblical Hebrew Word Order: The Interface of Information Structure and Formal Features. *ZAH* 15–16: 68–107.
Moshavi, A.
2006 The Discourse Functions of Object/Adverbial-Fronting in Biblical Hebrew. Pp. 231–45 in *Biblical Hebrew in Its Northwest Semitic Setting: Typological and Historical Perspectives*, ed. S. Fassberg and A. Hurvitz. Jerusalem: Magnes / Winona Lake, IN: Eisenbrauns.
Myhill, J.
1995 Non-Emphatic Fronting in Biblical Hebrew. *TL* 21: 93–144.
O'Connor, M.
2002 Discourse Linguistics and the Study of Biblical Hebrew. Pp. 17–42 in *IOSOT Congress Volume: Basel 2001*, ed. A. Lemaire. VTSup 92. Leiden: Brill.
Parker, S. B.
1999 The Composition and Sources of Some Northwest Semitic Royal Inscriptions. *SEL* 16: 49–62.
Schade, A.
2005 A Text Linguistic Approach to the Syntax and Style of the Phoenician Inscription of Azatiwada. *JSS* 50: 35–58.
2006a *A Syntactic and Literary Analysis of Ancient Northwest Semitic Inscriptions.* Lewiston, NY: Edwin Mellen.
2006b The Syntax and Literary Structure of the Phoenician Inscription of Yeḥimilk. *Maarav* 13: 119–24.
2008 Modal Prefixed Verb Forms in Phoenician: Pragmatic and Syntactic Considerations. Paper presented at the annual meeting of the Society of Biblical Literature. Boston, November 22.
Talstra, E.
1999 Reading Biblical Hebrew Poetry: Linguistic Structure or Rhetorical Device? *JNSL* 25: 101–26.
Westhuizen, J. P. van der
2002 Subject Fronting in the Shechem Letters. *JS* 11: 1–22.

The "Narrative Infinitive" in Phoenician and Its Background: A Discourse Analysis Approach

Andrés Piquer Otero

1. Introduction

In this paper, I will examine the use of the infinitive as the main verb in a sentence in narrative textual units in the Phoenician corpus.[1] The construction has been extensively studied in Phoenician and in other Semitic languages (Ugaritic, Biblical Hebrew, Amarna Canaanite),[2] but it still offers notable difficulties, both formal (problems to isolate forms due to the lack of vocalization) and functional (the absence of a precise definition of the opposition between infinitive and other possible narrative forms (perfective and imperfective).[3]

Considering this difficulty in proceeding on a purely morphological and morphosyntactic basis, my approach will apply the methodology

Author's note: The research leading to this paper has been produced within a Juan de la Cierva Research Contract funded by the Spanish Ministerio de Educación y Ciencia. It is part of the activity of the National R+D Project AUTHOR–Análisis Unificado de Textos Hebreos por Ordenador–directed by Prof. Luis Vegas Montaner at Universidad Complutense de Madrid.

1. Imperative or jussive uses will not be treated in this paper. See Krahmalkov 2001: 210–14; Segert 1976: 197).

2. Many are the studies and grammar that describe the phenomenon in Biblical Hebrew. See, for example, Meyer 1992: 403–7. The situation in Ugaritic is described in Sivan 1997: 123–26, and more extensively in Tropper 2000: 491–93. Cases in the Amarna Tablets were treated by W. L. Moran in several publications and have, more recently, been revisited systematically in Rainey 1996: 381–88.

3. I am adopting the perfective-imperfective terminology as a convenient and economic tool for referencing forms throughout the paper. This should not imply that my proposal espouses a particular tense or aspect value for the perfective-imperfective opposition. The reader may assume a formal equivalence between my use of perfective and "Suffix Conjugation" and imperfective and "Prefix Conjugation." Cases where the terms are applied in an explicit aspectual sense will be clearly commented on in the text.

of discourse analysis to a series of Phoenician inscriptions in which a "narrative" use of the infinitive has been traditionally detected in order to define its typological context(s). My categories of analysis derive from Niccacci's application of discourse analysis to Biblical Hebrew (see Niccacci 1986)[4] and follow the system I outlined in my discourse analysis-based study of the Ugaritic *Baal Cycle* (Piquer Otero 2007). Additionally, one of the problems that a typological analysis of Phoenician literature poses is the comparative dearth of different text types, given the stereotypical nature of royal inscriptions. Therefore, the analysis of Phoenician "narrative infinitive" uses will be complemented with a brief comparative study of other Northwest Semitic languages, Ugaritic and Amarna Canaanite.[5]

2. *"Narrative Infinitive" as a Category?*

Even without an explicit "narrative infinitive" label, Phoenician grammatical works present comments and explanations on the uses of the Infinitive Absolute that imply typological and supra-sentence structural concerns that are familiar to the discourse analysis methodology. For example, Segert (1976: 197) comments that the structure InfAbs-X "is used in the narrative sections of the royal inscriptions." Krahmalkov (2001: 211) speaks only of "past perfective": "[The perfective is] restricted to non sentence-initial position"; "[the infinitive absolute] was restricted to sentence-initial position" (see also 2001: 294). Krahmalkov (2001: 210) includes another category, "consecutive" infinitive, which must follow a previous sentence with a past perfective verb. This interest in word order and complementation/contrast relationships between sentences parallels the typical interests of discourse analysis approaches, though Krahmalkov does not explicitly adopt this methodology.

3. *Methodology: Applications of Discourse Analysis*

Considering these statements, I feel that some syntactic issues would benefit from that systematic application of a discourse analysis–

4. My typological classification of text types follows Longacre 1989.

5. Biblical Hebrew will be left out due to space concerns and the need for a particular methodological approach motivated by the variety of typological contexts and the additional challenge posed by the vocalization system. Adequate research into Biblical Hebrew uses should critically assess the Masoretic system, instead of simply accepting it as a basis for a syntactical study.

based methodology, which has already proven productive in the case of other Northwest Semitic languages, such as Biblical Hebrew and, more recently, Ugaritic (Greenstein 2006; Piquer Otero 2007). In the case of Phoenician, recent work by Aaron Schade (2005; 2006) has shown the value of a supra-sentence text-based analysis of Northwest Semitic inscriptions.

In the next three subsections, I will briefly outline the main methodological analysis elements of my approach. As in my study of the Ugaritic *Baal Cycle*, I will operate on two levels: a typological definition of text sections and a formal analysis (including word order) of the sentence structures used in different contexts (unit-opening, development, and closing). Finally, a cross-comparison of functional and formal data will hopefully lead to some conclusions on how sentences (and the verbal forms in them) function in a given text-type. The ultimate aim of these notes is to complement the observations of traditional "paradigmatic" grammars with a non-aprioristic survey of verbal usage in the texts themselves.

3.1. Main Line versus "Comment"

One of the basic concepts in discourse analysis as applied to Biblical Hebrew is the opposition between the "main line" of a text and a "comment."[6] The former presents the actions or statements by which the text advances; the latter introduces additional information that completes and nuances main line sentences but does not necessarily contribute to moving the action forward. Of course, in order to determine what constitutes the main line and the comment, a semantic (and literary) study of the text in question should be carried out in conjunction with a formal analysis. Main lines will be easier to establish in text-types that are organized through a sequential arrangement of actions (see below). As for comment, it should be distinguished from mere subordinate clauses: although a subordinate clause will act as a form of comment on the main sentence, not all comments require grammatical subordination (with or without particles). A series of sentences that takes place in the *background* (versus the *foreground* of the main line) would be a comment, even without any subordinate particle present.

6. See the formulation of the concept in Niccacci 1986: 14–21. Niccacci, nevertheless, speaks mostly of "narrative" versus "comment," because he does not develop a detailed text-type division according to functional typology.

3.2. *Text Types*

In the proposed typological classification that I have adopted (detailed in Piquer Otero 2007: 497–501), texts are divided in two main groups: narrative and direct speech discourse.[7] Narrative here is understood as a 3rd-person presentation of events by a narrator who stands outside the action presented in the text (with the possible exception of brief comments). Direct speech discourse is defined as the presentation of an utterance by a character identified explicitly within the text.[8] Direct speech discourse can be further divided according to the prevalent function of communication within a section: *Narrative Discourse* presents a series of events that took place in the past from the point of view of the speaker; *Predictive Discourse*, on the other hand, transmits events which, according to the speaker, will happen in the future; *Hortative Discourse* tries to elicit a response from the speaker's audience (expressions of commands, wishes, and so on are clear instances of this category); finally, *Expositive Discourse* introduces sentences in which the identification between an action or quality and its subject/actor takes priority over the presentation of actions as such. In sentence-level syntax, this function would be clearly associated with the nominal clause. In the field of Northwest Semitic literary materials, proclamations of all kinds (royalty, divinity) are stereotyped instances of Expositive Discourse. There is a certain degree of overlap within direct speech discourse types (for example, between Predictive and Hortative Discourse), but a primary semantic distinction may be based on the degree of sequential organization of the actions within the text (see Piquer Otero 2007: 566–69): Expositive Discourse presents statements in which a time-based sequence is not a priority element. Predictive and narrative texts seem to have a considerable degree of sequential organization. Hortative Discourse falls somewhere in between (commands, for instance, may or may not need to be fulfilled in a particular order). Finally Narrative Discourse has proven to be a complex category when one studies its sequential valence in Ugaritic texts: in some cases, it seems to be structured with sequential premises analogous to narrative

7. For a detailed presentation, see also Longacre 1989: 80–136. An up-to-date commentary on Longacre's textual typology can be found in Heller 2004.

8. In the application of this typology to narrative poems such as the *Baal Cycle* or certain Biblical Hebrew texts, this would be the direct speech by the characters within a story. In the Phoenician corpus, utterances by a named individual (identified as such within the inscription) would fall in the same category.

texts and to Predictive Discourse, while in others, it seems to be made of nonsequential series of actions.[9]

3.3. Textual Units, Clause Schemata, and Sentence Structures

A composition can be further divided into *sections* (mostly through contents and functionality, although formal markers can be parsed through analysis). Sections, in turn, are made up of *units*. These units can be delineated according to the context of the sentences that compose them: *opening* (or introduction), *development* (in the central part), and *closing*. A thorough analysis of a corpus can unveil patterns in the construction of each type:[10] whereas *development* constructions tend to follow the basic or default sentence structure for the text type in question, both opening and closing constructions are usually marked formally and functionally.[11] If one adds to this the different structures that mark a breach in the main line of discourse in order to introduce a comment (see above) within the unit, whether contrastive, backgrounding, or some other type, the analysis of a textual section involves defining and detecting a series of different *sentence structures* that may be correlated with different functions within the text. These structures can be simple (one sentence type, which can be repeated to form a multisentence series) or complex. Complex structures called *clause schemata* are made up of two or more sentence structures of a given type (or types) that appear together in a given functional context. A clear instance of a clause schema would be protasis-apodosis constructions.

Clearly, in the analysis of sentence structures, attention must be paid to *word order*. Traditionally, word order has been connected to rhetoric or poetic considerations and only recently has begun to be analyzed

9. Further research in this direction is marred by the dearth of Narrative Discourse sections in the Ugaritic corpus. In this sense, a comparative typological study with Phoenician can be elucidating for both languages, because according to the classification above, a large proportion of texts in Phoenician inscriptions would comprise Narrative Discourse sections (see below).

10. An extensive application of this parsing can be found in Piquer Otero 2007: 501–658. In the Phoenician (and other Northwest Semitic inscriptions) corpus, a remarkable instance of grammatical analysis performed in conjunction with textual sections and context can be found in Schade 2006.

11. Marking of beginnings and endings of textual sections has traditionally been acknowledged in grammars of Northwest Semitic languages and has occasionally posed as an explanation for "irregular" uses of verbal forms or word order, even though these instances have usually been studied from the point of view of rhetorics ("emphasis") and not as syntactic phenomena. See, for example, Tropper (2000: 706) on the opening, closing, and backgrounding use of the perfective.

as a syntactically relevant element.[12] In the application of discourse analysis to Biblical Hebrew (and Ugaritic), two concepts have proven useful in sentence analysis: focusing (placement of an element in the initial position of a sentence) and "complex nominal sentences." Formally, both structures imply a nominal element + verb word order (in contrast to the verb + nominal element order of the verbal sentence). Semantically and functionally, the difference between them would lie in the identification value of the nominal sentence (see Niccacci 1986: 103–6, 112–13; Piquer Otero 2007: 96–97): "It is [nominal element X] who performs [verbal action Y]." Focusing, on the other hand, does not imply a departure from verbal action series, and the position of a non-verbal element[13] in the initial position of the sentence contributes to the articulation of textual transitions, usually marking the beginning of a new unit by introducing a relevant element for the beginning textual section (main actor, a change in point of view or temporal-spatial circumstances, and others). It is evident that at times it will be problematic to determine the functional analysis when one is faced with an X + Verb structure in a given text. In these cases, the context must be examined carefully and the nominal/adverbial element carefully considered. Usually, an initial focus affects the whole unit it introduces, whereas the first element of a complex nominal sentence is more strictly bound to its verb on a one-on-one relationship.

4. The Selected Corpus

The previous paragraphs have introduced basic concepts for a discourse analysis approach to ancient Northwest Semitic texts. I will try to make the theory clearer by analyzing relevant texts for the "narrative" infinitive uses in Phoenician. In this, I will follow the inventory proposed by Krahmalkov for instances of "past perfect periphrastic" usage (Krahmalkov 2001: 211): the royal Kilamuwa inscription (*KAI* 24); the royal Azatiwada inscription (*KAI* 26); and two Byblian texts, the royal

12. Even discourse analysis scholars initially expressed some reluctance to apply their methodologies to poetic texts, thinking that "poetic phenomena" (emphasis, chiasmus, or parallelism) could mar the efforts of sentence structure parsing. See Niccacci 1986: 114–18; and compare with the more positive approach of Niccacci 2001.

13. Nominal (or pronominal) focuses are frequent, but a focused structure can also be constructed with adverbial elements or with a whole clause (initial comment, according to discourse analysis parsing) that will carry out the adverbial focus function. See the more detailed treatment of opening focused structures in Piquer Otero 2007: 522–42.

son of Sipitbaal inscription (*KAI* 9), and the royal Yehawmilk inscription (*KAI* 10).[14] For each text, I will illustrate how a discourse analysis approach to the use of infinitive clauses can contribute to a better understanding of this construction.

5. *Analysis of Phoenician Texts*

As mentioned above, I will proceed to a detailed presentation of InfAbs usage in four testimonies of Phoenician literature, that have been singled out as containing narrative usage of the infinitive in Krahmalkov 2001. Although there is no space for fully detailing the contextual framework of these clauses within the whole of each inscription, some cross-section discussion is needed. In this, I am greatly indebted to the detailed presentation of Schade 2006, which covers the Kilamuwa, Azatiwada, and Yeḥawmilk texts.

*5.1. The Kilamuwa Inscription (*KAI *24)*

Morphological analysis of the verbal forms in this inscription is a typical instance of the inherent difficulties in the parsing of infinitive forms as opposed to uses of the perfective. In this text, Schade's analysis presents a single case of the infinitive as the main verb of a sentence (2006: 69–70), whereas Krahmalkov's (2001: 211–12) survey includes quite a few more cases.[15] It is not coincidental that the disputed cases are sentences with a 3rd-person subject (explicit or not), whereas the only certain use of the infinitive appears with a 1st-person subject (lines 7–8).[16] The latter case will be examined in detail, beginning with example (1):

14. The construction is also attested once in a literary Punic text, the entrance monologue of Hanno in *Poenulus* 5.940–46a (the infinitive form appears in 942). Though interesting for a study of the syntactic structure, genre and chronology considerations present a considerable challenge for integrating this evidence with the other epigraphic materials. Therefore, the text will not be included in this survey, since it deserves its own full study. See Krahmalkov 1971; 1988; Gatwick 1971.

15. Basically the bulk of sentence-initial verbal forms in lines 2, 5–6. Krahmalkov's analysis of perfective forms is restricted to noninitial verbs ("Past Perfective III") or to "consecutive" verbs (which can appear clause-initially and continue a previous main declarative sentence). Evidently, the determination of "main" versus "consecutive" sentences cannot be achieved by pure formal analysis but requires a functional-discursive survey of the texts in question.

16. I have not pursued the possibility of a participle analysis. Though formally possible, the usage as a circumstantial clause would be quite rare in the context of the introduction of a new discourse actor (expressed as the 1cs pronoun.)

(1) Segment 4 (in Schade 2006)

wʾdr *ʿl=y* *mlk*
and=get.power.PERF.3MS over=PRON.3MS king.MS.NOM
dnnym ***w=skr*** ***ʾnk*** ***ʿl=y***
Danunian-MP.GEN and=hire.INF.ABS PRON.1CS over=PRON.3MS
mlk ***ʾšr*** *ʿlm-t* *y-tn*
king.MS.ACC Aššur.MS.GEN slave-FS.ACC give-IPFV.3MS
b=š *w=gbr* *b=sw-t*
for=sheep.MS.GEN and=man.MS.ACC for=garment-FS.GEN
'And the king of the Danunians obtained power over it; but I hired against him the king of Assyria; a slave girl he would give for a sheep, a man for a garment'. (*KAI* 24.7–8)

Accepting Schade's analysis of the passage, example (1) would constitute, in terms of textual typology, an instance of Narrative Discourse: Kilamuwa is the speaker (the self-reference is clear in *wskr ʾnk*). The discourse is carried over from the previous section, segment 3, lines 5–7, but here there is a contrastive change of actor/point of view, from Kilamuwa's father's house to the king of the Danunians (Schade 2006: 77). This is marked by the w-PERF X (new subject) structure. It is also noteworthy that there is a fundamental semantic change between segment 3 and segment 4: whereas segment 4 (my example [1]) presents *actions* (hence the Narrative Discourse proposed typology), segment 3 (my example [2]) has a prevalence of *states* (marked in bold):

(2) Segment 3 (in Schade 2006)

kn ***bt*** ***ʾb=y***
be.PERF.3MS house.MS.NOM father.MS.GEN=PRON.1CS
b=mtk-t ***mlk-m*** ***ʾdr-m*** *w=kl*
in=midst-FS.GEN king-MP.GEN powerful.MP.GEN and=all.NOM
šlḥ *yd* *l=lḥm* ***w=k-t***
send.PERF.3CP hand.FS.ACC to=fight.INF.CSTR and=PERF.be-1CS
b=yd ***mlk-m*** ***km*** ***ʾš***
in=hand.FP.GEN king-MP.GEN like.PREP fire.FS.GEN
ʾkl-t ***zqn*** ***w=km*** ***ʾš***
devour.PTCP-3FS.GEN beard.MS.ACC and=like.PREP fire.FS.GEN
ʾkl-t ***yd***
devour.PTCP-3FS.GEN hand.FS.ACC

'The house of my father was in the midst of powerful kings, and (they) all stretched the hand to fight. But I was in the hands of kings like fire which devours a beard and like a fire which devours a hand'. (*KAI* 24.5–7)

This expression of states is achieved through use of the verb *kn*. The only sentence with an action-oriented verb, *wkl šlḥ yd llḥm*, presents an X-Verb word order. This contrast could be marking a change of point of view within the section through focusing (from the king's father's house to the mighty kings around them), but it could also be analyzed as a complex nominal sentence ('and it was all [of them] who extended the hand to consume'). The unit is therefore defining a sort of descriptive frame in two parts or movements (Schade 2006: 76): the previous weakness of the royal house and Kilamuwa's strength. The X-Verb structure stands at the transition between both movements.

This structure is repeated in Segment 4 (my example [1]), which actually consists of a Narrative Discourse development of the previous depiction of Kilamuwa's stronger state. After stating that the king of the Danunians acquires power over his house, an action by Kilamuwa is introduced (hiring the king of Assyria); the result is the loss of power of the Danunian ruler.[17] Kilamuwa's action, *wskr ʾank ʿly mlk ʾšr*, stands as the transition between the power increase of the Danunian king and his ultimate humbling. If the previous transition sentence in segment 3 was an expanded comment-description, this one presents the actual *cause* that procures the change.

Nevertheless, it remains a problem to determine whether the bulk of the initial forms in these paragraphs (and in most of the inscription) are perfectives (following Schade's analysis) or infinitives (according to Krahmalkov's grammatical proposal). I will not attempt to challenge any grammatical proposal at large, but I will simply comment how this issue could be approached from the point of view of discourse analysis, cautiously adopting some notions similar to the "Past Perfective I" versus "Past Perfective III" word-order opposition. In the case of *KAI* 24, there is a majority of verb-initial sentences (not counting the presence of *w-*) and only a few X-Verb structures (together with simple nominal clauses), which are contextually defined, as in examples (3)–(5).

17. Due to the contents and general dynamics of the paragraph, it seems unlikely that the sentences *ʿlmt ytn bš wgbr bswt* refer to the king of the Assyrians. See Schade 2006: 78 and references therein.

(3) *ʾnk* *klmw* *br* *ḥy*[ʾ]
PRON.1CS Kilamuwa.MS.NOM son.MS.NOM Ḥayya.MS.GEN
'I am Kilamuwa, son of Ḥayya'. (*KAI* 24.1)

(4) *w=ʾnk* *klmw* *br* *tml*
and=PRON.1CS Kilamuwa.MS.NOM son.MS.NOM Tml.MS.GEN
m=ʾš *pʿl-t* *bl* *pʿl*
more=REL do-PERF.1CS no.NEG do.PERF.3CP
h=lpny=hm
ART=forerunner.MP.NOM=PRON.3MP
'And I, Kilamuwa, son of TML, am one who, more than what I did, their predecessors did not do'. (*KAI* 24.4–5)

(5) *ʾnk* *klmw* *br* *ḥyʾ*
PRON.1CS Kilamuwa.MS.NOM son.MS.NOM Ḥayya'.MS.GEN
yšb-t *ʿl* *ksʾ* *ʾb=y*
sit-PERF.1CS upon throne.FS.GEN father.MS.GEN=PRON.1CS
'It is I, Kilamuwa, who sat upon my father's throne'. (*KAI* 24.9)[18]

I will now present my proposal for an overarching textual pattern in example (6).

(6)

(A) *ʾnk klmw br ḥy*	(1, segment 1)
(B) . . .	(2–4, segment 2)
(A1) *wʾnk klmw br tml mʾš pʿlt bl pʿl hlpnyhm*	(4–5, segment 2 end)
(B_1) . . .	(5–8, segments 3–4)
(A2) *ʾnk klmw br ḥyʾ yšbt ʿl ksʾ ʾby*	(9, segment 5)
(B_2) . . .	(9–13, segment 6)

This tripartite structure in the first part[19] of the inscription is based on sentences with the recurring first element *ʾnk klmw*, an identification of

18. In the last two cases, one could pose a different clause parsing, with initial simple nominal clauses "I am Kilamuwa" followed by verbal sentences. This proposal would not change the initial focus nature of the Pronoun + Name phrase. My personal opinion is that a *casus pendens*-like focus, on the other hand, establishes a closer identity relationship between the speaker (Kilamuwa) and the deeds or comparisons with others established in the second part of the constructions.

19. Lines 14–16 have a different discourse type as their basis, because they refer to prospective events, to individuals who might not respect and preserve the inscription, and to the appropriate curses.

the speaker and main actor of the text as a whole. Taken together with Schade's proposed literary interlacing and contrastive relationships between textual segments (2006: 88–90), this recurrence defines an overarching pattern in the inscription: the monarch first introduces himself (as a simple nominal sentence), then states his capacity for action over any of his forerunners (X-PERF), and finally proclaims his ascendance to the throne (again X-PERF).

Following the typology outlined in the previous section of this paper, these sentences (A) would belong to Expositive Discourse. Each of them would be followed by a B section that further develops the A statements as Narrative Discourse[20] (details of Kilamuwa's ancestors; previous submission of the royal house and Kilamuwa's initiative; positive actions of Kilamuwa as a monarch) and in which the use of Verb-X structures is prevalent. In this sense, all the Verb-X sentences are following a sentence with an initial nominal element (the A declaration) and, therefore, could be considered either infinitive or perfective from the point of view of Krahmalkov's proposal if one does not limit the initial versus noninitial verb opposition to single-sentence instances but understands it in the larger frame of textual units or sections. The perfective chains would in fact be "continuation forms" (see Krahmalkov 2001: 178–79). This would be congruent with the appearance in the text of morphologically certain (1st-person) perfective forms (*kt*, line 6; *šty* ×2, line 11), which would construct the B Narrative Discourse series.

This would still leave the use of the infinitive in 24.7–8 unexplained. As anticipated above, I have interpreted this sentence as a comment that syntactically expresses a contrast-consequence to the previous action and textually also acts as a pivot and therefore defines the essential cause of the following statement.[21] Thus, the sentence *wskr ʾnk ʿly mlk ʾšr* could be interpreted as a comment within narrative discourse, further characterized by its cause-pivot role. This role would also be connected

20. It is worth noting that some of these Narrative Discourse sections are largely descriptive, as can be seen in the case of segment 3, commented on above. Evaluating the use of forms of *kn*, in this sense, would require an overarching analysis of the Phoenician corpus, which surpasses the limits of this paper. It could be said, nevertheless, that, against the nonsequential orientation of nominal clauses, a series of *kn*-X clauses would define a sequence of events, as can be seen in segments 1 (genealogy of previous rulers) and 3 (weakness of the house and Kilamuwa's initiative).

21. This statement, the weakening of the Danunian king, also departs from the Verb-X (and possibly PERF-X) in order to assume an X-IMPF structure. This would correspond to a past imperfective use (Krahmalkov 2001: 184) and a possible descriptive parenthesis in the narrative line.

to a change in actor perspective: whereas this section (segment 4 in Schade 2006) presents events from the point of view of the Danunian king (in contrast to segment 3, where Kilamuwa's House and Kilamuwa himself are the main actors), this comment introduces the relevant action taken by Kilamuwa. Thus, a brief (single sentence) narrative presentation would interrupt and interlace itself with the main narrative unit, introducing the key action of the discourse sequence from the angle of a different (and therefore rhetorically stressed) actor.

*5.2. The Royal Azatiwada Inscription (*KAI *26)*

The considerable length of this inscription and the abundance of infinitive clauses require a condensed treatment, given the space constraints of this essay. As I have noted previously, in many cases it is a challenge to identify a form as an infinitive or perfective, and the proposals in Krahmalkov's and Schade's works present noteworthy differences. Nevertheless, this inscription is longer and therefore richer in verb forms than *KAI* 24. This allows for a more precise parsing of recurring unit structures, because more contexts with formally distinct forms are available (namely, 1st-person perfective). These data are convincingly analyzed by Schade on the supra-sentence level to show how transition between textual units or segments is indicated by the shift from a perfective sentence to an infinitive sentence (Schade 2006: 25–58). My summary of the materials of *KAI* 26 will follow this proposal (adopting Schade's textual segmentation) and complement it with discourse analysis observation on the typology of the inscription's units and the function of the different structures.

The beginning of the inscription (segment 1; *KAI* 26.A.I.1) introduces the main actor (the ruler – main speaker in the monument) using a long nominal sentence, with multiple adverbial modifiers and relative clauses (it would be an instance of Expositive Discourse). After this, with the sole exception of segments 8 and 10 (*KAI* 26 A I.21–II.2 and 26 A II.17–19, respectively), all other text units begin with a perfective sentence and are continued by one or more InfAbs-X clauses.[22] This pattern is prevalent throughout the central (narrative) section of the inscription[23] and can be summarized in one overarching notion: the

22. The structural and poetic function of this contrast has been analyzed in detail in Schade 2006: 25–45.

23. Segments 11–14 have no structures with an absolute infinitive and, against the previous narrative text types, are markedly hortative (call for thanksgiving to the gods and a blessing for the rulers in 11; blessing of abundance for the population

perfective sentences construct a coherent discourse line (portrayal of Azatiwada's main events or actions), whereas the InfAbs-X sentences *expand* this line with additional information (secondary narrative lines) that completes the more general statements. Thus, the InfAbs-X clauses can be understood as a *narrative comment* (with a marked explanatory role). This can be seen in a more detailed presentation of selected section contents:

(7) Segment 2

pʿl=n *bʿl* *l=dnn-ym*
make.PERF.3MS=PRON.1CS Baal.MS.NOM for=Danunian-MP.GEN
l=ʾb *w=l=ʾm* *y-ḥw*
as=father.MS.GEN and=as=mother.FS.GEN CAUS-live.INF.ABS
ʾnk ***ʾyt*** ***dnn-ym*** ***y-rḥb***
PRON.1CS ACC Danunian-MP.GEN CAUS-be.wide.INF.ABS
ʾnk ***ʾrṣ*** ***ʿmq*** ***ʾdn*** . . .
PRON.1CS land.FS.ACC valley.MS.GEN Adana.MS.GEN

'Baal made me father and mother for the Danunians: I made the Danunians live; I expanded the land of the valley of Adana'. (*KAI* 26 A I.2–4)

Making the population live and enlarging the land would be concrete actions, that substantiate the general and poetic statement of becoming father and mother.

(8) Segment 3

w=kn *b=ym-t=y* *kl*
and=be.PERF.3MS in=day-MP.GEN=PRON.1CS all.NOM
nʿm ***w=mlʾ*** ***ʾnk*** ***ʿqr-t***
pleasure.MS.GEN and=fill.INF.ABS PRON.1CS barren-FS.ACC
pʿr ***w=pʿl*** ***ʾnk*** ***ss*** ***ʿl***
fertile.MS.ACC and=do.INF.ABS PRON.1CS horse.MS.ACC upon
ss
horse.MS.GEN

---

in 12; and customary curses against prospective defacers of the inscription in 13). Therefore, they will not be included or commented on here, except to note that the InfAbs-X construction as an independent sentence is notoriously absent from Hortative Discourse, as was the case in the previous Kilamuwa inscription. See Schade 2006: 46–57.

'And there was in my days all pleasure. . . . And I filled the barren with fertility and I made horse upon horse'. (*KAI* 26 A I.5–7)

The pleasures and abundance procured are detailed as fertility and military power.

(9) Segment 4

w=šbr-t *mlṣ-m* ***w=trk***
and=break-PERF.1CS scorn-PTCP-MP.ACC and=crush.INF.ABS
ʾnk ***kl*** ***h=rʿ*** *w=yṭnʾ* ***ʾnk***
PRON.1CS all.ACC ART=evil.MS.GEN and=place.INF.ABS PRON.1CS
bt ***ʾdny*** ***b=nʿm***
house.MS.ACC Adanaean.MS.GEN[24] in=pleasure.MS.GEN
w=pʿl ***ʾnk*** ***l=šrš*** ***ʾdny***
and=do.INF.ABS PRON.1CS for=root.MS.GEN Adanaean.MS.GEN
nʿm ***w=y-šb*** ***ʾnk*** ***ʿl***
pleasure.MS.ACC and=CAUS-sit.INF.ABS PRON.1CS upon
ksʾ ***ʾb=y*** *w=št*
throne.FS.GEN father.MS.GEN=PRON.3MS[25] and=set.INF.ABS
ʾnk *šlm* . . .
PRON.1CS peace.MS.ACC

'And I broke the scorners and I crushed all evil. . . . And I placed the house of Adana [alt., my lord] in pleasantness and I did pleasantness for the root of Adana [alt., my lord] and I made it sit upon the throne of its father and I set up peace'. (*KAI* 26 A I.8–11)

This case may seem less straightforward than the previous segments. Nevertheless, the breaking of the "scorners" is presented first and later developed with a detailed presentation of the restoration of the rightful lineage (and therefore dispelling of opposition).[26]

24. Here and in the following case: alternatively, 'of my Lord'. See Schade 2006: 29–31 and n. 26.

25. For the analysis of this clause, see Schade 2006: 29.

26. The option taken for the presentation of the data would have a clear rhetorical value: to previous "positive" statements in the main line (constructed with perfective forms), now an action is added with a change of point of view (the destruction of the scorners as a prerequisite for the reflourishing of the land); the "positive actions" appear as comment developments with infinitive structures.

(10) Segment 5

w=ʾp *b=ʾb-t* *pʿl=n*
and=also.CONJ in=fatherhood-FS.GEN make.PERF.3MS=PRON.1CS
kl *mlk* *b=ṣdq=y*
all.NOM king.MS.GEN in=righteousness.MS.GEN=PRON.1CS
w=bn ***ʾnk*** ***ḥmy-t*** ***ʿz-t***
and=build.INF.ABS PRON.1CS fortress-FP.ACC strong-FP.ACC
'And, also, every king appointed me for fatherhood because of my righteousness. . . . And I built strong fortresses'. (*KAI* 26 A I.12, 13–14)

The general statement about support and authority received from surrounding kings is developed with a concrete action (construction of fortresses to fight "bad men").[27]

(11) Segment 6

w=ʾnk *ʾztwd* *št=nm*
and=PRON.1CS Azatiwada.MS.NOM place.PERF.1CS=PRON.3MP
tḥt *pʿm=y* ***w=bn*** ***ʾnk***
under foot.DU.GEN=PRON.1CS and=build.INF.ABS PRON.1CS
ḥmy-t ***b=mqm-m*** ***hmt***
fortress-FP.ACC in=place-MP.GEN those.DEM.PL
w=ʿn ***ʾnk*** ***ʾrṣ-t*** ***ʿz-t***
and=subdue.INF.ABS PRON.1CS land.-FP.ACC strong-FP.ACC
b=mbʾ ***šmš*** . . .
in=coming.MS.GEN sun.MS.GEN
'And I, Azatiwada, placed them under my feet; and I built fortresses in those places. . . . And I subdued strong lands in the West'. (*KAI* 26 A I.16–17, 18–19)

The general statement (to attain victory over the "bad men" detailed in the previous section) is detailed with yet another reference to the construction of fortresses and a geographical reference (the West).

(12) Segment 7

w=ʾnk *ʾztwd* ***ʿn-t=m***
and=PRON.1CS Azatiwada.MS.NOM subdue.PERF-1CS=PRON.3MP

27. The relationship between syntax and contents configures a complex and effective chiastic presentation between segments 4 and 5. See Schade 2006: 32–27. This would underscore the shift of content focus between the two sections.

y-rd=m ***ʾnk***
CAUS-descend.INF.ABS=PRON.3MP PRON.1CS
y-šb=m ***ʾnk*** ***b=qṣ-t***
CAUS-settle.INF.ABS=them.MP PRON.1CS in=edge-FS.GEN
gbl=y ***b=mṣʾ*** ***šmš***
border.MS=PRON.1CS in=rising.MS.GEN sun.MS.GEN
'And I Azatiwada subdued them; I put them down; I placed them at the edge of my border in the East'. (*KAI* 26 A I.20–21)

Another proclamation similar in content to the beginning of segment 6, this time developed with sentences on the deportation and settlement of conquered peoples.[28]

(13) Segment 8
w=dnn-ym *y-šb-t* *šm*
and=Danunian-MP.ACC CAUS-settle.PERF-1CS there.ADV
w=kn *b=ym-t=y* *b=kl*
and=be.PERF.3MS in=day.M-P.GEN=PRON.1CS in=all.GEN
gbl *ʿmq* *ʾdn* . . .
border.MP.GEN valley.MS.GEN Adana.MS.GEN
'And the Danunians I settled there; and it was in my days in all the borders of the valley of Adana'. (*KAI* 26 A I.21–II.2)

The main line is continued here with a change of focus (from the king's actions to the Danunians, the people to be settled and to enjoy the new state of safety). The improved conditions of the kingdom are then described, but this time no absolute infinitive construction is used.[29]

28. As noted in Schade 2006: 38, an anadiplosis connects segments 6 and 7: *wʿn ʾnk ʾrṣt ʿzt / wʾnk ʾztwd ʿntnm*. This rhetorical figure is strongly linked to discourse syntax: a fact previously presented as expansion of a main-line action (peacemaking would ensure that neighboring kings make him a "father") is formulated here as a foregrounded action. On a supra-sentence level, the reference to West and East would also define a merismus for the totality of Azatiwada's reestablished kingdom. Each of the "geographical blocks" would be introduced by a X-PERF statement.

29. This could be a problem of verbal aspect: the actions presented in the relative clauses in this segment would be durative-recurring (and therefore expressed with imperfective forms; cf. Schade 2006: 39–40 and n. 41). Furthermore, one could propose an infinitive analysis for the verb in *wkn bymty bkl gbl* (as acknowledged in Schade 2006: 39 n. 42). Schade's proposal in line with a perfective analysis could find an additional argument in the semantic discourse analysis outlined below: the

(14) Segment 9a

w=kn *b=kl* *ym-t=y*
and=be.PERF.3MS in=all.GEN day.M-P.GEN=PRON.1CS
šbʿ . . . ***w=bn*** ***ʾnk***
abundance.MS.NOM and=build.INF.ABS PRON.1CS
h=qrt *z* ***w=št*** ***ʾnk***
ART=city-FS.ACC this.DEM and=place.INF.ABS PRON.1CS
šm ***ʾztwdy*** ***k***
name.MS.ACC[=PRON.3FS][30] Azatiwadaya.MS.ACC because

bʿl ***w=ršp*** ***ṣpr-m***
Baal.MS.NOM and=Rešep.MS.NOM stag-MP.GEN
šlḥ=n ***l=bnt***
send.PERF.MP=PRON.1CS to=build-INF.CSTR
w=bn=y ***ʾnk*** *b=ʿbr*
and=build.INF.ABS=PRON.3FS PRON.1CS by=grace.MS.GEN
bʿl *w=b=ʿbr* *ršp* *ṣpr-m*
Baal.MS.GEN and=by=grace.MS.GEN Rešep.MS.GEN stag-MP.GEN
b=šbʿ *w=b=mnʿm*
in=abundance.MS.GEN and=in=pleasantness.MS.GEN
'And there was abundance in all my days. . . . And I built it, this city, and I set its name as Azatiwadaya, because Baal and Rešep of the Stags sent me to build it. So I built it by the grace of Baal and by the grace of Rešep of the Stags, with abundance and pleasantness'. (*KAI* 26 A II.7, 9–13)

(15) Segment 9b

l=kny *mšmr* *l=ʿmq*
to=be.INF.CSTR protection.MS.GEN for=valley.MS.GEN
ʾdn *w=l=bt* *mpš*
Adana.MS.GEN and=for=house.MS.GEN Mopsos.MS.GEN
k *b=ym-t=y* *kn*
because in=day.M-P.GEN=PRON.1CS be.PERF.3MS

description of safety in the land is not a development of the settlement of the Danunians but another element in the main discourse line (Schade himself argues convincingly against an interpretation of the Danunians as the main focus for the entire section; I consider the Danunians to be focused in the first clause, to move the action forward from proclamations with Azatiwada as a focus, but this focus would not extend to the whole passage).

30. See Schade 2006: 42 n. 45.

l=ʾrṣ *ʿmq* *ʾdn*
for=land.FS.GEN valley.MS.GEN Adana.MS.GEN
šbʿ *w=mnʿm . . .*
abundance.MS.NOM and=pleasantness.MS.NOM
'to be protection for the valley of Adana and for the house of Mopsos; because in my days there was for the land of the valley of Adana abundance and pleasantness'. (*KAI* 26 A II.15–16)

This paragraph presents a new observation on the well-being of the kingdom in the main line. The development comments detail the building of the city and the deities' involvement in it. The section makes an explicit connection between the building of the city and the safety of the land, so the interpretation as an expansion of the general statement with a perfective verb would be supported by the text itself.

(16) Segment 10
w=bn ***ʾnk*** ***h=qrt*** ***z***
and=build.INF.ABS PRON.1CS ART=city.FS.ACC this.DEM
št ***ʾnk*** ***šm***
set.INF.ABS PRON.1CS name.MS.ACC[=PRON.3FS]
ʾztwdy ***y-šb*** ***ʾnk*** ***b=n***
Azatiwadaya.FS.ACC CAUS-dwell.INF.ABS PRON.1CS in=PRON.3FS
bʿl ***krntryš***
Baal.MS.ACC Krntryš.MS.ACC
'Now, I built this city; I set its name as Azatiwadaya; I made Baal *krntryš* to dwell in it'. (*KAI* 26 A II.17–19)

Segment 10, according to Schade's analysis of the text, is exceptional. It is the only one in the entire inscription that uses infinitive clauses only, without an initial perfective sentence of any kind; it is also marked by a strong degree of repetition when compared with the development of segment 9 with infinitive clauses.[31] Actually, it is the third time that the building of the city is mentioned. Although the three cases use the same verbal structure, InfAbs-X, it seems to me that their textual

31. The variation in the last clause, which still shares a reference to Baal with its correlate in segment 9, is clearly moving the text, content-wise, toward the final blessing in segment 11. This semantic progression is relevant for the syntactic explanation of the passage that I propose. The summary value of the section has also been discussed in Schade 2005: 50.

function (and in one case, also syntactical function) are different, as indicated by the semantics of the passage, represented by the schematic layout in example (17):

(17)

(A) *wbn ʾnk hqrt z wšt ʾnk šm ʾztwdy* *k bʿl wršp ṣprm šlḥn lbnt*	(14, segment 9A)
(B) *wbny ʾnk bʿbr bʿl wbʿbr ršp ṣprm bšbʿ wbmʿnm . . .* *lkny mšmr lʿmq ʾdn wlbt mpš* *k bymty kn lʾrṣ ʿmq ʾdn šbʿ wmnʿm . . .*	(15, segment 9B)
(C) *wbn ʾnk hqrt z št ʾnk šm ʾztwdy yšb ʾnk bn bʿl krntryš*	(16, segment 10)

Instance A presents the construction as detailed in the notes on segment 9 above; then a *k-* causative clause indicates the reason for the construction (in this case, a divine command from Baal and Rešep); instance B combines the two elements of A (building and divine mandate) and is further complemented with the specification of the practical functionalities of the building (to be protection for the valley of Adana and the House of Mopsos) and a final (and overarching for the whole inscription) cause: the well-being and prosperity of the kingdom. In this way, instances A–B are followed by a subordinate clause that progressively supplies additional information regarding the motivations for the building of the city. On the other hand, instance C has no associated hypotactic construction. It is followed by segment 11, which contains the usual prayers with jussive structures (Hortative Discourse). Nevertheless, a clear semantic link to the three references to building of the city would be that the prayers and instruction for sacrifices are logically addressed to Baal, the deity who features in instances A–C.

One could say that, in instance C, instead of a developing InfAbs-X sentence (or series) followed by a subordinate clause, we find an InfAbs-X series followed by a new discourse unit, which, additionally, implies a change in discourse type (from narrative to hortative). Segment 10 could then be understood as an *introduction* to the new discourse section of segment 11: the information on the construction of the city, already detailed in instances A–B of segment 9, is now retrieved to offer a background reference comment for the Hortative Discourse that follows (segment 11). This would produce, in addition to clear rhetorical structures (see Schade 2006: 43–45), a sort of "textual-syntactic chiasmus," where the information and sentence patterns, which close the narrative discourse that makes up the larger part of the inscription, are repeated as an introduction to the final unit. An alternative translation for segment 10 and the beginning of 11 could be: 'So, now that I have built this town and established its name as Azatiwadaya and caused Baal Krntryš to dwell in it, let now a sacrifice be brought to all molten images . . .' (that is, the following Hortative Discourse units).[32]

All in all, a text-syntax survey of this inscription seems to indicate that the use of InfAbs-X clauses is connected to contexts of continuation-specification of more general actions or situations expressed with perfective sentences; or, in section 10, to introductions-transitions (expressing retrieved information) to a new text type.[33]

5.3. The Yeḥawmilk Byblos Inscription (KAI *10)*

The syntax of this inscription regarding the use of infinitive clauses is especially difficult to interpret, given the presence of a morphologically ambiguous form (*wšmʿ ʾyt ql*, line 8) with an implicit 3FS subject. The degree of difficulty can be perceived clearly in Krahmalkov's grammar, where the author proposes a different analysis for the form in two sections of his book.[34] The form is especially relevant for a general vision of the syntax of Phoenician infinitive because, unlike the vast majority of cases, does not have a 1CS subject but a 3rd-person subject. Furthermore, quantitatively, it is a key constituent of the only narrative (Narrative Discourse) section of the inscription, which includes a comparatively small number of infinitive clauses (most of the section is made up of hypotactic subordinate clauses).

According to Schade's textual analysis (2006: 120–38), the inscription can be divided into five segments. The first segment is the

32. The hypotaxis and use of temporal adverbs ("now") in English are, of course, a mere device to convey the possible nuances in the use of the Phoenician InfAbs-X structure as initial comment to the Hortative Discourse. It is actually remarkable that the three clauses have no copula in between. This peculiarity could be related to the presence of *w-* at the beginning of the unit and at the beginning of section 11 as section connectors; whereas, in contrast, the clauses of section 10 are felt as a copula-less block or unit of meaning. See Piquer Otero 2007: 555–56, 722–25 for similar phenomena in Ugaritic.

33. This would complement Schade's observations on disjunction between textual units and its connection with syntax, which is one of the basic elements of analysis in Schade 2006.

34. See Krahmalkov 2001: 160 (for a perfective analysis), 214 (for an infinitive proposal). See also Schade 2006: 125–26 for further discussion on the syntax of this verb.

customary identification of the royal speaker, Yeḥawmilk (Expositive Discourse). Segments 3–5 present blessings and instructions (and prospective curses) for future successors in dealing with the monument (Hortative Discourse). Segment 2 presents a narrative discourse unit in which the king details how the goddess answered his prayer and how, consequently, he built the monument in her honor. The relevant sections for the analysis of infinitive clauses are detailed in examples (18) and (19):

(18) Segment 1

ʾnk *yḥwmlk* *mlk* *gbl* . . .
PRON.1CS Yeḥawmilk.MS.NOM king.MS.NOM Byblos.FS.GEN
ʾš *pʿlt=n* *h=rb-t*
whom.REL make-PERF.3FS=PRON.1CS ART=lady-FS.NOM
bʿl-t *gbl* *mmlk-t* *ʿl*
Baalat-FS.NOM Byblos.FS.GEN kingship-FS.ACC over
gbl
Byblos.FS.GEN
'I am Yeḥawmilk, king of Byblos . . . whom the Lady Baalat of Byblos made king over Byblos'. (*KAI* 10.1–2)

(19a) Segment 2a

w=qrʾ ***ʾnk*** ***ʾt*** ***rb-t=y***
and=call.INF.ABS PRON.1CS ACC lady-FS.GEN=PRON.1CS
bʿl-t ***gbl*** *w=šmʿ* *ʾyt*
Baalat-FS.NOM Byblos.FS.GEN and=hear.INF.ABS[35] ACC
ql ***w=pʿl*** ***ʾnk***
voice.MS.GEN[=PRON.1CS] and=make.INF.ABS PRON.1CS
l=rb-t=y ***bʿl-t*** ***gbl***
for=lady-FS.GEN=PRON.1CS Baalat-FS.GEN Byblos.FS.GEN
h=mzbḥ
ART=altar.MS.ACC
'And I called my Lady Baalat of Byblos and she heard my voice and I made for my Lady Baalat of Byblos the altar'. (*KAI* 10.2–3)

(19b) Segment 2b

w=h=ʿrp-t ***zʾ*** . . . ***pʿl*** ***ʾnk***
and=ART=portico.FS.ACC this.DEM make.INF.ABS PRON.1CS

35. Or: PERF.3FS

yḥmlk ***mlk*** ***gbl***
Yeḥawmilk.MS.NOM king.MS.NOM Byblos.FS.GEN
l=rb-t=y ***bʿl-t*** ***gbl***
for=lady-FS.GEN=PRON.1CS Baalat-FS.GEN Byblos.FS.GEN
km=ʾš ***qrʾ-t*** ***ʾt*** ***rb-t=y***
when.REL call.PERF-1CS ACC lady-FS.GEN=PRON.1CS
bʿl-t ***gbl*** *w=šmʿ*
Baalat-FS.GEN Byblos.FS.GEN and=hear.PERF.3FS
ql *w=pʿl* *l=y*
voice.MS.ACC[=PRON.1CS] and=make.PERF.3FS to=PRON.1CS
nʿm
pleasantness.MS.ACC
'So, this portico . . . I Yeḥawmilk king of Byblos made for my lady Baalat of Byblos, when I called to my lady Baalat of Byblos and she heard my voice and made to me pleasantness'. (*KAI* 10.6–8)

The first observation to be made is the function of the Narrative Discourse unit of segment 2: as in the other cases in the two inscriptions commented above, it follows an identification (Expositive Discourse) unit, segment 1 in this case. Further, content-wise, segment 1 indicates, via the relative clause *ʾš pʿltn hrbt bʿlt mmlkt ʿl gbl*, the grounds for Yeḥawmilk's gratitude. Thus, the first sentences of segment 2 (from *wqrʾ* . . . to *wpʿl* plus the long direct object series) are giving a detailed development (narrative account) of the generic statement on how the Lady made him king over Byblos and his thanksgiving actions. The textual function would therefore be similar to the cases seen in the Azatiwada text. A comparison with the previous inscription is also useful for analyzing the final part of segment 2, which presents a considerable level of repetition, both in vocabulary and in contents:[36] building of additional elements of the sanctuary and a repetition of the process of petition-response between king and goddess, this time expressed as a causal subordinate clause. Contextually, this level of repetition can be compared more precisely with segment 10 of the Azatiwada inscription commented on in §3.3 above: in both cases, we find two presentations

36. In fact, these repetitions constitute a chiastic layout that involves the relative clause at the end of segment 1 and the whole of segment 2, as mentioned in Schade 2006: 129–32. His analysis connects chiasmus in the contents pattern with a chiastic use of verbal forms. Here I am trying to extend those considerations to a discourse syntax level.

(via InfAbs-X clauses) of the same actions or events (with minor variants within a general picture): the first presentation would comment on or develop a previous exposition (rendered with PERF-X or X-PERF sentences); the second would appear as an introduction to the following Hortative Discourse section of the inscription (prayers, blessings, curses). Thus, it would be possible to interpret segment 2 as two symmetrical Narrative Discourse units with distinct textual functions,[37] and both blocks of InfAbs-X sentences would be commenting on other syntactical structures–one as expansion of Nominal Sentence (+ relative clause)–based Expositive Discourse, the other as an introductory-protasis comment of Hortative Discourse. Both textual uses would fit in the richer contexts (due to the length of the inscription) of the Azatiwada text. The first presentation of the construction of items explains the concrete form of the gratitude actions; the second acts as a bridge introducing the blessing (hence the gratitude would be iterated and, in turn, hope for future blessings would be expressed). Though there is a high degree of synonymy involved, the glide between two distinct text types (segments 1 and 3) seems to support analyzing §2 as a double bridging structure.

On a sentence-by-sentence level, we still need to determine whether the structure *wšmʿ ʾyt ql* of line 3 uses an infinitive or a perfective verb. It could either continue the InfAbs-X series initiated in the previous sentence or establish an action-consequence relationship with it.[38] Either choice would be compatible with the overarching use of infinitive-based Narrative Discourse units that is the focus of this paper.

*5.4. The Son of Sipitbaal Inscription (*KAI *9).*

This text has deteriorated a great deal and is ridden with lacunae that mar most efforts at placing clauses (themselves damaged) in a wider discourse context. In what may be read, the text follows the traditional discourse pattern: there is an identification of the monarch in line 1; then follows what seems to be a Narrative Discourse section (which includes the case for study in line 4); finally, line 5 presents the remains of a Hortative text that warns possible trespassers.

37. The contrast and continuity of functions, in turn, would be underscored by the symmetric-chiastic structure itself.

38. For the "consecutive" use of perfective forms, see Krahmalkov 2001: 178–79.

(20) [. . . *b*]*n* *šp̣tbʿl* *mlk* *gbl*
son.MS.NOM Šipiṭbaal.MS.GEN king.MS.GEN Byblos.FS.GEN
pʿl-t *l=y* *h=mškb* *zn*
make.PERF-1CS for=PRON.1CS ART=resting.place.MS.ACC this.DEM
'[. . . s]on of Sipitbaal, king of Byblos, made for myself this resting-place'. (*KAI* 9 A.1)

(21) ***w=ytn*** ***ʾnk***
and=give.INF.ABS PRON.1CS
'. . . and I gave [. . .]'. (*KAI* 9 A.4)

(22) [*ʾl* *t-pt*]*ḥ* *ʿ*[*lt* *h=mškb*]
NEG 2MS-open-JUSS upon[=PRON.1CS] ART=resting.place.MS.ACC
zn *l=rgz* *ʿṣm=y*
this.DEM to=disturb.INF.CSTR bone.MP.ACC=PRON.1CS
'[Do not open upon me] this [resting-place] to disturb my bones'. (*KAI* 9 A.5)

This inscription is very damaged, and only one verb form can be identified as part of an InfAbs-X clause structure: *KAI* 9 A, line 4: *wytn ʾnk* ʾ[. . .]. The context around it is deteriorated, so it is not clear what textual relationship it could have with the rest of the inscription, which, as far as the preserved materials indicate, follows a discourse pattern similar to the texts analyzed above: initial X-PERF in section A, line 1 and, if the reconstruction in *KAI* is accepted, a section of admonitions beginning in section A, line 5: Beyond the fact that the InfAbs-x clause appears right before the beginning of the prospective Hortative Discourse unit, no other discourse analysis information can be gathered from this damaged text.

6. Comparative Uses in Other Northwest Semitic Texts

6.1. Ugaritic Narrative Poetry: The Case of the Baal Cycle

Out of the whole Northwest Semitic corpus, it is probably Ugaritic that has the most remarkable number of similarities to Phoenician in the use of the InfAbs-X clause, as well as meaningful differences. A detailed taxonomy of usage has been produced by Tropper (2000: 491–96). Of the proposed values, I will focus on Tropper's "narrativer Gebrauch," because its contexts of use are more relevant for a comparison with the Phoenician structure examined in this paper.[39] Tropper himself provides a brief typological note in describing the general features of the "narrative infinitive": "Die meisten Belege [. . .] begegnen auffallend häufig in Einleitungspassagen zu wörtlichen Reden" (Tropper 2000: 491). I have proposed a more general introductory function, not necessarily linked to direct speech (Piquer Otero 2007: 680–85). Of course, this kind of textual parsing is limited by the Ugaritic writing system; my proposal approached the evidence through narrative contextual and semantic patterns, given the unavoidable obstacles for a statistical study. Within these material limitations, I have proposed three possible uses of the infinitive in narrative (and Narrative Discourse) contexts:

1. *Modal-mood comment*: An InfAbs-X clause appears at the beginning of a narrative section, introducing its main actor as the infinitive's subject and presenting a modal comment (as opposed to an action) about the subject; semantically, this comment tends to fall in the area of moods and feelings, as can be seen in the following two examples:[40]

(23) ***šmḫ*** *rbt ʾaṯ[rt] ym*
'Rejoicing the Lady Athirat of the Sea'. (*KTU* 1.4.II.28–29)

(24) ***yrʾu*** *bn ʾilm mt /* ***ṯṯʿ*** *ydd ʾil ǵzr*
'Fearing Divine Mot, becoming frightened Il's Beloved, the Champion'. (*KTU* 1.6.VI.30)

2. *Other narrative uses*: Besides some varied cases of ambiguous analysis,[41] a possible, though by no means certain, recurring structure is the infin-

39. The cognate-paronomastic use remains outside the independent clause structures; the imperative value is not especially useful for a comparison with Phoenician materials (because imperative series are not a part of the text types in the inscription corpus) and, besides, its parsing in Ugaritic is particularly difficult (even more so than narrative uses of the infinitive), given the consonantal identity of the infinitive and the imperative in the majority of cases (cf. Tropper 2000: 492: "Keiner der in Frage kommenden Belege ist jedoch unumstritten").

40. See also *KTU* 1.4.II.28–29; 1.4.V.20; 1.4.V.25 (feminine subjects); 1.4.V.35; 1.4.VI.35; 1.5.II.20; 1.6.III.14; 1.4.VII.21 (masculine subject, proposed analysis by comparison with the feminine structures).

41. For some of them, see Tropper: 2000: 484ff.

itive of the verb of speech introducing a direct style section.[42] Those structures could also be interpreted as a protasis of sorts to the direct speech unit, an initital comment specialized in text-type change marking. Its use in opposition to the more frequent formula with *wyʿn*-X could have a contrastive function of relating two speech utterances.

3. *Use in Narrative Discourse*: This is the well-known problematic case of Mot's speech in *KTU* 1.6.II.14–23. After a variegated use of structures and tenses,[43] three clauses use InfAbs-X sentences for a 1st-person narrative, twice in conjunction with the independent pronoun *ʾank*:

(25) ***ngš ʾank*** *ʾalʾiyn bʿl* / ***ʿdbnn ʾank*** *<k>ʾimr bpy* / *kllʾi bṯbrn q<n>y* ***ḫtʾu hw***
'I approached Mightiest Baal; I put him like a lamb in my mouth; like a kid, crushed he was in the pit of my throat!' (*KTU* 1.6 II 21–23)

The infinitives *close* the unit, a formal point in common with the Phoenician texts; though their syntactic relationship with the rest of the paragraph is hard to ascertain, it is clear that they climax Mot's speech (and the whole episode), as he reveals his devouring of Baal. This final report would constitute a different layer in Narrative Discourse, which plays off climax/contrast.[44] As in the Phoenician cases above, this difference in choice of structures achieves an effect, which is the distinction of the action as pivotal/singled out within a chain of discourse, be it as a detailed explanation or an ultimate conclusion.

6.2. Summary of Uses in the Akkadian of the Amarna Letters

Sentence structures with infinitive forms in lieu of a finite verb have been systematically treated in the classic works by W. L. Moran (1950a;

42. *wʿn* + DN 1.2.IV.7; 1.4.VI.7; 1.6.I.53; 1.6.I.53; 1.6.II.13; 1.6.VI.9*; *wṯn kṯr* 1.4.VI.3. See Tropper 2000: 483. Compare with Sivan 1997: 167 for a more cautious approach.

43. For a detailed proposal of syntactic and discursive overall structure for the passage, see Piquer Otero 2007: 450–53.

44. This contrast (and perhaps even the choice of different verbal forms) could be related to the structuring of the passage through ironic puns achieved by Mot's inversion of literary formulas from other sections in the *Cycle*. These patterns of "inversion of formulas" in the context of Mot as a "Chaos" entity and their relationship with syntax have been presented in Piquer Otero 2003.

1950b; 1952; 1961). More recently, the relevant passages have been re-examined and classified by A. F. Rainey in his exhaustive treatment of the Amarna tablets (Rainey 1996: 383–88). For the purpose of this paper, both Moran's and Rainey's conclusions would support the scenario delineated above for the Phoenician and Ugaritic instances: the vast majority of cases are not elements of the main line of discourse but fulfill a comment function:

1. *temporal use—EA* 137:49–51; 89:38–39;
2. *protasis use—EA* 118:37–39; 362:25–27; 132:30–35; 104:43–53; 109:44–46; 129:20–21; 129:40–42 (see Rainey 1996: 385–88).[45]

On sentence-order considerations, it is remarkable that the infinitive clause invariably comes before the sentence(s) that constitute the main line of discourse. This textual layout is quite similar to the Ugaritic use as a modal comment in narrative texts and similar to some of the Phoenician clauses outlined above.

3. *"past narrative" use* (*EA* 287:46–48; 73:11–14; 138:51–52; 116:10–12; see Rainey 1996: 384–85). The scarcity of attested cases compared with the data available in other ancient Northwest Semitic languages was striking for Gordon and Moran.[46] In my opinion, this overall picture would change if one considered that straightforward "past narrative" use is actually infrequent in (not to say absent from) Northwest Semitic syntax. In discourse analysis taxonomy, many of these cases can be rather explained as comment uses to a main discourse line: In *EA* 73:11–14 and 116:10–12, the infinitives follow and supplement a verb of perception or knowledge; in *EA* 287:46–48 the infinitive can be defining a framework for the following Hortative expression; the case of *EA* 138:51–52 could be similar (Narrative Discourse notice within a series of Hortative clauses), but the damaged context compromises any proposal.

45. In sentence-based syntax, this would be analyzed as a subordinate clause. Rainey further divides these cases into two more categories: (1) "as soon as" temporal relationships, and (2) "conditional sentences" (where the infinitive expresses the protasis; Rainey 1996: 385–88). In Moran 1952 there is a detailed argument against the structure's being "subordinates" or "hypotaxis." The concept of "comment" in discourse analysis does not require explicit syntactic subordination or hypotaxis but covers contexts where the infinitive clause seems to be defining a particular circumstance or condition within the text.

46. As noted in Rainey 1996: 384; see Gordon 1965: 80 (for Ugaritic); Moran 1950b: 169, 171 (for Phoenician and Biblical Hebrew).

The evidence from Amarna, as in the case of modal comments in the Ugaritic *Baal Cycle*, also points in the direction of a defined set of uses for infinitive clauses: expressions of protasis comments and, in a minority of attested cases, glides from another discourse type (Hortative) into Narrative Discourse. This is different from the Phoenician usage, but also, on the text syntax level, there is an interesting degree of continuity.

7. A Text Linguistic Pattern for the Infinitive Clause in Northwest Semitic?

In this study, I have outlined a brief discourse analysis commentary of select Northwest Semitic texts in which "narrative" values have been posed for clauses with infinitive forms.[47] Beginning with Phoenician inscriptions (perhaps the corpus with more "narrative" structures) and concluding with a summary of the Ugaritic and Amarna data, my typological analysis has identified a pattern of use in different discourse types. Although any sort of conclusion must be tempered by the lack of certitude on the morphological level of analysis,[48] contextualization of the clauses in their text types and units can offer some possible cross-language similarities.

The Ugaritic *Baal Cycle* exhibits infinitive clauses in a 3rd-person nondirect speech narrative line. A large proportion of the detectable uses are connected to an initial comment or to textual type change/ contrast. On the other hand, Phoenician cases appear in 1st-person Narrative Discourse (typologically distinct, though similar; see Piquer Otero 2007: 627–28). They are typologically closer to one Ugaritic instance with noninitial infinitives (*KTU* 1.6.II.14–23). In the Amarna corpus, the protasis function of the infinitive appears in different discourse types, both in the main text line and in reported speech. Possible "past narrative" uses, on the other hand, are a minority and, in distinct cases, are linked to the introduction of reported speech / discourse glides.

Phoenician infinitive clauses seem to exhibit two distinct patterns: either they follow a finite verb or, in a smaller number of cases, they initiate a section of discourse. In the latter cases, they are associated with a change in discourse type (from Narrative Discourse to Hortative Discourse in the Azatiwada text), clearly visible in the narrative-prayer/

47. With the notable exception of Biblical Hebrew, because of the methodological and extension concerns mentioned in n. 5 above.

48. Namely, the possibility that more infinitive forms are present but undetectable because they coincide in form with perfectives in unvocalized texts.

blessing typology of the Phoenician inscriptions. The contents of the infinitive clauses detail actions and, in a considerable number of cases, can be interpreted as a detailed expansion of actions or situations previously expressed with personal form verbs (mostly perfective structures). At times (the use in the Kilamuwa inscription), they present a contrastive statement (and a pivot function) in relation to the previously developed line of narrative discourse.

This interpretation leads to a cross-language picture in which infinitive clauses do not, in principle, function as constituents of the main line of a narrative sequence (whether in 3rd-person narrative or in narrative discourse direct speech). They are integral parts of narrative text types,[49] but their presence is associated with other sentence structures (with personal verbs, whether perfective or imperfective) that in cases where the text is long enough to yield meaningful contextual analyses, do configure the main line of discourse (though not exclusively of narrative type, as attested by EA 287 and by the Hortative Discourse–introduction use in Azatiwada).[50]

Though the Phoenician use tends to appear in clauses *following* other structures (whereas previous Canaanite evidence has a marked tendency to present *opening* infinitive clauses), a discourse analysis approach to these materials seems to define a basic shared use: the inclusion of contrast/glide markers in a text that could be defined as "comment" in text syntax terminology. This seems to become more productive in Phoenician, because longer series of infinitive clauses are produced. This also moves considerations from clause-based grammar into a necessary discourse analysis orientation, because syntactic relationships can be established between whole clause series.[51]

49. One must accept, however, that in a considerable number of cases the meaning-based distinction between main line and "expansion/contrast comment" can be rather tenuous and is perhaps a matter of personal interpretation. It is possible to think that the composers of the Phoenician corpus crafted, from various available options, a textual layout in which a discourse line (mostly using perfective verbs and based, at least partially, on identification units constructed with nominal clauses or X-PERF with nominal focus) was entwined by / complemented with Narrative Discourse units with verbs in the infinitive. Long infinitive series, such as the infinitives in Azatiwada, could point in the direction of a conventional/stylistic factor in usage, at least in some areas and moments of the inscription genre.

50. See the commentary on the Azatiwada text for a perfective-based line in the Expositive/Narrative Discourse block and an IMPF-based line in the final Hortative Discourse section.

51. This leads to the necessity for a combined study of rhetorical/syntactic features, because grammatical function reaches beyond single-clause items.

On the level of sentence structure, the picture sketched above would allow us to read infinitive clauses as complementation units that, based on their particular text function, may appear as introducing or following the main sentence. We would be speaking then of X [infinitive clause] + Verbal clause or Verbal clause + X [infinitive clause] schemata. The position of the X element as first member / focused comment or as an expansion/supplementation of the main sentence would vary between the different languages and depending on the particular textual functions (frame/protasis versus expansion). But in all cases, these uses hark back to the nominal quality of the infinitive form, which fits aptly with its function as part of a two-member schema together with another sentence (or with a unitary sentence block).[52] This should give us pause when we attribute to infinitive clauses syntactical values as replacement of / equivalent to finite verbs.

In conclusion, a typological study of context for the use of infinitive clauses oriented toward defining possible functions of main line versus comment or of combined/parallel discourse lines seems to be a productive line of research that will probably benefit from the survey of Biblical Hebrew evidence and from a case-by-case study of this briefly outlined evidence in longer publications, as well as a comparison with other uses in different text types ("imperative" usage in Hortative Discourse) that further define the syntax of a construction in a typological context.

---

52. This text syntax proposal would cover most of the functions outlined for Biblical Hebrew in Waltke and O'Connor 1990: 393–97.

Bibliography

Gatwick, A. S.
1971 Hanno's Punic Speech in the Poenulus of Plautus. *Hermes* 99:25–45.

Gordon, C. H.
1965 *Ugaritic Textbook: Grammar, Texts in Transliteration, Cuneiform Selections, Glossary, Indices.* AnOr 38. Rome: Pontifical Biblical Institute.

Greenstein, E. L.
2006 Forms and Functions of the Finite Verb in Ugaritic Narrative Verse. Pp. 75–102 in *Biblical Hebrew in Its Northwest Semitic Setting: Typological and Historical Perspectives,* ed. S. E. Fassberg and A. Hurvitz. Jerusalem: Magnes / Winona Lake, IN: Eisenbrauns.

Heller, R. L.
2004 *Narrative Structure and Discourse Constellations: An Analysis of Clause Function in Biblical Hebrew Prose.* HSS 55. Winona Lake, IN: Eisenbrauns.

Krahmalkov, C. R.
1971 The Punic Speech of Hanno. *Or* 39: 52–74.
1988 Observations on the Punic Monologues of Hanno in Poenulus. *Or* 57: 55–66.
2001 *A Phoenician-Punic Grammar*. HOSNME 54. Leiden: Brill.

Longacre, R. E.
1989 *Joseph—A Story of Divine Providence. A Text Theoretical and Textlinguistic Analysis of Genesis 37 and 39–48*. Winona Lake, IN: Eisenbrauns.

Meyer, R.
1992 *Hebräische Grammatik: Mit einem bibliographischen Nachwort von Udo Rüterswörden*. 3rd ed. Berlin: de Gruyter.

Moran, W. L.
1950a *A Syntactical Study of the Dialect from Byblos as Reflected in the Amarna Tablets*. Ph.D. dissertation, The John Hopkins University. [Repr., pp. 1–130 in Moran 2003.]
1950b The Use of Canaanite Infinitives Absolute as a Finite Verb in the Amarna Letters from Byblos. *JCS* 4:169–72. [Repr., pp. 151–57 in Moran 2003.]
1952 "Does Amarna Bear on Karatepe?" An Answer. *JCS* 6: 76–80. [Repr., pp. 165–72 in Moran 2003.]
1961 The Hebrew Language in Its Northwest Semitic Background. Pp. 54–72 in *The Bible and the Ancient Near East. Essays in Honor of William Foxwell Albright*, ed. G. E. Wright. Garden City, NY: Doubleday. Repr., Winona Lake, IN: Eisenbrauns, 1979. [Essay repr., pp. 197–218 in Moran 2003.]
1987 *Les letters d'el Amarna: Correspondance diplomatique du pharaon*, with V. Haas and G. Wilhelm. Trans. Dominique Collon and Henri Cazelles. LAPO 13. Paris: Cerf.
2003 *Amarna Studies: Collected Writings*, ed. J. Huehnergard and S. Izre'el. HSS 54. Winona Lake, IN: Eisenbrauns.

Niccacci, A.
1986 *Sintassi del verbo nella prosa biblica classica*. Jerusalem: Franciscan Printing.
2001 Poetic Syntax and Interpretation of Malachi. *LA* 51: 55–107.

Olmo Lete, G. del, and Sanmartín, J.
1996–2000 *Diccionario de la lengua ugarítica*. 2 vols. AuOrSup 7–8. Barcelona: AUSA.

Piquer Otero, A.
2003 The Laughing Face of Chaos / The Grinning Talk of Death. Paper presented at the annual meeting of the Society of Biblical Literature. Atlanta, November 24.
2007 *Estudios de sintaxis verbal en textos ugaríticos: El* Ciclo de Baal *y la "poesía bíblica arcaica."* Estella: Verbo Divino.

Rainey, A. F.
1996 *Canaanite in the Amarna Tablets: A Linguistic Analysis of the Mixed Dialect Used by the Scribes from Canaan*, vol. 2: *Morphosyntactic Analysis of the Verbal System*. HOSNME 25. Leiden: Brill.

Schade, A.
2005 A Text Linguistic Approach to the Syntax and Style of the Phoenician Inscription of Azatiwada. *JSS* 50: 35–57.
2006 *A Syntactic and Literary Analysis of Ancient Northwest Semitic Inscriptions*. Lewiston, NY: Edwin Mellen.

Segert, S.
1976 *A Grammar of Phoenician and Punic*. Munich: Beck.

Sivan, D.
1997 *A Grammar of the Ugaritic Language*. Leiden: Brill.

Tropper, J.
2000 *Ugaritische Grammatik*. AOAT 273. Münster: Ugarit-Verlag.

Waltke, B. K., and O'Connor, M.
1990 *An Introduction to Biblical Hebrew Syntax*. Winona Lake, IN: Eisenbrauns.

The Linguistic Position of Old Byblian

Holger Gzella

1. Introduction

As so often in Semitic epigraphy, any attempt to relate the language of the tenth-to-ninth-century inscriptions from Byblos (henceforth termed Old Byblian) to their background implies scrutinizing a tiny, difficult corpus in search of answers to major questions. The period to which these eight short texts date separated the Late Bronze Age from the early Iron Age and thus saw a radical linguistic transformation across the whole area of Syria–Palestine (see Gzella 2011a for a synopsis of this process). Akkadian, the lingua franca of the day, withdrew to the east whence it came, whereas several new, by-and-large clearly identifiable national languages appeared along the Mediterranean coast as well as in the plains. Together with their ancestors in the Bronze Age, which, except for Ugaritic, have only left indirect though significant reflexes in various Akkadian corpora, all these idioms are usually subsumed under the "Northwest Semitic" group. Their emergence is connected not only to the socioeconomic and cultural renaissance of places already inhabited, such as the Phoenician cities, but also to the steady growth of settlements in the highlands of Ephraim, Judah, and Transjordan into what may be labeled extended chiefdoms. Instead of syllabic cuneiform, the chancelleries of these recently established or revivified political entities adopted and standardized a form of alphabetic writing[1] that had been around but had remained in a basically experimental phase, for several centuries.[2] It seems quite reasonable to hypothesize that a change of

1. The term *alphabet* for writing systems that exclusively or predominantly represent consonantal phonemes is conventional, but some scholars prefer to use it only for scripts that use individual graphemes for both consonants and vowels. The alternate term for a consonant-only inventory of graphemes is *abjad*.

2. Millard 2011 gives a concise and up-to-date account of this process. The enigmatic "Byblos syllabary," based on pictograms, may cast further light on the history of writing at Byblos, but the present difficulties of interpretation render at-

script of this sort also echoed the novel self-awareness of rulers who had risen to power only recently and wished to recall their deeds in an innovative monumental prose style embraced by a fresh generation of scribes and administrators.

Important linguistic developments accompanied the same process: the Iron Age languages created new means of subject and object marking as a substitute for an older morphological case system, rearranged the distribution of the semantic categories of tense, aspect, and modality across a modified inventory of verbal forms,[3] and each acquired a definite article the main functions of which stabilized over the course of time. Contact promoted the spread of these features from center to periphery, depending on the prestige of the respective tongues and their speakers' social networks. Borrowing, convergence, and, as in Anatolia, language substitution are the obvious results. Regardless of their precise genetic affiliation (for the discussion around the nature and subdivision of "Northwest Semitic" has not yet settled),[4] the verbal and nominal systems of the Semitic languages in first-millennium Syria–Palestine thus conform to a common type quite different from the known Bronze Age material. Where, it may therefore be asked, does Old Byblian belong?

2. *Old Byblian and the Linguistic Background of Phoenician*

The roots of Old Byblian are covered in darkness. Unfortunately, no individual member of the "Canaanite" branch of Semitic—which includes Hebrew, Phoenician, Moabite, and perhaps some other Transjordanian languages fragmentarily attested in a handful of inscriptions—

tempts at a more comprehensive understanding of the transition from pictographic to alphabetic scripts in the region still somewhat premature.

3. The loss of word-final unstressed short vowels and subsequent paradigmatic leveling led to the merger of "long imperfect" (**yaktub-u*), "short imperfect" (**yaktub*), and "subjunctive" (**yaktub-a*) in many forms. Hence, the functions performed by these distinct conjugations were in part either absorbed by the remaining conjugations or taken over by newly emerging verbal paradigms due to grammaticalization (such as the "consecutive forms" in Hebrew). See Gzella 2004: 310–26.

4. Beyer (1984: 1.23 n. 1); and Lipiński (2001: 48–90), for example, posit a division into four branches according to the four cardinal points of the compass. While their classifications are not identical, both scholars prefer to assign the languages now commonly attributed to "Northwest Semitic" to either "North Semitic" (Ugaritic and Amorite) or "West Semitic" (Canaanite and Aramaic). For a succint outline of the current majority opinion, see Huehnergard 2005.

can be traced back from the first to the second millennium B.C. with any confidence. "Hebrew" and "Phoenician," to further complicate the matter, both act as umbrella terms for a number of different dialects. Several typical features of Canaanite as such, however, have indeed been identified in certain words and hybrid verbal forms in Akkadian letters sent from local rulers in Syria–Palestine to their Egyptian sovereigns in el-Amarna: the "Canaanite Shift" from */ā/ to /ō/ and the final vowel /-ī/ in the first-person-singular independent pronoun are both confirmed by the syllabic writing *a-nu-ki* /ʾanōkī/ 'I' in EA 287.66, composed in Jerusalem; the form *mu-še-ir-ti* 'I sent' in the same letter (EA 287.53) exhibits the concomitant shift of the 1S "perfect"[5] afformative from */-tu/ to /-tī/; according to a widespread interpretation of the spelling *ḫi-iḫ-bé-e* in EA 256.7 as /hiḫbiʾ/ 'he hid (X)', the old causative-stem prefix */ha-/ (originally */ša-/) was also attenuated to /hi-/ (see Huehnergard 1991: 285–86).[6]

Various scholars therefore assume that the Canaanite material in these letters reflects the vernacular of the respective places of origin. Letters from Byblos or Tyre would thus contain a "Western Canaanite" substrate, the forerunner of Phoenician, while the "Central (or: Southern) Canaanite" elements in the letters from Jerusalem are to be connected with the idiom that at a later stage became Hebrew.[7] However, the high degree of standardization in the Amarna letters despite the geographically fragmented and politically disunited area obscures possible instances of regional variation. For this reason, other models for clarifying the linguistic status of the letters have been proposed, not all of which render it feasible to work with the idea of substrate influence.[8]

5. The time-honored terms *perfect* and *imperfect* will be preferred over the purely morphological and equally widespread designations *suffix conjugation* and *prefix conjugation*, but their use does not entail any particular semantic interpretation. On matters of nomenclature, see also Gzella 2004: 64–68.

6. Cuneiform writing obscures some phonological traits of Canaanite, such as the loss of the Proto-Semitic interdentals, whereas distinctive morphological innovations such as the vowel harmony of the "perfect" of the doubling stem (*/qattila/ > /qittila/) and the possessive suffix of the first-person plural (*/-na/ > /-nu/, in analogy with the afformative of the 1PL "perfect") are unattested in the Amarna corpus.

7. So, for instance, Blau 1978: 36 n. 28; similarly Beyer 2006: 159–60. Segert (1976: §12.35) is less explicit but argues along the same lines.

8. C. Rabin (1971: 1150) already raised the question "whether the Canaanisms in the Tell el-Amarna Letters do not represent a common literary language rather than the actual spoken local forms." A similar view has been developed further in the light of contact linguistics by A. Gianto (2000 and elsewhere), according to whom these features are "institutionalized" and thus stem from firm scribal training.

Taking them seriously leads to the disconcerting effect that the dialectal landscape of the second millennium B.C. becomes even more elusive than is often supposed. Another hitherto underestimated source of information comprises a few letters in Ugaritic that were dispatched from Tyre or Byblos to the city of Ugarit (see Gzella 2010: 67–68). Some possible instances of substrate influence in these texts seem to foreshadow later linguistic developments in Phoenician.[9]

Therefore, it appears fair to say that, whatever their origins may have been, Hebrew, Phoenician, and the languages attested by the fringe corpora from Transjordan took their distinctive shape sometime during the transition phase between around 1200 and 900 B.C.[10] These years mark a crucial period in the history of the Semitic tongues and their speakers, since they are directly connected to the vexed question whether the biblical exodus tradition has any basis in fact or not. Linguistically speaking, they continue to be "Dark Ages," since the earliest continuous and datable texts in Phoenician, Aramaic, and related languages only appear in the course of the tenth century B.C. Some parts of the Hebrew Bible, especially certain compositions often grouped together as "Early Hebrew Poetry," may well be older, but they survive within a textual tradition shaped by centuries of transmission and editorial work. As a consequence, they can hardly be anchored in time and place, even if one accepts on linguistic grounds their generally archaic character. No doubt a common poetic diction links Ugaritic epic with at least the earliest pieces of Biblical Hebrew, but Hebrew does not count as a direct descendant of Ugaritic in terms of genealogical linguistics—that is, as an idiom that later "branched off" from a parent language.

A developmental view of Hebrew in its Syro-Palestinian setting would profit much from a careful look at the earliest epigraphic material. Phoenician deserves special interest for comparative purposes because of its numerous conservative aspects. (For a few case studies, see Israel 1991, with copious bibliographical references.) They suggest that this group of dialects, either due to the peripheral location of its speech area on the Mediterranean coast or thanks to its linguistic prestige was

9. A particularly interesting case is the use of the infinitive absolute with a 1s independent pronoun for a past event in *KTU* 2.38.23, a letter from the king of Tyre to the king of Ugarit.

10. The exact dates, especially the *terminus ad quem*, are controversial in current historical and archaeological research, depending on whether one accepts the traditional "high chronology," I. Finkelstein's "low chronology," or an intermediate framework ("modified low chronology").

not, or was not significantly affected by a number of innovations that spread in Judea and Transjordan.[11] For the same reason, eight approximately tenth-century Phoenician royal inscriptions, funerary and dedicatory, that have been discovered in the ancient city of Byblos allow for particularly valuable insights. It was indeed Byblos that, after the fall of Ugarit, appears to have taken over as the center of alphabetic writing for some time. The first continuous attestations of the Phoenician languages (that is, texts that contain more than just a few words or even single letters) are written in the Old Byblian variety. They were originally published between 1905 and 1945. Among the several collections of Semitic inscriptions in which they have been included, the edition in *KAI* (numbers 1–8), which is accompanied by a translation and a commentary, may count as the most serviceable for easy access to the material. For *KAI* 1, see now also Lehmann 2005 (with excellent photographs). Their dates can mainly be established on grounds of paleography and relative chronology. The latter depends on pieces of genealogical information provided by the texts themselves and, in turn, is moored in absolute chronology thanks to two recycled statues of Egyptian pharaohs, since their ruling periods are known (Amadasi Guzzo 1994: 180, 187–91).[12] Of this already small corpus, the interpretation of *KAI* 2 and 3 remains controversial up to the present day, *KAI* 5 is but fragmentarily preserved, and *KAI* 8 consists of barely three words, the last of which is damaged. However this may be, suffice it to say that "working with no data"[13] has its music, too!

Certain archaisms in phonology and morphology that will be discussed at greater length below distinguish Old Byblian as a corpus with a reasonable degree of consistency from later products of Byblian scribes to be dated between ca. 500 B.C. and the first century A.D. (at the latest). Except for a few tiny fragments, seals, and legends on coins, these are the texts included as numbers 9–12 in *KAI* together with a sarcophagus inscription from the Persian period treated most extensively

11. These innovations include most notably the relative particle *ʾšr* and the "consecutive imperfect" used for denoting sequences of past events in narrative.

12. On the date of *KAI* 1, which some previously assigned to the thirteenth century B.C., see Cook 1994. It seems now fairly clear for linguistic reasons that this text also belongs to the tenth century.

13. The phrase was coined by T. O. Lambdin (see Golomb 1987); it adequately summarizes the problems that any linguistic analysis of epigraphic fragments must face (see Miller 2004: 283).

by W. Röllig in 1974 and commonly referred to as "Byblos 13."[14] Later Byblian appears to differ from other contemporary varieties of Phoenician, especially in the 3MS possessive suffix (written with the grapheme {w} instead of {y})[15] and, at least partially, in its retention of the byforms *zn* and *zʾ* of the proximal demonstrative (normally *z*) already attested in Old Byblian (Segert 1976: §14.22; Gzella 2011b: 61). Although a consensus has not yet been reached about the dialectal subdivision of Phoenician (see Garbini 1977; and Röllig 1992: 83–87), the language variety of Byblos displays some differences as opposed to the idiom of Tyre and Sidon, which is often considered to be a kind of "Standard (or: Common) Phoenician."[16] Contact with this *koiné* may explain why some forms of Old Byblian have over the course of time been replaced by their "standard" counterparts (as already argued by Garbini 1977: 287; seconded by Garr 1985: 218), causing further convergence of the homeland dialects. Setting aside the languages of the western Mediterranean, inscriptions from Cyprus also seem to contain some peculiarities in their own right, such as the prosthetic glottal stop in the proximal demonstrative *ʾz* (Harris 1936: 9; Segert 1976: §14.26; Hackett 2004: 367). On the other hand, a short inscribed jar handle from Sarepta in Lebanon written in the "short alphabet" of Ugaritic cuneiform (*KTU* 6.70) but often considered to be an early Phoenician text, resembles Old Byblian in its use of the relative marker *z*. It could therefore be part of the same dialect group. One must keep in mind, however, that all epigraphic witnesses bear the marks of scribal traditions. Hence, they do not simply record spoken vernaculars and thus do not allow for a straightforward application of linguistic-geographical methods.

The traits of Old Byblian have been singled out in the various synchronic descriptions of Phoenician-Punic since Z. S. Harris's first historically sensitive treatment in 1936 (which still contains a number of interesting ideas not to be found elsewhere) as well as in more-modern studies on the linguistic map of Syria–Palestine at large, such as W. R.

14. Some different readings and interpretations have been proposed by Cross 1979 (with additional secondary literature). For additional bibliographical information, see Amadasi Guzzo 1994: 180.

15. For the reconstructed pronunciation /ō/ after consonants and /ē/ after vowels, see Gzella 2011b: 61. Note also the Byblian form of the 3MP suffix *-hm* /-hum/ as opposed to *-(n)m* /-(n)ōm/.

16. No obvious distinctions between the dialect of Tyre and the dialect of Sidon emerge from any known inscription.

Garr's dissertation issued as a book in 1985. A comprehensive and very balanced survey relating these and the later Byblian hallmarks to the rest of Phoenician was published by M. G. Amadasi Guzzo in 1994. Nonetheless, the data have not yet received a more rigorous diachronic treatment. It is the aim of the present essay to review these and other hallmarks with the purpose of placing them in a somewhat broader historical context, thereby depicting instances in the evolutionary process that eventually brought about the common basic type of nominal and verbal morphosyntax shared by the first-millennium Syro-Palestinian languages. Particular attention will be paid to Ugaritic, although—or, rather, because—it features less prominently in research on Phoenician than one might imagine given its geographic proximity and its value as a direct representative of second-millennium West or Northwest Semitic.[17] So this essay also attempts to emphasize the great and perhaps still somewhat underestimated value of Phoenician for historical-comparative approaches to Semitic.

3. Phonological Peculiarities

The most distinctive phonological feature of the Old Byblian inscriptions can be observed in a couple of 3MS "perfect" verbs belonging to the III-*y* class, that is, the forms spelled *ʿly* 'he ascended' (*KAI* 1.2; in the protasis of a conditional clause), *bny* 'he built' (*KAI* 4.1; 7.1), and *ḥwy* 'he restored' (factitive stem, *KAI* 4.2). Since they are consistently written with the grapheme {y}, the etymological word-final */a/ in this form of III-*y* verbs seems to have been preserved in Old Byblian. Similar spellings suggest that the same was the case in Ugaritic, contrary to Hebrew, Aramaic, and the Transjordanian languages. Hence, the examples just cited can with some confidence be reconstructed as /ʿalaya/, /banaya/, and /ḥiwwiya/, whereas later spellings such as *bn* (*KAI* 15 and 16, from Sidon, fifth century B.C.) point instead to a monophthongization of the etymological triphthong from */banaya/ to */banā/ and, following the "Canaanite Shift," eventually to /banō/. The Latino-Punic spelling *avo* confirms that the final vowel of the 3MS of such verbs was

17. Some, admittedly weak, isoglosses connect Ugaritic with northern Canaanite languages of the first millennium, above all Phoenician and northern Hebrew, even though Ugaritic must perhaps be treated as a language apart and not as another Canaanite variety (Gzella 2011a: 427). However, several scholars do group Ugaritic and Phoenician together as "Phoenic" within Canaanite (Ginsberg 1970).

indeed /ō/ (Friedrich and Röllig 1999: §176b).[18] Monophthongization of triphthongs is a common development in the West Semitic languages that eventually turned verbs with a root-final glide fully into verbs with a final long vowel. The details of its working vary in the individual idioms, but the shift of */awa/ and */aya/ to /ā/ was operational not only in Canaanite but also in Aramaic and in Arabic. Since monophthongization led to different results with triphthongs than with diphthongs, where */aw/ and */ay/ shifted to /ō/ and /ē/, respectively, it must have taken place sometime before the short, unstressed, word-final vowels disappeared. Otherwise, the hypothetical development of */banaya/ > */banay/ would have yielded the unattested form **/banē/.

It thus appears natural to conclude that, in general, short, unstressed, word-final vowels were not yet lost in Old Byblian (see, among many others, Amadasi Guzzo 1994: 182), at least if one subscribes to the theorem of the "exceptionlessness" of sound changes as it was formulated by the Neo-grammarians in the nineteenth century. An inference of this sort would imply that the nominal and verbal system of Old Byblian at large was considerably at variance with the system of later Phoenician and the other first-millennium Canaanite and Aramaic languages but looked more like Ugaritic or Classical Arabic. In an earlier type of West Semitic preserved by these latter idioms, short vowels in an identical environment also marked inflectional case endings and distinguished between various types of the "imperfect" conjugation, each with its own semantic profile in the tense-aspect-mood matrix. This

18. The Tiberian pointing of Biblical Hebrew, by contrast, records /ā/ instead of /ō/ for the cognate form (that is, *bānā*). This seeming exception to the Canaanite Shift has been explained as an Aramaism in the vocalization by, for example, Beyer (1969: 63), who also suggests that the original vowel was indeed /ō/, indicated by the *mater lectionis* {h}. Similarly, but antedating this possible Aramaism by several centuries, the /ā/ is attributed by Bauer and Leander (1922: 410) to the "Sprechweise der jüngeren Schicht" based on their theory of Hebrew as a mixed language. An alternative explanation, favored by many older grammarians (see also Pardee 2003–4: 323), would proceed from the hypothesis that the *qameṣ* in Tiberian Hebrew corresponds to an originally short or at least not properly long /a/. Its quantity was thus described as "anzeps" by Brockelmann 1908: 627, whose idea that a contraction of */awa/ and */aya/ to /a/ due to the loss of intervocalic glides took place already in Proto-Semitic (1908: 619) has of course been disproved by the Ugaritic and Old Byblian examples discovered since then. A slightly more modern variety of the latter hypothesis argues that the quantity of the etymological phoneme differed from the quantity of its realizations in the historical languages. Finally, one may suppose with equal reason that the /a/ vowel in Hebrew results from paradigm pressure by analogy with the corresponding form in all other classes of verbs (Joüon and Muraoka 2006: 189 n. 4).

reasoning derives some support from the absence of a special particle acting as a direct object marker in the same corpus, which suggests that the morphological accusative case still signaled the grammatical role of the direct object or at least that no other means distinguishing subject and object had yet taken the place of inflectional case marking; later Byblian has *ʾ(y)t*, the usual *nota obiecti* in Phoenician.[19]

Alternative explanations, however, cannot be excluded. All three examples of III-*y* verbs, to be sure, occur in traditional phrases that express a king's building activities and a curse formula. It is thus not impossible that they preserved a morphological archaism or even simply an obsolete, historical spelling differing from contemporary usage or pronunciation, especially since they all reflect only one particular grammatical form—the 3MS of the "perfect" conjugation. The lack of the *nota obiecti* could be explained by emphasizing the obvious fact that an emerging category does not become regular in use immediately but needs time to consolidate, and it may long have been optional in Phoenician anyway (Garr 1985: 192). While the problem of the actual status of spellings such as *ʿly*, *bny*, and *ḥwy* must remain unsolved, further evidence does single out the language of the Old Byblian inscriptions as a transition phase marked by a certain amount of inconsistency in the behavior of the word-final short vowels. It thus appears that more caution is needed when one draws conclusions about the nominal and verbal system on the basis of these forms.

In this respect, the occurrence of a third person masculine singular "imperfect" *wygl* 'he uncovers' in the Aḥīrōm inscription (*KAI* 1.2) proves significant. The verbal root *gly* no doubt belongs to the same class as √*bny* and √*ʿly*,[20] so at a first glance, the spelling without the letter {y} suggests that *ygl* is a "short imperfect." Depending on the thematic vowel of the "imperfect," the vocalization would thus be /wa-yagl/ or /wa-yigl/ (Friedrich and Röllig 1999: §177a). Its use together with /wa-/ is sometimes even adduced as proof that early Phoenician had a "consecutive imperfect" similar to Classical Hebrew prose. On the other hand, this form occurs in the protasis of a conditional clause, where one

19. See the references in Friedrich and Röllig 1999: §255. There are several different ways that languages can compensate for the loss of case morphemes due to phonological processes.

20. It does not matter whether it was originally a III-*w* or III-*y* root in Proto-Semitic, as some scholars suppose (such as Brockelmann 1916: 149). According to Ugaritic spellings such as *tgly*, the merger with the III-*y* class was already very advanced in second-millennium Northwest Semitic.

would not normally expect a "short imperfect";[21] for the "short imperfect" most naturally appears in main clauses, which is just the syntactical implication of its pragmatic use as a narrative conjugation that was first associated with the foreground or mainline story.[22] As a consequence, the Semitic languages that did have a productive "consecutive imperfect," such as Classical Hebrew and Moabite, switched to the "perfect" or the "long imperfect" when "backgrounded" information conveyed in subordinate clauses interrupts the mainline action (see Gzella 2004: 318–20 for a very brief sketch of this analysis). The logical conclusion is that, at least on syntactical grounds, *wygl* must be understood as a "long imperfect" (Gzella 2009b, with a more detailed discussion). From this point of view, the juxtaposition of the "perfect" *ʿly* and the "long imperfect" *wygl* in the protasis of a conditional clause would establish a difference between the central element of the condition and a more general prerequisite: "if someone, having conquered (*ʿly*) Byblos, uncovers (*wygl*) this sarcophagus: the scepter of his kingship may wither away."[23]

Whereas the syntactical explanation just outlined is entirely plausible, it seems to be contradicted by orthography and morphology. For if *ygl* can only be a "long imperfect," its spelling must point to a

21. As pointed out to me by Robert Holmstedt (private communication), the protasis in Deut 32:41, introduced by a conditional particle, contains both a "perfect" and an "imperfect" *wtʾḥz* 'and [sc. my hand] takes hold'. The latter verb could be parsed as a "short imperfect," even though the form as such is of course ambiguous. The fact that Deuteronomy 32 is commonly included among the oldest biblical texts adds further weight to this interesting passage for a better understanding of *KAI* 1.2. Alternatively, the "imperfect" in Deut 32:41 may be analyzed as a "long imperfect" introducing a consecutive clause ('so that my hand takes hold'; cf. Driver 1892: 178). For *KAI* 1.2, however, the interpretation of *wygl* as expressing the result seems less apt on contextual grounds, because the event triggering the curse (that is, opening the king's sarcophagus) would then be part of a subordinate proposition. Lev 15:24, on the other hand, furnishes a morphologically clear example of a "short imperfect" *wthy* in a similar construction. The Masoretes pointed this verb as a jussive (*ū-ṯhī*), but since a jussive in the protasis of a legal prescription would be difficult to understand, it has been suggested that one revocalize it as a "consecutive imperfect" (*watthī* 'and [sc. her impurity] came [upon him]') indicating a subsequent event (Blum 2008: 120–21) or assume that the verb is jussive in form but not in meaning (cf. Driver 1892: 213).

22. Presumably, the use of either "perfect" or "short imperfect" in the protasis after *ʾn*, which is typical for Classical Arabic (see Reckendorf 1895: 686–87; Tietz 1963: 16–21), cannot be compared directly with the switch from the one to the other in the same clause, as in *KAI* 1.2.

23. Already Brockelmann (1947: 67) cursorily alluded to a similar distinction between prerequisite (*konstatierende Voraussetzung*) and main event (*Hauptsache*), but he did not relate this interpretation to the question what type of form *ygl* actually is.

contracted form of the etymological */yagliyu/ (assuming the thematic vowel was /i/) or */yiglayu/ (if the thematic vowel was /a/ and therefore triggered the dissimilation of the preformative vowel */ya-/ > /yi-/ according to the so-called "Barth-Ginsberg Law"), either to be written **ygly*. Following the normal rule of monophthongization of */iyu/ to /ī/ in Canaanite, this would lead to */yaglī/ or */yiglī/. Subsequently, in Canaanite and Aramaic, stressed word-final */ī/ was often lowered to /ē/, or, more precisely, an open /ę̄/ (/ɛ:/ in IPA notation), just like the *Tiefenform* of the masculine singular participle */bāniyu/ became /bōnē/ 'building' in Canaanite (Brockelmann 1908: 144).[24] Forms ending in */-ayu/, by contrast, were presumably leveled in analogy with /-iyu/ (cf. Bauer and Leander 1922: 407). Hence, the expected vocalization of the "long imperfect" should be /yaglē/ or /yiglē/. The long final vowel would of course not be indicated in writing, because the Old Byblian inscriptions do not generally employ *matres lectionis*. But how can it be that the one triphthong in the "imperfect" underwent monophthongization while the other, in the "perfect," did not? Avoiding speculations about the exact workings of this sound shift, one must take into consideration that contracted and uncontracted spellings of III-*y* verbs, including the same root *gly*, plainly coexist in Ugaritic (Bordreuil and Pardee 2004: 70; 2009: 48–49, with a somewhat different interpretation of the data).[25] Most of the attested forms that exhibit monophthongization belong to the "imperfect" conjugation, whereas the "perfect" forms and infinitives that display the same peculiarity are relatively few. These uncontracted examples also may simply represent historical writings. But a similar irregularity applies to the merger of III-*w* and III-*y* verbs in Ugaritic, Canaanite, and Aramaic: here, too, the Ugaritic cor-

24. The /ē/ is evidenced not only by the later vocalization traditions of Hebrew and Aramaic but also by the vowel letter {h} in Old Aramaic inscriptions, which, as a rule, does not denote /ī/. Some scholars, to be sure, assume that it results directly from the contraction of the diphthongs */ay/ and */iy/ in III-*y* roots (see, for instance, Degen 1969: §19). However, a contraction of */iy/ to /ē/ without any intermediate step would be difficult to explain on phonological grounds. Moreover, the monophthongization of alleged */ay/ in III-*y* verbs in Old Aramaic would, at any rate, have produced a closed /ẹ̄/ (or /e:/ according to IPA conventions), to be indicated by the vowel letter {y}. As a consequence, it is much more plausible to assume that first a triphthong was monophthongized to /ī/ and only thereafter was lowered to /ē/.

25. Attempts to explain away this phenomenon by referring to distinct temporal, aspectual, or modal functions are unconvincing because no consistent difference in meaning can be observed.

pus still has a 3FS "perfect" *atwt* /ʾatawat/ 'she came' from the original root *ʾtw*, whereas the "imperfect" had already been transferred to the III-*y* class as evidenced by the spelling *tity* /taʾtiyū/ 'they came', a 3MP "short imperfect." This obviously hints at an intermediate stage of the underlying process in Ugaritic in which the "imperfect" again turns out to be more easily susceptible to phonetic change (as perceptively noted by Huehnergard 2005: 179). Regardless of whether the evidence for both contracted and uncontracted spellings comes down to a question of orthography alone or indeed to a question of phonology and morphology, their coexistence is a fact. Hence, nothing prevents one from taking *ygl* as a "long imperfect" /yaglē/ or /yiglē/ despite the presence of the "perfect" *ʿly* /ʿalaya/ without monophthongization in the same clause. The interpretation of *ygl* as a "long imperfect" is therefore not only possible, given the spelling conventions of Old Byblian, but also likely for syntactical considerations. So it clearly deserves preference over the view that *ygl* is a "short imperfect" /yagl/ or /yigl/, which seems equally unobjectionable on orthographic grounds but can hardly be accepted for a subordinate clause. The monophthongization of /iyu/, or /ayu/, in Old Byblian is thus at least indirectly attested. On the whole, then, the attested forms of III-*y* verbs neither confirm nor refute the presence of word-final short vowels[26] but reinforce the idea that the language of these inscriptions, or their orthographic garb, reflects a transition period.

Apart from the behavior of triphthongs, which arguably constitute a special case, there appears to be only one piece of phonetic evidence directly bearing on the question at stake here: the sandhi writings *byḥ[mlk* (*KAI* 6.1) and *byḥmlk* (*KAI* 7.3) 'son of Yaḥūmilk' for ordinary **bn yḥmlk*, and perhaps also *bklby* 'son of Kalbay' (*KAI* 8), imply that the /n/ of *bn* /bin/ was assimilated to the following glide (Garr 1985: 40–43).[27] This, in turn, would only be possible if /bin/ lacked a case ending and had thus become a proclitic element. It is now generally assumed that the case vowel was preserved on a bound-form noun in Ugaritic,

---

26. Pace Garr 1985: 61 ("since final short vowels did not drop in verbal forms, it is inferred that they did not drop in nouns"); Amadasi Guzzo 1994: 182 ("La verosimile conservazione delle vocali finali brevi dei casi, che si deduce dalla conservazione di - Y nei verbi di terza debole").

27. An assimilation of this sort, however, did not happen with a following glottal stop, as in *bn ʾḥrm* (*KAI* 1.1) or *bnʾlbʿl* (*KAI* 7.2). It is unattested in later Byblian (see *KAI* 9.1; 10.1; 11; 12.2–3).

the system of which comes closest to the ancestor of Old Byblian,[28] but its absence in a particular unsuffixed bound form on its own does not prove that the whole inflectional case system had disappeared. Rather, one might see these forms as symptoms of a gradual breakdown. In addition to this, a fixed expression such as "son of X" can easily count as a composite name, so these three examples may not be representative of all nouns (pace Friedrich and Röllig 1999: 48, 145). The value of this evidence for determining the status of inflectional case marking in Old Byblian is thus doubtful.

Another remarkable feature of phonology concerns the apheresis of /ʾa-/ in the word /ʾaḥ-/ (< *ʾaḫ-/) 'brother'. It is a well-known fact of Phoenician that almost every attestation of this word in compound names, especially /ʾAḥīrōm/ 'My brother is exalted', exhibits a loss of the first syllable. Because it occurs not only in Phoenician alphabetic writings such as *ḥrm* but also in the Hebrew Bible (*Ḥīrām* in 2 Sam 5:11, 1 Kgs 5:15), cuneiform sources (*Ḫi-ru-um-mu* in a list of foreign kings bringing tribute to Tiglath-pileser III), and several Greek historians (Ειρωμος),[29] it certainly reflects a genuine sound change rather than an aberrant spelling. Exceptions are rare and at least in part controversial (details in Amadasi Guzzo 1994: 181). Incidentally, the Semitic word for 'one' underwent a similar development in Aramaic from *ʾaḥad-/ to /ḥad/,[30] so this phenomenon by itself is not unparalleled. However, the Aḥīrōm sarcophagus, unfortunately the only tenth-century witness that contains such a name, still has a reflex of the more original form (*KAI* 1.2). Harris suggested that the instance of aphaeresis under discussion presupposes a reduction of the vowel /a/ (Harris 1936: 31–32, also with a reference to Aramaic); hence, it would have been the result of a gradual process. Interestingly, the variant spelling *iḫ* instead of the more usual *aḫ* in Ugaritic, where two of the five total attestations occur in a letter sent from Byblos,[31] reveals the same instability of this vowel. The use of the grapheme {ʾ} in the Aḥīrōm inscription, of course, says

28. For the peculiar shortened form *ḥ* instead of *ḥy* in an oath formula, see Gzella 2007: 545.

29. Friedrich and Röllig (1999: 161) give a fairly extensive summary of the evidence.

30. See Huehnergard (1995: 275), who nonetheless correctly voices doubts about its diagnostic value for distinguishing Aramaic from other Semitic languages. Brockelmann (1908: 110, 257) mentions several other examples in Aramaic.

31. Lines 2 and 3 of *KTU* 2.44, the other examples being 2.41.18, 4.123.23, and 4.780.2. See Gzella 2010: 68 n. 57.

nothing about the quality or quantity of the following vowel, but in light of the second-millennium evidence, it would be quite reasonable to believe that it was indeed already reduced, thereby hinting at the emerging phenomenon of later Phoenician in the Old Byblian corpus.

The different spellings of the 3MS suffix also mirror a phonetic process. Here also the Aḥīrōm inscription has the original /-hu/ or /-hū/,[32] indicated by the grapheme {h}, on both nouns (only attested in the genitive) and verbs. Evidently, it corresponds to the proto-West Semitic form. In Old Byblian after the Aḥīrōm sarcophagus, however, the intervocalic /h/ between the suffix and the case or linking vowel of the noun seems already to have disappeared, which becomes clear from the form *šntw* 'his years' in *KAI* 4.5. This led to a diphthong, the reflex of which in the consonantal orthography was {w} (if not patterned after the form after vowels). Later stages of Phoenician and Punic, including later Byblian, attest to several different forms, the origins of which are not yet well understood.[33] Consequently, the 3MS suffix in *KAI* 1 can only be an archaism.

4. Morphology and Morphosyntax

A resurvey of certain morphological features of Old Byblian deviating from Standard Phoenician leads to results that are similar to results from the preceding investigation into the phonology. Not all phenomena, it is true, bear on a developmental perspective, because some of them appear to be dialectal differences, not necessarily archaisms. This

32. The quantity of the final vowel in the personal pronouns, possessive or object suffixes, and endings of the "perfect" conjugation is an unsolved problem in comparative Semitics, because the individual languages exhibit conflicting evidence. See, for example, the tables in Lipiński 2001: 306–7, 314–15, and 368–69.

33. For the time being, see Friedrich and Röllig 1999: 66; and especially Hackett 2004: 374–76; Gzella (2011b: 61) has a reconstruction of the purported pronunciation. This part of Phoenician grammar in particular will benefit from more research. Amadasi Guzzo (1994: 184–85) gives an overview of the situation in later Byblian. Variants in the spelling of certain suffixes in Standard Phoenician point to a preservation of the old genitive at least in suffixed forms. The survival of the genitive also in nonsuffixed nouns into later periods is still debated but does not necessarily follow from the situation with possessive suffixes (see Friedrich and Röllig 1999: §217). Phoenician personal names in cuneiform sources constitute the only direct evidence from ancient times for the presence or absence of case vowels on nonsuffixed nouns. Apart from problems of syllabic writing and fluctuating spelling conventions (Friedrich and Röllig 1999: §92 bis), however, personal names often preserve archaisms and are thus unlikely to represent the spoken language of their day faithfully anyway.

applies first and foremost to the demonstrative pronouns. Within the Old Byblian corpus, a masculine-singular form for the proximal deixis ('this') spelled *zn*, and supposedly vocalized /zinā/, is attested in the Aḥīrōm sarcophagus inscription, where it modifies a direct object (1); in the Aḥīrōm graffito, it seems to occur after a preposition (2).

(1) *ʾrn* *zn*
sarcophagus DEM
'[sc. who uncovers] this sarcophagus'. (*KAI* 1.2)

(2) *tḥt* *zn*
under DEM
'below this' or 'underneath'. (*KAI* 2.3)

Moreover, the Yaḥūmilk inscription contains an instance of the plural form *ʾl* /ʾil(l)ē/ modifying the nominal host (*nomen rectum* in traditional terminology) of a bound form as a direct object (3):

(3) *kl* *mpl-t* *h-bt-m* *ʾl*
all ruin-FP ART-house-MP DEM
'[sc. he restored] the ruins of all these buildings'. (*KAI* 4.2–3)

Proximal demonstratives regularly contain a */ḏ/ element, which became /z/ in Canaanite, in the singular and the consonantal phonemes /ʾ/ and /l/ in the plural, not only in Phoenician and other Canaanite languages, but also in Aramaic and Arabic. The situation in Old Byblian closely resembles Aramaic, the proximal demonstrative of which is */ḏenā/, whereas its Hebrew counterpart /zē/ has a different etymology; Ugaritic *hnd* is so distinct from either, both formally and functionally, that it cannot be compared directly. No common parent form can thus be reconstructed–not for proto-Northwest Semitic and certainly not for Proto-Semitic. Later Byblian, by contrast, also has a form spelled *z*, as does Standard Phoenician (see Friedrich and Röllig 1999: §113).[34] The fifth-century Yeḥawmilk inscription from Byblos (*KAI* 10), by contrast, uses *zn* and *z* for the masculine singular side by side, but since

34. Inscriptions from Cyprus regularly display a form expanded by a prothetic glottal stop (*ʾz*), but this is no doubt simply a phonetic alternate (Harris 1936: 54). Many scholars also reconstruct [*z*]*n* for the seventh-century Ur box (*KAI* 29.1), but, if correct, this would be an isolated instance.

both crop up in the same environment, there is no obvious functional difference. Harris, however, accurately noted that *zn* only appears when the demonstrative is separated from its noun and suggests that "it may have been felt to be more emphatic" (Harris 1936: 54).[35] Apparently, older Byblian *zn* was first reduced to a by-form for certain pragmatic purposes and later fully replaced by *z*. This instance of substitution may have taken place under the influence of Standard Phoenician; alternatively, the Old Byblian relative marker *z*, to be discussed below, could have taken over as a demonstrative by means of a parallel development. In any case, the form *zn* thus constitutes a dialectal peculiarity of Old Byblian, later competing with *z*, but it does not need to be more archaic than the standard form, especially since deictics are often expanded by /n/ and other elements in Semitic.[36]

In light of the behavior of the demonstratives, the substitution of the determinative-relative marker *z* /zū/ in Old Byblian, as already indicated, can be better explained. This form is obviously a reflex of the Common Semitic determinative–relative pronoun */ḏū/ (Ugaritic *d* / dū/), which was once inflected for case, like its cognate in Classical Arabic, and the original genitive form of which, */ḏī/, has become the normal masculine-singular demonstrative pronoun in Hebrew (with */ḏī/ > /zę̄/) and the relative marker in Aramaic (later > /dī/ > /d(a)-/). It occurs at the beginning of at least four Old Byblian inscriptions (*KAI* 1.2, 4.1, 6.1, 7.1; reconstructed in 5.1) and can in principle be translated either '*this* sarcophagus [house, votive image, wall] X made' or 'sarcophagus [etc.] *that* X made'.[37] Within Phoenician-Punic as such, this pattern is typical for Old Byblian but appears already on the Sarepta jar handle that was inscribed with Ugaritic cuneiform (*KTU* 6.70). After the Old Byblian period, however, *z* was replaced by the Standard Phoenician

35. Compare *ʿl pn ptḥy z* 'facing this engraving of mine' with *ʿl ptḥ ḥrṣ zn* 'above this golden engraving' (*KAI* 10.5). The respective constructions are practically identical: both instances of the demonstrative modify a noun governed either by another noun in the construct state or by a preposition—that is, two instances in which a Semitic language with inflectional case marking would require a genitive. Any semantic difference would be hard to demonstrate on the basis of these examples alone. For other proposals, see Amadasi Guzzo 1994: 185 with n. 47.

36. The connection between the feminine counterpart *zʾ*, which in Byblian is only attested in the Yeḥawmilk inscription, and Standard Phoenician *z* still must be thoroughly investigated. It does not fall within the scope of the present paper.

37. A clear-cut decision is impossible to make on grammatical grounds alone, but the interpretation as a relative seems to be preferred by most scholars. See Gzella 2006: 4.

relative particle *ʾš*. Both are unrelated, and the revivified, extensive discussion about the latter's etymology can be bypassed here (see Holmstedt 2007), even though it has some bearing on the present argument; for if *ʾš* proves to be not a secondary by-form of /ʾašar/ but a reflex of East Semitic /ša/, as some (though not all) scholars suppose, one cannot simply classify *z* as an archaism. Whatever the origin of the respective forms may be, the replacement of the one by the other could have been triggered, for disambiguating purposes, by the change of the masculine-singular demonstrative *zn* to *z*. Supposing that Standard Phoenician *z* was pronounced /zū/, it could not be distinguished anymore from the relative marker.[38] The ambiguity of *z*, which also perplexes modern scholars, would therefore have played a role in the morphological change.

A more obvious archaism is the use of *hʾt*, the former 3MS oblique pronoun in the Yaḥūmilk text (*KAI* 4.2) instead of the usual Old Byblian (*KAI* 1.2), Byblian (*KAI* 10.9, 15), and Standard Phoenician *hʾ* (see Friedrich and Röllig 1999: §110). Its nearest cognate, Ugaritic *hwt*, is known as a nonnominative variant meaning 'of his' or 'him', but this distinction must have been neutralized later, because *hʾt* in *KAI* 4.2, provided in example (4), clearly refers to the subject that it reinforces (perhaps it originated in fronted direct objects).

(4)	*hʾ-t*	*ḥwy*	*kl*	*mpl-t*	*h-bt-m*	*ʾl*
	he-OBL	restore.3MS.PERF	all	ruin-FP	ART-house-MP	DEM

'he (alone?) restored the ruins of all these buildings'. (*KAI* 4.2–3)

This "emphatic" use resembles the occurrence of the nominative pronoun in fronted position in the Aḥīrōm inscription, given in example (5).

(5)	*w-hʾ*	*y-mḥ*	*spr-h*
	and-he-NOM	3MS-efface.IMPF	inscription-3MS.GEN

'and as for him—may his own inscription be effaced'. (*KAI* 1.2)

The reason underlying this variation may be that, in the earlier text, the collapse of inflectional case marking was not yet completed, whereas

38. Harris (1936: 55) also briefly suggested that there may have been a connection between these developments, but he did not go into detail.

the construction in *KAI* 4 presupposes the loss of a distinction between nominative and oblique case. Hence, *hʾt* may have become a short-lived by-form that left no traces in the later history of Phoenician, whereas the old 3MP oblique form *hmt* was generalized. Incidentally, this suggests that the case system fully broke down only in the period between *KAI* 1 and *KAI* 4—that is, during the course of the first half of the tenth century B.C. The Yaḥūmilk inscription may therefore represent a stage of the language before a neat distribution of the nominative and nonnominative form across singular and plural had been achieved. On the other hand, 3MS forms of III-*y* verbs continued to be spelled with {y} even in the very same text, as *bny* 'he built' (*KAI* 4.1) and *ḥwy* 'he restored' (*KAI* 4.2) demonstrate. Of course, it is possible that orthography lagged behind innovations in the language itself and that these spellings are merely historical. The evidence is thus insufficient for a consistent explanation of seemingly contradictory facts, and in all likelihood they reflect a linguistic stage in transition.

One of the most interesting facets of Old Byblian is that it provides a snapshot of the genesis of a grammaticalized definite article in several Semitic languages between the tenth and the ninth centuries B.C.: Phoenician, Hebrew, Moabite, the various manifestations of Old Aramaic, and Arabic, as well as Old South Arabian. The respective forms point to distinct morphological resources that cannot easily be reduced to one common ancestor. Their functions and determinative force also seem to have differed in the beginning and converged only later. However, Canaanite (that is, Phoenician, Hebrew, and Moabite) /ha-/ with gemination of the following consonant in all likelihood derives from an older deictic or presentative marker /han/, the transformation of which into a definite article was apparently in an embryonic stage already in Ugaritic.[39] The Old Byblian corpus illustrates the speed with which this development took place, since the article /ha-/ is still lacking in the Aḥīrōm inscription, even in a construction (6) where it would normally be expected,

(6)	*w-y-gl*	*ʾrn*	*zn*
	and-3MS-uncover.IMPF	sarcophagus	DEM

'and uncovers this sarcophagus'. (*KAI* 1.2)

39. This hypothesis has gained support from new findings; see Gzella 2007: 543.

but appears at most a few decennia later in (7) the report of Yaḥūmilk's building achievements (in fact, the earliest datable attestation of this category; Amadasi Guzzo 1994: 183):

(7) *h'-t* *ḥwy* *kl* *mpl-t* *h-bt-m* *'l*
he-OBL restore.3MS.PERF all ruin-FP ART-house-MP DEM
'he (alone?) restored the ruins of all these buildings'. (*KAI* 4.2–3)

In older Phoenician, the article is most frequently used either with noun phrases that are already marked as definite by a demonstrative and function as direct objects, or with nouns governing a relative clause. Hence, it has been suggested that it does not mark definiteness exclusively but exercises its determinative force in a broader context of syntactical dependence and subordination (see Gzella 2006).[40]

It would be most revealing for the nature of linguistic change in Semitic to discover connections between the rise of a morphological expression of definiteness and the other innovations that did distinguish the type of the first-millennium Syro-Palestinian languages from their predecessors. Recent work on Germanic, for instance, has endeavored to identify a direct correlation by which the appearance of a grammaticalized definite article coincided with fundamental changes in the marking of verbal aspect (so Leiss 2000; see also Gzella 2006: 1–2). The discussion in Semitic, by contrast, has focused on the origin of the respective forms rather than on the functional conditions that promoted the emergence of such a category. However, exploring this little-known side of the interaction between nominal and verbal system could lead to important results. First of all, one cannot deny a basic affinity between the perfective aspect (or the idea of punctuality closely associated with it)[41] and definiteness (or contextual identifiability), because a verbal form positively marked for punctuality at times attracts a nominal form positively marked for definiteness. Conversely, generic noun phrases are generally, yet not always, accompanied by verbs associated with du-

40. Stempel (2008) comes to a similar conclusion from a different perspective and states that the article in Canaanite (among other languages) has been reanalyzed as having developed from an original relative pattern. Unfortunately, he ignores both the Ugaritic evidence for an ancestor form */han/ and the peculiarities of the datable epigraphic material.

41. For the outline of a theoretical framework correlating aspect and *Aktionsart*, or situation type, see Gzella 2004: 90–100.

rativity or iterativity (see Lyons 1999: 180). Semitic languages also furnish suitable examples.[42]

Even if the so-called definite article in Semitic did not, or did not exclusively serve as an expression of definiteness *sic et simpliciter* at the very beginning, it no doubt had a bearing on the phenomenon of deixis and identifiability. For this reason, its transformation from a deictic marker into a morphological category coincided with one particular fundamental change in the verbal system: in the older Semitic languages that acquired a proper definite article (that is, Canaanite, Aramaic, and Arabian), the narrative "short imperfect" as the verbal form most strongly marked for past tense and perfectivity was marginalized. (Since the "perfect" covers a number of different nuances of past tense, including states, it bears a much lesser degree of markedness in terms of perfectivity.) The loss of the "short imperfect" with past-tense function is of course evident in Phoenician, including, as has been demonstrated above, the Aḥīrōm sarcophagus. The same applies to the highly diversified Aramaic language family.[43]

By contrast, in Classical Hebrew and some Transjordanian idioms such as Moabite, the same conjugation underwent a radical metamorphosis by amalgamating with the conjunction /wa-/ into a new grammaticalized "consecutive imperfect" confined to the clause-initial position. This explanation also accounts for the situation in Classical Arabic, although, unlike first-millennium Canaanite and Aramaic, Classical Arabic largely preserved the basic structure of the "Central Semitic" verbal system, with its opposition of a "perfect" *kataba* and three different "imperfect" conjugations, *yaktub*, *yaktubu*, and *yaktuba* (see Gzella 2004: 311–17). Nonetheless, Classical Arabic in fact reduced the functional range of the "short imperfect" *yaktub* from a universal past narrative form to negations in the past (*lam yaktub*). Hence, it is not altogether

42. For a striking instance from Qumran Aramaic, see Gzella 2004: 259–61: a passage from the *Genesis Apocryphon* (21:28) uses periphrastic constructions for past durativity with two verbs lacking a direct object, but switches to the "perfect" (which is marked for punctuality when juxtaposed with a periphrasis with the verb 'to be' and a participle) for the third verb, which takes a definite direct object. Kapeliuk (2006: 388) points to an interesting phenomenon of a similar kind in Urmi Neo-Aramaic.

43. The question whether the few possible instances of this function in Old Aramaic texts, all prefixed by /wa-/, are retentions from an older stage, actual "long imperfects," or borrowings from Canaanite (for a brief discussion, see Gzella 2004: 322–24), does not affect its by-and-large insignificant role in Old Aramaic. Hence, the argument proposed here works with all current interpretations of these forms.

implausible to posit that the semantic interface between definiteness and perfective aspect played a role in the genesis of a definite article in Semitic. The major processes that brought about a younger type of Semitic therefore seem to exhibit a considerable degree of interaction. Admittedly, however, it seems less easy to assess the situation in other Arabian languages such as Sabaic, because the origin and function of the "imperfect"-type conjugation there is still debated. One should also note that an association between eroding perfectivity marking in the verbal system and emerging definiteness marking in the nominal system does not seem to be a major typological tendency, so further in-depth research would be needed.

Yet another area in which nominal and verbal system interact closely is the grammatical expression of voice.[44] Once again, the Aḥīrōm inscription displays a noteworthy peculiarity in that it contains two examples of the Gt-stem formed by a /t/-infix after the first root consonant (which is unattested not only in the whole of later Phoenician and Punic but also in the rest of Old Byblian): *tḥtsp* /tiḥtasip/ 'may it (his sceptre) become defoliated (or: break)'[45] and *thtpk* /tihtapik/ 'may it (his throne) collapse' (*KAI* 1.2).[46] Both are 3FS "short imperfects" from the roots *ḥsp* and *hpk*, respectively, expressing deontic modality; they occur in a curse formula and refer to potential usurpers of Byblos who might dare to open Aḥīrōm's sarcophagus. The Gt-stem serves as a reflexive or mediopassive[47] counterpart to the unmarked G-stem and can be reconstructed for Common Semitic. Hence, it must be a retention from an older stage of the language, just as in Ugaritic, Moabite, and Aramaic.[48] Since the passive system of Phoenician defies reconstruction, only more-or-less

44. For a more extensive diachronic treatment of the passive system in Hebrew and closely related languages, see Gzella 2009a.

45. The exact meaning of this verb is controversial.

46. Friedrich and Röllig 1999: §150, with a somewhat misleading translation as passives. Pace Garr 1985: 120, it is not at all clear whether the Gt in Old Byblian had usurped the meaning of the passive counterpart to the G-stem normally associated with the N-stem or the apophonic G-passive.

47. Reflexivity and middle voice have a considerable overlap because, in the former, the agent performs the grammatical roles of both subject and object whereas, in the latter, the agent is more generally affected by the action.

48. In Aramaic, the /t/-morpheme was transformed into a prefix, following a common development in languages. There is one example of a /t/-infix in the Old Aramaic Gozan inscription (*KAI* 309.23: *ygtzr* 'may it disappear', literally: 'may it cut itself off'), which has been explained as an archaism by some and as being influenced by the Akkadian Gt-stem by others. See also Gzella 2009a: 302.

inspired guesses can be made concerning the distribution of differing semantic nuances across the available morphological means. The lack of Gt-forms in other Phoenician and Punic texts may in theory be a simple coincidence, but their vanishing over the course of time seems much more likely than their preservation. With the presence of both a medio-passive "N"-stem and an "internal," apophonic passive (which, however, is not clearly attested in Phoenician), the Gt-stem in Canaanite at large would have had a comparatively low degree of markedness and could thus have dropped out easily. At least, this is what happened in Hebrew, the passive system of which would initially have resembled the passive of Phoenician: in view of the fact that Hebrew has very few fossilized remainders of the Gt-stem,[49] this category must have disappeared from living use at a relatively early stage; as a consequence, other stems broadened their functional range.[50] Aramaic, by contrast, which preserved the Gt-stem (in the form of a tG-stem) and even expanded its meaning to a genuine passive once the apophonic passives had dropped out, lacked an N-stem in its earliest manifestations, so that the semantic profile of the Gt-stem would have been less ambiguous there than in Canaanite. As a consequence, it appears fairly safe to treat the two Gt-"imperfects" in the Aḥīrōm sarcophagus as distinctive features of Old Byblian–and perhaps even of its oldest representative only.[51]

5. Additional Lexical Features

In addition to characteristic phonetic traits and core elements of the morphology, the lexicon of the Old Byblian corpus appears to be somewhat at variance with Standard Phoenician. The historical significance of these few differences, however, is hard to evaluate. They do not add much to the general picture but apparently do not militate against the conclusions drawn so far either. First of all, the use of an otherwise unattested conditional particle *ʾl* distinguishes the Aḥīrōm sarcophagus (*KAI* 1.2) from the rest of Old Byblian (*KAI* 3.3), which, just like Phoenician in general, has *ʾm* (see Friedrich and Röllig 1999:

49. For example, some archaic place-names such as Eshtaol or Eltekeh (Bauer 1917: 410) and a couple of forms from the root *pqd* 'to muster' in Judg 20:15, 17; 21:9 (Blau 1957: 386).

50. The verbal root *hpk* with the medial meaning 'to collapse', for instance, is attested in the G and N stems in Hebrew.

51. So, too, Amadasi Guzzo 1994: 182, yet without historical-linguistic arguments.

§257e).[52] There is no consensus about the precise etymology of *ʾl*, but several scholars relate it to the various deictic markers containing an /l/ attested in Semitic languages.[53] This sort of reanalysis of a deictic element as a conditional particle indeed occurs frequently, yet one cannot identify either *ʾl* or *ʾm* as the typologically more archaic form. If, moreover, the interpretation of *ʾm* in *KAI* 3.3 as an oath particle instead of a conditional conjunction proves correct,[54] the reason for the coexistence of both words in Old Byblian appears to have been functional rather than diachronic. Thus, all one can say is that *ʾm* was generalized in later Byblian—a development that was perhaps triggered or at least reinforced by contact with Standard Phoenician.

Equally ambiguous in terms of diagnostic value is the deictically neutral use of the preposition *b*, sometimes called *bet separativum*, in the expression *bmṣrm* 'from Egypt' (*KAI* 5.2) as opposed to the more common instances which require a translation 'in(to)', 'by', or 'with'. This ambiguous use occurs frequently in Ugaritic, which does not have an "ablative" preposition /min/, and in Early Hebrew poetry, but quite seldom in later Hebrew compositions (for a survey, see Althann 1997: 5–24). Within Hebrew, it must therefore count as an archaism. Phoenician, however, does not seem to have had the preposition /min/ until the fourth century B.C. (e.g., *KAI* 33.2; see Zevit 1975: 107–9), so *b* and *l* would naturally have assumed its role in earlier periods. An ablative use of *b* thus appears more archaic on a spectrum of the entire history of Phoenician, yet it does not constitute a peculiarity of Old Byblian, even though other examples are hard to find.[55]

Last but not least, Old Byblian uses the term *ʾdtw* 'his lady', a feminine counterpart to Common Semitic /ʾadān-/ 'lord', as a title for the city goddess of Byblos (*KAI* 5.2; 6.2; 7.4; also in *KAI* 29). The later Yeḥawmilk inscription, by contrast, has *rbt*, which essentially carries a

52. Note that the examples also include an instance from later Byblian (*KAI* 10.13, twice).

53. See Garr 1985: 116. Brockelmann (1947: 65–66) summarizes several older proposals. Brockelmann's own solution—namely, that this form derives from a verbal root meaning 'to be mighty' and that by implication the conditional clause is not introduced by any particle—has not won acceptance in recent scholarship.

54. Suggested by McCarter and Coote (1973: 19), who translate: "I have sworn: 'You shall by no means receive a grant!' "

55. The hypothesis that *km nbš ytm bʾm* in the ninth-century Kilamuwa inscription (*KAI* 24.13) means something along the lines of 'like the disposition of an orphan (taken from its) mother' would perhaps yield another example, but this is of course just one of many possibilities for understanding the passage in question.

very similar meaning (*KAI* 10.2, 3; see Amadasi Guzzo 1994: 184). Apart from these, no convincing cases have been identified in which Old Byblian uses a different word from a later Phoenician word for the same thing. Lexemes or semantic shifts confined to this dialect did not find their way into formulas and patterns that were presumably part of a broader literary tradition.

6. *Conclusion*

Conflicting evidence in the Old Byblian corpus renders it difficult for us to extract a coherent picture from the few surviving texts. From a linguistic point of view, the Aḥīrōm inscription without doubt turns out to be the most archaic, since at least three differences from the other seven witnesses are conditioned by chronological factors: the preservation of the glottal stop in personal names containing the word /ʔaḥ/ 'brother', pointing to a period halfway through the process of phonetic reduction, which may have begun in the second millennium; the presence of a 3MS suffix spelled *-h*, indicating that the etymological /-h/ of the suffix had not yet disappeared; and the lack of a definite article, hinting at the still-ongoing grammaticalization of this item. It is also quite possible to posit that the Gt-stem had already dropped out during the Old Byblian period in order to reduce "overhead" in the inventory of medio-passive forms; however, since none of the other inscriptions contains a verbal form in which this stem would be likely, judgment must be suspended. As a purely lexical item, the conditional particle *ʾl* seems less significant for purposes of classification but likewise sets the earliest direct representative of this dialect apart. The many similarities, by contrast, justify a date slightly earlier than *KAI* 2–8 and almost rule out the possibility that the Aḥīrōm text was composed in the thirteenth century B.C.[56] Thanks to a peripheral location and a conservative scribal tradition, some Byblian features could survive into Persian and Hellenistic or, depending on the controversial date of *KAI* 12, perhaps even Roman times (as sagaciously noted in Amadasi Guzzo 1994: 187). Nonetheless, the language would have been greatly influenced by the prestigious dialect of Tyre and Sidon.

Together with the rest of Old Byblian, *KAI* 1 reflects an intermediate stage of Canaanite between the second-millennium and the first-

56. Amadasi Guzzo (1994: 184) also concludes that such an early date, often assumed in earlier scholarship, is unlikely on the basis of both language and script.

millennium type. The main difference between these two types consists of the impact that the disappearance of the short word-final vowels had on the structure of the nominal and verbal systems. Following the loss of inflectional case markings, on the one hand, the rearrangement of the nominal categories may not yet have been finalized, as the preservation of at least some triphthongs and the absence of a direct-object marker suggest. However, a reanalysis of an old oblique form of the 3MS pronoun as reinforcing the subject reveals that the former nominative, genitive, and accusative cases were not fully distinguished in all environments. This view is supported by the possible loss of case endings on at least some nouns in the construct state. There are, on the other hand, no traces of a corresponding morphological distinction among "short imperfect," "long imperfect," and "subjunctive" as is characteristic of the older Semitic type. The past-tense use of the "short imperfect" is likewise unattested. The rise of a grammaticalized definite article during the first half of the tenth century B.C. might have developed from this situation because it compensated the reduction or loss of a category strongly marked for past tense and perfective aspect by producing a new item that formally highlighted definiteness.

By allowing a glimpse into the workings of precisely the driving forces that shaped the Syro-Palestinian languages of the first millennium, the Old Byblian inscriptions contribute to our understanding of the history of Semitic at a crucial moment. It is most unfortunate that there are so few of these inscriptions. On a less abstract level, the evidence put together here could also stimulate one to readdress the question about the relationship between Old Byblian and Standard Phoenician—or, rather, the local dialect on which Standard Phoenician is based. Many scholars, who rightly point to the archaic character of the Aḥīrōm inscription especially, assume that Old Byblian antedates Tyro-Sidonian (see, for instance, Garr 1985: 230–31). However, the true archaisms of tenth-century Old Byblian cannot be compared directly with the situation in eighth-century Standard Phoenician. Instead, both may have taken shape at the end of the second millennium, but this problem of Phoenician dialectology can only be tackled by means of a comprehensive study of the Semitic material from Bronze Age Syria–Palestine.

Bibliography

Althann, R.
1997 *Studies in Northwest Semitic.* BibOr 45. Rome: Pontifical Biblical Institute.

Amadasi Guzzo, M. G.
1994 Lingua e scrittura a Biblo. Pp. 179–91 in *Biblo: Una città e la sua cultura,* ed. E. Acquaro et al. Rome: Consiglio Nazionale delle Ricerche.

Bauer, H.
1917 Kanaanäische Miszellen. *ZDMG* 71: 410–13.

Bauer, H., and Leander, P.
1922 *Historische Grammatik der hebräischen Sprache des Alten Testamentes.* Halle: Max Niemeyer.

Beyer, K.
1969 *Althebräische Grammatik.* Göttingen: Vandenhoeck & Ruprecht.
1984–2004 *Die aramäischen Texte vom Toten Meer samt den Inschriften aus Palästina, dem Testament Levis aus der Kairoer Geniza, der Fastenrolle und den alten talmudischen Zitaten.* 2 vols. and supplement. Göttingen: Vandenhoeck & Ruprecht.
2006 Das biblische Hebräisch im Wandel. Pp. 159–80 in *"Der Odem des Menschen ist eine Leuchte des Herrn" (Gedenkschrift Agus),* ed. R. Reichman. Heidelberg: Carl Winter.

Blau, J.
1957 Über die t-Form des Hifʿil im Bibelhebräisch. *VT* 7: 385–88.
1978 Hebrew and North West Semitic: Reflections on the Classification of Semitic Languages. *HAR* 2: 21–44.

Blum, E.
2008 Das althebräische Verbalsystem: Eine synchrone Analyse. Pp. 91–142 in *Sprachliche Tiefe: Theologische Weite,* ed. O. Dyma and A. Michel. Biblisch-theologische Studien 91. Neukirchen-Vluyn: Neukirchener Verlag.

Bordreuil, P., and Pardee, D.
2004 *Manuel d'ougaritique.* 2 vols. Paris: Geuthner. [Translated into English as Bordreuil and Pardee 2009.]
2009 *A Manual of Ugaritic.* LSAWS 3. Winona Lake, IN: Eisenbrauns.

Brockelmann, C.
1908–13 *Grundriß der vergleichenden Grammatik der semitischen Sprachen.* 2 vols. Berlin: Reuther & Reichard.
1916 *Semitische Sprachwissenschaft.* Berlin: Göschen.
1947 Kanaanäische Miszellen. Pp. 61–67 in *Festschrift Otto Eißfeldt,* ed. J. Fück. Halle: Max Niemeyer.

Cook, E. M.
1994 On the Date of the Linguistic Dating of the Phoenician Ahirom Inscription (*KAI* 1). *JNES* 53: 33–36.

Cross, F. M.
1979 A Newly-Published Inscription of the Persian Age from Byblus. *IEJ* 29: 40–44.
Degen, R.
1969 *Altaramäische Grammatik der Inschriften des 10.–8. Jh. v. Chr.* AKM 38/3. Wiesbaden: Franz Steiner.
Driver, S. R.
1892 *A Treatise on the Use of the Tenses in Hebrew and Some Other Syntactical Questions.* Oxford: Clarendon. [Repr. with an introduction by W. R. Garr, Grand Rapids, MI: Eerdmans, 1998.]
Friedrich, J., and Röllig, W.
1999 *Phönizisch-Punische Grammatik.* 3rd ed. by M. G. Amadasi Guzzo with W. R. Mayer. AnOr 55. Rome: Pontifical Biblical Institute.
Garbini, G.
1977 I dialetti del fenicio. *Annali dell'Istituto Orientale di Napoli* 37: 283–94.
Garr, W. R.
1985 *Dialect Geography of Syria–Palestine, 1000–586 B.C.E.* Philadelphia: University of Pennsylvania Press. [Repr., Winona Lake, IN: Eisenbrauns, 2004.]
Gianto, A.
2000 Amarna Akkadian as a Contact Language. Pp. 123–32 in *Languages and Cultures in Contact,* ed. K. Van Lerberghe and G. Voet. OLA 96. Leuven: Peeters.
Ginsberg, H. L.
1970 The Northwest Semitic Languages. Pp. 102–24 in *The World History of the Jewish People.* First Series, *Ancient Times (Patriarchs and Judges).* vol. 2: *Patriarchs,* ed. B. Mazar. Tel Aviv: Jewish History Publications.
Golomb, D. M., with Hollis, S. T., eds.
1987 *"Working with No Data": Semitic and Egyptian Studies Presented to Thomas O. Lambdin.* Winona Lake, IN: Eisenbrauns.
Gzella, H.
2004 *Tempus, Aspekt und Modalität im Reichsaramäischen.* VOK 48. Wiesbaden: Harrassowitz.
2006 Die Entstehung des bestimmten Artikels im Semitischen: Eine "phönizische" Perspektive. *JSS* 51: 1–18.
2007 Some Penciled Notes on Ugaritic Lexicography. *BiOr* 64: 527–67.
2009a Voice in Classical Hebrew against Its Semitic Background. *Or* 78: 292–325.
2009b Ein auffälliger Konditionalsatz in der Aḥīrōm-Inschrift (*KAI* 1). Pp. 63–71 in *Philologisches und Historisches zwischen Anatolien und Sokotra: Analecta Semitica in Memoriam Alexander Sima,* ed. W. Arnold et al. Wiesbaden: Harrassowitz.
2010 Variation in the Ugaritic Letters and Some Implications Thereof. Pp. 58–70 in *Society and Administration in Ancient Ugarit,* ed. W. H. van Soldt. Leiden: Nederlands Instituut voor het Nabije Oosten.

2011a Northwest Semitic in General. Pp. 425–51 in *Semitic Languages: An International Handbook*, ed. S. Weninger et al. Handbücher zur Sprach- und Kommunikationswissenschaft 36. Berlin: de Gruyter.

2011b Phoenician. Pp. 55–75 in *Languages from the World of the Bible*, ed. H. Gzella. Berlin: de Gruyter.

Hackett, J. A.

2004 Phoenician and Punic. Pp. 365–85 in *The Cambridge Encyclopedia of the World's Ancient Languages*, ed. R. D. Woodard. Cambridge: Cambridge University Press.

Harris, Z. S.

1936 *A Grammar of the Phoenician Language*. AOS 8. New Haven, CT: American Oriental Society.

Holmstedt, R. D.

2007 The Etymologies of Hebrew *ʾăšer* and *šeC-*. *JNES* 66: 177–91.

Huehnergard, J.

1991 Remarks on the Classification of the Northwest Semitic Languages. Pp. 282–93 in *The Balaam Text from Deir Alla Re-evaluated*, ed. J. Hoftijzer and G. van der Kooij. Leiden: Brill.

1995 What Is Aramaic? *ARAM* 7: 261–82.

2005 Features of Central Semitic. Pp. 155–203 in *Biblical and Oriental Essays in Memory of William L. Moran*, ed. A. Gianto. BiOr 48. Rome: Pontifical Biblical Institute.

Israel, F.

1991 Some Conservative Features of Phoenician in the Light of Geographic Linguistics. Pp. 729–44 in *Semitic Studies in Honor of Wolf Leslau on the Occasion of His Eighty-Fifth Birthday*, ed. A. S. Kaye. Wiesbaden: Harrassowitz.

Joüon, P., and Muraoka, T.

2006 *A Grammar of Biblical Hebrew*. Rev. ed. SubBi 27. Rome: Pontifical Biblical Institute.

Kapeliuk, O.

2006 The Neo-Aramaic Tense System in the Light of Translations from Russian. Pp. 381–90 in *Loquentes linguis: Studi linguistici e orientali in onore di Fabrizio A. Pennacchietti*, ed. P. G. Borbone et al. Wiesbaden: Harrassowitz.

Lehmann, R. G.

2005 *Dynastensarkophage mit szenischen Reliefs aus Byblos und Zypern*, vol. 1/2: *Die Inschrift(en) des Aḥīrōm-Sarkophags und die Schachtinschrift des Grabes V in Jbeil (Byblos)*. Mainz: Zabern.

Leiss, E.

2000 *Artikel und Aspekt: Die grammatischen Muster von Definitheit*. Berlin: de Gruyter.

Lipiński, E.

2001 *Semitic Languages: Outline of a Comparative Grammar*. 2nd ed. OLA 80. Leuven: Peeters.

Lyons, C.
1999 *Definiteness*. Cambridge: Cambridge University Press.
McCarter, P. K., Jr., and Coote, R. B.
1973 The Spatula Inscription from Byblos. *BASOR* 212: 16–22.
Millard, A.
2011 The Alphabet. Pp. 14–27 in *Languages from the World of the Bible*, ed. H. Gzella. Berlin: de Gruyter.
Miller, C. L.
2004 Methodological Issues in Reconstructing Language Systems from Epigraphic Fragments. Pp. 281–305 in *The Future of Biblical Archaeology: Reassessing Methodologies and Assumptions*, ed. J. K. Hoffmeier and A. Millard. Grand Rapids, MI: Eerdmans.
Pardee, D.
2003–4 Review of *Ugaritische Grammatik*, by Josef Tropper (AOAT 273; Münster: Ugarit-Verlag, 2000). *AfO* 50: 1–404. http://orientalistik.univie.ac.at/fileadmin/documents/Rezension_Tropper_AOAT273.pdf.
Rabin, C.
1971 Semitic Languages. Pp. 1149–57 in vol. 14 of *Encyclopaedia Judaica*, ed. C. Roth. Jerusalem: Keter.
Reckendorf, H.
1895 *Die syntaktischen Verhältnisse des Arabischen*. Leiden: Brill. [Repr., 1967.]
Röllig, W.
1974 Eine neue phönizische Inschrift aus Byblos. Pp. 1–15 in *Neue Ephemeris für Semitische Epigraphik* 2, ed. R. Degen, W. W. Müller, and W. Röllig. Wiesbaden: Harrassowitz.
1992 Die Phönizische Sprache: Bemerkungen zum gegenwärtigen Forschungsstand. Pp. 76–94 in *Karthago*, ed. W. Huß. Wege der Forschung 654. Darmstadt: Wissenschaftliche Buchgesellschaft.
Segert, S.
1976 *A Grammar of Phoenician and Punic*. Munich: Beck.
Stempel, R.
2008 Zur Geschichte des bestimmten Artikels in den semitischen Sprachen. Pp. 551–59 in *Chomolangma, Demawend und Kasbek: Festschrift für Roland Bielmeier zu seinem 65. Geburtstag*, vol. 2: *Chomolangma*, ed. B. Huber, M. Volkart, and P. Widmer. Halle: International Institute for Tibetan and Buddhist Studies.
Tietz, R.
1963 *Bedingungssatz und Bedingungsausdruck im Koran*. Ph.D. dissertation, Tübingen University.
Zevit, Z.
1975 The So-Called Interchangeability of the Prepositions *b*, *l*, and *m(n)* in Northwest Semitic. *JANES* 7: 103–12.

Phoenician Case in Typological Context

Rebecca Hasselbach

1. Introduction and Methodology

As is well known, Semitic languages are attested for a time period of roughly 4,700 years—from the earliest attestation of Semitic personal names in Sumerian cuneiform sources from roughly 2600 B.C. until today—which is a time depth unequaled by any other language family. Given this long and continuous attestation, we might expect that Semitic would play a prominent role in the general study of language and the development of current linguistic theories such as Generative Grammar, Optimality Theory, Functional Linguistics, Pragmatics, and Discourse Analysis. However, Semitic languages have been marginal at best in establishing these linguistic trends and, more importantly, in their application, especially with regard to the study of ancient languages.[1]

The study and analysis of ancient Semitic languages is primarily based on the methodologies of comparative and historical linguistics as developed on the basis of Indo-European in the nineteenth century. The historical and comparative method has been quite successful for the reconstruction of individual languages, sub-branches, and certain features of the language family as a whole. However, as useful and necessary as it is to work from a historical and comparative perspective,

Author's note: I would like to thank Martin Worthington for sharing his unpublished manuscript on Neo-Assyrian with me.

1. There have been notable exceptions, such as the work of McCarthy and Prince, who based much of their work in generative phonology and morphology on Semitic, and Chomsky's master's thesis, which is based on Hebrew. These works, however, are hardly referred to by Semitists. Furthermore, the formative studies of generative linguistics were based on English, despite Chomsky's early work on Hebrew (Izre'el 2002: 13). Discourse analysis has become more prominent in recent years, although primarily in the study of modern Semitic languages (see Khan 2002).

this methodology often reaches its limits, especially when it comes to features for which the data available in the individual languages are too diverse and/or ambiguous to allow for certainty in reconstruction.

It is in cases such as these that it can be useful to turn to linguistic typology. A typology of languages tries to establish common principles in the formation of languages based on cross-linguistic comparison (Croft 2003: 4). One of the most important results of typological studies gained so far is the discovery that there are constraints to linguistic variation—that is, languages do not vary infinitely. The constraints that can be formulated are commonly referred to as linguistic "universals"; in other words, typological universals are the underlying principles that restrict language variation (Croft 2003: 5).[2] In addition, typologists have established hierarchies (such as the animacy and case-marking hierarchies) and functional principles that attempt to explain the attested constraints.

Although typologies and functional principles have primarily been established on the basis of modern languages, it is commonly accepted that typological observations are as valid for dead languages as for living languages. Consequently, when we try to reconstruct or trace the development of a linguistic feature in a given language or language family, the constraints imposed by typologies should prevent us from proposing reconstructions that violate these cross-linguistic tendencies. Typologies can thus help us to evaluate proposed reconstructions and even lead us further back in reconstructing developments that occurred prior to the stages of a language or language family that can be reconstructed with the historical and comparative method. The integration of linguistic typology into the reconstruction and analysis of ancient Semitic languages is thus highly desirable in order to put proposed reconstructions on a firmer methodological base.

Given these facts, it is noteworthy that typology is almost absent in the field of comparative Semitics. Only few scholars, such as Talmy Givón (e.g., Givón 1980; 1991), have worked on Semitic (although mostly on modern Semitic languages) using a typological approach. In order to advance our understanding of Semitic, it would be helpful to integrate the methodologies and results of linguistic typology into the analysis of the language family.

2. As Croft (2003: 5) states, "Language universals reflect the belief that there exist linguistic properties beyond the essential definitional properties of language that hold for all languages."

There is one important methodological point that must be considered, however: despite the fact that typologies summarize the most commonly found linguistic patterns and developments in large samples of languages, they are not exceptionless universals. Consequently, before applying the results of typological studies to any given language or language family regarding developments that cannot sufficiently be proven by the available data, one must first establish that the respective language(s) conform to cross-linguistic tendencies in related aspects. This means, for example, before trying to reconstruct the whole case system, expression of grammatical roles and relations, and the alignment of Proto-Semitic with reference to typological data, one must first investigate whether or not it is possible to apply linguistic typology to Semitic languages, and whether the developments we can trace with regard to its case systems conform to cross-linguistic tendencies.

I have recently argued that the case system of Phoenician behaves according to principles established by language typologies with respect to the process underlying the loss of morphological case markers and case syncretism (Hasselbach 2011). I also suggested that the same process can be observed in Akkadian, although for the latter language I did not provide a detailed investigation. In the present essay, I wish to follow up on the comparison of the Phoenician and Akkadian case systems and the implications that the parallels found in these languages might have for the examination of Semitic languages in general.

Let me first summarize the basic typological premises used for this investigation. In the world's languages, there are three main ways in which case can be expressed: (1) by synthetic constructions, that is morphological case markers; (2) by analytical constructions that primarily consist of adposition plus noun; and (3) by position, that is, word order (Blake 2001: 10–12; Anderson 2006: 2).[3] The present investigation will focus on the first type, inflectional case markers.

Inflectional case markers can undergo certain cross-linguistically attested developments. For example, individual case morphemes can be neutralized. This process results in the formal merger of two or more inflectional endings and is commonly referred to as "syncretism" (Blake

3. Certain tendencies concerning combinations of morphological case marking and word order can be observed. The word order SVO, for example, is commonly employed in languages that do not mark case morphologically but primarily use word order to express grammatical relations. VSO is often found in languages with mixed systems, while SOV is primarily used in languages that make extensive use of morphological case marking.

2001: 19). Cross-linguistically, syncretisms occur according to certain tendencies. In Latin, for example, the nominative and accusative tend to merge morphologically in the neuter declination. They form a clear opposition to the dative and ablative, which likewise tend to merge (Blake 2001: 21). The merger of nominative and accusative versus dative and ablative can be explained on a functional level. The nominative and accusative primarily encode verbal arguments—the Agent of a transitive verb A, the subject of an intransitive verb S, and the Patient P—while the dative and ablative are more frequently found after prepositions (Blake 2001: 22, 30; Anderson 2006: 2).[4] This implies that the morphological merger or syncretism of cases often reflects similarities in verbal argumentation: cases that are closer to each other in the frequency of their occurrence as verbal arguments are more likely to fall together morphologically than cases that vary greatly in this respect. In addition, the nominative and accusative are what is often referred to as "core" or "grammatical" cases. These cases include nominative, ergative, accusative, and dative. The ablative, instrumental, and others, on the other hand, are referred to as "semantic" cases, which primarily express location. The nominative and accusative are thus functionally closer to each other than, for example, the nominative and ablative, a fact that again facilitates a morphological merger (Blake 2001: 31–33, 173). It is important to note that the morphological merger of cases has no impact on the original function of each case, which is preserved.

In addition to morphological mergers, case markers can be lost by phonological processes. Languages do not usually prevent the loss of case inflection caused by regular sound changes. Case in languages of this sort is simply expressed by alternate means, such as word order and/or adpositions (Blake 2001: 169). It is important to note that, when the inflectional case system is lost or in the process of being lost, case marking tends to be preserved on independent and bound pronouns—that is, nouns and pronouns do not need to behave in the same manner with respect to case inflection, as can easily be exemplified by English. Compare, for example, "I (NOM) saw him (ACC)" and "He (NOM) saw me (ACC)" versus "The man (NOM) saw the rat (ACC)" and "The rat (NOM) saw the man (ACC)" (Blake 2001: 170).[5]

---

4. The genitive is primarily adnominal—that is, it is not used as a verbal argument (Blake 2001: 149).

5. When a language only has a two-case system, it usually consists of a nominative versus oblique distinction (rather than a simple nominative versus accusative) with the oblique covering a wide range of functions (Blake 2001: 156).

2. Overview of Inflectional Case Systems in Semitic

As is well known, various Semitic languages such as Classical Arabic (1), Akkadian (2), and Ugaritic (3) share the same vocalic case suffixes in the singular, dual, and plural.

(1) Classical Arabic: masculine noun

	SINGULAR	DUAL	PLURAL
NOM	*-u-*	*-ā-*	*-ū-*
GEN	*-i-*	*-ay-*	*-ī-*
ACC	*-a-*	*-ay-*	*-ī-*

(2) Old Babylonian: masculine unbound noun

	SINGULAR	DUAL	PLURAL
NOM	*-u-*	*-ā-*	*-ū*
GEN	*-i-*	*-ī-* (<**ay*)	*-ī*
ACC	*-a-*	*-ī-* (<**ay*)	*-ī*

(3) Ugaritic: masculine unbound noun (see Tropper 2000: 338)

	SINGULAR	DUAL	PLURAL
NOM	*-u-*	*-ā-*	*-ū-*
GEN	*-i-*	*-ē-* (<**ay*)	*-ī-*
ACC	*-a-*	*-ē-* (<**ay*)	*-ī-*

In the singular, we have evidence for a triptotic system consisting of a nominative marked by *-u*, a genitive by *-i*, and an accusative by *-a*. The dual and plural have a diptotic system with a nominative versus oblique opposition marked by *-ā* in the nominative dual, **-ay* in the oblique dual, *-ū* in the masculine nominative plural, and *-ī* in the masculine oblique plural.[6]

Other Semitic languages such as Geʿez have a reduced system of case inflection (4).

6. In the following paradigms, only masculine forms are given since these are representative of the case inflection of each language. The only difference in the feminine is that it has a short case vowel in the plural instead of a long one.

(4) Geʿez: singular and plural unbound noun

	SINGULAR/PLURAL
NOM	-*Ø*
GEN	-*Ø*
ACC	-*a*

In Geʿez, the reduced system can be explained by the loss of final short vowels: short /i/ and /u/ regularly merged to /ə/, which was subsequently lost in word-final position (*i*, *u* > *ə*; *ə* > *Ø* / _#), while short /a/ was preserved in all environments. The loss of /i/ and /u/ and the preservation of /a/ resulted in the diptotic inflection of non-accusative versus accusative that was extended to the plural by analogy.

Other Semitic languages such as Hebrew and Aramaic do not distinguish case morphologically. Vestiges of former case vowels, however, can still be found in the linking vowels that connect singular nouns and possessive suffixes in Hebrew and Aramaic. These linking vowels were fixed in vowel harmony with the original suffix vowel, illustrated in (5) and (6).

(5) Hebrew

malk-ō < **malkuhu* (NOM)
king-his.MS
'his king'

malk-ēḵ < **malkiki* (GEN)
king-your.FS
'your king'

malk-əḵā < **malkaka* (ACC)[a]
king-your.MS
'your king'

a. For the reconstruction of the final vowel as short see Hasselbach 2004.

(6) Syriac

malk-eh < **malkihi* (GEN)
king-his.MS
'his king

malk-eḵ(y) < **malkiki* (GEN)
king-your.FS'
'your king'

malk-an < **malkana* (ACC)
king-our.CP
'our king'

The linking vowels indicate that both Hebrew and Aramaic originally had some reflex of the same three case vowels in the singular as attested in Classical Arabic, Akkadian, and Ugaritic.

Given this evidence, we can state with considerable certainty that Semitic at an early stage had an inflectional case system with three morphological case markers in the singular and two in the dual and plural, which reflect three cases: the nominative, genitive and accusative–the genitive and accusative being syncretized in the dual and plural (7).[7]

(7) Proto-Semitic: masculine noun[8]

	SINGULAR	DUAL	PLURAL
NOM	*-u-*	*-ā-*	*-ū-*
GEN	*-i-*	*-ay*	*-ī-*
ACC	*-a-*	*-ay-*	*-ī-*

3. Case Inflection in Phoenician and Akkadian

The following sections provide a closer look at the attestations and developments of the case systems of Phoenician and Akkadian.

7. This reconstructed case system greatly simplifies a more complex situation, since it does not account for certain features such as the diptotic declension of certain nominal patterns and proper names in Classical Arabic and Ugaritic and the distribution of vocalic markers in the earliest Semitic proper names, which indicate that the earliest Semitic case system probably differed from the reconstruction proposed here. Nevertheless, it is certain that Semitic at some time before the split into East and West Semitic had developed a case system as the one attested in Classical Arabic, Akkadian, and Ugaritic. It is thus possible to use this common reconstruction as a working hypothesis in the present context.

8. For this reconstruction and presentation of the case system of classical Semitic languages, see, for example, Lipiński 2001: 267; Huehnergard 2004: 149.

3.1. Phoenician[9]

In order to understand the development and evidence of case markers in Phoenician, we must first establish the case system of its ancestor, early Canaanite. Evidence for early Canaanite exists in the Canaanizing tablets from Tell El-Amarna dating to the fourteenth century B.C. These texts exhibit a fully productive case system for nouns and adjectives that is in accordance with the case inflection of Classical Arabic (Rainey 1996: 1.161). Since Akkadian still had a productive inflectional system at that point as well, the question arises whether the case markers attested in the Amarna letters are genuine Canaanite forms or whether they reflect Akkadian morphology. The fact that the case inflection is part of the underlying Canaanite and not merely a feature of Akkadian is proven by occurrences of Canaanite glosses that show morphological case inflection, such as examples (8)–(10), which in part do not conform to Akkadian morphology (Rainey 1996: 1.164).

(8) *ru-šu-nu*
rušu-nu
head.NOM.SING-1CP.GEN
'our head'

(9) *ta-aḫ-ta-mu*
taḥta-mu
below.ACC-3MP.GEN
'beneath them'

(10) *le-lá-ma*
night.ACC-and
'at night'

Furthermore, contrary to Akkadian usage, nouns sometimes have case vowels in the construct and before pronominal suffixes, a fact that is attributed to West Semitic influence (Rainey 1996: 1.174).[10]

In addition to the previously mentioned vestiges of case vowels before pronominal suffixes in Hebrew, the evidence from the Amarna letters allows us to reconstruct a fully productive inflectional case system

9. Parts of this investigation of the Phoenician case system are based on Hasselbach 2011.

10. Examples include *ba-aš-ta-ka* 'your honor' in the accusative.

for Proto-Canaanite that had the same basic case affixes as those given for Proto-Semitic. The ancestor of Phoenician thus had a fully productive case-marking system.

Let us now turn to Phoenician itself. The dialects relevant for the present investigation are Byblian, Old and Standard Phoenician. As is well known, these dialects are written in an entirely consonantal script. The vocalic case suffixes of the singular and plural are thus never expressed in the orthography. There is, consequently, no direct evidence for the status of case inflection in nouns. Nevertheless, the presence or absence of case vowels can, at least to a certain degree, be inferred from other orthographic features, which I will discuss in the following.

In Old Byblian and Old Phoenician, word-final /n/ of the first noun in a construct assimilates to the first consonant of the next word, as in examples (11)–(12):

(11) *byḥmlk*
biy-yaḥūmilk (< *bin-Y.)
son.CSTR-PN
'son of Yaḥūmilk'. (*KAI* 6.1, 7.3, Old Byblian)

(12) *bklby*
bik-kalbay (< *bin-K.)
son.CSTR-PN
'son of Kalbay' (*KAI* 8, Old Byblian)

Nouns that have a glide as the third root radical lose the final glide, as in example (13):

(13) *qn* *ʾrṣ*
qōnV ʾarṣ (< **qōniyV ʾarṣi*)
creator.CSTR earth
'the creator of the earth'. (*KAI* 26 A III.18, Old Phoenician)

The phrases in *KAI* 6 and *KAI* 26 reflect the nominative, designating the subjects of their clauses, while *KAI* 8 is in the genitive. The assimilation of /n/ and the loss of the final glide can only be accounted for by the absence of the final case vowel in the singular construct, which in these cases are the final short vowels of the nominative and genitive, /u/ and /i/. Consequently, the loss of most if not all case vowels on nouns in the construct must have occurred no later than the late eleventh or early tenth centuries B.C. (Friedrich and Röllig 1999: §92).

Furthermore, in Standard Phoenician, we find two different sets of possessive suffixes for 1cs, 3ms, and 3fs on singular nouns used in different syntactic contexts. If the noun is in the nominative, these suffixes are not indicated in the writing, while if the noun is in the genitive, the suffixes have a final <Y>; see example (14).[11] For the following reconstruction see Huehnergard (1991: 187).

(14) Phoenician Possessive Suffixes: Nominative and Genitive

1cs nom *-C-Ø* = */-ī/* < **-ī*
1cs gen *-i-Y* = */iya/* < **-iya*

3ms nom *-C-Ø* = */-ō/*[a] < **-ahu*
3ms gen *-i-Y* = */-iyu/* < **-ihu*

3fs nom *-C-Ø* = */-ā/* < **-aha*
3fs gen *-i-Y* = */-iya/* < **-iha*

a. The vocalization of the 3ms suffix is taken from Greek transcriptions, which express this suffix vowel as /-ō/, such as βαραχω 'may he bless him' (Krahmalkov 2001: 69).

The pronominal suffixes of the nominative reflect a merger with the forms that developed on the basis of suffixes originally attached to nouns in the accusative. The latter are the result of vowel contractions that occurred after the loss of intervocalic /h/ (15).

11. There is one exception in which the genitive suffix is not indicated in the orthography, for which, see Krahmalkov 2001: 52. The distinction between a nominative and genitive in the 1cs is only preserved in the earliest stage of Phoenician, that is, Old Phoenician and the Kilamuwa inscription from Samʾal. In the rest of Phoenician, beginning with the Karatepe inscription, the 1cs suffix is most commonly written <Y> independent of case (Friedrich and Röllig 1999: §234). For less frequently occurring spellings without <Y>, see Krahmalkov 2001: 50. The distinction in the 3s suffixes remains throughout Standard Phoenician but is lost in Late Punic (Krahmalkov 2001: 50). Byblian differs from the following presentation in that it does not have distinct forms for pronominal suffixes in the nominative and genitive (Hackett 2004: 375). See also Krahmalkov (2001: 50–59) for Byblian. The 3ms possessive suffix in early Old Byblian is generally written with <H>, reflecting the original suffix consonant /h/. Friedrich and Röllig (1999: §234) assume that the original case vowels were preserved before this suffix.

(15) Phoenician Possessive Suffixes: Accusative

3MS ACC **malkahu > *malkaw > malkō*

3FS ACC **malkaha > *malkā*

The possessive suffix derived from the original accusative was then analogically extended to the nominative.

The forms with <Y> in the genitive are the result of the palatalization of the original /h/ of the suffix after the high front vowel /i/ (16).[12]

(16) Phoenician Possessive Suffixes: Genitive

3MS GEN **malkihu > malkiyu*

3FS GEN **malkiha > malkiya(:)*

The different forms of the possessive suffixes that emerge in Standard Phoenician indicate that the case distinction before pronominal suffixes, at least the distinction between nominative/accusative and genitive, must have been preserved until these suffixes developed. Although we do not have any evidence for the respective possessive suffixes in Old Phoenician, the distinction between nominative/accusative and genitive suffixes in Standard Phoenician still makes it very likely that the distinction of at least two cases was preserved longer on nouns with possessive suffixes than on nouns in construct without suffixes. Also note that case vowels in Phoenician never underwent the same vowel harmony with the original suffix vowel as attested in Hebrew and Aramaic mentioned above. Most importantly, the distribution of the suffixes according to case–nominative/accusative versus genitive–clearly indicates the merger of nominative and accusative and the preservation of the genitive in the pronominal system.

---

12. A similar distinction is found in 3MP suffixes, for which the nominative is written <M> and the genitive <NM>. For a discussion of these forms, see Huehnergard 1991: 187, 192. The accusative suffixes likewise have different forms based on the form of the verb to which they are attached. When the verbal stem ends in a consonant, the 3MS suffix is not written, but when the verbal form ends in a vowel, the suffix is written as <Y> (Hackett 2004: 376). This distribution shows the same phonologically motivated palatalization of /h/ after vowels as suggested for nouns. The palatalization occurred after final /ī/ and /ū/, as in *bnty* 'I built it' versus *yšbt* 'I sat down' (the latter form of the 1CS is attested in Old Byblian, Byblian, Old Phoenician and Phoenician) and *brky* 'they blessed him'. No verbal forms ending in final /ā/ are attested (Friedrich and Röllig 1999: §§187–90).

The status of vocalic case markers outside nouns in the construct and with possessive suffixes is more difficult to establish. The status of final short /a/ can in part be inferred by an orthographic change that took place during the transition from Old Byblian to later Byblian. In Old Byblian, III-*w*/*y* roots are usually written with a final glide, as in *ʿly* 'he ascended' and *bny* 'he built', which indicates the preservation of the original final vowel of the 3MS perfect. The verbal forms can therefore be vocalized as /ʿalaya/ and /banaya/, respectively. In all other dialects of Phoenician, including Old Phoenician, the third root letter is not indicated in the writing, as in *ḥz* 'he saw', vocalized as /ḥazō/ (Friedrich and Röllig 1999: §§92, 174). The absence of any orthographic representation of the glide indicates that the original final short vowel, /a/ in all these cases, was not present any longer (Friedrich and Röllig 1999: §280).[13]

The loss of final short /a/ and most likely /u/ is further indicated by the aforementioned analogical extension of the form of the possessive suffix on nouns in the accusative to nouns plus suffix in the nominative. This formal merger was most likely caused by the merger of nominative and accusative in unbound nouns and adjectives, and this in turn implies the loss of final short /a/ and /u/ (Huehnergard 1991: 188).[14]

The merger of nominative and accusative on unbound nouns is confirmed by the emergence of the direct-object marker *ʾyt* in Standard

13. The development that resulted in the final long vowel of III-*y* roots in Phoenician is, of course, the contraction of the original triphthong. Nevertheless, the forms from Old Byblian indicate that the triphthong, and thus the final /a/, was still preserved. Another indication that Old Byblian preserved final short vowels at least to a certain degree is the occurrence of what seem to be accusatives of direction, such as *gbl* 'to Byblos', to be vocalized /gubla/ with the final /a/ representing the accusative case vowel (Friedrich and Röllig 1999: §280).

14. It is important to note that there is no direct evidence for the loss of final /u/ besides the merger of nominative and accusative, which might theoretically also reflect a merger into *-u*. Participles of III-*y* roots, which would have preserved final /y/ in the orthography if they had had a final case vowel, are written without /y/ in Old Byblian—the only dialect in which the final triphthong would have been preserved; however, note that the one attestation we have is in the construct. Imperfects of III-*y* roots could also theoretically provide evidence for the preservation or loss of final /u/ (a distinction between long and short imperfect is preserved and noticeable in forms that distinguish these forms by the presence or absence of final *-na*—that is, the 2FS, 2MP, and 3MP), but unfortunately we only have evidence for the short imperfect in Old Byblian, which, again, is the one dialect in which original *yaqtulu* and *yaqtul* would have been distinguished orthographically. The final triphthong had contracted in all other Phoenician dialects (Friedrich and Röllig 1999: §§64b, 134, 177).

Phoenician, since the merger of nominative and accusative must logically have preceded the emergence of this morpheme.[15] The direct-object marker first occurs in an inscription from Cyprus that dates to the end of the ninth century B.C.; this datum conforms with the aforementioned distinction between certain possessive suffixes according to case that emerges in Standard Phoenician and the attested loss of final short /a/ in the transition of Old Byblian to Byblian. All these features combined indicate that Phoenician lost final short /a/ and probably /u/ at the beginning of the first millennium B.C.

An important question that still requires clarification is whether the genitive on unbound nouns was lost at the same time as the nominative and accusative. Friedrich and Röllig suggest that all short vowels were lost at the beginning of the first millennium B.C.,[16] while Huehnergard assumes that the binary inflection attested in the pronominal system was also preserved in the nominal inflection, since it would not make sense to preserve case marking only before pronominal suffixes (Huehnergard 1991: 188 n. 11).[17] Huehnergard's argument is not necessarily valid though, since, as mentioned above, it is a cross-linguistic phenomenon that pronouns tend to preserve case distinction longer than nouns. Consequently, the preservation of a genitive versus non-genitive distinction in parts of the pronominal system is no indication that the same distinction is also present in the nominal system. The question whether the genitive was preserved on nouns, therefore, still requires further investigation.

The inscriptional evidence for Phoenician does not provide us with any information regarding the status of final short /i/. We therefore must look at evidence outside the genuine Phoenician textual material, such as transcriptions of proper names into other writing systems, in particular Neo-Assyrian cuneiform. However, one must be aware that

15. The use of the direct-object marker is not mandatory. It is primarily used before definite nouns, but even here its use seems to be optional (Friedrich and Röllig 1999: §275). Garr assumes that the direct object is usually unmarked in Standard Phoenician, and that the direct-object marker is used to mark contrast and emphasis; he states: "In Standard Phoenician, then, the *nota accusativi* marked objects that were of particular interest to the author, its use was subject to individual style" (Garr 1985: 192).

16. Friedrich and Röllig (1999: §217) include final short /i/ in this statement.

17. Recent treatments of Phoenician grammar, such as Hackett's, follow Huehnergard's analysis (Hackett 2004: 374). Friedrich and Röllig (1999: §217), on the other hand, assume that the opposition of genitive and non-genitive was only preserved before pronominal suffixes on singular nouns.

the transcriptions can, of course, reflect the grammar of the underlying language, especially when, as in our case, the case system of the transcribed language is similar to that of the language into which the transliterations were made. The investigation of transcriptions can thus only lead to tentative results.

In the scholarly literature, we find different opinions on whether or not Phoenician names in cuneiform transcriptions indicate the preservation of case vowels. Friedrich and Röllig state that cuneiform transcriptions of Phoenician names from the Neo-Assyrian and Neo-Babylonian periods (ninth–fifth centuries B.C.) show no evidence of a productive system of inflectional case marking. CV signs at the end of a word are used when the Phoenician word ends in a consonant cluster that could not be expressed in cuneiform writing. For example, the sign PA is used for a final syllable ending in CP instead of AB to avoid resolving of the final cluster (Friedrich and Röllig 1999: §§92, 217, 256). Segert, on the other hand, states that especially in the early period "case endings may be reflected in some transcriptions" (Segert 1976: 114).[18] An important aspect neglected by Friedrich and Röllig is distinguishing between different time periods within the transcribed material. Table 1 provides representative names in chronological order.[19]

Table 1: Phoenician Names in Cuneiform Transcriptions[a]

Shalmaneser III (858–824 B.C.)			
ma-ti-nu-ba-ʾa-li 'gift of Baal' (Shalm. ii 93)	NOM CSTR -*u*		GEN -*i*
a-du-nu-ba-ʾa-li 'Baal is Lord' (Shalm. ii 94)	NOM -*u*	(PRED)	NOM -*i*
Tiglath-pileser III (744–727)			
ḫi-ru-um-mu 'my brother is exalted' (Tigl. III 9.51)	–		NOM -*u* (PRED)
[*ma*]-*ta-an-bi-ʾi-il* 'gift of Baal' (Tigl. III 67.60)	NOM CSTR -*Ø*		GEN -*Ø*

18. Segert (1976: 114) quotes names transcribed at the time of Shalmaneser III, such as *ma-ti-nu-ba-ʾa-li* 'gift of Baʿl' and *a-du-nu-ba-ʾa-li*, both of which employ the nominative correctly. The case marking in the first name cannot reflect Assyrian usage since Assyrian would not mark case on a construct noun. Latin and Greek transliterations from the fifth century B.C. on clearly do not reflect case vowels.

19. This list is based on Benz 1972. The elements *abdi* 'servant' and *milki* 'king/Milk' are always written in the same way, regardless of position or syntactic context. Other **qatl* nouns such as **baʿl* do not follow the same convention of resolving the final consonant cluster orthographically by writing final <Ci>. It is unlikely that the guttural in **baʿl* was lost since it is indicated by <ʾV / Vʾ> in most cases, and thus *ʿabd*, *milk*, and *baʿl* all have the same underlying nominal pattern *qVtl*, which, consequently, is not likely to be the reason for the different orthographic representations of the final syllable.

si-pí-it-ti-bi-ʾi-li 'judgment of Baal' (Tigl. III 67 Rs 7)	NOM CSTR *-i*	GEN *-i*
Sennacherib (704–681)		
bu-du-DINGIR 'by the hands of Il' (Senn. ii 55)	GEN P *-u*	–
ma-lik-ram-mu 'Malik is exalted' (Senn. ii 57)	NOM *-Ø*	NOM *-u*
mi-in-ḫi-im-mu 'compassionate (one)' (Senn. ii 50)	NOM *-u*	–
tu-ba-ʾa-lum 'Baal is with him' (Senn. ii 51)	–	NOM *-um*
ú-ru-mil-ki 'Milk is light' (Senn. ii 53)	NOM *-u* (PRED)	*milki*
Esarhaddon (680–669)		
ab-di-mil-ku-ut-ti 'servant of Milkot' (Esar. ii 65)	*abdi*	GEN *-i*
a-bi-ba-ʾa-li 'Baal is my father' (Esar. v 61)		NOM *-i*
a-ḫi-mil-ki 'Milk is (my) brother' (Esar. v 62)		*milki*
ba-ʾa-li 'Baal' (Esar. iii 17)	NOM *-i*	
ba-ʾa-lu 'Baal' (Esar. v 55)	NOM *-u*	
ma-ta-an-ba-ʾa-al 'gift of Baal' (Esar. v 60)	NOM CSTR *-Ø*	GEN *-Ø*
mil-ki-a-ša-pa 'Milk has added' (Esar. v 59)	*milki*	PERF *-a*
Assurbanipal (668–631)		
a-bi-ba-ʾa-al 'Baal is (my) father' (Assrb. ii 82)		NOM *-Ø*
a-bi-mil-ki 'Milk is (my) father' (Assrb. ii 84)		*milki*
a-du-ni-ba-ʾa-al 'Baal is Lord' (Assrb. ii 82)	NOM *-i*	NOM *-Ø*
a-zi-ba-ʾa-al 'Baal is my protection / strength' (Assrb. ii 82)		NOM *-Ø*
ba-ʾa-al 'Baal' (Assrb. ii 49)	NOM *-Ø*	
ba-ʾa-al-ḫa-nu-nu 'Baal has shown favor' (Assrb. ii 84)	NOM *-Ø*	PERF *-u*
ba-'a-al-ia-šu-pu 'Baal has added' (Assrb. ii 83)	NOM *-Ø*	PERF *-u*
ba-'a-al-ma-lu-ku 'Baal has reigned' (Assrb. ii 84)	NOM *-Ø*	PERF *-u*
bu-di-ba-al 'by the hands of Baal' (Assrb. ii 83)	GEN P *-i*	GEN *-Ø*
ia-ḫi-mil-ki 'Milk may live' (Assrb. ii 58)		*milki*
ia-ki-in-lu-u 'Ilu may establish' (Assrb. ii 63)		NOM *-u*
ša-pa-ṭí-ba-al 'Baal has judged' (Assrb. ii 83)	PERF *-i* (PRED)	NOM *-Ø*
Seventh-century economic and legal sources		
ab-di-a-zu-zi 'servant of strength (?)' (ADD 285.rev. 4)	*abdi*	GEN *-i*
ab-di-ḫi-mu-nu 'servant of Hammon' (ADD 425.15)	*abdi*	GEN *-u*
ab-di-mil-ki 'servant of Milk' (ADD 1040.5)	*abdi*	*milki*
ab-di-^{d}*sam-si* 'servant of Shamash' (ADD 1.3)	*abdi*	GEN *-i*
ab-di-si-ḫar 'servant of dawn' (ADD 254.rev. 4)	*abdi*	GEN *-Ø*
a-du-na-i-zi 'Strength is Lord' (ADD 26.1)	NOM *-a*	NOM *-i*
a-du-na-iz 'Strength is Lord' (ADD 3.3)	NOM *-a*	NOM *-Ø*
a-ḫu-ut-mil-ki 'Milk is sister' or 'sister of Milk' (ADD 894.5)	NOM (CSTR) *-Ø*	*milki*
gi-ri-ba-ʾa-al 'Client of Baal' (ADD 775.7)	NOM *-i*	GEN *-Ø*
gír-ṣa-pu-nu 'Client of Zaphon' (ADD 832.12)	NOM *-Ø*	GEN *-u*
ia-ta-na-e-li 'El has given' (ADD 621.2)	PERF *-a*	NOM *-i*
sa-mu-na-ia-tu-ni 'Eshmun has given' (ADD 160.rev. 11)	NOM *-a*	PERF *-i*

a. The texts are quoted according to the sigla provided in Benz 1972.

In the earliest inscriptions dating to the reigns of Shalmaneser III, Tiglath-pileser III, and Sennacherib, the nominative is mostly employed correctly, independent of the position of the element and its function—that is, whether it is the subject or predicate. However, already in this early period there are cases in which the nominative is either indicated by the wrong vowel or is not indicated at all. Non-indication occurs in one case in which the nominative subject is the first element of the name, and wrong indication by *-i* is attested once in the nominative subject in second position. Since the wrong indication occurs just one line down in the same text, in which *ba-ʾa-li* is indeed in the genitive and the second element of a name as well, this wrong indication might have been caused by an incorrect analogy or an error in copying by the scribe.

Nouns in the nominative construct behave irregularly, as one would expect from genuine Phoenician material; this suggests that constructs had lost case vowels at the beginning of the first millennium B.C. The first name under Shalmaneser seems to imply that the construct preserved its case vowel *-u*; however, this example is exceptional. In other instances, the construct either does not have a vowel, or it imitates the Assyrian form, as in *sipitti* 'judgment'. The loss of case marking on the construct also explains why the element *abd* 'servant' is consistently written with final *-i*. It only appears in the construct and thus would not have had a final case vowel.

In the early seventh century, that is, in the inscriptional material from Esarhaddon, the nominative is most frequently indicated by *-i*. From the time of Assurbanipal on, the nominative is most commonly not indicated, regardless of whether it occurs on the first or second element of a name. The orthographic representation of the nominative in these transcribed names indicates that the nominative was still, at least in part, preserved in the earliest material from the ninth to eighth centuries B.C. Since this corresponds to the case system of Neo-Assyrian, it is almost impossible to draw conclusions regarding the underlying Phoenician system, although the evidence may indicate that the original nominative case vowel *-u* was preserved longer than commonly assumed. From the early seventh century on, we can clearly trace the loss of the nominative in all positions. This situation might reflect Phoenician grammar, since Neo-Assyrian preserved this case marker.[20]

20. Neo-Assyrian has a NOM/ACC *-u* and a GEN *-i* (Hämeen-Anttila 2000: 77). For a more detailed discussion, see §3.2 below.

For the genitive, we have significantly less evidence than for the nominative. In the material from the ninth to early seventh centuries, the genitive is usually employed correctly, although spellings without a case vowel occasionally occur as well. From the seventh century on, we also find wrong spellings of the genitive and more frequent omissions of the final case vowel, especially in legal and economic texts. This situation does not correspond to Neo-Assyrian grammar, for which, see §3.2 below.

The evidence from the names in transcription also show that final *-a* was lost from an early period on since the perfect is most frequently written with final *-u* or *-i*, which has no basis in either Phoenician or Neo-Assyrian grammar.

If we can trust the evidence from the Neo-Assyrian transcriptions, the following picture emerges: the status of the nominative case vowel is uncertain because of its congruence with Assyrian usage in the early periods, although it seems it was lost at least from the early seventh century on. The genitive *-i* was at least partially preserved up to the late eighth century B.C. but probably disappeared by the early to mid-seventh century, after which it is not attested in cuneiform transcriptions any longer.[21] The fact that the evidence from transcriptions does not always conform to Neo-Assyrian grammar regarding the loss of the nominative and genitive case vowels, especially in the evidence from the seventh century B.C., might indicate that we are dealing with genuine Phoenician forms, although it has to be stressed that conclusions based on the transcriptions have to remain tentative.

Nevertheless, the names seem to confirm that Phoenician had a binary case inflection, genitive versus non-genitive, in both the nominal and pronominal system in the early first millennium B.C. This system was most likely lost on nouns in the unbound state no later than the seventh century, that is, earlier than it was lost on pronominal suffixes. This observation is contrary to the previously mentioned assumptions in this section that the genitive was preserved throughout the history of Phoenician, and it confirms cross-linguistic observations that independent and bound pronouns tend to preserve case distinction longer than nouns and adjectives.

21. The loss of the genitive is, according to Krahmalkov, also attested in the nouns *ʾb* and *ʾḥ* before pronominal suffixes, which regularly use the nominative vowel /ū/ before suffixes from the second half of the first millennium B.C. on, as in Poenulus *me sem abuca* 'what is the name of your father?' and Neo-Punic *labunom* 'for their father' (Krahmalkov 2001: 129).

3.2. Akkadian

The following paragraphs review the case inflection of unbound and bound nouns without pronominal suffixes in Sargonic Akkadian and the main periods of Babylonian and Assyrian. The discussion focuses on the inflection of masculine-singular nouns since these are representative for most changes and developments.

In Sargonic Akkadian, the triptotic inflection on unbound singular nouns is fully preserved and corresponds to the traditional Proto-Semitic reconstruction (17).

(17) Sargonic Akkadian Nominal Inflection

	Unbound	Bound w/o Pronominal Suffixes
NOM	*-u-m*	-Ø (*-u* rare)
GEN	*-i-m*	*-i*
ACC	*-a-m*	-Ø

On bound singular nouns, the nominative and accusative are generally not marked, although very few exceptions in which we find a nominative vowel *-u* on masculine-singular nouns do occur. The genitive *-i* is regularly preserved, as reflected in the paradigm provided under (17) (Hasselbach 2005: 182).[22]

The Old Babylonian nominal inflection differs from Sargonic Akkadian in that it lost the distinctive genitive ending on bound singular nouns, which is only preserved in a few vestige forms (18).

(18) Old Babylonian Nominal Inflection

	Unbound	Bound w/o Pronominal Suffixes
NOM	*-u-m*	-Ø (*-u* occasionally in poetry)
GEN	*-i-m*	-Ø (*-i* rare)
ACC	*-a-m*	-Ø (*-u* occasionally in poetry)

The nominative *-u* on bound nouns is occasionally attested in Old Babylonian poetry, where it marks both the nominative and the accusative (von Soden 1995: §64a).[23] In nonliterary Old Babylonian, the bound form of the noun is most commonly unmarked for case.

22. The accusative *–a* is not attested on MS bound nouns in Sargonic Akkadian.
23. The nominal declension of early Babylonian corresponds to that of Old Babylonian (Whiting 1987: 11).

In Old Assyrian, the inflection of unbound nouns follows the common triptotic case marking (19).

(19) Old Assyrian Nominal Inflection

	Unbound	Bound w/o Pronominal Suffixes
NOM	*-u-m*	*-Ø* (*-u* rare)
GEN	*-i-m*	*-Ø*
ACC	*-a-m*	*-Ø*

The most commonly found form in the construct is with zero-ending.[24] The original nominative ending *-u* is preserved in a few vestige forms in both literary and nonliterary texts (Hecker 1968: §62d).[25]

In Middle Babylonian (20) nonliterary and literary texts, the case inflection is fully productive on unbound nouns, while the bound form is not marked for case (Aro 1955: 65).[26] The use of wrong case endings is rare and primarily occurs in late Middle Babylonian texts. Middle Assyrian corresponds to Middle Babylonian.[27]

(20) Middle Babylonian Nominal Inflection

	Unbound	Bound w/o Pronominal Suffixes
NOM	*-u*	*-Ø*
GEN	*-i*	*-Ø*
ACC	*-a*	*-Ø*

In the dialects discussed so far, the unbound form of singular nouns remained stable except for the loss of mimation in Middle Babylonian and Middle Assyrian. In the bound form, we start with a binary inflection of genitive versus non-genitive in Sargonic Akkadian that was lost in subsequent periods of Akkadian, except in some vestige forms in

24. There are also noun types that end in *-i*. Zero-marking and final *-i* can occur on the same word, although the distribution of these two endings is mostly phonologically conditioned: stems that end in two consonants usually have no final vowel in the construct, as do stems ending in a vowel and stems ending in a single consonant or the feminine ending *-at* (Hecker 1968: §63b–d).

25. The triptotic case inflection on construct nouns is preserved on typical nouns with vocalic endings, *kalu-*, *abu-*, *aḫu-*, and *pū-*. Cases on these nouns are only rarely confused (Hecker 1968: §62b–c).

26. Mimation was lost at this stage of Babylonian (Aro 1955: 65). For Middle Babylonian royal inscriptions, see Stein 2000: 32.

27. For Middle Assyrian, see Mayer 1971: 48.

mostly literary and poetic texts in Old Babylonian and Old Assyrian. The most significant changes in the nominal inflection occurred, as is well known, in Neo-Assyrian and Neo-Babylonian.

Neo-Assyrian texts attest a binary case system on unbound nouns in the singular with opposition between nominative/accusative and genitive (21).

(21) Neo-Assyrian Nominal Inflection (after 1000 B.C.)

	Unbound	Bound w/o Pronominal Suffixes[a]
MS NOM	*-u*	*-Ø*
MS GEN	*-i/e*	*-Ø*
MS ACC	*-u*	*-Ø*

	NOM	OBL
MP	*-ī*	*-ī*
FP	*-ti*	*-ti*

a. The construct occasionally appears with unexpected final *-i*, although zero-marking is more common (Luukko 2004: 169).

The nominative and accusative merged morphologically and are expressed by the original vowel of the nominative, *-u*. The genitive is preserved and indicated by *-i* (Hämeen-Anttila 2000: 77; Luukko 2004: 166). Subject and object are usually distinguished by word order, although in cases in which ambiguities can arise, the direct object is alternatively expressed by the preposition *ana* plus a noun in the genitive. The plural only has one form that reflects the original oblique (Hämeen-Anttila 2000: 77).[28]

Exceptions to this system, such as occasional use of the genitive ending *-i/-e* for the nominative, are rare in texts from the early first millennium B.C.[29] In material from the late Neo-Assyrian period—that is, from the time of Esarhaddon and Assurbanipal—the case system was subject to further change. According to Worthington, the genitive ending *-i/-e* began to lose its stability in this late period, at least in masculine-singular nouns with strong roots (Worthington n.d.: 205). The inconsistencies in

28. The same is true for the plural of masculine adjectives with *-ūt-* (which also merged into the original oblique case, *-ūti*) and the particularizing plural *-ānī* (Hämeen-Anttila 2000: 77).

29. These exceptions are occasionally attested in letters; see Luukko 2004: 168.

the writing of the genitive singular in late Neo-Assyrian indicate that Neo-Assyrian was in the early process of losing the entire morphological case system.

In Neo-Babylonian, only a few texts attempt to use case endings correctly. In literary texts, such as royal inscriptions, the use of case endings on unbound nouns is mostly irregular (Stein 2000: 33). The original nominative ending *-u* is found in all three cases in the singular and is the most frequently attested vocalic ending. The ending *-i* is still often used for the genitive but also occurs for other cases, while the accusative *-a* is only rarely attested. In late Neo-Babylonian inscriptions, nouns can have *-Ø* endings in the singular, while in the plural, the original masculine-singular *-ū* tends to replace the oblique ending *-ī* (Stein 2000: 33).

In Neo-Babylonian letters, we find a picture similar to the royal inscriptions (22).

(22) Neo-Babylonian Nominal Inflection: Royal Inscriptions

	Unbound	Bound w/o Pronominal Suffixes
MS NOM	*-u*	*-Ø*
MS GEN	*-i*/*-u*	*-Ø*
MS ACC	*-u* (*-i* / *-a* rare)	*-Ø*
MP NOM	*-ū*	
MP OBL	*-ū*/*-ī* (less frequently)	

The nominative and accusative have merged and are frequently expressed by *-u*, while the genitive is mostly, although not in all cases, expressed by final *-i*/*-e* (Woodington 1982: 63). This indicates the almost complete loss of case distinction in the nominal inflection, although the still frequently attested use of *-i* for the genitive singular suggests that the genitive was initially preserved longer than the nominative and accusative. Thus, also the Babylonian case system most likely underwent a stage in which it had the binary opposition of genitive and non-genitive.

The evidence cited so far shows that the loss of morphological case marking on bound and unbound nouns attested at various periods of Akkadian always occurred according to the same basic process. We first find a merger of nominative and accusative, resulting in a binary case system of genitive and non-genitive, and the subsequent loss of all three original vocalic case markers. This development is attested in Sargonic Akkadian, where it applies to bound nouns, and in Neo-Assyrian and Neo-Babylonian, where it occurred with unbound nouns. The rare appearance of nominative and accusative nouns in the construct with *-u* that are attested in Old Babylonian poetry are of special interest. If these forms are reflections of an earlier situation, they indicate that Babylonian did not simply merge the singular nominatives and accusatives because of the loss of final short /a/ and /u/ but first underwent a morphological merger of the two cases into the original nominative marker, similar to what we can observe with respect to Neo-Assyrian unbound nouns. Then it lost the nominative/accusative case marker, resulting in the zero-marking of both the nominative and accusative attested in most Old Babylonian texts.

A binary case system of genitive and non-genitive is, of course, also well known from singular nouns with pronominal suffixes that have distinct genitive forms throughout Akkadian, as in (23) and (24):

(23) *kalab-šu*
dog.CSTR-3MS.GEN
'his dog'. (NOM/ACC)

(24) *ana kalbī-šu*
to dog.CSTR.GEN-3MS.GEN
'for his dog'. (GEN)

This differs from bound nouns without pronominal suffixes, such as (25) and (26):

(25) *kalab awīl-im*
dog.CSTR man-GEN.SING
'the dog of the man'. (NOM/ACC)

(26) *ana kalab awīl-im*
to dog.CSTR man-GEN
'for the dog of the man'. (GEN, after Sargonic Akkadian)

The distinction between a genitive and nominative/accusative before pronominal suffixes is also regularly found in dialects that were in the process of losing case distinction altogether, such as Late Neo-Assyrian and Neo-Babylonian.[30]

Thus there was a similar development in Akkadian and Phoenician regarding the loss of case inflection.

4. Conclusion

The evidence from Akkadian and Phoenician with regard to morphological case marking shows a very similar development in the two languages.

In Phoenician, we have clear evidence from spellings of personal names and nouns in the construct with final weak roots that singular nouns in construct had lost their final case vowels at the earliest stage of Phoenician available to us. In the pronominal system, nominative and accusative had merged morphologically, while genitive remained distinct. There is also a great likelihood that unbound nouns first lost final /a/ and /u/ (although we cannot be certain that these two vowels were lost at the same time), while /i/ was preserved for a longer period. If we can trust the evidence from Phoenician transcribed into Neo-Assyrian, this binary case system was subsequently lost on unbound nouns around the seventh century B.C.

Akkadian attests the same basic development. Morphological case distinction first collapsed on nouns in the construct, with Sargonic Akkadian attesting to a binary case system of genitive and non-genitive. This binary system was subsequently lost, resulting in the total absence of case distinction in construct nouns. After the loss of mimation beginning in Late Old Babylonian, case vowels also began to be lost on unbound nouns. Neo-Assyrian attests to the initial merger of nominative and accusative into one morphological case, while the genitive again remained distinct. Neo-Babylonian had lost all inflectional case markers at least at its latest stage.

In both Phoenician and Akkadian, case distinction between nominative/accusative and genitive was preserved before pronominal suffixes, even after case inflection on unbound nouns was lost completely. Thus, in both languages, we find the following process: the loss of case inflection begins with the syncretism of nominative and accusative in the

30. In Neo-Assyrian, the genitive generally remained distinct before pronominal suffixes (Luukko 2004: 139). The same is true for Neo-Babylonian (Woodington 1982: 73).

singular. In Neo-Assyrian (unbound nouns) and most likely at an early stage of Old Babylonian (construct nouns), this merger resulted in the marking of both cases by the original nominative marker *-u*. In Phoenician, the possessive suffixes leveled for the original accusative form. Unfortunately, we have no unambiguous evidence for the beginning of the merger of unbound nouns in Phoenician, so it is not possible to say whether Phoenician likewise had a merged case expressed by either the original nominative or the accusative vowel. The syncretism of nominative and accusative resulted in a binary case system of genitive versus nominative/accusative. The next step was the loss of the nominative/accusative marker, which left a case system that had a morphologically marked genitive and a zero-marked nominative/accusative. Subsequently, the genitive was lost, resulting in the absence of morphological case distinction on both unbound and bound nouns. However, case distinction based on the previous binary case system was still preserved in the pronominal system at this stage. Last, case distinction also disappeared in the pronominal system, which is a stage attested in Neo-Punic.

The parallel development in Phoenician and Akkadian is the most significant observation of the present investigation with regard to the relationship of these languages and language typology. The merger of nominative and accusative is, as mentioned in the introduction, a well-known phenomenon among the world's languages that can be explained by the fact that these cases had a functional overlap in their use as verbal arguments, as opposed to the genitive, which is solely adnominal in Semitic. The strong tendency in Akkadian and Phoenician to first merge nominative and accusative and to preserve the genitive can thus be explained on a functional basis. The multiple-step process outlined above that can be traced in Akkadian and Phoenician also suggests that the loss of case inflection was not solely determined by phonological factors, that is, the loss of final short vowels, but also by functional criteria. Consequently, the underlying process was more complex than is usually assumed.

It is the conformity with cross-linguistic observations that makes Semitic languages such as Akkadian and Phoenician interesting for typological studies and vice versa. Revealing the conformity of Akkadian and Phoenician to what has been observed regarding case marking in other languages and language families lays a foundation for applying typological and functional theories to these languages and other branches of Semitic and for further studies of case and the marking of grammatical relations in Semitic that must rely more heavily on typological data.

Bibliography

Anderson, J. M.
2006 *Modern Grammars of Case*. Oxford: Oxford University Press.

Aro, J.
1955 Studien zur mittelbabylonischen Grammatik. *Studia Orientalia* 20.

Benz, F. L.
1972 *Personal Names in the Phoenician and Punic Inscriptions: A Catalog, Grammatical Study and Glossary of Elements*. Rome: Pontifical Biblical Institute.

Blake, B. J.
2001 *Case.* 2nd ed. Cambridge: Cambridge University Press.

Croft, W.
2003 *Typology and Universals.* 2nd ed. Cambridge: Cambridge University Press.

Friedrich, J., and Röllig, W.
1999 *Phönizisch-Punische Grammatik*. 3rd ed. by M. G. Amadasi Guzzo with W. R. Mayer. AnOr 55. Rome: Pontifical Biblical Institute.

Garr, W. R.
1985 *Dialect Geography of Syria–Palestine, 1000–586 B.C.E.* Philadelphia: University of Pennsylvania Press. [Repr., Winona Lake, IN: Eisenbrauns, 2004.]

Givón, T.
1980 The Binding Hierarchy and the Typology of Complements. *Studies in Language* 4:333–77.
1991 *Syntax: A Functional-Typological Introduction*, vol. 2. Amsterdam: Benjamins.

Hackett, J. A.
2004 Phoenician and Punic. Pp. 365–85 in *The Cambridge Encyclopedia of the World's Ancient Languages*, ed. R. D. Woodard. Cambridge: Cambridge University Press.

Hämeen-Anttila, J.
2000 *A Sketch of Neo-Assyrian Grammar*. SAAS 13. Helsinki: The Neo-Assyrian Text Corpus Project.

Hasselbach, R.
2004 Final Vowels of Pronominal Suffixes and Independent Personal Pronouns in Semitic. *JSS* 49: 1–20.
2005 *Sargonic Akkadian: A Historical and Comparative Study of the Syllabic Texts*. Wiesbaden: Harrassowitz.
2011 Early Canaanite and Old Aramaic Case in the Light of Language Typology. Pp. 101–11 in *Grammatical Case in the Languages of the Middle East and Europe: Acts of the International Colloquium: Variations,*

concurrence, et evolution des case dans divers domaines linguistiques, ed. M. Fruyt, M. Mazoyer, and D. Pardee. Chicago: Oriental Institute.

Hecker, K.
1968 *Grammatik der Kültepe-Texte*. Rome: Pontifical Biblical Institute.

Huehnergard, J.
1991 The Development of the Third Person Suffixes in Phoenician. *Maarav* 7: 183–94.
2004 Afro-Asiatic. Pp. 138–59 in *The Cambridge Encyclopedia of the World's Ancient Languages*, ed. R. D. Woodard. Cambridge: Cambridge University Press.

Izre'el, S.
2002 Introduction: With Some Notes on the Russian School of Semitic Linguistics. Pp. 13–20 in *Semitic Linguistics: The State of the Art at the Turn of the 21st Century*, ed. S. Izre'el. IOS 20. Winona Lake, IN: Eisenbrauns.

Khan, G.
2002 The Study of Semitic Syntax. Pp. 151–72 in *Semitic Linguistics: The State of the Art at the Turn of the 21st Century*, ed. S. Izre'el. IOS 20. Winona Lake, IN: Eisenbrauns.

Krahmalkov, C. R.
2001 *A Phoenician-Punic Grammar*. HOSNME 54. Leiden: Brill.

Lipiński, E.
2001 *Semitic Languages: Outline of a Comparative Grammar*. 2nd ed. OLA 80. Leuven: Peeters.

Luukko, M.
2004 *Grammatical Variation in Neo-Assyrian*. SAAS16. Helsinki: Neo-Assyrian Text Corpus Project.

Mayer, W.
1971 *Untersuchungen zur Grammatik des Mittelassyrischen*. Neukirchen-Vluyn: Neukirchener Verlag / Kevelaer: Butzon & Bercker.

Rainey, A. F.
1996 *Canaanite in the Amarna Tablets: A Linguistic Analysis of the Mixed Dialect Used by the Scribes from Canaan*. 4 vols. Leiden: Brill.

Segert, S.
1976 *A Grammar of Phoenician and Punic*. Munich: Beck.

Soden, W. von
1995 *Grundriss der akkadischen Grammatik*. 3rd ed. Rome: Pontifical Biblical Institute.

Stein, P.
2000 *Die mittel- und neubabylonischen Königsinschriften bis zum Ende der Assyrerherrschaft*. Wiesbaden: Harrassowitz.

Tropper, J.
2000 *Ugaritische Grammatik*. Münster: Ugarit-Verlag.

Whiting, R. M.
1987 *Old Babylonian Letters from Tell Asmar*. Chicago: University of Chicago Press.
Woodington, N. R.
1982 *A Grammar of the Neo-Babylonian Letters of the Kuyunjik Collection*. Ph.D. dissertation, Yale University.
Worthington, M.
n.d. *Linguistic and Related Aspects of Neo-Assyrian Royal Inscriptions*. Unpublished MS.

A Brief Case for Phoenician as the Language of the "Gezer Calendar"

Dennis Pardee

1. Introduction

This case can be particularly brief because its principal function is to move suggestions made over the last two decades out of the category of the review (and there, sometimes, in the subcategory of the footnote)[1] into a forum in which some of my colleagues in Northwest Semitic studies might read and evaluate the proposal.[2] In its briefest form, the claim is that, in our present state of knowledge, the combination of morphological and syntactic features requires that the identification of the language of the Gezer text as Phoenician be preferred. The argument itself is briefly stated, but the attempt to give at least a broad view of the history of the linguistic analysis of this text and, to a lesser extent, of its philological interpretation has resulted in rather voluminous footnotes.

Author's note: My thanks to R. Hasselbach for reading and commenting on various drafts of this paper; also B. Sass, with whom a lively e-mail discussion was engaged and who was kind enough to send me the prepublication manuscript of Finkelstein, Sass, and Singer-Avitz 2008.

1. My basic proposal was made in a review of Gibson 1982 (Pardee 1987: 139 n. 20); the proposal made there was referenced in a review of Renz 1995 (Pardee 1997b: 217); the arguments were repeated with emphasis on the morphological aspect in a review of Briquel-Chatonnet and Lozachmeur 1998 (Pardee 2001: 136–37). The one departure from the review genre was in an encyclopedia article on the Gezer Calendar (Pardee 1997a), where the basic arguments were provided in very brief form, and the inscription was said to be "northern Hebrew or Phoenician" (Pardee 1997a: 401).

2. Though the first review cited in n. 1 is mentioned by Dobbs-Allsopp et al. (2005: 158), in their discussion of the morphology of the word *yrḥw* in the Gezer inscription, my correlation of the morphological analysis with the syntactic analysis and the conclusion drawn therefrom in regard to the linguistic identification of the Gezer inscription go unmentioned in their remarks on syntax (2005: 158) and in those on linguistic classification (2005: 156–57).

In spite of the absence of a clear archaeological context for the inscription, it was considered "a showpiece of early Hebrew inscriptions" (Pardee 1997a: 400),[3] with little contest, for something like half a century after the editio princeps (Gray 1909; Lidzbarski 1909a; and Pilcher 1909).[4] In recent years, various proposals have been made to identify the language as Phoenician or Canaanite[5] or, more specifically,

---

3. In an influential and oft-cited article, Albright (1943: 18; see also p. 25) claimed that the inscription "is written in perfect classical Hebrew"; Cross and Freedman (1952: 46–47) treated this inscription in the chapter on Hebrew inscriptions in their classic study of Northwest Semitic orthography; Dobbs-Allsopp et al. (2005: 155–65) include it in their collection of Hebrew inscriptions, despite their explicitly stated view that the language is best described as "South Canaanite" (2005: 156).

4. Under a common title, each of these authors provided his own reading and interpretation of the text. Doubts began being cast on the identification as Biblical Hebrew as early as 1939 and picked up steam in the mid-1950s; see the following notes for some examples.

5. To my knowledge (and I thank B. Sass for the reference), the first to cast doubt on the simple identification of the language as Hebrew was Harris (1939: 24): "In Gezer there was found a calendar inscription which clearly represents the local dialect, not that of Jerusalem; it is of the 9th century and is written in the Phoenician alphabet." Garbini (1954–56) once denied the identification of the language as Biblical Hebrew, but he did not make a specific proposal for its linguistic identity, arguing only for its archaicity (moreover, the proposal was based primarily on an untenable morphological analysis, which robs it of much of its value); two decades later, in the process of establishing a comparison with the script of the Manaḥat sherd, he was referring to the script as "pienamente fenicia" (Garbini 1974: 589); but shortly thereafter, he identified the language as "una forma di ebraico arcaico morfologicamente diverso da quello biblico" (Garbini 1977: 294); a few years later still, however, he identified the language as "diversa dall'ebraico" (Garbini 1983: 31); he has most recently claimed that this language would be a "manifestazione tardiva della lingua cananaica parlata nella città nel periodo del Tardo Bronzo" (Garbini 2006: 98). Naveh's apparently evolving views are also of interest: as early as 1968, he observed that "no specifically Hebrew features can be distinguished in the script of the Gezer Calendar" (Naveh 1968: 69), but in n. 3, he identified the language as Hebrew for historical reasons; a very similar statement appeared two years later (Naveh 1970: 277) and a briefer formulation a little over a decade later (Naveh 1984: 61: "a Hebrew used it [i.e., the Phoenician script] for writing the Gezer calendar"); but, as early as in 1972, he had declared his preference "to leave open the question of whether it [i.e., the Gezer Calendar] was written in an archaic Hebrew, in a northern Hebrew dialect, or in Phoenician" (Naveh 1972: 187), and in 1978, he observed that "the late tenth-century B.C. Gezer Calendar is still written in the Phoenician script, and perhaps even in the Phoenician language" (Naveh 1978: 33); in his book-length study of the early alphabetic inscriptions, he affirmed that the "script of the Gezer Calendar . . . is identical with that of the tenth-century Phoenician inscriptions" and went on to claim, with no historical qualifiers, that it contains no "lexical or grammatical features that preclude the possibility of it being Phoenician" (Naveh 1982: 76). In 1969, Brown identified the inscription as "Canaanite" without giving

as "Philistian,"—that is, the Canaanite dialect adopted by the Philistines.[6] The morphological argument adduced below for *yrḥ* (month.MS=its.3MS) rules out the latter identification, however, if one agrees that the Ekron inscription is typical of "Philistian," for 'his lady' is written *ʾdth* (lady.FS=his.3MS) in this inscription,[7] whereas the Gezer text shows *Ø* for the 3MS pronominal suffix on a singular noun, as is the case in Standard Phoenician[8] (see also below, §2.3, especially n. 31). Truth be told, the identification as Canaanite cannot be ruled out, because we have no early first-millennium Canaanite inscriptions that are not identifiable as belonging to one of the known Cisjordanian or Transjordanian languages/dialects. The same is true to a lesser extent of Samarian Hebrew, if we accept that the Samarian inscriptions do indeed represent a

---

his reasons (Brown 1969: 2). In 1976, Millard criticized Naveh for allowing historical considerations to influence his decision on the language of the inscription (Millard 1976: 132). One year later, Lipiński referred to the language as "an archaic southern Palestinian dialect" (Lipiński 1977: 82; the phrase is presented as being in agreement with the views of Gibson, who in fact used the phrase "an archaic Hebrew dialect"; Gibson 1971: 1). In 1983, Dahood proposed a Phoenician identification because of the missing definite article and the monophthongization of diphthongs (Dahood 1983: 597–98). In the same year, A. F. Rainey remarked: "it could just as well be Phoenician (Canaanite)" (Rainey 1983: 630). My proposal to identify the language as Phoenician on morphosyntactic grounds came a few years later (Pardee 1987: 139 n. 20). Beyer once indicated that the Gezer inscription should be included in the Phoenician-Punic group but without giving his reasons (Beyer 1984: 23 n. 2.), and Freedman once asked the largely rhetorical question: "The language is Hebrew or Canaanite or Phoenician or what?" (Freedman 1992: 4). At about the same time, Briquel-Chatonnet was remarking that "on ne sait si elle [the Gezer inscription] était rédigée en hébreu ou dans une autre langue de Palestine appartenant au groupe cananéen" (Briquel-Chatonnet 1992: 100–101). More recently, Schüle has classified the text as Phoenician for the same morphosyntactic reasons as I have adduced, mentioning also the orthographic argument (Schüle 2000: 37–38), while McCarter has preferred the Canaanite option: ". . . is probably most safely described as a South Canaanite dialect" (*COS* 2.222). This opinion was quoted favorably by Dobbs-Allsopp et al. (2005: 156–57). As we saw above in this note, this was also the end-point of Garbini's peregrination. On the strictly paleographical question, see below and additional references in n. 27.

6. Lemaire (1997: 162; 1998a: 54; 1998b: 487; 2000: 247; 2006: 182, 184, 193). Before the recognition of the existence of "Philistian" inscriptions in a form of Canaanite, Lemaire resisted a firm classification according to the categories of Phoenician, Canaanite, or Israelite Hebrew (see Lemaire 1981: 10–11).

7. The editio princeps is Gitin, Dothan, and Naveh 1997.

8. *-h* is still used as the 3MS pronominal suffix on singular nouns in the Ahiram inscription, the date of which is much debated but which, in any case, is representative of Old Byblian, as opposed to Standard Phoenician, where the 3MS pronominal suffix on a singular noun is *-Ø* in the nominative/accusative and *-y* in the genitive.

northern dialect of Hebrew,[9] for the morphosyntactic categories necessary for a comparison along multiple parameters are not yet attested; here, however, an orthographic argument may be adduced against the identification.[10] Thus, either of these identifications would presently be based on absence of data or, in the latter case, against one class of data. Hence my claim that the identification as Phoenician must be preferred in our present state of knowledge.

2. *Criteria Used to Identify the Language*

2.1. Morphology

As is well known to all who have studied the Gezer text, the principal grammatical *crux interpretum* lies in the analysis of *-w*, which appears four times on the word *yrḥ* 'month', in the phrases descriptive of agricultural activity throughout the year, in contrast to *-Ø*, which appears on the other four occurrences of the term. Two principal types of solutions have been offered:[11] the orthographies reflect (1) case endings, where

9. On this question, see the studies cited below in n. 29.

10. Many scholars who hold to the identification of the language as Hebrew, even as "good Biblical Hebrew" (Albright 1943: 22) or even "perfect classical Hebrew" (1943: 18, 25), identify the dialect as Samarian/Israelite because of the writing *qṣ* line 7 (e.g., Albright 1943: 24; Cross and Freedman 1952: 47; Yun 2005: 745) but, as I remark below, the absence of *matres lectionis* in this inscription does not match the orthographic practice of the writers of the Samaria ostraca (Albright simply argued, and forcefully, that the Gezer Calendar witnesses an earlier and more conservative orthography in the writing of Israelite Hebrew [Albright 1943: 24–25]). The presence of the suffixal form *-w* on a dual/plural noun does not tell us whether its actual pronunciation reflects Israelite Hebrew (Cross and Freedman 1952: 46–47; *KAI* 2.181), Phoenician, or a putative Canaanite dialect; what we can say is that the relevant form is not yet attested in Samarian Hebrew, while one finds *-w* in both Phoenician and Judean Hebrew. Thus the presence of the form as such is useless for choosing among these possibilities and the phonetic reconstruction can only be hypothetical and follow the reconstruction of this suffix (a particularly vexed question, as all specialists know) in the language to which one decides to attribute the inscription.

11. The most thorough overview may be found in Renz (1995: 32–34). Three positions not canvassed by Renz: (1) The earlier reading, *yrḥn*, was abandoned progressively after Lidzbarski's initial objections (tentatively in 1909a: 27; more forcefully in 1909b), and it was put to rest definitively by Albright (1943: 24); (2) Aartun took the *-w* as an enclitic particle (Aartun 1973: 2; 1974: 43–44)—a solution that is not totally dissimilar from Lidzbarski's very early attempt to explain the *-w* as *waw compaginis* (Lidzbarski 1909a: 27 n. 1 [an editorial addition citing an oral communication from Lidzbarski]; 1909b); (3) the *-w* would in fact be a separate word, the

-w represents (a) /ō/ < /ā/ (the proto–West Semitic nominative dual ending),[12] (b) /ū/ (the proto–West Semitic nominative plural ending),[13] or (c) a dual morpheme with consonantal /w/,[14] while orthographic *-Ø* represents either phonetic /Ø/, on the assumption that the short case vowel has dropped, or else a vocalic remnant of the case vowel; (2) pronominal suffixes, with *-w* representing consonantal /w/ after a long vowel resulting from the contraction of a case/number morpheme[15] with the old 3MS pronominal suffix /-hu/, while orthographic *-Ø* represents a long vowel resulting from the contraction of a short case vowel with the same pronominal morpheme.

In spite of the favor that the explanation as a dual morpheme /ō/ has enjoyed since first being proposed by Ginsberg, this solution must be rejected out of hand for three principal reasons: no Canaanite language/dialect of the first millennium has retained a productive dual,[16]

well-known conjunction (Gray 1909: 31; Ronzevalle 1909: 109), an idea kept alive far past its time by W. H. Shea (1993).

12. The proposal appears to have been made first by Ginsberg in a review that appeared in Hebrew (1935: 49), then in an expanded English form of the same review (1936a: 146); also in 1936, he referred readers of an article on an unrelated topic to the review just cited (1936b: 178). This is not the place to trace the fortunes of this explanation; the interested reader can follow back based on the references in Sivan 1998: 102; and Dobbs-Allsopp et al. 2005: 157–58.

13. This analysis of the *-w* has been the basis of Garbini's various proposals regarding the linguistic classification of the text (some of which are cited above, n. 5).

14. Lemaire 1975: 17; 1998a: 54; Lipiński 1977: 82; Halpern 1987: 132; Tropper 1993. The details of these proposals vary considerably; see discussion below, esp. n. 20.

15. Most who have preferred this analysis of the form *yrḫw* have explicitly included the parsing as a dual, beginning with Albright (1943: 24), continuing with Honeyman (1953: 54–55), including myself (1987: 139 n. 20, where the putative dual form is qualified as "productive or frozen") and, more recently, such eminent scholars as Renz (1995: 32), Sivan (1998), and McCarter (*COS* 2.222 n. 1). For the necessary qualifications, see below, esp. n. 21.

16. Judging from Rainey's presentation of the data from the Amarna tablets (Rainey 1996a: 1.136–39), the dual may still have been productive in fourteenth-century Canaanite: though only words for parts of the body that occur in pairs are cited, both cases, the nominative and the oblique, are attested according to Rainey's analysis (the problem with this explanation is that the /ā/ of the nominative form has not shifted to /ō/). Albright once suggested (1944: 21) that *ma-ga-RI-ma* in Taanach 2:8 be read *ma-ga-re-ma* and interpreted as the Canaanite dual ending attached to the Akkadian word for 'wheel' (this view was accepted by Sivan [1984: 111–12], while nothing is said about it in the most recent edition of the text [Horowitz and Oshima 2006: 132–34]). Whether or not some of the claims for dual pronominal and verbal forms in Biblical Hebrew are correct (e.g., Rendsburg 1982)–and such forms appear

no Canaanite language/dialect of the first millennium has retained the nominative form of the dual as a frozen form (Albright 1943: 24; Honeyman 1953), and the orthography of this inscription is otherwise conservative, with no certain example of the use of *matres lectionis* (Albright 1943: 24; Cross and Freedman 1952: 46–47; Zevit 1980: 6; Rainey 1983: 630).[17] Accepting that these two anomalies would have been combined in a single form passes the bounds of sound grammatical method.[18] Explaining *-w* as plural /ū/ meets similar objections: no trace of the nominative plural ending /ū/ is retained in any other Canaanite language/dialect, and the representation of such as vowel by a *mater lectionis* is entirely unexpected in this inscription.[19] The analysis as a consonantal marker of the dual is not subject to the orthographic criticism, but it is even less plausible that so archaic a morpheme would have been retained in a first-millennium Canaanite language.[20]

It is thus necessary to conclude that the two endings, *-w* and *-Ø*, represent pronominal suffixes: the first the 3MS pronominal suffixed to the

to me to be at best vestigial—there can be no doubt that dual nominal forms were not produced spontaneously to represent two tokens of an entity in Standard Biblical Hebrew, and the same must be said of the other Canaanite languages (without further data, there is no reason to see *mʾtn* 'two hundred' in Moabite [*KAI* 181.20] as anything but a frozen dual, while *ṣhrm* 'noon' in line 15 of the same inscription cannot, of course, be a Moabite dual).

17. As is well known, *-w* and *-y* are used in Samalian to represent nominative and oblique case endings in the plural; but Samalian represents an early usage of *matres lectionis* characteristic of Aramaic, and the plural is not the dual.

18. Dobbs-Allsopp et al. (2005: 158) judge that "given the evidence of the Zenjirli inscriptions . . . one cannot rule it [i.e., that *-w* represents a case ending] out completely." I must disagree: the grammatical and the orthographic factors conjoined require that this explanation be ruled out. (One must, of course, always qualify a statement of this sort in terms of possible future discoveries; but, in our present state of knowledge, the hypothesis may not be retained as a viable alternative.)

19. See Rainey's forceful statement (1983: 630).

20. References for this analysis may be found in n. 14. Tropper's proposal (1993) that the old nominative dual morpheme would have been /aw/ in symmetry with the oblique morpheme /ay/ is theoretically more sophisticated than Lemaire's proposal (1975: 17) for an original form /-awim/ that would subsequently have shifted to /-ayim/ (Lipiński's proposal [1977] appears to assume the opposite development, though it is indicated in the briefest possible form, "*-aw* < *-ay*"), it nevertheless remains in the realm of theory, with no attested tokens of the phenomenon in any Canaanite language/dialect. Halpern's idea that "The ending could have been generated locally by attachment of 'nominative' *-u* to nominative dual *-ā* " is overtly driven by the need to find an explicitly marked dual form here—an inadequate basis for so bizarre a reconstruction of the form (see esp. nn. 21 and 36).

coalesced dual/plural form;[21] the second the same suffix on the singular noun,[22] probably functioning as a subject.[23] Only (post-Ahiram) Phoenician shows this distribution of forms.[24]

21. For my views on the historical process involved in the loss of the dual as a productive grammatical number and the loss of case endings in the Northwest Semitic languages, see Pardee 2011. It is necessary to define the form of the noun as "the coalesced dual/plural form" rather than simply as a dual, because the latter analysis assumes that the dual was still productive (an option that I left open in my 1987 note [137 n. 20] but that I now consider untenable for the reason stated above); Dobbs-Allsopp et al. (2005: 157) state correctly that "there is no formal distinction between the two [viz., the dual and the plural]." If the unlikelihood of the existence of a productive dual is granted, one might still claim that a frozen dual form was retained for this word, as is the case for some words designating time in Biblical Hebrew: for example, the words for 'day' and for 'year'. This hypothesis would have no direct basis in attestations, however, for neither of the words for 'month' in Biblical Hebrew, *yeraḥ* and *ḥōdeš*, is attested in the dual form, and the same is true of Phoenician.

22. To my knowledge, the correct analysis of the two orthographies is to be credited first to Albright (1943: 24): "In the dual with a pronominal suffix of the third person masculine singular there is a consonantal *waw*, while in the corresponding singular form there is none" (Albright translated the pronominal suffix 'his' and explained it as referring to the person performing the activity in question). This morphological analysis was adopted by Cross and Freedman (1952: 46–47 n. 11), who also mentioned P. Skehan's oral suggestion that the suffixes might be taken as proleptic; a similar analysis had been proposed earlier by Ringgren (1949: 127–28), with reference, however, only to the form *yrḥw*, which he took as a singular noun: "the month of harvest" (1949: 128). The first to conjoin the two analyses explicitly was, again to my knowledge, Honeyman (1953), who analyzed *yrḥw* as a dual noun, *yrḥ* as a singular. To my knowledge, the first to adduce the conjoined morphosyntactic analysis in favor of the identification of the language of the inscription as Phoenician was I (1987: 139 n. 20), and the only other scholar to draw the same conclusion explicitly from this analysis has been Schüle (2000: 37–38).

23. Honeyman (1953: 55) once suggested that the word *yrḥ* might be functioning as an (adverbial) accusative. In Phoenician, of course, the nominative and accusative functions are marked identically in these pronominal forms.

24. See, for example, Friedrich and Röllig 1999: 65–66. The case for *-Ø* as the orthography of the 3MS suffix on a singular noun in the nominative/accusative is clearest; the case for *-w* on plural nouns is less clear though the phenomenon is attested in the Byblian dialect at a relatively late date (*KAI* 10.9, *ymw* 'his days') and, earlier, on the noun *ʾdt* 'lady', which may take the suffixes as appropriate for a masculine-plural noun (that is, as a feminine-plural noun with appended suffixes appropriate for a masculine-plural noun, as in Hebrew). Within the hypothesis of a Phoenician identification of the language of the Gezer inscription, it may be posited either that it is in the Byblian dialect or that the orthography *-w* was more widespread in the ninth century, before the shift to *-y*, as we know it in Standard Phoenician. Judean Hebrew shows *-h* and *-w*/*-yw*; "Philistian" shows *-h* for the pronoun on a singular noun, plural unattested; while neither form is attested for Israelite Hebrew; nor certainly for whatever Canaanite dialects may still have been spoken in the area of Gezer in the early first millennium. Tropper expressly rejects the morphological

2.2. *Syntax*

Though less clear-cut, the syntactic argument may nonetheless be cited as relevant. Ringgren (1949), who first proposed what I consider to be the correct syntactic analysis, remarked that the use of proleptic pronominal suffixes is more common in Phoenician and in Late Biblical Hebrew than in Standard Biblical Hebrew. If the orthographies *-w*/*-Ø* represent pronominal suffixes, they are best interpreted as proleptic,[25] and the entire structure of the text is thus based on prolepsis. This sort of structure must be considered an argument for the Phoenician linguistic identification.[26]

2.3. *Other Criteria*

Many who have studied this inscription have invoked paleographic, orthographic, or phonetic criteria in assigning a linguistic classification.

---

analysis of *yrḥ* as bearing a pronominal suffix, because he would expect the suffix to be represented in the orthography: "Die geforderte Form müßte aber angesichts des orthographischen Befundes in den frühen byblischen und hebräischen Inschriften entweder *yrḥh* or *yrḥw* lauten." If the inscription is not identified as being in Old Byblian or in Hebrew, however, the objections disappear.

25. As indicated above (n. 22), this analysis was first proposed in print by Honeyman in 1953, anticipated by a year as an oral suggestion by Skehan to Cross and Freedman (who do not declare a preference). Taking the suffixes not as proleptic but as referring to an entity not named in the inscription (unless it were the possible personal name inscribed on the left margin of the plaque) whose activities would be listed was Albright's understanding (see also above, n. 22), an interpretation that apparently is still accepted by scholars who translate the pronominal suffixes as 'his' (though this is not always made explicit, for example, in the case of McCarter [*COS* 2.222]). Some who have accepted the explanation as proleptic suffixes are: Donner and Röllig (*KAI* II 181); A. F. Rainey in an editorial note in the English translation of Aharoni's edition of the Arad ostraca (Rainey apud Aharoni 1981: 32); Rainey (1983: 630; 1996b: 70); Renz (1995: 33); Schüle (2000: 37–38); Dobbs-Allsopp et al. (2005: 158, 160).

26. By simple sign count or word count, prolepsis is certainly more common in the Karatepe Phoenician inscription (the origin of Ringgren's observation) and in other Phoenician texts (some others of which were also cited by Ringgren) than in the comparatively immense corpus of Standard Biblical Hebrew. I am unaware of a detailed analysis of the phenomenon in Late Biblical Hebrew. Since the proposal is to identify the inscription as Phoenician, however, the extent to which the phenomenon occurs in Late Biblical Hebrew is irrelevant. Tropper rejects the analysis of the forms in the Gezer text as bearing proleptic suffixes (1993: 228: "läßt sich aus syntaktischen Gründen kaum halten") apparently because prolepsis is not characteristic of Biblical Hebrew. I draw this conclusion because the only authority cited is Young (1992: 364), who referred with apparent favor to Albright's description of the text as being "in perfect classical Hebrew," accepted the analysis of the *-w* on *yrḥw* as a plural ending, and was apparently unaware of the use of proleptic pronouns in Phoenician.

2.3.1. Though I do not pretend to be an expert in the paleography of first-millennium inscriptions, it appears from the expert discussions that the paleographic criterion is moot.[27]

2.3.2. Accepting that the *-w* of *yrḥw* must be a consonant for the reasons adduced above, the Gezer inscription shows no example of a *mater lectionis* and differs, therefore, from orthographic practices of Biblical

27. We saw above (n. 5) that Harris and Naveh, among others, consider the script to be indistinguishable from Phoenician. Most recently, Finkelstein, Sass, and Singer-Avitz (2008) conclude that the script of the Gezer inscription is "local, or Philistian." Cross, one of the strongest proponents of the classification of the language as Hebrew, can say no better than: "I believe that the first rudimentary innovations that will mark the emergent Hebrew script can be perceived in the Gezer Calendar, but they are faint at best" (Cross 1980: 14). Bordreuil observed that, epigraphically speaking, the inscription "ne présente aucune caractéristique permettant de le considérer" as being Hebrew; he concluded that geographical and chronological considerations "accréditeraient . . . l'idée d'un texte exécuté par un lapicide d'origine cananéenne" (Bordreuil 1992: 144). Going back in time, Birnbaum proposed a date for the Gezer inscription in the first half of the ninth century by comparison with the scripts of inscriptions of diverse linguistic origins (Birnbaum 1942) and subsequently defended this method with the following remarks: "If . . . we put the alphabets of the Ahiram, Abibaal and Elibaal inscriptions, of the Arslan Tash Ivories, and of the Mesa Stele, side by side with that of the Gezer Tablet, we realize that there is no difference in the basic forms or in the style" (Birnbaum 1944: 213); in his later monumental study of the Hebrew scripts, he classified the inscription explicitly as "Palaeo-Hebrew" and preferred an earlier rather than later dating in the first half of the ninth century (Birnbaum 1971: part 1.35–42); his comparative method remained unchanged in this publication and was defended briefly: "Our earliest material does not, of course, represent the oldest stage of the Palaeo-Hebrew script. There can be no doubt that the Hebrews had been employing it for several centuries previously–it was the general alphabet of the whole region" (1971: part 1.33). The one exception to this general consensus is in the work by Tappy et al. (2006: 26–42), who include the Gezer inscription among the inscriptions that represent a script described as "an inland development of the mature Phoenician tradition of the early Iron Age" (2006: 26); they cite Cross (1980: 14) as an authority for their view that "in the tenth century [the script] already exhibits characteristics that anticipate the distinctive features of the mature Hebrew national script" (Tappy et al. 2006: 27–28) without noting Cross's highly qualified statement in regard to the Gezer inscription itself (quoted here above). The only features cited as characteristic of this script and present in the Gezer inscription are the elongation of vertical strokes and the rounding of some angles; how much weight may be placed on these features is beyond my competence to determine. If, in the future, this view of the script of the Gezer inscription should take hold among expert paleographers, that would constitute a stronger argument for a non-Phoenician linguistic identification for it appears less plausible to claim that a user of an evolving non-Phoenician script would be writing in the Phoenician language than to claim that an as yet undifferentiated script of Phoenician origin was being used to write Phoenician.

Hebrew,[28] Samarian Hebrew,[29] and Philistian.[30] Accepting that the -*Ø* of *yrḥ* corresponds to the 3MS pronominal suffix on a singular noun may rule out the hypothesis that this inscription represents an archaic form of Samarian Hebrew or Philistian for orthographic reasons: it may be judged unlikely that the -*h* that is attested in inscriptions representing these dialects would have been adopted subsequently as the *mater lectionis* for a vowel that had long been /-ô/ and for which there was no orthographic tradition based on the historical writing with -*h*. (Here one remarks that the writing with -*w* characteristic of the tradition reflected in the Masoretic Text constitutes a modification of the historical writing with -*h* characteristic of the pre-exilic inscriptions in Judaean Hebrew, a matter discussed in Pardee 2011.)

2.3.3. The orthography of *qṣ* without -*y*- reflects the monophthongization of the /ay/ diphthong and is thus one of the elements eliminating this inscription from the Judean-Hebrew category and hence from the Biblical Hebrew category, where the word is /qayiṣ/, with consonantal /y/, as well as from the Philistian category.[31] It fits, however, the identifications as Samarian Hebrew or Phoenician, where the /y/ of

28. As is well known (details provided in Cross and Freedman 1952: 45–57).

29. Israel 1986; 1989; Briquel-Chatonnet 1992. Cross and Freedman (1952: 47) concluded from the presence of *qṣ* (see following remark) that "the dialect of the Gezer Calendar was North Israelite, as opposed to Judahite"; but this conclusion requires the further conclusion that the orthographic practices visible in the Samaria ostraca were not followed in the Gezer text, a conclusion toward which Freedman later "lean[ed]" (1992: 4).

30. On the orthography of the longest of these texts, the Ekron inscription, see Byrne 2002.

31. Lemaire (2000: 248) claims that {qṣ} may show that "certaines diphtongues" were monophthongized in Philistian; the qualification is necessary because of the presence of the the form {byt} in one of the Tell Qasile ostraca, which belong to the core group of Philistian inscriptions according to Lemaire and the scholars who preceded him in identifying this body of texts. Lemaire suggests (2000: 248 n. 81) that the orthography was due to the fact that the word *byt* in the Tell Qasile ostracon is part of a place-name, his thinking apparently being that the orthography represents the actual pronunciation of the place name as /bayt ḥôrōn/ by its Judean inhabitants. Taking the writing at face value, however, one can see that it constitutes a second feature, alongside the writing of the third-person pronominal suffix with -*h*, differentiating Philistian from the language and orthography of the Gezer inscription. The problem with giving any weight to the Qasile datum is the uncertain origin of these inscriptions, which were on sherds found on the surface of the tell (Maisler 1950–51: 208), which means that their dating is by pottery type and paleography and that their real origin is uncertain (as was kindly pointed out to me by B. Sass).

qayl-base nouns is neither retained nor represented historically in the orthography.

3. *Interpretation*

With the two principal aspects of the morphosyntactic analysis of the Gezer inscription in place and with no counter evidence from the areas of paleography, orthography, and phonetics, the text may be plausibly identifed as Phoenician and interpreted along the following lines. Though not strictly speaking a calendar, because activities are indicated rather than month names and because these activities number 8 rather than 12,[32] a correct analysis of the pronominal suffixes permits the global interpretation of the text as describing a 12-month sequence of agricultural pursuits.[33] These divisions of the year are expressed as a list of 8 distinct activities, beginning at the fall equinox with the gathering in of the produce of that season and ending with the harvesting of the late-summer fruits. The activities, to the extent that the terms are correctly interpreted, represent 8 months of harvesting diverse crops and 4 months of sowing. The following translation is intended to be somewhat literal and is laid out by structure rather than according to the lines on the limestone plaque; words placed in parentheses are considered to be implied but not stated explicitly. The referent of the proleptic suffix is indicated in brackets and preceded by an arrow (→). The modern months are indicated in brackets to the right of the translation.[34] The interpretation is defended only where deemed relevant and necessary.

---

32. One cannot agree with Lemaire's assertion that the text "est essentiellement une liste de noms de mois" (1981: 11): there are only eight of these terms, and nothing allows the conclusion that any of these terms designating agricultural activities would ever have functioned as month names.

33. The basic view of the text as reflecting a twelve-month sequence has been accepted by so many scholars over the years, irrespective of the morphosyntactic analysis preferred, that it may be described as a commonplace and left undocumented.

34. The word *late* in the equivalents is meant to express the fact that the beginning of the solar year with the fall equinox would only rarely have coincided directly with the beginning of the year as defined in terms of the lunar cycle. Exactly what device was used in the Gezer region in ca. 900 B.C. for keeping the lunar year roughly in synchronism with the seasonal cycle is unknown. My discussion in the following notes of the appropriate dates for some of the agricultural activities is predicated (as has been the case for most discussions of this sort in the past) on the assumption of a sequence of months beginning with the actual fall equinox–that is, not on the assumption of a year in which a series of uncorrected lunar years has resulted in the new year beginning no less than a month (or more, depending on the criteria in use) before the fall equinox.

yrḥw *ʾsp*
yaraḥ=êw ʾasōp
months.MP=its.MS[→ *ʾsp*] gather.INF[35]
Its (two)[36] months:[37] ingathering,[38] [*late September–late November*]

---

35. Though certainly nominal, the precise analysis of the form following *yrḥ*/ *yrḥw* in each entry as a common noun or as a verbal noun is uncertain; and, in the former case, the precise form of the noun is uncertain while, in the latter, the choice between what is known in Hebrew grammar as the infinitives construct or absolute is uncertain. Friedrich and Röllig (1999: 84) assume the existence of both in Phoenician and emphasize the usage of the latter with a following independent pronoun as a narrative construction (1999: 192–93). If *kl* in the sixth entry is indeed from the III-weak root denoting completion (see below, n. 42), only analysis as the infinitive "absolute" (< /qatāl/ in the G-stem, plausibly /qattāl/ in the D-stem [Piel]) is possible, for the infinitive "construct" of such roots bears afformative *-t* (1999: 174).

36. Sivan's (1998) entire presentation—and in this respect he is following in a long line of predecessors, for example, his mentor Rainey (see esp. Rainey 1983: 630 and 1996b: 70)—appears to be based on the presupposition that, if the text does not state the number *two* explicitly (he is arguing for the forms' being dual), then the forms in question must be plural and must express the plural. If, however, the text is a quasi-calendar and reflects agricultural usage, the number *two* need not be expressed. Whether or not the text reflects scribal training or a non-scholarly mnemonic device, as many have held over the years (for the former, see *COS* 2.222; for the latter, see the classic study in Albright 1943), the strict structure corresponding to a sequence of agricultural activities ending in *qṣ*, which, if the form was /qêṣ/ < /*qayṣ/, may have meant both 'summer fruits' and 'end' (if, in this language, /*qiṣṣ/ became /qēṣ/), makes of the text a sort of puzzle in which the number *two* must be filled in wherever the nonsingular form appears. As remarked above (n. 21), is not impossible that a frozen dual may have been retained for the word *yrḥ*, in which case the distinction between the dual and the plural (this noun plausibly being built on a *qatl* base, as in Hebrew) would have been expressed in the nominal stem: historically /yarḥ + ay + hu/ in the dual, /yaraḥ + ay + hu/ in the plural. Such a supposition, however, is not necessary for the forms bearing *-w* to be intelligible in their context as referring to two months.

37. If the *-w* does indeed correspond to the 3MS pronominal suffix and have as its point of reference the following noun, each entry is probably a phrase rather than a sentence—that is, the relationship between the suffixed noun and the following noun is that of a quasi-genitive rather than that of subject–predicate. Hence, instead of 'are' in parentheses in the translation, I use a colon, the intent of which is to reflect a basic understanding 'the months of it [i.e., of gathering]' ≈ 'two months of ingathering'. The clearest proleptic suffixes in the Karatepe inscription are certainly quasi-genitival (*l šbtnm dnnym* 'for their dwelling [i.e., of the Danunians]' [*KAI* 26 A I.17–18]; *l tty bʿl* 'with regard to his giving [i.e., of Baal]' [III.4]), and it avoids the odd logical connection between subject and predicate that would be A of B is B ('the months of it [i.e., gathering] are gathering'). My thanks to A. Butts for sorting out these hypothetical options for me.

38. Because the olive harvest is the last of the season and because olives are typically gathered from the ground, rather than being snipped (as are grape clusters) or plucked (as are the soft fruits), the typical activity for these two months is some-

yrḥw	*zrʿ*	
yaraḥ=êw	zarōʿ	
months.MP=its.MS[→ *zrʿ*]	sow.INF	
its (two) months: sowing,		[*late November–late January*]

yrḥw	*lqš*	
yaraḥ=êw	laqōš	
months.MP=its.MS[→ *lqš*]	do.late.sowing.INF	
its (two) months: late sowing,		[*late January–late March*]

yrḥ	*ʿṣd*	*pšt*	
yarḥ=ô	ʿaṣōd	pišt[39]	
month.MS=its.MS[→ *ʿṣd pšt*]	chop.INF	flax.MS	
its month: flax harvest,[40]			[*late March–late April*]

times said to be the harvesting and pressing of olives (e.g., Albright 1943: 22 n. 30—see discussion in Dobbs-Allsopp et al. 2005: 158–59). One must not forget, however, that certain types of nuts ripen at the same time as olives and are harvested in the same manner, that is, from the ground after the tree has been shaken. One should also not push the use of √ʾSP too strongly: the phrase *ʾispû yayin wĕqayiṣ wĕšemen* (Jer 40:10) shows that the verb was used not only for the fruits themselves but for a variety of agricultural products (indeed, Dalman [1909: 118] was of the opinion that *ʾsp* in the Gezer inscription expresses the gathering of the fruit "*to the house*" [italics his], not the harvest itself—a position that appears extreme in view of the agricultural reality of certain crops' being harvested from late September until into November).

39. If the form of the verbal noun is indeed the infinitive "absolute" (see above, n. 35), the rection would be accusatival rather than genitival.

40. The phrase denotes the chopping of the woody flax stem near its base, almost certainly with a tool, the blade of which is at right angles to the handle rather than parallel to it (see Albright 1943: 22 n. 35): judging from the range of activities assigned to it, the *maʿăṣād* in Biblical Hebrew denotes an 'adz'-like tool rather than an 'ax' (stated in terms of American usage, in which an *adz* is a stronger implement than a *hoe* and refers to tools of various sizes that are used either in agriculture or in wood-working). It has been averred that flax harvest could not have occurred in March (see discussion in Renz 1995: 35; or in Dobbs-Allsopp et al. 2005: 160–61); but a great many varieties of flax are planted in Syria–Palestine, some that are in fact harvested as early as March (see, e.g., Post 1932–33: 1.248–53; Zohary 1966–86: part 2, text, 258–64). Taking twentieth-century practice as the only criterion for interpreting a text that dates to the Iron Age and concluding that the harvesting of flax in March is impossible (Borowski 1987: 35) can only be described as an artificial limitation of the possibilities. Albright's general comment applies particularly to this entry: "The agricultural operations clearly follow the time-schedule of the Shephelah or low hill-country, not that of the central district, which averages more than 2000 feet higher and lags several weeks behind the low lands" (Albright 1943: 25). If the inscription is in the Phoenician language, the form of the word for the flax plants must be /pišt/, for the feminine form corresponding to Hebrew /pištā^{h}/ would be *pštt* in Phoenician. The use of /pišt/ would correspond to the masculine form /pēšet/

yrḥ	*qṣr*	*šʿrm*
yarḥ=ô	qaṣīr[41]	šiʿōrīm
month.MS=its.MS[→ *qṣr šʿrm*]	harvest.MS	barley.MP
its month: barley harvest,		[*late April–late May*]

yrḥ	*qṣr*	*w*	*kl*
yarḥ=ô	qaṣīr	wa	kallô
month.MS=its.MS[→ *qṣr*]	harvest.MS	and.CONJ	complete.INF
its month: (wheat) harvest and completion,[42]			[*late May–late June*]

in Josh 2:6, where the phrase /pištē^{y} hāʿēṣ/ refers to recently harvested flax stalks that have been spread out on a roof to dry (the Hebrew plural would refer to the multiple stalks, while the Phoenician singular would be a collective). Albright (1943: 22 n. 34) argued that the feminine form was required (he took the morpheme to be /ā/ written defectively) because, in his view, the masculine singular form did not exist and because the feminine form would have been used in Biblical Hebrew to denote the standing crop. The word *pṯt* is, however, well attested in Ugaritic, albeit with the meaning of the product rather than of the plant, and *pšt* is attested in Punic. The use of the masculine form in the Gezer inscription may only indicate that the emphasis was not on the growing plants, in which case the feminine form would indeed be expected, but on the harvesting of the plant in view of obtaining the product from it. However this may be, the use of the masculine plural in the following line (*qṣr šʿrm*) and in Biblical Hebrew for the harvesting of barley and wheat shows that, though one may legitimately query why the masculine singular form was used, the assertion that the feminine form is expected, even required, may not be granted the same legitimacy. The treatment of flax as mentioned in passing in the Rahab story, by the way, belies the assertion that flax was an import product in ancient Palestine to the point that it would not have been mentioned in a text such as the Gezer inscription (Talmon 1963): judging from the mention in Joshua 2 of the spreading of the flax stalks on the roof of the house (which was done for the purpose of drying the stalk before the fibers were detached from it), one must conclude that the teller of the story knew exactly what the process was for proceeding from the flax plant itself to the cloth derived from it.

41. The noun denoting the activity is here vocalized as a common noun because of the frequency of usage of the *qatīl* base noun in Hebrew in formulas such as this one.

42. That is, the completion of the grain harvest. Because it appears likely that *kl* here and the verb *ykl* in the primary Meṣad Ḥashavyahu inscription designate the same reality, one may eliminate the interpretation of *kl* as the noun meaning 'all'. Furthermore, the notion of *completion* fits the context of the Meṣad Ḥashavyahu inscription, I believe, better than does that of *measuring* (see Pardee et al. 1982: 21; Lindenberger 2003: 110). The same may be said of this inscription, where "measuring" the harvest would be of no calendrical interest (as one must grant that it might have been in the context of the Meṣad Ḥashavyahu inscription), whereas the marking of the completion of the grain harvest is relevant to an agricultural "calendar." Moreover, as Lemaire has argued (1971: 64–68), the reapers of this text would not have done the threshing that must precede any possible measuring (this argument does not, of course, apply to the much briefer formulation of the Gezer Calendar).

yrḥw *zmr*
yaraḥ=êw zamōr
months.MS=its.MS[→ *zmr*] prune.INF
its (two) months: (vine) pruning,[43] [*late June–late August*]

yrḥ *qṣ*
yarḥ=ô qêṣ
month.MS=its.MS[→ *qṣ*] summer.fruit.MS
its month: summer fruits. [*late August–late September*]

4. Conclusion

In light of the most plausible interpretation of the forms *yrḥw* and *yrḥ* and in terms of the presently attested linguistic data for the area, the language of the text commonly known as the Gezer Calendar is best identified as Phoenician. For scholars who find this to be historically or geographically implausible,[44] the identification as an unknown Canaan-

43. According to this list of activities, the ambiguous term *zmr*, which denotes the act of 'pruning' in Biblical Hebrew, designates an activity that occurred from late June to late August. Because, according to later traditions and premodern practice, the grape harvest did not begin until July or August and the best grapes for making wine were not harvested until September (see the sources cited in Pardee 2000: 157 n. 24), it appears necessary to conclude that the activity mentioned in the Gezer text is what is known in modern usage as 'green pruning'—that is, canopy management to provide ideal sun/shade conditions for the grapes (for some early formulations of this explanation, see Février 1948: 36–37; Albright 1943: 23 n. 38). The grape harvest itself would therefore have been one of the activities of the last month of the year, designated *qṣ* in this text (dogmatism is, however, out of place: some varieties of grapes may well have ripened during the last part of the two-month period designated as "pruning"-time; here one should keep in mind that the same tool used for pruning may have been used for severing the bunch of grapes from the vine). Because the last month of the year was considered typical of the grape harvest at Ugarit (see Pardee 2000: 156–58), it is reasonable to suppose that the same month would not have been too early for the grape harvest at Gezer, located some 400 kilometers to the south. This possibility is put forward in opposition to Dobbs-Allsopp et al. (2005: 158–59), who come down strongly in favor of the idea that the grape harvest occurred during the first month, the activities of which were subsumed under *ʾsp* in this text.

44. The proposed identification as Phoenician is meant to be purely linguistic and to say nothing about the ethnicity of the inhabitants of Gezer in ca. 900 B.C. One intellectual odyssey is recorded above in n. 5: Naveh began by insisting on the Hebrew character of the text on the basis of 1 Kgs 9:16 but stated himself more reservedly in other publications. Renz (1995: 31–32; 1997: 5) may be cited as another example: he recognizes that the script represents a stage preceding any differentiation from the Phoenician type but voices no doubts about the Hebraic nature of the language and discusses the inscription in terms of the biblical references and "national" origins.

ite language/dialect cannot be ruled out, but it rests, by definition, on the absence of data. While a similar combination of morphological and syntactic data are not yet attested that would permit a decision to identify it as Samarian Hebrew or as Philistian, the orthographic conventions observed by the scribe of the Gezer Calendar are different from the conventions of these poorly attested dialects/languages; the writing of the third-person pronominal suffix with *-h* in the Ekron inscription constitues an argument against the identification of the Gezer inscription as Philistian, and the form *byt* in one of the Tell Qasile ostraca may constitute a similar argument. In sum, according to presently known data, the paleography, orthography, morphology, and syntax of the Gezer Calendar correspond only to the norms of Phoenician.

Bibliography

Aartun, K.

1973 Die hervorhebende Endung *-w*(V) an nordwestsemitischen Adverbien und Negationen. *UF* 5:1–5.

1974 *Die Partikeln des Ugaritischen.* Vol. 1. AOAT 21/1. Kevelaer: Butzon & Bercker / Neukirchen-Vluyn: Neukirchener Verlag.

Aharoni, Y.

1981 *Arad Inscriptions.* Jerusalem: Israel Exploration Society.

Albright, W. F.

1943 The Gezer Calendar. *BASOR* 92: 16–26.

1944 A Prince of Taanach in the Fifteenth Century B.C. *BASOR* 94: 12–27.

Bartoloni, P., et al., eds.

1983 *Atti del I Congresso Internazionale di Studi Fenici et Punici: Roma, 5–10 Novembre 1979.* Rome: Consiglio Nazionale delle Ricerche.

Beyer, K.

1984 *Die aramäischen Texte vom Toten Meer.* Göttingen: Vandenhoeck & Ruprecht.

Birnbaum, S. A.

1942 The Dates of the Gezer Tablet and of the Samaria Ostraca. *PEQ* 74: 104–8.

1944 On the Possibility of Dating Hebrew Inscriptions. *PEQ* 76: 213–17.

1971 *The Hebrew Scripts.* Leiden: Brill.

Bordreuil, P.

1992 Sceaux inscrits des pays du Levant. Cols. 86–212 in vol. 12, fasc. 66 of *Supplément au Dicitionnaire de la Bible.* Paris: Letouzey & Ané.

Borowski, O.

1987 *Agriculture in Iron Age Israel.* Winona Lake, IN: Eisenbrauns.

Briquel-Chatonnet, F.

1992 Hébreu du nord et phénicien: Étude comparée de deux dialectes cananéens. *OLP* 23: 89–126.

Briquel-Chatonnet, F., and Lozachmeur, H., eds.

1998 *Proche-Orient ancien: Temps vécu, temps pensé. Actes de la Table-Ronde du 15 novembre 1997 organisée par l'URA 1062 «Etudes Sémitiques».* Antiquités Sémitiques 3. Paris: Maisonneuve.

Brown, J. P.

1969 *The Lebanon and Phoenicia: Ancient Texts Illustrating Their Physical Geography and Native Industries*, vol. 1: *The Physical Setting and the Forest.* Beirut: American University of Beirut.

Byrne, R.

2002 Philistine Semitics and Dynastic History at Ekron. *UF* 34: 1–23.

Cross, F. M.

1980 Newly Found Inscriptions in Old Canaanite and Early Phoenician Scripts. *BASOR* 238: 1–20.

Cross, F. M., Jr., and Freedman, D. N.

1952 *Early Hebrew Orthography. A Study of the Epigraphic Evidence.* AOS 36. New Haven, CT: American Oriental Society.

Dahood, M.

1983 Some Eblaite and Phoenician Month Names. Pp. 595–98 in vol. 2 of *Atti del I Congresso Internazionale di Studi Fenici et Punici*, ed. P. Bartolini et al. Rome: Consiglio Nazionale delle Ricerche.

Dalman, G.

1909 Notes on the Old Hebrew Calendar-Inscription from Gezer. *PEFQS* 118–19.

Dobbs-Allsopp, F. W.; Roberts, J. J. M.; Seow, C. L.; and Whitaker, R. E.

2005 *Hebrew Inscriptions: Texts from the Biblical Period of the Monarchy with Concordance.* New Haven, CT: Yale University Press.

Février, J. G.

1948 Remarques sur le calendrier de Gézer. *Semitica* 1: 33–41.

Finkelstein, I.; Sass, B.; and Singer-Avitz, L.

2008. Writing in Iron IIA Philistia in the Light of the *Tel Zayit/Zeta Abecedary*. *ZDPV* 124: 1–14.

Freedman, D. N.

1992 The Evolution of Hebrew Orthography. Pp. 3–15 in *Studies in Hebrew and Aramaic Orthography*, e. D. N. Freedman, A. D. Forbes, and F. I. Andersen. Biblical and Judaic Studies the University of California, San Diego 2. Winona Lake, IN: Eisenbrauns.

Friedrich, J., and Röllig, W.

1999 *Phönizisch-Punische Grammatik.* 3rd ed. by M. G. Amadasi Guzzo with W. R. Mayer. AnOr 55. Rome: Pontifical Biblical Institute.

Garbini, G.

1954–56 Note sul «calendario» di Gezer. *AION* 6: 123–30.

1974 Note epigrafiche, vol. 3: Le iscrizioni «protocananaiche» del XII e XI secolo a.C. *AION* 34: 584–90.

1977 I dialetti del fenicio. *AION* 37: 283–94.

1983 Chi erano i fenici? Pp. 27–33 in vol. 1 of *Atti del I Congresso Internazionale di Studi Fenici et Punici*, ed. P. Bartolini et al. Rome: Consiglio Nazionale delle Ricerche.

2006 *Introduzione all'epigrafia semitica*. Studi sul Vivino Oriente antico 4. Brescia: Paideia.

Gibson, J. C. L.

1971 *Textbook of Syrian Semitic Inscriptions*, vol. 1: *Hebrew and Moabite Inscriptions*. Oxford: Clarendon.

1982 *Textbook of Syrian Semitic Inscriptions*, vol. 3: *Phoenician Inscriptions Including Inscriptions in the Mixed Dialect of Arslan Tash*. Oxford: Clarendon.

Ginsberg, H. L.

1935 Review of D. Diringer, *Le iscrizioni antico-ebraiche* (Florence, 1934). *BJPES* 2/3–4: 48–49.

1936a Review of D. Diringer, *Le iscrizioni antico-ebraiche* (Florence, 1934). *ArOr* 8: 146–47.

1936b The Rebellion and Death of Baʿlu. *Or* 5: 161–98.

Gitin, S.; Dothan, T.; and Naveh, J.

1997 A Royal Dedicatory Inscription from Ekron. *IEJ* 47: 1–16.

Gray, G. B.

1909 An Old Hebrew Calendar Inscription from Gezer. *PEFQS* 30–33.

Halpern, B.

1987 Dialect Distribution in Canaan and the Deir Alla Inscriptions. Pp. 119–39 in *"Working with No Data": Semitic and Egyptian Studies Presented to Thomas O. Lambdin*, ed. D. M. Golomb. Winona Lake, IN: Eisenbrauns.

Harris, Z.

1939 *Development of the Canaanite Dialects: An Investigation in Linguistic History*. AOS 16. New Haven, CT: American Oriental Society.

Honeyman, A. M.

1953 The Syntax of the Gezer Calendar. *JRAS* 53–58.

Horowitz, W., and Oshima, T.

2006 *Cuneiform in Canaan: Cuneiform Sources from the Land of Israel in Ancient Times*. Jerusalem: Israel Exploration Society and Hebrew University.

Israel, F.

1986 Études sur le lexique paléohébraïque: Les ostraca de Samarie et l'hébreu du Nord. *JA* 274: 478–79.

1989 Studi di lessico ebraico epigrafico I: I materiali del Nord. *Langues Orientales Anciennes: Philologie et Linguistique* 2: 37–67.

Lemaire, A.

1971 L'ostracon de Meṣad Ḥashavyahu (Yavneh-Yam) replacé dans son contexte. *Semitica* 21: 57–79.

1975 *Zāmīr* dans la tablette de Gezer et le Cantique des Cantiques. *VT* 25: 15–26.

1981 *Les écoles et la formation de la Bible dans l'ancien Israël*. OBO 39. Fribourg: Éditions Universitaires / Göttingen: Vandenhoeck & Ruprecht.

1997 Review of J. Renz. *Handbuch der althebräischen Epigraphik*, vol. 1/1: *Text und Kommentar*, 1995. *BiOr* 54: 161–66.

1998a Les formules de datation en Palestine au premier millénaire avant J.-C. Pp. 53–82 in *Proche-Orient ancien: Temps vécu, temps pensé*, ed. F. Briquel-Chatonnet and H. Lozachmeur. Antiquités Sémitiques 3. Paris: Maisonneuve.

1998b Review of J. Renz. *Schrift und Schreibtradition*, 1997. *BiOr* 55: 486–87.

2000 Phénicien et philistien: paléographie et dialectologie. Pp. 243–49 in *Actas del IV congreso internacional de estudios fenicios y púnicos, Cádiz, 2 al 6 de Octubre de 1995*, vol. 1, ed. M. E. Aubet and M. Barthélemy. 4 vols. Cádiz: Universidad de Cádiz.

2006 Hebrew and Aramaic in the First Millennium B.C.E. in the Light of Epigraphic Evidence (Socio-Historical Aspects). Pp. 177–96 in *Biblical Hebrew in Its Northwest Semitic Setting: Typological and Historical Perspectives*, ed. S. E. Fassberg and A. Hurvitz. Jerusalem: Magnes / Winona Lake, IN: Eisenbrauns.

Lidzbarski, M.

1909a An Old Hebrew Calendar Inscription from Gezer. *PEFQS* 26–29.

1909b The Old Hebrew Calendar-Inscription from Gezer. *PEFQS* 194–95.

Lindenberger, J. M.

2003 *Ancient Aramaic and Hebrew Letters*. 2nd ed. SBLWAW 14. Atlanta: Society of Biblical Literature.

Lipiński, E.

1977 North-west Semitic Inscriptions. *OLP* 8: 81–117.

Maisler [Mazar], B.

1950–51 The Excavations at Tell Qasile: Preliminary report. *IEJ* 1: 194–218.

Meyers, E. M., ed.

1997 *The Oxford Encyclopedia of Archaeology in the Near East*. 5 vols. New York: Oxford University Press.

Millard, A. R.

1976 The Canaanite Linear Alphabet and Its Passage to the Greeks. *Kadmos* 15: 130–44.

Naveh, J.

1968 A Palaeographic Note on the Distribution of the Hebrew Script. *HTR* 61: 68–74.

1970 The Scripts in Palestine and Transjordan in the Iron Age. Pp. 277–83 in *Near Eastern Archaeology in the Twentieth Century: Essays in Honor of Nelson Glueck*, ed. J. A. Sanders. Garden City, NY: Doubleday.

1972 Review of J. C. L. Gibson. *Textbook of Syrian Semitic Inscriptions*, vol. 1: *Hebrew and Moabite Inscriptions*, 1971. *IEJ* 22: 187–88.

1978 Some Considerations on the Ostracon from ʿIzbet Ṣarṭah. *IEJ* 28: 31–35.

1982 *Early History of the Alphabet: An Introduction to West Semitic Epigraphy and Palaeography*. Jerusalem: Magnes.

1984/1981 Inscriptions of the Biblical Period. Pp. 59–68 in *Recent Archaeology in the Land of Israel*, ed. H. Shanks. English ed. Washington, DC: Biblical Archaeology Society, 1984. [Hebrew ed., ed. B. Mazar. Jerusalem: Israel Exploration Society, 1981.]

Pardee, D.

1987 Review of J. C. L. Gibson. *Textbook of Syrian Semitic Inscriptions*, vol. 3: *Phoenician Inscriptions Including Inscriptions in the Mixed Dialect of Arslan Tash*, 1982. *JNES* 46: 137–42.

1997a Gezer Calendar. Pp. 400–1 in vol. 2 of *The Oxford Encyclopedia of Archaeology in the Near East*, ed. E. M. Meyers. New York: Oxford University Press.

1997b Review of J. Renz. *Handbuch der althebräischen Epigraphik*, vol. 1/1: *Text und Kommentar*, 1995. *WO* 28: 216–20.

2000 *Les textes rituels*. Ras Shamra–Ougarit 12. Paris: Recherche sur les Civilisations.

2001 Review of F. Briquel-Chatonnet and H. Lozachmeur, eds. *Proche-Orient ancien: Temps vécu, temps pensé*, 1998. *JAOS* 121: 134–37.

2011 Vestiges du système casuel entre le nom et le pronom suffixe en hébreu biblique. Pp. 113–21 in *Grammatical Case in the Languages of the Middle East and Europe: Acts of the International Colloquium—Variations, concurrence et évolution des cas dans divers domaines linguistiques, Paris, 2–4 avril 2007*, ed. M. Fruyt, M. Mazoyer, and D. Pardee. SAOC 64. Chicago: Oriental Institute.

Pardee, D., et al.

1982 *Handbook of Ancient Hebrew Letters*. SBLSBS 15. Chico, CA: Scholars Press.

Pilcher, E. J.

1909 An Old Hebrew Calendar Inscription from Gezer. *PEFQS* 33–34.

Post, G. E.

1932–33 *Flora of Syria, Palestine and Sinai: A Handbook of the Flowering Plants and Ferns, Native and Naturalized, from the Taurus to Ras Muhammad and from the Mediterranean Sea to the Syrian Desert*. 2nd rev. ed., J. W. Dinsmore. American University of Beirut, Publications of the Faculty of Arts and Sciences, Natural Science Series 1, 2. Beirut: American Press.

Rainey. A. F.

1983 Review of Z. Zevit. *Matres Lectionis in Ancient Hebrew Epigraphs*, 1980. *JBL* 102: 629–34.

1996a *Canaanite in the Amarna Tablets. A Linguistic Analysis of the Mixed Dialect Used by Scribes from Canaan*. 4 vols. HOSNME 25. Leiden: Brill.

1996b Review of J. M. Sasson et al., eds. *Civilizations of the Ancient Near East*, 1995. *BAR* 22/6: 70–71, 76.

Rendsburg, G.

1982 Dual Personal Pronouns and Dual Verbs in Hebrew. *JQR* 73: 38–58.

Renz, J.

1995 *Handbuch der althebräischen Epigraphik*, vol. 1/1: *Text und Kommentar*. Darmstadt: Wissenschaftliche Buchgesellschaft.

1997 *Schrift und Schreibtradition: Eine paläographische Studie zum kulturgeschichtlichen Verhältnis von israelitischem Nordreich und Südreich.* Abhandlungen des Deutschen Palästina-Vereins 23. Wiesbaden: Harrassowitz.

Ringgren, H.
1949 A Note on the Karatepe Text. *Oriens* 2: 127–28.

Ronzevalle, S.
1909 The Gezer Hebrew Inscription. *PEFQS* 107–12.

Schüle, A.
2000 *Die Syntax der althebräischen Inschriften: Ein Beitrag zur historischen Grammatik des Hebräischen.* AOAT 270. Münster: Ugarit-Verlag.

Shea, W. H.
1993 The Song of Seedtime and Harvest from Gezer. Pp. 243–50 in *Verse in Ancient Near Eastern Prose*, ed. J. C. de Moor and W. G. E. Watson. AOAT 42. Kevelaer: Butzon & Bercker / Neukirchen-Vluyn: Neukirchener Verlag.

Sivan, D.
1984 *Grammatical Analysis and Glossary of the Northwest Semitic Vocables in Akkadian Texts of the 15th–13th c.* B.C. *from Canaan and Syria.* AOAT 214. Kevelaer: Butzon & Bercker / Neukirchen-Vluyn: Neukirchener Verlag.
1998 The Gezer Calendar and Northwest Semitic Linguistics. *IEJ* 48: 101–5.

Talmon, S.
1963 The Gezer Calendar and the Seasonal Cycle of Ancient Canaan. *JAOS* 83: 177–87.

Tappy, R. E., et al.
2006 An Abecedary of the Mid-Tenth Century B.C.E. from the Judaean Shephelah. *BASOR* 344: 5–46

Tropper. J.
1993 Nominativ Dual **yariḥau* im Gezer-Kalendar. *ZAH* 6: 228–31.

Young, I.
1992 The Style of the Gezer Calendar and Some 'Archaic Biblical Hebrew' Passages. *VT* 42: 362–75.

Yun, I.-S. A.
2005 The Transjordanian Languages during the Iron Age II. *UF* 37: 741–66.

Zevit, Z.
1980 *Matres Lectionis in Ancient Hebrew Epigraphs.* ASOR Monograph Series 2. Cambridge, MA: American Schools of Oriental Research.

Zohary, M.
1966–86 *Flora Palestina.* 4 parts in 8 vols. Jerusalem: Israel Academy of Sciences and Humanities.

Index of Authors